Social Skills for Teenagers With Developmental and Autism Spectrum Disorders

Social Skills for Teenagers With Developmental and Autism Spectrum Disorders

THE **PEERS** TREATMENT MANUAL

ELIZABETH A. LAUGESON
AND FRED FRANKEL

Routledge
Taylor & Francis Group
New York   London

Routledge
Taylor & Francis Group
711 Third Avenue
New York, NY 10017

Routledge
Taylor & Francis Group
27 Church Road
Hove, East Sussex BN3 2FA

© 2010 by Taylor and Francis Group, LLC
Routledge is an imprint of Taylor & Francis Group, an Informa business

International Standard Book Number: 978-0-415-87203-4 (Paperback)

Library of Congress Cataloging-in-Publication Data

Laugeson, Elizabeth A.
    Social skills for teenagers with developmental and autism spectrum disorders : the PEERS treatment manual / Elizabeth A. Laugeson & Fred Frankel.
        p. ; cm.
    Includes bibliographical references and index.
    ISBN 978-0-415-87203-4 (pbk. : alk. paper)
    1. Autistic youth--Rehabilitation. 2. Autism in adolescence--Social aspects. 3. Developmental disabilities--Patients--Rehabilitation. 4. Developmental disabilities--Social aspects. I. Frankel, Fred H. II. Title.
    [DNLM: 1. Autistic Disorder--therapy. 2. Adolescent. 3. Friends. 4. Interpersonal Relations. WM 203.5 L374s 2010]

RJ506.A9L38 2010
616.85'88200835--dc22   2009037538

Visit the Taylor & Francis Web site at
http://www.taylorandfrancis.com

and the Routledge Web site at
http://www.routledgementalhealth.com

This book is dedicated to our families, whose love
and support have made this work possible.

Contents

Preface...**xxi**

Acknowledgments ....**xxiii**

Authors..**xxv**

SECTION I INTRODUCTION

1 Introduction...**3**

Use of This Manual... 3

Required Personnel.. 4

Who May Benefit From PEERS?.. 5

Organization of the Manual.. 5

    Parent Session Therapist Guide 9

    Parent Handout 9

    Teen Session Therapist Guide... 10

    Teen Activity Guide... 11

Research Evidence 11

Using PEERS in the School Setting... 13

Use of This Manual With Young Adults.. 13

SECTION II PREPARING FOR TREATMENT

2 Preparing for Treatment..**17**

Screening... 17

Phone Screening Script... 18

PEERS Phone Screen Data Sheet.. 21

    Program for the Education and Enrichment of Relational Skills 21

    Family Information... 21

    Identifying Information 21

Parent and Teen Intake Interview 22

    Greeting 22

    Teen Interview... 22

    Parent / Guardian Interview 23

Wrap-Up 25

Teen Intake Interview Checklist.. 27

Global Impressions...28
Welcome to PEERS! (Sample Welcome Letter) 29
    Meeting Location...29
    Parking...29
    Your Teen Will Learn 29
Forming Groups..30
    Composition of the Group...30
    Physical Facilities...30
    Behavioral Control Techniques...30
    Required Materials...31
    Providing Food and Beverages...32
    Initial Start-Up Challenges 32
    Buzzwords..33
    Outcome Assessments...33

SECTION III   TREATMENT SESSIONS

3   **Session 1: Introduction and Conversational Skills I—Trading
    Information...37**
    Parent Session Therapist Guide..37
        Guiding Principles of the Parent Session 37
        Opening Remarks..40
        Introduction..42
        What to Expect From the Group...43
        Methods...43
        What Not to Expect From the Group..43
        Characteristics of Good Friendships...44
        Didactic Lesson: Trading Information 44
        Rules for Trading Information...45
        Homework Assignments 45
        How to Help Your Teen Do His or Her Homework...........................46
        Final Administrative Comments...47
    Parent Handout 1: Introduction and Conversational Skills I—Trading
    Information...48
        What to Expect From the Group...48
        Methods...48
        What Not to Expect From the Group..48
        Rules for Trading Information...49
        Homework Assignments 49
        How to Help Your Teen Do His or Her Homework...........................50
    Teen Therapist Guide—Session 1: Introduction and Conversational
    Skills I—Trading Information 51
        Guiding Principles of the Teen Session...51
        Handling Misbehavior 53

Set-Up and Opening Remarks 53
Opening Remarks 54
Rules for the Group 54
   Rules 54
Overview of PEERS 54
   Reason for the Group 54
   Structure of the Sessions 55
   Earning Points 55
Discussion Questions 56
   Characteristics of Good Friendships 56
Didactic Lesson: Rules for Trading Information 57
Role-Play Exercise 59
Behavioral Rehearsal 59
Homework Assignments 60
Teen Activity: Jeopardy 60
Reunification 61
Homework Assignments 62
Calculate Points 62
Teen Activity Guide: Session 1 62
  "Jeopardy" 62
   Materials Needed 62
   Rules 63
   "Jeopardy" Answer Sheets 65

4 Session 2: Conversational Skills II—Two-Way Conversations 67
Parent Session Therapist Guide 67
  Guiding Principles of the Parent Session 67
   Approaches to Challenging Parent Behaviors That Appear in
   This Session 69
  Homework Review 70
  Didactic Lesson: Sources of Friends / Two-Way Conversations 70
   Sources of Friends 71
  Rules for Having a Two-Way Conversation 71
  Homework Assignments 73
Parent Handout 2: Conversational Skills II—Two-Way Conversations 74
  Sources of Friends 74
  Rules for Having a Two-Way Conversation 74
  Homework Assignments 75
Teen Therapist Guide—Session 2: Conversational Skills II—Two-Way
Conversations 76
  Guiding Principles of the Teen Session 76
  Rule Review 77
  Homework Review 77
  Discussion Questions 78

Common Conversational Topics for Boys and Girls 79
Didactic Lesson: Rules for Having a Two-Way Conversation 79
Role Play 86
Behavioral Rehearsal 87
Homework Assignments 87
Teen Activity: Jeopardy 88
Reunification 88
Homework Assignments 89
Calculate Points 89
Teen Activity Guide: Session 2 90
"Jeopardy" 90
Materials Needed 90
Rules 90
"Jeopardy" Answer Sheets 93

5   Session 3: Conversational Skills III—Electronic Communication ... 95
Parent Session Therapist Guide 95
Guiding Principles of the Parent Session 95
Homework Review 96
Didactic Lesson: Choosing Appropriate Friends / Electronic
Communication 97
Rules for Starting and Ending a Phone Call 98
Rules for Leaving a Voice-Mail Message 99
Rules for Phone Calls / Text Messages / Instant Messages / E-mail 100
Rules for Using the Internet 101
Homework Assignments 102
Parent Handout 3: Conversational Skills III—Electronic Communication....103
Rules for Starting and Ending a Phone Call 103
Rules for Leaving a Voice-Mail Message 104
Rules for Phone Calls / Text Messages / Instant Messages / E-mail 104
Rules for Using the Internet 105
Homework Assignments 105
Teen Therapist Guide—Session 3: Conversational Skills III—Electronic
Communication 107
Guiding Principles of the Teen Session 107
Rule Review 108
Homework Review 108
Didactic Lesson: Electronic Communication 109
Rules for Starting and Ending a Phone Call 109
Rules for Phone Calls / Text Messages / Instant Messages / E-mail 113
Rules for Using the Internet 115
Behavioral Rehearsal 116
Homework Assignments 117
Teen Activity: Jeopardy 117

Reunification 118
Homework Assignments 119
Calculate Points 120
Teen Activity Guide: Session 3 120
"Jeopardy" 120
Materials Needed 120
Rules 120
"Jeopardy" Answer Sheets 123

6   Session 4: Choosing Appropriate Friends 125
Parent Session Therapist Guide 125
Guiding Principles of the Parent Session 125
Homework Review 126
Didactic Lesson: Sources of Friends 126
Importance of Having a Crowd or Clique 127
Sources for Friendships 128
Homework Assignments 129
Parent Handout 4: Choosing Appropriate Friends 132
Sources for Friendships 132
Homework Assignments 133
Teen Therapist Guide—Session 4: Choosing Appropriate Friends 135
Guiding Principles of the Teen Session 135
Rule Review 136
Homework Review 136
Didactic Lesson: Choosing Appropriate Friends 137
Identifying Different Crowds 138
Importance of Having a Crowd or a Group 139
Identifying Which Group You Fit in With 139
Homework Assignments 141
Teen Activity—Trading Information: Personal Items 142
Reunification 142
Homework Assignments 143
Calculate Points 144
Teen Activity Guide: Session 4 144
"Trading Information: Personal Items" 144
Materials Needed 144
Rules 145

7   Session 5: Appropriate Use of Humor 147
Parent Session Therapist Guide 147
Guiding Principles of the Parent Session 147
Homework Review 148
Didactic Lesson: Appropriate Use of Humor 148
Rules About Using Humor 149
Humor Feedback 150

What to Do With Humor Feedback 151
Homework Assignments 151
Parent Handout 5: Appropriate Use of Humor 154
Rules About Using Humor 154
Humor Feedback 155
What to Do With Humor Feedback 155
Homework Assignments 156
Teen Therapist Guide—Session 5: Appropriate Use of Humor 158
Guiding Principles of the Teen Session 158
Rule Review 158
Homework Review 159
Didactic Lesson: Rules About Using Humor 160
What to Do With Humor Feedback 164
Behavioral Rehearsal 164
Homework Assignments 166
Teen Activity—Trading Information: Personal Items 167
Reunification With Parents 167
Homework Assignments 168
Calculate Points 169
Teen Activity Guide: Session 4 170
"Trading Information: Personal Items" 170
Materials Needed 170
Rules 170

8   Session 6: Peer Entry I—Entering a Conversation.........................171
Parent Session Therapist Guide 171
Guiding Principles of the Parent Session 171
Homework Review 172
Didactic Lesson: Peer Entry 173
Steps for Slipping Into a Conversation 173
Homework Assignments 175
Parent Handout 6: Peer Entry I—Entering a Conversation 177
Steps for Slipping Into a Conversation 177
Homework Assignments 178
Teen Therapist Guide—Session 6: Peer Entry I—Entering a Conversation..181
Guiding Principles of the Teen Session 181
Rule Review 181
Homework Review 181
Didactic Lesson: Slipping Into Conversations 184
Good Times and Places to Make Friends 184
Good Choices for Friends 185
Steps for Slipping Into a Conversation 185
Role Play 189
Homework Assignments 191

Teen Activity: Slipping Into Conversations 192

Reunification With Parents...193

    Watch 193

    Wait 193

    Join 194

Homework Assignments 194

Calculate Points 196

Teen Activity Guide: Session 6 196

  "Slipping Into Conversations" 196

    Materials Needed 196

    Rules 196

9   Session 7: Peer Entry II—Exiting a Conversation.......................... 199

Parent Session Therapist Guide..199

  Guiding Principles of the Parent Session 199

  Homework Review...200

  Didactic Lesson: Exiting Conversations 201

  Slipping Out of a Conversation...202

  Homework Assignments 203

Parent Handout 7: Peer Entry II—Exiting a Conversation 205

  Rules for Slipping Out of a Conversation...............................205

  Homework Assignments 206

Teen Therapist Guide—Session 7: Peer Entry II—Exiting a Conversation.. 208

  Guiding Principles of the Teen Session...................................208

  Rule Review 208

  Homework Review...209

  Didactic Lesson: Slipping Out of Conversations 210

  Rules for Slipping Out of a Conversation...............................211

  Steps for Slipping Out of a Conversation...............................212

  Role Play 213

  Slipping Out of a Conversation You Already Joined................216

  Role Play 216

  Homework Assignments 217

  Teen Activity: Slipping In and Out of Conversations 218

  Reunification With Parents...219

  Homework Assignments 219

  Calculate Points 220

Teen Activity Guide: Session 7 221

  "Slipping In and Out of Conversations" 221

    Materials Needed 221

    Rules 221

10   Session 8: Get-Togethers 223

Parent Session Therapist Guide... 223

  Guiding Principles of the Parent Session 223

Homework Review 224
Didactic Lesson: Get-Togethers 225
   What Parents Should Expect During the Get-Togethers 226
Suggestions for Activity-Based Get-Togethers 226
   Parents' Jobs for Having Good Get-Togethers 228
   Rules for Having a Good Get-Together 228
   Teens' Jobs for Having Good Get-Togethers 228
Homework Assignments 230
Parent Handout 8: Get-Togethers 232
Suggestions for Activity-Based Get-Togethers 232
Parents' Jobs for Having Good Get-Togethers...................................232
Teens' Jobs for Having Good Get-Togethers 233
   Before the Get-Together 233
   At the Beginning of the Get-Together 233
   During the Get-Together...233
   End of the Get-Together 234
Homework Assignments 234
Teen Therapist Guide—Session 8: Get-Togethers 236
Guiding Principles of the Teen Session 236
Rule Review 237
Homework Review 237
Didactic Lesson: Rules for Having a Good Get-Together 238
   Before the Get-Together 238
Suggestions for Activity-Based Get-Togethers 240
   At the Beginning of the Get-Together 241
Role Play 242
   During the Get-Together... 243
   End of the Get-Together 245
Role Play 246
Homework Assignments 246
Teen Activity: Get-Togethers 247
Reunification...247
Homework Assignments 248
Calculate Points 248
Teen Activity Guide: Session 8 249
   "Get-Togethers" 249
      Materials Needed 249
      Rules...249

11 Session 9: Good Sportsmanship 251
Parent Session Therapist Guide..251
Guiding Principles of the Parent Session 251
Homework Review 252
Didactic Lesson: Good Sportsmanship...253

Rules for Good Sportsmanship 253

Homework Assignments 254

Parent Handout 9: Good Sportsmanship 256

Rules for Good Sportsmanship... 256

Homework Assignments 257

Teen Therapist Guide—Session 9: Good Sportsmanship........................ 258

Guiding Principles of the Teen Session....................................... 258

Rule Review 258

Homework Review 258

Didactic Lesson: Rules for Good Sportsmanship 259

Homework Assignments 262

Teen Activity: Get-Togethers and Good Sportsmanship 262

Reunification.. 263

Homework Assignments 264

Calculate Points 264

Teen Activity Guide: Session 9 265

"Get-Togethers and Good Sportsmanship"................................... 265

Materials Needed 265

Rules... 265

12 Session 10: Rejection I—Teasing and Embarrassing Feedback 267

Parent Session Therapist Guide...267

Guiding Principles of the Parent Session 267

Homework Review.. 268

Didactic Lesson: Teasing and Embarrassing Feedback...................... 269

Tease-the-Tease... 269

Handling Embarrassing Feedback 271

Homework Assignments 272

Parent Handout 10: Rejection I—Teasing and Embarrassing Feedback........274

Tease-the-Tease..274

Homework Assignments 275

Teen Therapist Guide—Session 10: Rejection I—Teasing and
Embarrassing Feedback 277

Guiding Principles of the Teen Session... 277

Rule Review 278

Homework Review 278

Didactic Lesson: Tease-the-Tease.. 279

Role Play 283

Behavioral Rehearsal 284

Handling Embarrassing Feedback 285

Homework Assignments 286

Teen Activity: Get-Togethers and Good Sportsmanship 287

Reunification... 287

Homework Assignments 288

Calculate Points 289
Teen Activity Guide: Session 10 289
   "Get-Togethers and Good Sportsmanship" 289
      Materials Needed 289
      Rules 289

13 Session 11: Rejection II—Bullying and Bad Reputations 293
   Parent Session Therapist Guide 293
      Guiding Principles of the Parent Session 293
      Homework Review 294
      Didactic Lesson: Bullying and Bad Reputations 295
         How to Handle Bullying 295
         Tips for Changing a Bad Reputation 296
      Homework Assignments 298
   Parent Handout 11: Rejection II—Bullying and Bad Reputations 299
      How to Handle Bullying 299
      Tips for Changing a Bad Reputation 299
      Homework Assignments 300
   Teen Therapist Guide—Session 11: Rejection II—Bullying and Bad
   Reputations 302
      Guiding Principles of the Teen Session 302
      Rule Review 302
      Homework Review 303
      Didactic Lesson: Bullying and Bad Reputations 304
      Handling Bullying 305
      Bad Reputations 307
         Tips for Changing a Bad Reputation 307
      Homework Assignments 309
      Teen Activity: Good Sportsmanship and Outdoor Activities 310
      Reunification With Parents 310
      Calculate Points 311
   Teen Activity Guide: Session 11 312
      "Good Sportsmanship and Outdoor Activities" 312
         Materials Needed 312
         Rules 312

14 Session 12: Handling Disagreements 313
   Parent Session Therapist Guide 313
      Guiding Principles of the Parent Session 313
      Homework Review 314
      Didactic Lesson: Handling Disagreements 314
      Handling Disagreements 315
      Homework Assignments 316
      Suggestions for How to Present the Graduation 317
         Teen Session 317

     Parent Session 318
     Graduation Ceremony 318
   Parent Handout 12: Handling Disagreements..............................319
    Handling Disagreements...319
    Homework Assignments 320
   Teen Therapist Guide—Session 12: Handling Disagreements 322
    Guiding Principles of the Teen Session............................322
    Rule Review...322
    Homework Review 323
    Didactic Lesson: Handling Disagreements 324
    Role Play 327
    Behavioral Rehearsal 330
    Homework Assignments 330
    Graduation Announcement..331
     Parent Session 331
     Graduation Ceremony 331
    Teen Activity: Good Sportsmanship and Outdoor Activities 332
    Reunification With Parents...332
    Homework Assignments 333
    Calculate Points 333
   Teen Activity Guide: Session 12 334
    "Good Sportsmanship and Outdoor Activities"................334
     Materials Needed 334
     Rules.. 334

15 **Session 13: Rumors and Gossip....................................337**
   Parent Session Therapist Guide..337
    Guiding Principles of the Parent Session 337
    Homework Review 338
    Didactic Lesson: Rumors and Gossip 339
    Rules for Handling Rumors and Gossip 339
     How to Avoid Being the Target of Gossip.....................339
     What to Do When You Are the Target of Gossip 340
    Homework Assignments 341
    Suggestions for How to Present the Graduation 342
     Telling Parents About the Teen Session.......................342
     Telling Parents About the Parent Session 343
     Telling Parents About the Graduation Ceremony.........343
   Parent Handout 13: Rumors and Gossip..............................344
    Rules for Handling Rumors and Gossip 344
     How to Avoid Being the Target of Gossip.....................344
     What to Do When You Are the Target of Gossip 344
    Homework Assignments 345
   Teen Therapist Guide—Session 13: Rumors and Gossip 347

Guiding Principles of the Teen Session...347
Rule Review..347
Homework Review..347
Didactic Lesson: Rumors and Gossip 349
Rules for Handling Rumors and Gossip 350
Role Play 352
Behavioral Rehearsal...353
Homework Assignments..353
Graduation Announcement..354
Parent Session..354
Graduation Ceremony 354
Teen Activity: Good Sportsmanship and Outdoor Activities 355
Reunification With Parents...355
Homework Assignments 356
Calculate Points..356
Teen Activity Guide: Session 13 357
"Good Sportsmanship and Outdoor Activities".....................................357
Materials Needed 357
Rules..357

16   **Session 14: Graduation and Termination..................................... 359**
Parent Session Therapist Guide..359
Guiding Principles of the Parent Session 359
Administer Posttreatment Outcome Measures 360
Homework Review... 360
Didactic Lesson: Final Thoughts / Where to Go From Here.................361
Where to Go From Here 361
Reunification and Graduation Ceremony 364
Parent Handout 14: Where to Go From Here 366
Final Thoughts...366
Teen Therapist Guide—Session 14: Graduation and Termination 369
Guiding Principles of the Teen Session...369
Administer Posttreatment Outcome Measures 369
Homework Review...369
Teen Activity..370
Calculate the Points..370
Graduation Prizes...371
Reunification and Graduation Ceremony 371

17   **Case Examples 373**
Case Example: "Martin" 373
Case Example: "Tina"...375
Case Example: "Daniel" 376

References **379**

List of Key Terms **383**

Appendices **385**
    Assessment Measures.. 385
    Session Materials 385

Appendix A.. **387**
    Test of Adolescent Social Skills Knowledge (TASSK)................................... 387
    Test of Adolescent Social Skills Knowledge (TASSK)................................... 389
        Administration 389
        Scoring Key.. 389

Appendix B **393**
    Quality of Play Questionnaire—Parent (QPQ-P)...393
    Quality of Play Questionnaire—Adolescent (QPQ-A)[2] 394
    Quality of Play Questionnaire 395
        Administration 395
        Scoring Key (Both Parent and Teen Versions) 396

Appendix C.. **397**
    Phone Roster 397

Appendix D **399**
    Planned Absence Sheet... 399

Appendix E **401**
    In-Group Phone Call Assignment Log 402
        Week 1.. 402
        Week 2.. 402
        Week 3.. 402
        Week 4.. 402
        Week 5.. 402
        Week 6.. 402

Appendix F **403**
    PEERS Weekly Point Log 404

Appendix G **405**
    PEERS Good Sportsmanship Point Log.. 406

Appendix H **407**
    PEERS Homework Compliance Sheet 408

Appendix I **409**
    Graduation Flyer..410

Author Index **411**

Subject Index.. **413**

Preface

This manual is the product of the postdoctoral fellowship of Elizabeth Laugeson, Psy.D., with the mentorship of Fred Frankel, Ph.D., ABPP. Funding for Laugeson's postdoctoral fellowship was provided by a Ruth L. Kirschstein National Research Service Award through the National Institutes of Health Training Grant NIH T32-MH17140 (Andrew Leuchter, Principal Investigator).

The intervention, as well as the manual, is based in large part upon the structure and experiences of Children's Friendship Training (Frankel & Myatt, 2003). The tradition of Children's Friendship Training is evidenced based, deriving in part from developmental research on how socially successful children form and maintain quality friendships and in part on the results of extensive empirical testing on clinic patients. Both interventions include parents as a formal and integral part of the intervention. Both are manualized, meaning an important structure is imposed on sessions, which is necessary for improvement in social skills. The program is individualized to the needs of each client through weekly review of homework. This affords an opportunity to discuss barriers to implementation and address how to overcome these barriers.

The content of Children's Friendship Training has been developed and used with over 1400 families in 150 groups and 3 funded research studies. More than 80 Ph.D.- and M.S.W.-level therapists have been trained to use the manualized treatment approach. Reflecting that there is a core set of social skills that carry one through life, many of the chapters in this manual are developmentally appropriate enhancements of Children's Friendship Training, so that the treatment modules are similar (permission to use those modules in this manual has been granted by the authors). For example, one of the first tasks of friendship at any age is to be able to join groups of same-aged peers. Children enter groups more in the context of play, and teens and adults enter groups more in the context of conversations. The current manual took many of the content elements of Children's Friendship Training as its core. In extrapolating the intervention for use with teens, it was necessary to adapt or extensively modify most of the modules (Sessions 1, 2, 6, 8, 9, 10, and 14). Several new modules were added that apply to key social elements of the adolescent world (Sessions 3, 4, 5, 7, 11, 12, and 13).

Acknowledgments

This work would not have been possible without the love and support of my family and friends, who inspire me to work hard and live life to its fullest. In particular, I wish to thank Lance Orozco and Janet Tate for their unwavering love and encouragement; and Jennifer Wilkerson, Carrie Raia, and Blair Paley for their constant friendship and support.

To our incredible research team, we most particularly wish to acknowledge the tireless efforts and dedication of Ashley Dillon, Clare Gorospe, Jennifer Sanderson, Ruth Ellingsen, Alex Gantman, Catherine Mogil, Jilly Chang, and Martha Wang for the warmth and compassion they show to every one of our PEERS families.

I wish to thank my wonderful friends and colleagues at the University of California, Los Angeles (UCLA) and The Help Group; I am ever grateful for your support of this work. I am also eternally grateful for the steadfast guidance and friendship of Andrew Leuchter, who has been the most generous of mentors and without whose support the development of this intervention would have remained a vision, as opposed to a reality.

Finally, I wish to gratefully acknowledge and thank the amazing families who have participated in our research to develop this intervention. It has been a gift to know you all, and it is through your perseverance and commitment that this work has been brought to life.

Elizabeth A. Laugeson

I would like to thank my wife, Susan, and children, Seth, Rachel, and Sarah for their love and support. In adapting this from Children's Friendship Training, the families that came to us for help with teens have taught us much and helped to make our intervention work for them.

Fred Frankel

Authors

Elizabeth Laugeson, Psy.D., is a licensed clinical psychologist specializing in social skills training for children and adolescents with autism spectrum disorders and other developmental disabilities. She is a clinical instructor in the Department of Psychiatry and Biobehavioral Sciences at UCLA Semel Institute for Neuroscience and Human Behavior and is the Director of The Help Group—UCLA Autism Research Alliance. Dr. Laugeson is also the Associate Director for the UCLA Children's Friendship and Parenting Program and Director of the UCLA Early Childhood Clubhouse Program. She received her doctorate in psychology from Pepperdine University in 2004 and completed postdoctoral training through an NIH T32 postdoctoral research fellowship at UCLA in 2007. She has been a principal investigator and a collaborator on a number of research studies investigating the effectiveness of social skills training for children with autism spectrum disorders, mental retardation, fetal alcohol spectrum disorders (FASDs), and attention-deficit-hyperactivity disorder (ADHD).

Fred Frankel, Ph.D., is a professor of medical psychology in the Department of Psychiatry and Biobehavioral Sciences at the UCLA Semel Institute for Neuroscience and Human Behavior. He is the Founder and Director of the UCLA Parenting and Children's Friendship Program. He has been principal investigator on two National Institute of Mental Health (NIMH)-funded studies of social skills training for children with ADHD and autism spectrum disorders, coprincipal investigator on one Centers for Disease Control and Prevention (CDC)-funded study of social skills training for children with fetal alcohol spectrum disorders (Mary O'Connor, Principal Investigator [PI]), and one interdisciplinary training grant for research in childhood psychosis (Peter Tanguay, PI). He is a coinvestigator in the NIH-funded Center for Autism Intervention Research Network (Connie Kasari, PI) and the Drown Foundation–funded pediatric overweight prevention grant (Wendy Slusser, PI). He has published more than 46 peer-reviewed studies on autism, ADHD, developmental disabilities, FASDs, and childhood obesity. He has been a guest reviewer for the *Journal of Autism and Developmental Disabilities, Pediatrics,* the *Journal of Abnormal Child Psychology, Child Psychiatry and Human Development,* and the *Journal of Child and Adolescent Psychopharmacology.* Dr. Frankel joined the UCLA faculty in 1973 and has three children, aged 24, 5, and 2 years old.

INTRODUCTION 1

Chapter 1

Introduction

Use of This Manual

PEERS (Program for the Evaluation and Enrichment of Relational Skills) is a parent-assisted intervention focusing on teens in middle school and high school who are having difficulty making or keeping friends. It is the developmental extension of an evidence-based program known as Children's Friendship Training (Frankel & Myatt, 2003). PEERS has been field tested most extensively on teens with autism spectrum disorders (ASDs), to a limited extent on teens with developmental disabilities and fetal alcohol spectrum disorders (FASDs), and is currently undergoing testing with teens with attention-deficit-hyperactivity disorder (ADHD).

The intervention includes separate parent and teen sessions that meet at the same time for 90 minutes each week over a 14-week period. The group focuses on skills like having conversations; entering and exiting conversations; using electronic forms of communication; choosing appropriate friends; handling teasing, bullying, and other forms of social rejection; handling arguments and disagreements with friends; and having appropriate get-togethers with friends, including how to be a good host and a good sport. When the manual is used as described, in the middle of the intervention therapists will often hear parent reports such as, "My teen (with an autism spectrum disorder) no longer stays in his room when company comes, but comes out to interact more." By the end of the intervention, many teens will be having regular get-togethers with a small group of peers. For more detailed accounts of typical treatment outcomes, see Chapter 17, "Case Examples."

This manual is meant to be used as a complete program in its entirety. Each session is based upon what has come before. It can be implemented either as an outpatient program, as described here, or as a school-based program where teens meet during or immediately after school and parents meet at a more convenient time for them.

The orientation of the manual is behavioral, in the sense that material is presented as a series of steps to be followed by parents and teens and the main focus is in getting parents and teens to do homework assignments (that is, generalize what they learn in session to home, community, and school). The program is unique in that it follows a unique format initiated by Children's Friendship Training, it involves parents as an integral component of the intervention, and it focuses on "get-togethers." These are features present in no other known social skills programs. Parent handouts and delivery techniques have been modified over the years based upon over 150 groups conducted with Children's Friendship Training and dozens of groups with PEERS. These techniques have been taught to beginning therapists through our psychology and psychiatry training programs at University of California, Los Angeles (UCLA), and to dozens of mental health professionals and educators in the community. Therapists need not have much experience running social skills groups or groups in general in order to be effective, but they should have background knowledge in working with teens with different forms of developmental disabilities and their parents. We ask experienced therapists to suspend judgment based upon their theoretical orientations and give these behavioral techniques a try, given the previous success of the program.

Required Personnel

In order to run the groups concurrently, it will be necessary to have a teen group leader and a parent group leader. These leaders should have extensive experience working with families in the targeted population (e.g., autism spectrum disorders, developmental delays, attention-deficit-hyperactivity disorder). Yet these leaders need not have experience running social skills groups. Generally, PEERS groups are run by mental health professionals (e.g., psychologists, psychiatrists, social workers, marriage and family therapists), but teacher-/educator-facilitated groups have also been successful. Teen group leaders should have previous experience working with teens and knowledge of high-functioning autism (when relevant) to run groups of teens with this diagnosis. Hibbs et al. (1997) suggest that the following types of therapists might be suited better for an intervention that involves a manual: those more comfortable with psychoeducational approaches (e.g., parent training), and "crossover" professionals (e.g., teachers, school counselors, or primary health care paraprofessionals).

In addition to having a teen group leader and a parent group leader, it will be essential to have one to two coaches to assist in the teen group. Coaches should be trained to handle repeated teen misbehavior and should be supervised by group leaders during weekly case conference meetings. The coaches should be competent in discussing resolution of any misbehavior with parents and teens.

Coaches will also be responsible for demonstrating social skills with the teen group leader via role-play exercises presented to teens. It has been found that undergraduate psychology students with background courses in developmental disabilities or child psychology and having relevant clinical experience with teens (e.g., summer camp counselor) are adequate for this role. Coaches should be trained to do each role play before the session during a weekly case conference. It may be helpful to have them read the role-play scripts (provided in each Teen Session Therapist Guide) until they get the appropriate affective components. The parent group may be conducted by a single therapist.

Who May Benefit From PEERS?

As you will see below, the intervention was developed for teens with autism spectrum disorders, and we are confident that teens with ASD may show lasting benefits from PEERS. The program developers are currently piloting PEERS on a clinic sample of teens with ADHD and having a good clinical response. Because PEERS targets skills development rather than correction of social mistakes and because the steps to making and keeping friends seem to be the same, regardless of the diagnosis of the teen, PEERS may have widespread applicability. We suspect that any teen who does not know the steps to forming and maintaining friendships could benefit from PEERS. In support of this contention, Children's Friendship Training, upon which PEERS is based, was originally developed for children with ADHD. Later studies demonstrated the applicability to children with fetal alcohol spectrum disorders (O'Connor et al., 2006), ASD (Frankel, Myatt, Whitham et al., 2009), and problems with obesity (Frankel, Sinton, & Wilfley, 2007). We encourage professionals using PEERS with other populations to write to the authors.

Organization of the Manual

PEERS is conducted as a structured class on social skills necessary for teens to make and keep friends and improve their reputation among peers. An overview of all of the treatment sessions is presented in Table 1.1. This manual is intended to serve as a step-by-step outline for each session. We find that an outline rather than a script facilitates a more spontaneous sounding presentation of the material, is easier to follow for the therapist, and allows for the therapist to ad lib with material consistent with each lesson. As therapists become more comfortable with our approach, additional therapist material is helpful in getting the major points of each session across. This manual is meant to be used at the time of each session. Memorization is neither required nor encouraged. Families seem comfortable with the therapists having the manual open in front of them as they guide the parents and teens through the skills. The rationale is that the therapist

Table 1.1 Overview of Treatment Sessions

Session	Didactic Lessons	Homework Review	Teen Activity	Materials Needed	Homework Assignment
1	Introduction and Conversational Skills I: Trading Information	None	Jeopardy	Board, markers, name tags, Jeopardy answer sheets, scissors, pens	1. In-group call 2. Practice trading info with parent
2	Conversational Skills II: Two-Way Conversations	1. In-group call 2. Practice trading info with parent	Jeopardy	Board, markers, name tags, Jeopardy answer sheets, scissors, pens	1. In-group call 2. Practice trading info with parent
3	Conversational Skills III: Electronic Communication	1. In-group call 2. Practice trading info with parent	Jeopardy	Board, markers, name tags, Jeopardy answer sheets, scissors, pens	1. In-group call 2. Practice phone call with parent 3. Sources of friends 4. Personal item
4	Choosing Appropriate Friends	1. In-group call 2. Practice phone call with parent 3. Sources of friends 4. Personal item	Trading information: Personal items	Board, markers, CD player, speakers, headphones, magazines	1. In-group call 2. Out-of-group call 3. Sources of friends 4. Personal item
5	Appropriate Use of Humor	1. In-group call 2. Out-of-group call 3. Sources of friends 4. Personal item	Trading information: Personal items	Board, markers, CD player, speakers, headphones, magazines	1. In-group call 2. Out-of-group call 3. Sources of friends 4. Humor feedback 5. Personal item

#	Session	Homework	Didactic lesson	Materials	Homework assigned
6	Peer Entry I: Entering a Conversation	1. In-group call 2. Out-of-group call 3. Sources of friends 4. Humor feedback 5. Personal item	Trading information: Personal items	Board, markers, CD player, speakers, headphones, magazines	1. Slipping in 2. In-group call 3. Out-of-group call 4. Humor feedback 5. Personal item
7	Peer Entry II: Exiting a Conversation	1. Slipping in 2. In-group call 3. Out-of-group call 4. Humor feedback 5. Personal item	Trading information: Personal items	Board, markers, CD player, speakers, headphones, magazines	1. Slipping in 2. Out-of-group call 3. Indoor game
8	Get-Togethers	1. Slipping in 2. Out-of-group call 3. Indoor game	Get-togethers	Board, markers, indoor games	1. Get-together 2. Slipping in 3. Indoor group game
9	Good Sportsmanship	1. Get-together 2. Slipping in 3. Indoor game	Get-togethers and Good sportsmanship	Board, markers, indoor games	1. Get-together 2. Being a good sport 3. Slipping in 4. Indoor game
10	Rejection I: Teasing and Embarrassing Feedback	1. Get-together 2. Being a good sport 3. Slipping in 4. Indoor game	Get-togethers and Good sportsmanship	Board, markers, indoor games	1. Get-together 2. Being a good sport 3. Tease-the-tease 4. Outdoor equipment
11	Rejection II: Bullying and Bad Reputations	1. Get-together 2. Being a good sport 3. Tease-the-tease 4. Outdoor equipment	Good sportsmanship and Outdoor activities	Board, markers, outdoor equipment	1. Get-together 2. Tease-the-tease 3. Handling bullying/bad reputations 4. Outdoor equipment

(Continued)

Table 1.1 (Continued) Overview of Treatment Sessions

Session	Didactic Lesson	Homework Review	Teen Activity	Materials Needed	Homework Assignment
12	Handling Disagreements	1. Get-together 2. Tease-the-tease 3. Handling bullying/bad reputations 4. Outdoor equipment	Good sportsmanship and Outdoor activities	Board, markers, outdoor equipment	1. Get-together 2. Tease-the-tease 3. Handling bullying/bad reputations 4. Handling disagreements 5. Outdoor equipment
13	Rumors and Gossip	1. Get-together 2. Tease-the-tease 3. Handling bullying/bad reputations 4. Handling disagreements 5. Outdoor equipment	Good sportsmanship and Outdoor activities	Board, markers, outdoor equipment	1. Get-together 2. Handling rumors/gossip 3. Tease-the-tease 4. Handling bullying/bad reputations 5. Handling disagreements
14	Graduation and Termination	1. Get-together 2. Handling rumors/gossip 3. Tease-the-tease 4. Handling bullying/bad reputations 5. Handling disagreements	Graduation party and Ceremony	Graduation diplomas, food, beverages, decorations, movies, TV, DVD player, CDs, CD player, graduation prizes	None

needs to be sure to cover all the necessary elements of the skills being taught. It is not meant to be read aloud (except for the Parent Handouts). Each chapter is set up to provide a brief overview of the guiding principles of each session. Each session contains therapist guides for concurrent parent and teen sessions. Sessions must be highly structured to maintain the focus of the lesson. The sections are divided as listed below.

Parent Session Therapist Guide

Each "Parent Session Therapist Guide" (with the exception of Session 1) is broken down into the following sections:

- **Guiding Principles of the Parent Session**—There is a lot of material in each session. The major focus of the session is presented in this section to help the group leader place the appropriate emphasis on the most important material and to address process issues.
- **Homework Review**—Putting the homework review at the beginning of the session underlines the importance of homework completion and allows sufficient time to troubleshoot homework problems. It is during this section that the intervention will be individualized to the specific needs of each family. This section generally takes about 50 to 60 minutes of the 90-minute session time.
- **Homework Assignment**—This section provides a description of how the parent group leader should present the Parent Handout and homework for the following week. For ease of presentation, the "Parent Handout" is embedded in the "Parent Session Therapist Guide." Portions of the "Parent Handout" are in **bold type** within the "Parent Session Therapist Guide" so the group leader need only look in one place while delivering session material. "Parent Handouts" give an overview of the homework assignment and the lesson for the week. The "Parent Handout" provides the major structure for the parent session and describes in detail the parent's part of the homework assignment, as well as a review of the teen didactic lesson. This section generally takes about 20 to 30 minutes of the 90-minute session time. The remaining 10 to 20 minutes is spent on reunification with teens and homework negotiation (see the section "Teen Session Therapist Guide," below).

Parent Handout

"Parent Handouts" appear in the section just following the "Parent Session Therapist Guide." The handouts are suitable for photocopying purposes and should be distributed to parents during each corresponding session. Extra handouts should be available for previously missed sessions, but providing handouts prior to sessions where there is not a planned absence is discouraged.

Teen Session Therapist Guide

Each "Teen Session Therapist Guide" (with the exception of Session 1) is broken down into the following sections:

- **Guiding Principles of the Teen Session**—Similar to the parent session, the major focus of the session is presented in this section to help the group leader place appropriate emphasis on the most important material and to address potential process issues.

- **Rule Review**—A brief overview of the rules for the group is presented in this section but should only be reviewed beyond the first session if group members are engaging in frequent rule violations.

- **Homework Review**—As with the parent session, reviewing the homework at the beginning of the session underlines the importance of homework completion and allows sufficient time to troubleshoot homework problems, thereby individualizing the intervention to the specific needs of each teen. This section generally takes about 20 to 30 minutes of the 90-minute session time.

- **Didactic Lesson**—The didactic material for teens is usually presented using a Socratic method or through the use of role play/exercises to keep the teens involved and engaged and give them a feeling of competence that they (at least collectively) already know much of the material and are generating the rules themselves. This section generally takes about 30 minutes of the 90-minute session time.

- **Behavioral Rehearsal**—One way for teens to begin to translate the material into their daily lives is to practice newly learned skills in session while receiving performance feedback from the group leader and coaches. The behavioral rehearsal section includes suggestions for guided practice to help promote generalization of skills.

- **Homework Assignment**—In this section, the teen group leader briefly provides an overview of the homework assignments for the coming week. By assigning weekly homework corresponding to new and previous lessons, the teen group leader presents a formal way in which the teens will begin to generalize the newly learned skills outside of the session.

- **Teen Activity**—To a large degree, teens should have a choice of whether they continue to come to group. If they do not find the sessions fun and rewarding, they will be more likely to drop out. The teen activity is not only a fun part of the session, but it also affords additional opportunities to practice newly learned skills to varying degrees. A "Teen Activity Guide" appears at the end of the teen section of each chapter. This section generally takes about 20 minutes of the 90-minute session time.

- **Reunification**—Teens and parents come together in the same room at the end of the session. The teen group leader facilitates the teens' review of what they learned in the session by using "buzzwords." The buzzwords are found in ***bolded and italicized type*** throughout the manual. These key words are pointed out to both parents and teens to serve as shorthand for discussing the important content of each session. The review of the lesson and buzzwords is followed by the teen group leader formally announcing the homework assignment for the coming week. The treatment team (including group leaders and coaches) then briefly and privately individually negotiates with each teen and parent how to work together to ensure that the assignment is completed. This section generally takes about 10 to 20 minutes of the 90-minute session time.

■ **Calculate Points**—Each week teens are earning points toward a graduation party with graduation prizes. Points are earned by completing homework assignments and through group participation and appropriate following of the rules. Teen coaches should calculate the number of individual and group points each session (see the Point Log in Appendix F). The calculating of points should be done out of the teens' awareness, and disclosing the number of individual and total points is discouraged.

Teen Activity Guide

The last section of each chapter includes a "Teen Activity Guide" to help the teen group leader and coaches effectively facilitate the socialization activity.

■ **Materials Needed**—A list of materials needed for the activity is presented in the "Teen Activity Guide." Items should be secured prior to the start of the group, when possible.

■ **Rules**—Specific instructions on how to facilitate the activity are provided in this section, including how to coach and give points during the activity and how to debrief the teens at the end.

Research Evidence

Although typically, developing teens often learn basic rules of social etiquette through observation of peer behavior and specific instruction from parents (Gralinski & Kopp, 1993; Rubin & Sloman, 1984), some adolescents may require further instruction, particularly those with developmental delays or autism spectrum disorders. Learning to make and keep friends may be especially difficult for adolescents with ASD, because the natural development and transmission of necessary peer etiquette requires generally positive and sustained interaction with peers and learning from best friends. Frequent isolation, which is common among adolescents with ASD, may make deficits in the knowledge of peer etiquette more pronounced. Furthermore, when gone untreated, many adults with ASD end up lacking the community connections and friendships that are taken for granted by typically developing persons (Baxter, 1997). Thus, teaching the skills necessary to make and keep friends may have significant lifelong impact for persons with ASD.

Among typically developing children, best friendships become stable by about the fourth grade (Frankel, 1996; McGuire & Weisz, 1982). Having one or two best friends is of great importance to later adjustment, can buffer the impact of stressful life events (Miller & Ingham, 1976), and correlates positively with self-esteem and negatively with anxious and depressive symptoms (Buhrmester, 1990). In typically developing children, best friends may promote the development of social competence, but conflicts with acquaintances may inhibit future social interaction.

Although it is clear that teaching social skills to adolescents is an important treatment priority, much of the literature on social skills training for adolescents with ASD has focused on interventions with younger children in the lower ranges of social functioning (Wolfberg & Schuler, 1993). Few social skills interventions have been devoted to investigating the efficacy of social skills training for teens who are less socially impaired, such as teens with Asperger's disorder or high-functioning autism (Marriage, Gordon, & Brand, 1995). Even among the social skills intervention studies conducted with this population, most have not been formally tested in terms of improving social competence or developing close friendships, and they have not assessed social functioning in situations outside of the treatment setting, such as using parent or teacher reports.

The lack of evidence-based social skills instruction to improve social competence and promote the formation of friendships for adolescents with developmental and autism spectrum disorders is what inspired the development of this manual. In 2009, the first randomized controlled trial of PEERS was published in the *Journal of Autism and Developmental Disorders* (Laugeson, Frankel, Mogil, & Dillon, 2009). This study compared 17 teens receiving PEERS with a matched delayed treatment control group of 16 teens, 13 to 17 years of age with ASD. Results revealed, in comparison with the control group, that the treatment group significantly improved their knowledge of social skills, increased frequency of hosted get-togethers, and improved overall social skills as reported by parents. Social skills improvement reported by teachers showed a strong trend toward improvement but was not significant, possibly due to a poor return rate of questionnaires from teachers. At the time of writing this manual, this study is composed of one of the largest number of subjects reported in the treatment outcome literature for older adolescents with ASD.

In a second study of PEERS, currently in preparation for publication, previous findings were repeated for a group of 28 middle school and high school teens with ASD and further showed a significant decrease in autism symptoms related to social responsivity. Results from a comparison of teens receiving the PEERS intervention to those waiting for treatment revealed a significant increase in parent-reported social skills and social responsivity, increased frequency of hosted get-togethers, and improvement in knowledge of social etiquette. These gains were maintained for all measures except teen reports of hosted get-togethers at the end of the 3-month follow-up assessment period. Teen reports of hosted get-togethers declined significantly during the follow-up period; however, 7 of 12 parents reported improvements from baseline to follow-up. We suspect from this data that get-togethers, when parents are present, are better than get-togethers maintained in the community setting and other teens' homes. This finding further promotes parent involvement in get-togethers as a means of ensuring continued gains during follow-up.

These combined findings suggest that the use of PEERS as a parent-assisted social skills intervention leads to improvement in friendship skills for adolescents with ASD. The combined sample of 61 subjects makes these results more compelling. Attrition rates were low in both studies with 33 completers and 6 dropouts (14.6%) in the first study and 28 completers and 4 dropouts in the second study (12.5%). In contrast, Frankel and Simmons (1992) report as many as 43% to 59% drop out during the course of most outpatient treatment.

Using PEERS in the School Setting

In 2008, PEERS underwent pilot testing in a school setting through a collaboration with Autism Spectrum and Treatment (ASTAR) in Seattle, Washington, and the Lake Washington School District. This pilot study was conducted as a therapist-facilitated, parent-assisted after-school program. Results were encouraging and consistent with previous findings.

At the time of writing this manual, the PEERS intervention is currently being tested for effectiveness through The Help Group's Village Glen School, a non-public school for children with ASD in the greater Los Angeles area. The study, funded by the Nathan and Lily Shapell Foundation, is being conducted as part of The Help Group–UCLA Autism Research Alliance, and will test the effectiveness of improving friendship skills among over 80 middle school children with ASD. Using a teacher-facilitated model, an adapted version of the PEERS intervention will be implemented in the classroom daily for 20 to 30 minutes per day. Parents will receive weekly psychoeducational handouts instructing them on key features of the program and how to best support their teens' efforts to improve their friendships. Treatment outcome for this 14-week intervention will be compared to the usual social skills curriculum at the Village Glen School.

Use of This Manual With Young Adults

Young adulthood encompasses many challenges, including school transition, finding employment, building a social network, increasing household tasks, and developing romantic relationships. All of these areas require a certain degree of mastery of social skills that many young adults with autism are sadly lacking. Untreated, these social difficulties may lead to symptoms of depression, anxiety, social isolation, and loneliness. Although research on ASD has been extensive in the child and adolescent literature, there has been a void in research-validated services for young adults with autism.

At the time of writing the current manual, a research study to test the effectiveness of using an adapted version of the PEERS manual to improve friendship skills in young adults 18 to 23 years of age with ASD is underway also through The Help Group–UCLA Autism Research Alliance. Parents and caregivers will be included in weekly classes that teach young adults the rules of social etiquette. During the 14-week intervention, core skills necessary to making and keeping friends will be addressed, including social communication, choosing appropriate friendships, organizing social activities, dealing with social rejection, resisting social pressures and exploitation, dating etiquette, and more.

PREPARING FOR TREATMENT

Chapter 2

Preparing for Treatment

Screening

Prior to admission to the group, we recommend that a prescreening phone interview and an intake interview be conducted to establish appropriateness for the group and to describe expectations for participation. The primary purpose in conducting these interviews is to identify whether the teen has adequate verbal abilities that will ensure he or she is able to follow the didactic lessons presented in the groups, to make sure the teen is motivated to attend, to ensure that there are no behavioral issues that would prohibit participation (i.e., aggressive behavior), and to ensure that parents agree to do their parts in the homework assignments. It is essential that only teens who are interested in participating in the groups be admitted to the program.

A prescreening phone interview can generally be conducted in approximately 10 to 15 minutes and need not be conducted by a licensed clinical therapist (see "Phone Screening Script" and "PEERS Phone Screen Data Sheet"). During this prescreening interview, it will be essential to verify that the teen is of average to above average intelligence to ensure that he or she will be able to follow the course material, which is presented through verbal instruction. It is highly recommended that the parent or guardian be informed of the strict guidelines with regard to verbal abilities and willingness to participate. A sample PEERS "Phone Screening Script" appears below and is intended to screen teens who would benefit from PEERS as well as begin to get necessary background information. The "Phone Screen Data Sheet" also appears below and will help to complete the screening process.

Phone Screening Script

"Thank you for calling!"

[Ask parent name.]

Q: Who referred you to our program or how did you find out about us?

Let me tell you a little more about the program. PEERS is a parent-assisted intervention for teens in middle school and high school who are having difficulty making or keeping friends.

> *There are separate parent and teen sessions that meet at the same time for 90 minutes each week over a 14-week period. The group focuses on skills like having conversations; entering and exiting conversations; electronic forms of communication, including making phone calls to friends; choosing appropriate friends; handling teasing, bullying, and other forms of rejection; handling arguments and disagreements with friends; and having appropriate get-togethers with friends, including being a good host and a good sport. Parents are taught how to help their teens make and keep friends by acting as social coaches outside of the group. During the teen session, teens are presented with a lesson and then practice whatever skill they just learned while participating in socialization activities or playing board games, card games, or outdoor sports. Homework assignments are also given each week to make sure teens are practicing the skills they are learning. The class meets* (insert day and time). *The classes are 14 weeks long, and the next classes begin on _____ and end on _____. The same parent must be able to attend at least 11 of the 14 sessions to be enrolled.*

→ Exclude if parents need to trade off attending, if the family will miss more than three sessions, or if the family will miss the first two sessions.

Q: Is this something you might be interested in?

> [If no, provide referrals from a list of alternative social skills groups.]
> [If yes, continue below.]

Q: Does this group sound like something that your teen would be interested in attending?

It's important for you to know that we do not force anyone to participate in these groups. That means your teen must be willing to attend the groups voluntarily. Do you need more time to discuss this with your teen?

> [If not a problem, continue with phone screen.]

Great! I first need to ask you a few questions about you and your teen in order to determine if he or she is eligible for our program. All of your answers will be confidential. I will also need to obtain your contact information so we can mail you our enrollment materials.

Q: What is your teen's first and last name? (Confirm spelling.)

Q: How old is your teen?

Q: What is your teen's date of birth?

Q: What grade is your teen currently in?

[Must be in middle school or high school. Exclusion if teen is in college; even if teen is still 17.]

Q: What is the name of the school your teen attends?

Q: Does your teen receive any special services at the school he or she is enrolled in?

If in special education, ask: *What grade level is the work he or she is doing?*

[Exclude if teen is working below a sixth-grade level.]

Q: What problems or issues does your teen have making or keeping friends?

No friends at school

Cannot make new friends

Does not keep friends

No get-togethers

Teased or bullied

Aggressive with friends

Does not get invited to others' houses or birthday parties

Other kids do not like the teen

→ Exclude if:

Teen does not have verbal skills

Teen does not agree to attend voluntarily

→ Possible exclusion if:

Teen strongly prefers to isolate self from others [Probe if teen is nevertheless interested in the group—if so, then do not exclude.]

Q: Does your teen have a group of friends at school?

Q: Does your teen have get-togethers with peers? Or does your teen have friends over?

Q: How do those get-togethers usually go?

Q: What types of games or activities does your teen like to play?

Q: Does he or she play any sports?

Q: Is he or she in any clubs or extracurricular activities?

Q: Does your teen have any significant behavioral issues at home?

Q: Has your teen's teacher reported that your teen has any significant behavioral issues at school?

→ Exclude if teen has significant behavioral problems such as:

Violent, aggressive behavior toward adults or teens

Inability to function without one-on-one aide

Teen not able to function within a group setting

Teen does not respond to limit setting

Q: Has your teen ever received any type of psychological or medical diagnosis?

→ Exclude if:

Teen has severe speech or articulation issues

Lower functioning autism

Physical or medical disability (unable to engage in sports activities)

Visually or hearing impaired

Major mental illness (schizophrenia, bipolar disorder, major depression)

Q: Is your teen on any medication? [Obtain name and dosage information.]

As I mentioned before, there is a parent portion of our program which requires one parent to attend on a consistent basis. The other parent is also always welcome to attend.

Q: Who will be attending the program with your teen?

   →   Exclude if parents need to trade-off attending.

Q: Just to confirm, what is your relationship to your teen (e.g., Are you his biological mother?)

Q: Is this a two-parent or single-parent home?

Q: Does your teen have any siblings? [Obtain ages and gender of siblings.]

It sounds like our program may be appropriate for your teen. In order to enroll your teen in the program, I will mail you out a packet of questionnaires to complete. It will take you about 20 to 30 minutes to fill out the forms and return them. When we get the forms back from you, we will call you to schedule a 1-hour intake appointment with you and your teen to determine if our program is appropriate and if it is something that will benefit your teen. After you complete the intake and if we feel your teen will benefit from the class, then he or she is officially on the waiting list to start the next available class. You will not be placed on the waiting list until we've received your packet and you've completed your intake appointment.

Q: Do you have any other questions I can answer for you?

Great! Thanks for your call. You should be receiving the packet in the mail in a few days. Please remember that enrollment is limited, so please return your packet as soon as possible. If you have any further questions please feel free to give us a call back.

PEERS Phone Screen Data Sheet

Program for the Education and Enrichment of Relational Skills

Screened by:			Date:
Teen Name:	M	F	Date of Birth (DOB):
Age:	Grade:		School:
Referent:			

Family Information

Family type:

☐ Bio parents ☐ Adoptive parents ☐ Foster ☐ Group home

☐ Two-parent ☐ Single-parent ☐ Other: _____

Who will attend intake:

☐ Bio-mom ☐ Bio-dad ☐ Step-mom ☐ Step-dad

☐ Other: _____

Identifying Information

Parent(s) Name:	
Address:	
E-mail:	
Home Phone: Work Phone: Cell Phone:	
Diagnosis:	Meds:
IQ score/classification:	School setting:
Inclusion Criteria (check all that apply)	Exclusion Criteria (check all that apply)
☐ Teen is in middle or high school ☐ IQ above 70 ☐ Social problems ☐ Teen and parent fluent in English ☐ Parent/guardian willing to participate ☐ Teen willing to participate	☐ Major mental illness (schizophrenic, bipolar). Specify: ☐ Physical disability (preventing outdoor play). Specify: ☐ Medical conditions (preventing participation). Specify:
Behavioral Problems (check all that apply)	
☐ Inappropriate classroom behavior ☐ Trouble with home/school work ☐ Violence/aggression ☐ Fire setting ☐ Stealing	☐ Severe property destruction ☐ Argumentative/tantrums/disobeying ☐ Parent afraid of child ☐ Previously hospitalized for behavior ☐ Other (specify):
Social Problems (check all that apply)	
☐ No get-togethers ☐ No friends at school/community ☐ Socially isolated/withdrawn ☐ Social anxiety ☐ Trouble making friends ☐ Trouble keeping friends	☐ Inappropriate peer group ☐ Aggressive or mean to peers ☐ Teased/bullied ☐ Rejected by peers ☐ Socially awkward ☐ Trouble understanding social cues
Comments:	

Parent and Teen Intake Interview

It is highly recommended that an intake interview be conducted with both parents or guardians and teens prior to admission in the treatment group. This intake interview can generally be conducted within 50 minutes. The recommended structure of the interview includes a 5-minute greeting with both the parent or guardian and teen; a 20-minute private interview with the teen; a 20-minute private interview with the parent or guardian while the teen completes the pretreatment assessments; and a 5-minute wrap-up with both parent or guardian and teen. The waiting period between interviews can often be a useful time to have the parents or guardians and teens complete any outstanding pretreatment questionnaires.

Greeting

It is helpful to begin the intake interview with a brief greeting welcoming the family and orienting them to the intake procedures. You might begin by saying: *I wanted to take a few minutes to meet with you to explain what we will be doing today. First, I want to make sure that everyone has a clear understanding of why we're meeting today. (Teen's name), Do you have a clear understanding of why you're here?* At this point, you will want to give the teen the opportunity to explain his or her understanding of the appointment and address any misunderstandings about the nature of the visit. If the teen is unsure about the purpose of the meeting, you might say: *We have a group for teens about your age where we teach you to make and keep friends. The group meets once a week for about 14 weeks and if you participate in the group, both you and your parent(s) will attend the group. We're meeting today to find out if this group is a good fit for everyone. In order to figure out whether this is the right group for you and your parent(s), I'd like to ask you some questions about school, your friends, and what you like to do. Would that be alright?*

Assuming the teen agrees to answer your questions, you will want to continue by explaining the structure of the intake appointment. You might say: *Now that we're all clear about why we're here, I'd like to take some time to speak with each of you individually. I was hoping to meet with (teen's name) for about 20 minutes and then with (parent's name) for about 20 minutes. While each of you is waiting, I have a few forms for you to fill out. These forms will give me a better understanding of what's happening with (teen's name) socially. At the end of the hour, we'll all meet up again and talk about whether or not this group seems to be a good fit for everyone. Does that sound alright?*

Teen Interview

At the beginning of the teen interview, it may be useful to spend a few moments describing the intervention to the teen. You might say: *As you know, I'm going to be asking you some questions about your school, friends, and things you like to do. Before I do that, I'd like to take a few moments to tell you a little more about our groups. Our program is known as PEERS, and the purpose of our group is to help teens learn to make and keep friends. We do this by teaching you important skills that are needed in friendships; things like how to have an appropriate conversation, how to walk up to other teens and join their conversations, and how to have get-togethers with friends. We also teach you skills that help you handle conflict with peers; things like how to handle teasing and bullying, how to resolve an argument with a friend, and even how to change a bad reputation. We not only teach you these skills, but we have you practice them in the group each week and then outside of the group between sessions. There are usually about 8 to 10 teens in the group, all around the same age as you. While you're attending the teen group, your parent(s) will be attending their own group in a separate room. The idea behind the parent group is that we're trying to teach your parents what you're learning and help them to identify places where you might be able to make new friends. The great news is that the groups are usually fun and most of the teens who participate in PEERS are able to improve their friendship skills by the end of the 14 weeks. Does that sound like something you might be interested in? Do you have any questions about the program?* You will then want to address any questions raised by the teen and then proceed with the teen intake interview (see the "Teen Intake Interview Checklist").

During the teen interview, it will also be important to establish rapport with the teen and make it clear that his or her participation in the group is entirely the teen's decision. You will want to make it clear that the teen has to want to participate in order to be included in the group. If the teen is reluctant to agree to participation, it is strongly advised to wait until the teen agrees before admitting him or her into the group. In this case, the teen should be required to communicate his or her interest in participation directly to the interviewer before moving forward. In cases in which the teen is unwilling to give his or her assent to participate in the group, the interviewer should feel free to discontinue the intake interview and reconvene with the parent and teen to discuss this issue. The parent should be informed that the teen is unwilling to agree to participate in the group and the interview cannot continue until the teen has given his or her assurances that he or she wants to receive treatment. In such cases, it is common for parents to pressure their teen to agree to treatment. In this event, it is advisable that the interviewer be very cautious about continuing with the intake interview. Including families in which teens are reluctant to participate often leads to a lack of group cohesion and higher rates of attrition.

Parent / Guardian Interview

During the parent or guardian interview, you will want to obtain a thorough history of the teen's social, psychological, medical, and developmental history. In particular, you will want to get a description of any previous or current psychiatric diagnoses, as well as a comprehensive description of any current or previous psychiatric evaluations or treatments (including medication). It will be important to spend a substantial amount of time allowing the parent or guardian to describe his or her concerns about their teen's social problems, while considering whether these concerns are sufficiently addressed through the PEERS curriculum, or whether a different treatment is indicated or additional referral is required.

This is the time when you carefully describe what is expected of the parent or guardian during the intervention. Specifically:

■ The same parent should attend each session.
■ The teen should have enough unscheduled time so that get-togethers with new friends made during the intervention can easily happen.
■ The parents have to commit to try to find extracurricular activities in which to enroll their teen as the group starts. Material in PEERS is designed to help them do this, but they have to be sufficiently motivated to carry this through.
■ Parents have to understand that the intervention is highly structured with an agenda for each session and homework assignments specifically designed to promote friendships. There will be little time for parent support functions or to talk about issues other than problems in getting the homework done.
■ Parents should agree that their teen needs the intervention or have them reconsider taking part in the group. They will not be able to change the format of the sessions or goals of the treatment.
■ Parents should also understand that the purpose of this group is to give the teens enough skills to make their own friends. The other teens in the group will be present for the purpose of practicing these skills. For good reasons, they will not be allowed to socialize in any way with the other teens in the group for the 14 weeks of PEERS (see Box 2.1 for a detailed explanation). Note that some of the teen homework assignments require making phone calls to other group members. The homework is only to practice specific conversational skills, not to arrange social contacts between group members. Teens are assigned a different group member to call each week. This assignment eventually expands to include calls to teens who are not in the group. From Box 2.1, it is evident that prohibiting within-group social contacts also applies to groups run at a school program and for teens who happen to know each other prior to starting PEERS. For teens who share an acquaintance with other group members prior to the treatment, it is recommended to have them agree to cease social contacts while they are participating in the group.

At the end of the parent or guardian interview, you should discuss your decision about the appropriateness of treatment for the family. In the event that the teen is appropriate for the PEERS intervention, you will want to give the parent the opportunity to decide whether he or she wants to participate in the treatment before meeting with the teen again. In the event that the teen is not found to be appropriate for treatment, you will want to explain the nature of these reasons and be willing to provide appropriate referrals.

**BOX 2.1 REASONS TO PROHIBIT SOCIAL CONTACT
BETWEEN GROUP MEMBERS DURING THE INTERVENTION**

1. Inconsistent with the skills being presented:
   a. The teens may not actually want to socialize with each other. The prohibiting of social contact with other group members allows them a graceful way to avoid an uncomfortable situation.
   b. The parents may rightfully feel the teens should not be friends with each other.
2. Introducing negative affect between group members:
   a. After-session social contacts introduce competition and bad feelings between some group members through the forming of cliques.
   b. Organizing get-togethers with other group members before the presentation of this skill has occurred may result in negative interactions between the teens.
   c. Conflict between group members resulting from outside group social contact may lead to tension within the group and possibly early withdrawal from the group.
3. Prohibiting between-session contacts allows parents and teens to:
   a. Report freely on homework assignments, without concern of making a group member feel left out.
   b. Speak their minds to each other, without worrying about alienating a "potential friend."
   c. Maintain credibility in their efforts to help each other solve social problems.

Source: Frankel & Myatt, 2003.

Wrap-Up

Once you establish eligibility in the program with the parent or guardian, you will want to take a few minutes to meet with the parent or guardian and teen to share the news with the teen and give the family information about how to proceed. In cases in which the teen has been accepted into the program, you might say: *It looks like you and your parent will be joining our program. As you know, our groups meet every week for 90 minutes over a 14-week period. The next group begins* [give the specific date]. *I have some information about the groups that I'd like to share with you and I'd be happy to answer any final questions you may have.* At this point, it is helpful to provide the family with a "Welcome Letter" that provides comprehensive information about the start date, the time and location of the groups, driving and parking information, and a brief list of the skills that will be taught. Within this "Welcome Letter" it is also advisable to notify families that regular attendance and arriving on time are imperative to the success of the program (see sample "Welcome Letter"). Be sure to notify parents or guardians that they will need to make arrangements not to have siblings in session. An exception to this rule would be the involvement of older adult siblings who may be helpful in facilitating successful participation (e.g., including an English-speaking adult sibling when a parent is non-English speaking in an English-only group).

Teen Intake Interview Checklist

1. Did your parents tell you why you're here today?
   ☐Gave correct answer ☐Did not know ☐Incorrect
2. We have a class that teaches teens how to make and keep friends. Is that something you might be interested in?
   ☐Yes ☐No ☐Don't know
3. I would like to find out about the things you like to do. Do they have a time at your school when you are free to hang out with other teens (lunch, before/after school)?
   ☐Yes ☐No (skip Question #4)
4. What do you usually do during that time?
   ☐Spend time with other teens ☐Alone
5. Are there teens that you usually hang around with at school?
   ☐Yes ☐No (skip to Question #9)
6. What are their first names?
   ☐Provides no names ☐Provides a few names ☐Provides four or more names
7. Are they in the same grade as you?
   ☐Same grade ☐Older ☐Younger ☐Adults
8. How do you usually meet up?
   ☐We decide together ☐Same place every day ☐I find out where they are
9. What kind of things do you usually do with your friends outside of school?
   ☐Talk/hang out ☐Shop/go to the mall ☐Phone/Internet
   ☐Sports/clubs: _____ ☐Games: _____ ☐Other: _____
10. Have you been on any teams or clubs?
    ☐No ☐Yes:
11. What games do you have in your home that you like to play?
    ☐None ☐Board/card games: _____ ☐Sports: _____
    ☐Electronic/video games: _____ ☐Other: _____
12. Do you ever have get-togethers with friends?
    ☐Yes ☐No (end interview)
13. What kinds of things do you like to do with your friends when you have get-togethers?
    ☐Talk/hang out ☐Games ☐Watch TV/movies ☐Listen to music
    ☐Video games/electronics ☐Sports: _____ ☐Other: _____
14. When was the last time you had a get-together?
    Within the last: ☐Week ☐Month ☐Longer than 1 month
15. What was the teen's name?
    ☐Gave name: _____ ☐Could not remember
16. What did you do together (prompt for complete answer)?
    ☐Mixed activities ☐Exclusively electronic/video games and/or TV
17. Reported interest in a class that teaches teens how to make and keep friends:
    ☐Not interested, has plenty of friends
    ☐Showed interest by asking questions about the class
    ☐Stated interest in the class

Global Impressions

Oriented ×3 (person, place, time)?   □Yes □No
Mood and affect appropriate to the situation? □Yes □No
Established rapport with the examiner? □Readily   □Eventually   □Never
Cognitive abilities: □Below average   □Average   □Above average
Social maturity: □1 to 2 years below age level □Age level □Above age level

(Adapted with permission from Frankel & Myatt, 2003.)

Welcome to PEERS! (Sample Welcome Letter)

- You are confirmed to attend the next PEERS group, which is scheduled to start on _____ and will be held from _____ to _____ **p.m.**
- Regular attendance and coming on time is imperative for getting the full benefit of the program. **We recommend that you wait for the next group if you already know you will be missing three or more sessions or will be absent for the first two sessions.** We typically meet consistently on a weekly basis and schedule around major holidays. A planned absence sheet and schedule will be distributed during the first session.
- It is important that the **same parent** attend every session. Teens have weekly assignments that require parental supervision (i.e., making or receiving phone calls from other group members, calling friends on the telephone to practice conversational skills, having get-togethers with friends not in the group). **Other parents are always welcome to attend, but we strongly discourage parents from switching off each week.**
- We ask that you please **do not** bring siblings to group sessions.
- Dr. _____ will lead the teen group, and Dr. _____ will lead the parent group. Other trained therapists and graduate students may assist with the groups under direct supervision.
- **If applicable,** all payment or copayments will be collected at the beginning of session. Only Visa, MasterCard, American Express, check, or exact cash will be accepted. Information regarding fees and insurance coverage will be discussed during the first session.

Meeting Location

- We will meet at: _____
- The groups will be meeting in the same location on a weekly basis.
- *See enclosed map.*

Parking

- *See enclosed parking information.*

Your Teen Will Learn

• How to use appropriate conversational skills	• How to be a good host during get-togethers
• How to find common interests in conversations	• How to choose appropriate friends
• How to enter and exit conversations between peers	• How to be a good sport
• How to use appropriate humor	• How to handle arguments with peers
• How to use electronic communication	• How to change a bad reputation
• How to handle rumors and gossip	• How to handle teasing and bullying

If you have any questions, please contact our staff at XXX-XXX-XXXX.

Forming Groups

Composition of the Group

The recommended PEERS group size should be between 7 and 10 teens per group. Each specific group of teens needs to be limited in their range of psychopathology. It has been repeatedly observed in the PEERS social skills groups that teens with ASD are often most comfortable and appear to thrive more successfully with other teens with ASD. Therefore, homogenous groups for teens with ASD are encouraged. Teens with ADHD and other social behavioral problems have generally been observed to be less accepting of teens with ASD in the groups and may therefore benefit from a separate group in order to minimize attrition. With regard to age and grade level, the groups may have a wider range providing there is more than one teen at each age level. Girls and boys are easily mixed without problems. Historically, boys are more likely to present for social skills treatment, so it is likely that groups will be composed of fewer girls. It is recommended that groups with only one female member be avoided, unless the family willingly agrees.

Physical Facilities

It is helpful to create a classroom atmosphere for the parent sessions and the didactic segment of the teen sessions. The teen room should have a whiteboard and markers with tables and chairs for teens to sit facing the board. The parent room should have chairs arranged in a large circle and enough space for all parents to be seated together at the same time. Teen Sessions 11 through 13 are conducted on an outside play area used to teach skills for outdoor games and sports and should resemble a schoolyard as much as possible. It should have sports equipment such as a basketball hoop, soccer goal net, or volleyball net and should be fully fenced in for safety. In the event that such outdoor accommodations are not possible, teen session activities for Sessions 11 through 13 will need to be modified for indoor games as described in Sessions 8 through 10. Parent and teen rooms and the outside play area should be as close as possible to each other for quick transport of teens during each session.

Behavioral Control Techniques

Most behavioral problems are addressed through the screening process. If the teen willingly agrees to participate in the group he or she will mostly behave. However, some teens may be disruptive in the group and will require further behavioral intervention to modify these disruptions. The teen group leader should draw the line with three types of behaviors: disruption of other teens (e.g., engaging in behaviors that distract or disturb other group members from the lesson), disrespect for the group leader or other teens (e.g., teasing, bullying, making rude comments), and agressive behavior or threats of agression. Explicit guidelines for handling behavioral disturbances are presented in the "Teen Therapist Guide—Session 1."

Required Materials

The following materials will need to be available for the groups:

- A "Phone Roster" with each participant's name and a phone number where he or she can be easily reached for in-group phone call assignments. This roster should be distributed to parents on the first session of the group (see the "Phone Roster" in Appendix C). Parents will need to provide an appropriate phone number at intake and give consent to have this information released to other group members.
- A "Planned Absence Sheet" should be distributed to parents during the first session and completed by each teen's parent indicating which session(s) they will miss (see the "Planned Absence Sheet" in Appendix D). This sheet should not include information about the didactic lesson presented each week so as to avoid parents picking and choosing sessions they wish to attend.
- An "In-Group Phone Call Assignment" sheet will be needed to track phone assignments in the teen group during Sessions 1 through 6. Keeping careful track of which teens are assigned to call one another will enable the teen group leader to switch the order or "caller" and "receiver" for these phone calls and ensure that teens call different group members throughout this process (see the "In-Group Phone Call Assignment" sheet in Appendix E).
- A "Weekly Point Log" will be needed to track the individual and group points in the teen session each week. This log should include the name of each teen, along with individual and group totals for points used toward the distribution of graduation prizes in Session 14 (see the "Teen Therapist Guide—Session 1" for a description of the point distribution). A sample "Weekly Point Log" is provided in Appendix F.
- A few copies of the "Good Sportsmanship Point Log" will be needed in Sessions 9 through 13 to track teens' attempts at good sportsmanship during both indoor games and outdoor sports activities. The number of point logs needed will be determined by the number of personnel in the teen group. Each member of the teen group treatment team should track good sportsmanship compliance for a specified group of teens. A sample "Good Sportsmanship Point Log" is provided in Appendix G.
- "Homework Compliance Sheets" are highly recommended to track weekly progress and completion of homework assignments. The sheets may be completed by the parent group leader and the teen group coaches during the sessions. They should include both the parent and teen names, and when relevant, age, grade, diagnosis, and school placement will provide

useful information to group leaders. These sheets should be filed for future reference and used to track treatment compliance during the weekly case conference. A "Homework Compliance Sheet" for the parent and teen groups is provided in Appendix H.

■ A dry erase board with markers for keeping track of teens' points and writing buzzwords and relevant lesson points will be an essential tool for the teen group room.

■ Additional materials needed for teen session activities are provided in the "Teen Activity Guide" at the end of each teen session.

Providing Food and Beverages

Providing food and beverages seems to be common practice among outpatient groups for teens with ASD and developmental disabilities. The PEERS social skills groups have been run with and without food and beverages. The advantage of providing food and beverages is that groups can be scheduled at regular meal times, the meal may help teens to remain seated throughout the homework review, and the meal may provide opportunities for unstructured coaching on table manners. The disadvantage is that session time is taken up with distribution of these items and sometimes creates an unwelcome distraction from the session material. The bottom line is that the groups run just as well with or without food and beverages.

Initial Start-Up Challenges

The most difficult part of the start-up process occurs during the formation of the first few groups. Referral sources have often not been alerted to the inclusion criteria of the groups or what they may provide, and no "track record" has been established (either in the capacity to form adequate groups or the ability to benefit teens). In order to start a group, parents of teens with comparable characteristics must be enrolled within about a 2-month period of each other. Any longer than this and parents will usually not want to wait or will lose confidence that you can provide the intervention that has been described to them. You should not compromise on the above criteria in order to get the initial groups underway; however, a minimum of six teens in a group is essential. This is the "critical mass" or the minimal number of participants that feels like a "group" to both participants and group leaders. Other compromises could risk the "word-of-mouth" reputation of your fledgling clinical enterprise. Seven or eight participants is a safer number to start, as absences will be less likely to take the group below critical mass. Recommended maximum group size is 10, as this allows parents and teens adequate time for discussion within a 90-minute session.

Buzzwords

Terms that are ***bold and italicized*** in either the teen or parent session material are buzzwords and represent important concepts from the curriculum. The buzzwords represent complex social behaviors that can be identified in just a few simple words.

Try to use the buzzwords as much as possible to develop a common language between therapists, parents, and teens. In both sessions, when you get to the first instance of a buzzword in the therapist guide, try to emphasize the words in speaking, and in teen sessions write them down on the board.

Outcome Assessments

Standardized assessment is an essential part of treatment. It is how the intervention program maintains quality control and is the most objective assessment of treatment outcome. Group leaders will be more apt to deliver the manualized treatment if they know that participants will fill out evaluations geared toward measuring improvement. We list the assessments we have used in our published studies as they are readily available and have demonstrated substantial change after our treatment. They also impose little demands upon parents and teens to complete. They should be administered as a packet sent to parents to complete before or during the intake interview, and completed again during the last treatment session.

> *Social Skills Improvement System (SSIS)* (Gresham & Elliott, 2008)—The SSIS, replacing the Social Skills Rating System (SSRS) (Gresham & Elliott, 1990) consists of 76 items and takes approximately 15 minutes to complete. Questionnaires may be completed independently by the teen's parent and teacher. The items are rated as either "Never," "Sometimes," or "Very Often." The Social Skills and Problem Behaviors scales were derived from factor analysis. Gresham and Elliott (2008) reported the psychometric properties of the parent and teacher forms for teens. For ages 13 to 18, Coefficient alphas were above .77 for parents and .75 for teachers. Test–retest reliability was above .73 for parents and .75 for teachers. Higher scores on the Social Skills scale indicate better social functioning, and lower scores on the Problem Behavior scale indicate better behavioral functioning.
>
> *Social Responsiveness Scale (SRS)* (Constantino, 2005)—The SRS is a 65-item rating scale that measures the severity of autism spectrum symptoms as they occur in natural social settings. Completed by the parent and the teacher, the SRS takes about 15 minutes to complete and provides a clear picture of the teen's social impairments, assessing social awareness, social information processing, capacity for reciprocal social communication, social anxiety or avoidance, and autistic preoccupations and traits. It is appropriate for use with children from 4 to 18 years of age.

Friendship Qualities Scale (FQS) (Bukowski, Hoza, & Boivin, 1994)—The FQS is a teen self-report measure that assesses the quality of best friendships. It consists of 23 Likert-scale items, ranging from 1 to 5, from five different subscales (companionship, closeness, help, security, and conflict) and takes approximately 5 minutes to complete. Teens are instructed to identify their best friend and keep this friendship in mind while completing this measure. For example, items include, "My friend and I spend all of our free time together." The total score ranges from 23 to 115, with higher scores reflecting better-quality friendships. According to the authors, coefficient alphas for subscales range from .71 to .86. Confirmatory factor analysis supported the factor structure of the subscales and comparisons between ratings by reciprocated versus nonreciprocated friends supported the discriminant validity of the scales (Bukowski et al., 1994).

Test of Adolescent Social Skills Knowledge (TASSK) (Laugeson et al., 2009) —The TASSK is a 26-item criterion-referenced test developed for PEERS to assess the teen's knowledge about the specific social skills taught during the intervention. Two items were derived from key elements of each of the 13 didactic lessons. Teens are presented with sentence stems and asked to choose the best option from two possible answers. Scores range from 0 to 26, with higher scores reflecting greater knowledge of teen social skills. Coefficient alpha for the TASSK was .56. This moderate level of internal consistency was acceptable, given the large domain of questions on the scale. The TASSK takes approximately 5 minutes to complete and is presented in Appendix A.

The Quality of Play Questionnaire (QPQ) (Frankel & Mintz, 2009)—The QPQ consists of 12 items administered to parents and teens independently to assess the frequency of get-togethers with peers over the previous month and the level of conflict during these get-togethers. It takes approximately 2 to 3 minutes to complete. The 10 items that make up the conflict scale ask for individual parent and teen ratings of peer conflict (e.g., "criticized or teased each other"). The last two items ask parents and teens to individually estimate the number of invited and hosted get-togethers the teen has had over the previous month. The QPQ was developed through factor analysis of 175 boys and girls. Coefficient alpha was .87 for the conflict scale. This scale also demonstrated convergent validity with the SSRS problem behaviors scale (*rho* = .35, *p* < .05) and significantly discriminated community from clinic-referred samples (*p* < .05). Reported frequency of hosted and invited get-togethers also significantly discriminated community from clinic samples (*p*'s < .005). Spearman correlation between teen and parent ratings at baseline for the randomized controlled trial of PEERS was .55 for the conflict scale, .99 for the frequency of hosted get-togethers, and .99 for the frequency of invited get-togethers (deleting reports of "0" get-togethers resulted in correlations of .97 and .94, respectively, all *p*'s < .001). The adolescent and parent versions (QPQ-A and QPQ-P) are presented in Appendix B.

TREATMENT SESSIONS

Chapter 3

Session 1
Introduction and Conversational Skills I—Trading Information

Parent Session Therapist Guide

Guiding Principles of the Parent Session

The purpose of the first parent session is to orient parents to the structure of the group and solidify the expectations for treatment. This is the main point of the first session for parents so that the content of the didactic lesson is limited. The development of clear expectations and session structure cannot be understated, as without these core components, the session plan may more easily get sidetracked, thereby minimizing the effectiveness of the intervention.

At the time of writing this manual, very few effective programs for remediation of friendship problems in children and adolescents exist, and of those that have an evidence base, these programs are not in widespread use among practitioners. Consequently, parents of teens entering PEERS are often discouraged through years of efforts at trying to help their children using methods that have not worked. They often come with varying degrees of desperation. On the one hand, they hope you can help them, and on the other hand, they may show high levels of resistance. They sometimes assume that their teen will not change as a result of treatment, probably because this is what has happened with numerous experiences they have had before. They sometimes even assume in their predictions of homework compliance that their teen will not change, which may lead them to be sluggish to do their parts of the homework assignments.

You will find that most parents who enroll their teens want and need your help and are rewarding to work with. They will be grateful to you for providing the group and anxious to do their best to complete homework assignments. Once they see improvement in their teen they will be excited. They are nurturing and sustaining for therapists also. However, there may be a subset of parents who present problems, most often ascribed to narcissistic symptoms that they may have. Perhaps 90% of all problems in the groups are generated from less than 10% of all parents. This section along with much of the structure of the parent sessions is aimed at addressing the symptoms of these parents, so that their teens will stand a better chance of benefiting from PEERS, and the help provided to the other parents in the group will not be diminished. Closely adhering to the group structure we have provided is the best overall means of insuring that most parents and teens benefit from PEERS. Deviating from the structure runs the risk of turning the intervention into a support group for their day-to-day family problems, and at worst gripe sessions about their teens. With Frankel and Myatt (2003) serving as a treatment basis, and our own experiences with parents of teens, we have successfully employed several techniques to overcome these resistances and pitfalls.

It is important to recognize these symptoms and quickly take appropriate action before difficult and challenging parents derail the group. Recent research suggests that the number of symptoms of personality disorder exist on a continuum, with the number of symptoms correlating with the outcome more than the presence or absence of a *Diagnostic and Statistical Manual of Mental Disorders* (4th ed.) (*DSM-IV*) diagnosis (Marlowe, Kirby, Festinger, Husband, & Platt, 1997). Expression of these traits in parent sessions can seriously undermine the therapist's goals if not addressed promptly. Listed in Box 3.1 are the more commonly observed symptoms of narcissism that are likely to impact group treatment process.

Because the first session intentionally does not have as much didactic content in the parent session, the tendency is to race too fast over the Parent Handout, just reading it. What happens in this case is that the group leader will finish way before the end of the session and wait for the teens to come back into the room. This may allow a parent with narcissistic symptoms to exhibit one of the behaviors listed in Box 3.1. To head this off, the group leader might go around the room, asking parents to read one point in the handout and then reflect on what it means to them. Go over the homework assignment in minute detail. Many parents will need this additional clarification. Ask for questions after you finish presenting the homework assignment. Only answer questions that are relevant to the handout. Questions that are addressed in later sessions should be saved for those sessions. You might say: *That's a really important question and we will get to that eventually. We're not there yet, so hold onto that question and we'll get back to it in a future session.* Questions that do not relate to the intervention (e.g., "What causes autism?" "Is there a cure for autism?") should be clearly classified as such. In this case you might say: *While that's a good question, I want to be careful to keep us focused on our goal for PEERS, which is to help our teens make and keep friends. We have only enough time for this and we should all be cautious not to get*

BOX 3.1 PARENT CHARACTERISTICS LIKELY TO NEGATIVELY IMPACT TREATMENT PROGRESS

- *Controlling*
  The more obvious example of this is the parent who insists that sessions accommodate for their teen's needs immediately. A less obvious example is the parent who asks when the group leader will get to the topic of their immediate concern. You can refer this parent to the first Parent Handout to help you with this.

- *Needs to be the center of attention*
  Examples of this are the parent that rushes to make excuses about homework they did not attempt to do (impinging upon the time of those who completed the assignments), or talking about how hard their lives are. In this case, it will be important to redirect the discussion back to parents who were able to complete the assignment.

- *Needs their teen to represent them in the world in ways that meet the parents' emotional needs*
  Examples are parents who try to turn the session into gripe sessions about their teens. We deal with this in the first session by having the parent say the thing they like best about their teen and redirecting them if they do not do this.

- *Tries to minimize the importance of the group*
  Examples include the parent who reports on a get-together their teen had instead of their attempts to do the assigned homework. Or the parent who indicates that his teen was too busy with schoolwork to complete the homework assignment. Another example is the parent who casually indicates that their teen did not want to do the homework assignment when the time came, disregarding the fact that it is the parent's job to facilitate these assignments. The group leader can minimize this by asking for parents who were successful in homework assignments to raise their hands, and call on those parents first. This supports the group focus and also shows that the homework was "doable."

side-tracked." This redirection turns out to be comforting to parents as they know exactly what to expect and more easily focus upon what PEERS has to offer.

For a completely off-track question, you also can use the structure of the group to help by saying something like: *We have a lot to cover today and unfortunately we do not have time to discuss that right now.* For particularly challenging groups, you might need to write the agenda down on the board to highlight this point. It can also be helpful from the outset to let parents know that you may need to interrupt them from time to time by saying something like: *We have a lot of material to cover each week, so I may have to occasionally interrupt you to keep us focused, but please understand that this is necessary to keep us on track so you can all get the full benefit of the program.* In cases where parents are bringing up problems that may be impacting treatment, it is best to meet with them outside of the group, rather than derail the group process, and be prepared to provide additional referrals if necessary.

The first series of homework assignments, the in-group phone calls and eventually the out-of-group phone calls, is based upon the innovation introduced by Frankel and Myatt (2003). The phone call is used as a means for parents to implement and monitor the generalization of conversational techniques taught in session. Practice occurs in front of the parent who is instructed on how to intervene at this "teachable moment" to improve the teen's conversational skills. The in-group phone calls are easy to complete because both parties to the call negotiate when the call will take place ahead of time. The initial assignment of easy-to-complete homework tasks sets the expectation that homework can be done and will be completed.

Opening Remarks

- Begin by welcoming the group.
- Go around the room and have parents introduce themselves in the following specific manner. Have them say:
  - Their name
  - Their teen's name and age
  - One favorite thing they like about their teen
- Repeat things that the parent liked best about his or her teen succinctly after each parent finishes. This will help keep them on track.
- Discourage any parents from saying negative things about their teen. (You may need to gently interrupt them and restate the request for the favorite thing they like about the teen.)
- Discourage chitchat at first to set appropriate expectations. (Do not get involved in a conversation with only one parent and try not to allow parents to get into distracting side conversations.)
- *Review Issues of Confidentiality*
  - Review limits to confidentiality (this will vary according to the region within which one practices):
    - *If we have information that a teen is being abused or neglected or that there is risk of harm to that person or others, we will report this information to the proper authorities.*
  - Encourage group members to keep what they hear in the group confidential:
  - *We want you and your teen also to maintain confidentiality. Please don't discuss things brought up here with anyone outside of the group. But please remember we can't control whether all of you are following this instruction.*

- ▪ *Explain the Purpose of the Group*
  - PEERS is a social skills group to help teens make and keep friends.
  - We focus on teaching the following skills:
    - How to use good conversational skills
    - How to appropriately use electronic communication (phones, text messaging, instant messaging, e-mailing, Internet)
    - How to enter and exit conversations with peers
    - How to choose appropriate friends
    - How to use humor appropriately
    - How to have a successful get-together with friends
    - How to be a good sport
    - How to handle teasing and bullying
    - How to change a bad reputation
    - How to handle arguments and disagreements with friends
    - How to handle rumors and gossip
  - We will be meeting once a week for 90 minutes for the next 14 weeks.
  - There will be a teen group and a parent group that meet in separate rooms at the same time.
  - Parents will be told what the teens are talking about in the teen group.
  - Parents will be talking to teens and helping them with the skills they learn in PEERS.
  - At the end of the 14 weeks, we will have a graduation party and ceremony.
- ▪ *Explain the Structure of the Parent Sessions*
  - The session begins with a review of the previous homework assignment (approximately 50 to 60 minutes).
    - You and your teen will be given homework assignments each week to practice the newly learned skills.
    - The level of parental involvement in homework completion depends on what your teen feels comfortable with:
      - ▪ This will be determined through negotiation with the treatment team during reunification at the end of every session.
      - ▪ You must at least discuss the homework with your teen.
    - We will only focus on *completed* homework assignments:
      - ▪ This means that if you did not complete your assignment, we will not be spending time talking about why it did not happen, unless to troubleshoot a problem.
      - ▪ The success of the program depends on the completion of the homework assignments.
  - The next portion of the group is when we go over the homework for the coming week (approximately 20 to 30 minutes):
    - You will receive a Parent Handout each week with the homework assignment and a brief description of the lesson.

- ■ We encourage you to save these handouts and even store them in a binder.
- ■ We also encourage you to share the handouts with other family members who might be called upon to help your teen with his or her social skills.
  - – At the end of the session, we will have a reunification with teens in which we will review the lesson and insure that you and your teen agree on the homework to be done before you leave (approximately 10 to 20 minutes).
- ■ *Briefly Explain the Structure of the Teen Sessions*
  - – Each teen session begins with homework review, including troubleshooting any problems related to the completion of the assignment (approximately 20 to 30 minutes).
  - – This is followed by the didactic lesson for the week (approximately 30 minutes).
  - – Then there is a behavioral rehearsal in which teens practice the newly learned skills in the session (approximately 20 minutes) in the context of:
    - • Socialization activities
    - • Indoor games
    - • Outdoor games and sports
  - – The session ends with a reunification with parents in which the lesson is reviewed and the homework assignment is negotiated among parents, teens, and members of the treatment team (approximately 10 to 20 minutes).
- ■ *Explain What Will Happen If Teens Misbehave in the Group*
  - – The teen group leader will be in communication with parents throughout the 14 weeks of PEERS.
  - – If the teen misbehaves during the group, the teen will be given a warning.
  - – If the teen continues to misbehave, he or she will be given one final warning.
  - – If the teen's behavior does not improve, the parent will be called out of session and the teen group leader or coach will discuss the problem with the parent and teen and decide how best to proceed.
- ■ If the teen's misbehavior is a continuous problem, the teen group leader will discuss possible solutions to the problem with the parent, which may include early termination.

Introduction

- ■ Distribute the Parent Handout:
  - – When you pass out the handout, immediately start reading it, otherwise it loses its impact.
- ■ Go around the room and have parents take turns reading the Parent Handout:

- Do not have parents read the handout if you suspect that one or more parents are language or reading impaired. (This can often be determined from the completion of the questionnaires at the intake interview.)
- Sections in **bold print** come directly from the Parent Handout.
- Terms that are ***bold and italicized*** are buzzwords and represent important concepts from the curriculum:
  - The buzzwords represent complex social behaviors that can be identified in just a few simple words.
- Try to use the buzzwords as much as possible to develop a common language between therapists, parents, and teens.

What to Expect From the Group

1. **To help your teen learn how to make and keep friends.**
2. **To help you more effectively support your teen's efforts at finding suitable friends.**
3. **To help you more effectively support your teen's ability to make new acquaintances and develop close friendships.**
4. **To help you foster your teen's independence with his or her social relationships.**

Methods

1. **Each teen session will involve brief instruction to your teen about how to handle challenging social situations.**
2. **You will be briefed about each teen session.**
3. **During each session, your teen will rehearse the skills being taught.**
4. **You and your teen will be given homework assignments every week for home and school in order to practice the skills being taught.**
5. **Previous homework will be reviewed each week in the parent and teen groups.**
6. **The two most important jobs parents have in this group are to:**
   a. **Involve your teen in activities where he or she can meet other teens.**
   b. **Help your teen arrange get-togethers with friends.**

What Not to Expect From the Group

1. **This is not a support group or a group to help you find out about psychological disorders or developmental issues.**
2. **Your teen will not improve unless you attend regularly and come on time.**
3. **Your teen will not improve unless he or she attempts to do each homework assignment.**

4. **Your teen may not make lasting friendships with other members of the group. This is a skills training group not a "friendship matching" group. You will not be allowed to socialize with other group members during the group.**
    a. **[Have parents verbally agree as a group to no social contacts with other group members during the treatment.]**
5. **We are not treating all of your teen's problems; we are only focusing on friendships.**

Characteristics of Good Friendships

■ Explain: *The name of this group is PEERS. And peers are sometimes also friends or potential friends. The purpose of this group is for our teens to learn to make and keep friends. Which means it's important for us all to agree on what makes a good friend so that we can help them find the most suitable friends.*

■ Explain the elements of good friendships with parents (allow them to discuss and add to the list):
    – Common Interests
        • Similar interests, likes, hobbies (e.g., you have things in common)
    – Self-Disclosure/Share Secrets
        • Feel comfortable sharing private thoughts, feelings, stories (e.g., you feel comfortable sharing your secrets)
    – Understanding
        • Mutual understanding (e.g., you understand one another)
    – Conflict Resolution
        • Can solve potential arguments and conflicts without hurting the friendship (e.g., if you argue or disagree, you can make up and still be friends)
    – Mutual/Shared/Equal
        • A shared friendship; reciprocal in nature (e.g., you are equals; you both share the friendship; no one dominates the other person)
    – Affection/Care
        • A friendship based on fondness, warmth, and caring for one another (e.g., you both care about the other person)
    – Commitment/Loyalty/Trust
        • A friendship based on loyalty, allegiance, and trust (e.g., you are loyal to each other; you trust each other)

Didactic Lesson: Trading Information

■ Say: *The first lesson the teens are learning tonight is how to **trade information** (this is our first buzzword). Trading information is what people naturally do in a conversation and it involves the sharing or exchange of thoughts, ideas, and interests. The most important goal of trading information is to find* *common interests so that you can find out if there are things you might enjoy talking about or doing together.*

- Go around the room and have parents take turns reading the Parent Handout:
  - Sections in **bold print** come directly from the Parent Handout.

Rules for Trading Information

- *Ask the other person about himself or herself* (e.g., their interests, hobbies).
- After the other person finishes, *answer your own question:*
  - *Share something related about yourself* (e.g., your interests, likes, hobbies).
- *Find common interests*:
  - Identify things you can talk about.
  - Identify activities you can do together.
  - Find out what he or she does not like to do—so you can avoid doing these things.
- *Share the conversation*:
  - Give the person a chance to ask you a question or make a comment.
  - Pause occasionally to let the other person direct the conversation.
    - If the person does not say anything—follow up with another question or comment.
  - You may need to assess to make sure the person is interested in the conversation:
    - Are they participating in the conversation (e.g., talking to you, asking questions)?
    - Are they making eye contact?
    - Are they trying to walk away?
    - What is their body language saying? (e.g., are they facing you or facing away?)
- *Do not get too personal at first*:
  - This may make the other person uncomfortable.
  - May be less willing to talk to you in the future.

Homework Assignments

- The parent group leader should go over the homework assignment and troubleshoot any potential problems with parents:
  1. Parents should practice *trading information* with his or her teen this week
     a. Go over the rules for trading information with the teen before practicing.
     b. *Find a common interest* to share with the group.

2. ***In-Group Call***
   a. **Before the Call:**
      i. **Before leaving the group, parents should arrange for their teen to call another member of the group to practice conversational skills.**
         1. **The teen group leader will assign the phone calls each week and will read the call assignment aloud during the reunification.**
      ii. **Set up a day and time to make the call.**
      iii. **Negotiate where the parent will be during the call.**
      iv. **Go over the rules for *trading information* with their teen before the call.**
   b. **During the Call:**
      i. **Teens should trade information on this phone call.**
      ii. ***Find a common interest* to report back to the group.**
   c. **After the Call:**
      i. **Parents and teens should discuss the phone call and identify *common interests* and troubleshoot any problems.**

How to Help Your Teen Do His or Her Homework

- ***Troubleshoot Problems***
  - ***Offer suggestions when your teen is struggling with a new skill.***
    - **Suggestions can often be given with statements that start with: *How about if....***
      - **Example: *How about if next time you are trading information, you ask your friend what he likes to do, too?***
  - **Do not overtly tell your teen that he or she did something wrong.**
    - **This may discourage your teen or make him or her feel embarrassed.**
    - **Example: *You didn't trade information the right way!***

Note: Make note of parents offering excuses for why their teen will have trouble with the first homework assignment. Some parents are "helicopter parents" or "hoverers" and will try to do the assignments for their teen or try to provide too much prepping. Have these parents back off the first time to see how it works before stepping in to help their teen out. Discourage these parents from coaching or providing scripts during phone calls. It is better to practice with the teen before the phone call, rather than during it.

Final Administrative Comments

■ Go over the Phone Roster with the parents. (This should have been created prior to the start of groups, listing all of the parents' and teens' first names and phone numbers.)
  – Tell them they will use this phone roster for the in-group calls.
  – Parents should note the day and time of the scheduled call each week on this sheet.
  – Parents should let us know if they wish to have a different number used for the in-group call roster or if there are any errors on the current roster.
    • In the event that there are changes, a new roster should be distributed the next week.
■ Go over the Planned Absence Sheet
  – Remind parents that it is extremely important for them to attend all sessions.
  – If they need to miss a session, they should indicate that on the Planned Absence Sheet and return to the treatment team no later than the second session.
  – You might consider rescheduling a session if there are several absences planned that week.

Parent Handout 1: Introduction and Conversational Skills I—Trading Information

What to Expect From the Group

1. To help your teen learn how to make and keep friends.
2. To help you more effectively support your teen's efforts at finding suitable friends.
3. To help you more effectively support your teen's ability to make new acquaintances and develop close friendships.
4. To help you foster your teen's independence with his or her social relationships.

Methods

1. Each teen session will involve brief instruction to your teen about how to handle challenging social situations.
2. You will be briefed about each teen session.
3. During each session, your teen will rehearse the skills being taught.
4. You and your teen will be given homework assignments every week for home and school in order to practice the skills being taught.
5. Previous homework will be reviewed each week in the parent and teen groups.
6. The two most important jobs parents have in this group are to:
   a. Involve your teen in activities where he or she can meet other teens.
   b. Help your teen arrange get-togethers with friends.

What Not to Expect From the Group

1. This is not a support group or a group to help you find out about psychological disorders or developmental issues.
2. Your teen will not improve unless you attend regularly and come on time.
3. Your teen will not improve unless he or she attempts to do each homework assignment.
4. Your teen may not make lasting friendship with other members of the group. This is a skills training group, not a "friendship matching" group. You will not be allowed to socialize with other group members during the group.
5. We are not treating all of your teen's problems; we are only focusing on friendships.

Rules for Trading Information

- ■ ***Ask the other person about himself or herself*** (e.g., his or her interests, hobbies).
- ■ After the other person finishes, ***answer your own question***:
  - – ***Share something related about yourself*** (e.g., your interests, likes, hobbies).
- ■ ***Find common interests***
  - – Identify things you can talk about.
  - – Identify activities you can do together.
  - – Find out what he or she does not like to do—so you can avoid doing these things.
- ■ ***Share the conversation***
  - – Give the person a chance to ask you a question or make a comment.
    - • Pause occasionally to let the other person direct the conversation.
    - • If the person does not say anything—follow up with another question or comment.
  - – You may need to assess to make sure the person is interested in the conversation:
    - • Are they participating in the conversation (e.g., talking to you, asking questions)?
    - • Are they making eye contact?
    - • Are they trying to walk away?
    - • What is their body language saying? (e.g., are they facing you or facing away?)
- ■ ***Do not get too personal at first***
  - – This may make the other person uncomfortable.
  - – May be less willing to talk to you in the future.

Homework Assignments

1. Parents should practice ***trading information*** with their teen this week.
   a. Go over the rules for ***trading information*** with the teen before practicing.
   b. ***Find a common interest*** to share with the group.
2. ***In-Group Call***
   a. Before the Call:
      i. Before leaving the group, parents should arrange for their teen to call another member of the group to practice conversational skills.
      ii. Set up a day and time to make the call.
      iii. Negotiate where the parent will be during the call.
      iv. Go over the rules for ***trading information*** with the teen before the call.

   b. During the Call:
      i. Teens should ***trade information*** on this phone call.
      ii. ***Find a common interest*** to report back to the group.
   c. After the Call:
      i. Parents and teens should discuss the phone call and identify ***common interests*** and troubleshoot any problems.

How to Help Your Teen Do His or Her Homework

■ ***Troubleshoot Problems***
   – ***Offer suggestions*** when your teen is struggling with a new skill.
     • Suggestions can often be given with statements that start with: "How about if…."
      ■ Example: "How about if next time you are trading information, you ask your friend what he likes to do, too?"
     • Do not overtly tell your teen that they did something wrong.
      ■ This may discourage them or make them feel embarrassed.
      ■ Example: Do not say something like, "You didn't trade information the right way!"

Teen Therapist Guide—Session 1: Introduction and Conversational Skills I—Trading Information

Guiding Principles of the Teen Session

The primary goal of the first teen session is to orient the teens to the structure of the group and establish group cohesion through a brief didactic lesson and behavioral exercise. It will be very important for the group leader to establish clear expectations in the first group and to minimize any misbehavior.

Assuming the guidelines for conducting intake interviews were followed, all of the teens in the group should be participating voluntarily. By only including teens who want to participate in the intervention, you will minimize behavioral disturbances and misbehavior. In the very early stages of the intervention, it is common for teens to exhibit the "too cool for school syndrome." They may act as if they do not need the intervention and they do not belong in the group, as an awkward means to "save face." It is common for one or two group members to behave in this way, particularly older teens. It is recommended that the group leader not attempt to engage in a debate with these teens about why they should participate in the program. This will only serve to embarrass other group members who were eager to participate. Instead, in an attempt to normalize the experience, the group leader should speak generally about the benefits of improving friendships, explaining that making and keeping friends can be difficult and that everyone (including parents and the treatment team) can stand to learn more about the process.

A controlled classroom environment is important to ensure that the teens can get the maximum benefit from the didactic portion of the session. Group members should have to raise their hands in order to speak and teens should not be allowed to talk over one another or engage in long or overly personal storytelling. Establish these expectations by presenting the rules for the group. In order to ensure that the teens are compliant with these rules, it will be helpful to present the rules by having the teens explain why each of these rules is important. This discussion will help them be more willing to comply with the rules.

If a teen launches into an unrelated discussion, the teen group leader should avoid allowing the teen to get too far off track by redirecting him or her by saying: *Is this on topic?* The group leader should also not hesitate to redirect tangential teens who give overly lengthy responses to questions, as this also takes away from the group. In such cases, it can be helpful to say: *Okay, we're going to have to move on. We have a lot to cover.* If the teen persists, you might say: *If we have time later, we can talk about that.* However, it is not advisable to revisit the topic, as this only reinforces tangential comments.

It is very important for the group leader to establish a fun environment for the group. Creating a fun atmosphere involves getting the teens actively engaged in the process of generating the rules for the lessons. PEERS uses a specific curriculum involving concrete rules and steps for social etiquette. The process by which

BOX 3.2   HOW TO HANDLE MISBEHAVIOR IN THE GROUP

- The teen group leader should be in communication with parents throughout the 14 weeks of PEERS.
- If the teen misbehaves during the group he or she should be given a warning (e.g.: *This is a warning. If you continue to _____, I will have to call in your parent.*).
- It is acceptable to give a few warnings before enlisting the help of parents, so long as the teen makes some response to each warning.
- If the teen continues to misbehave after repeated warnings, give him or her one final warning (e.g.: *This is your final warning, if you continue to _____, I will have to go get your parent.*).
- If the teen's behavior does not improve, call the teen's parent out of the parent room.
- Find a neutral location where only the teen group leader or (preferably) the coach, teen, and parent are present.
- Briefly explain the behavioral problem.
- Notify the teen and parent that the teen is welcome to come back to the group when he or she is prepared to behave appropriately (e.g.: *I am going to give you both some time to talk. When you're ready to behave appropriately, you are free to come back to the group.*).

these points are generated is through a Socratic method of questioning, as well as through modeling and role-play exercises. The former involves asking specific questions in such a way that you elicit the response you were seeking. The latter involves specific demonstrations of both appropriate and inappropriate behaviors, in order to generate the rules for a more complex series of social behavior (e.g., demonstrating what it looks like to be a "conversation hog" and then asking: *What did I do wrong in that conversation?*). These techniques of instruction are used to keep the teens' attention during the didactic lessons and help them to more readily buy into the skills being taught. Teens are far more likely to believe what you have to teach them if they and their peers are generating the rules, rather than the group leader.

When presenting the rules and steps for social etiquette, avoid asking open-ended questions like: *Does anyone have any ideas about how to have a good conversation?* Questions like this are too broad and often result in inappropriate responses from the teens who do not yet know the rules of social etiquette. Instead, stick to the questions outlined in the didactic portion of this manual.

Finally, the group leader and coaches should avoid being silly and making jokes with the teens, as this may result in a loss of control of the group and difficulty in staying on track.

Handling Misbehavior

We do not advise explaining the process of handling misbehavior to the teens (before they actually misbehave), as this may only serve as a dare for them to misbehave. Begin setting limits for behavior immediately. This means if a teen talks out of turn, you might say: *I need you to raise your hand.* If a teen inappropriately laughs at someone else's comment, you might say: *I need everyone to be respectful of one another.* If a teen tries to make jokes and assume the role of the "class clown," you might say: *I need everyone to be serious.* These comments will help redirect the teens toward the behavioral expectations you have established, while avoiding being too punitive at first. If the teen persists in his or her limit testing, it can also be helpful to open the discussion up to the group by saying: *Why is it important to raise your hand, be serious, be respectful of other group members?* By using this method, you are applying peer pressure without directly calling out the misbehaving teen. It will be natural for teens to test limits initially, but if you address these situations with respect, you will be able to minimize the negative effects.

Alternatively, two types of misbehavior that should receive immediate consequences involve verbal or physical attacks. This includes simulated or pretend fighting. It is never acceptable for a teen to be teased, bullied, or physically threatened in any form during the group. These rare instances should result in immediate removal of the teen from the group. Parents should be called outside of the parent group and informed of the incident in the presence of their teen. Depending on the seriousness of the incident, the teen may return to the group once the matter has been adequately addressed. It is critical for all teens to feel safe in the group and for these types of incidents to be addressed immediately. It is important to have a coach who is trained to handle this issue while the teen group leader continues with the rest of the group.

Set-Up and Opening Remarks

When the teens enter the room, write their names on the board and leave room for awarding points after each name (points will be given for homework completion and participation). This will be the same procedure each week of the group.

Given that teens have different learning styles, it is suggested that when presenting the rules of social etiquette, that buzzwords or brief bullet points relating to rules and steps be written on the board. These rules and steps should remain on the board for the entire session (not to be erased), as the teens may need to rely on them for their behavioral rehearsal exercises. Thus, the therapist will have to allot room on the board for both the lesson and the distributing of points.

Be sure teens remain seated throughout the session, raising hands to make statements or ask questions; otherwise, the session could get out of control. It may be helpful to have a meal (e.g., pizza) and beverages while they are listening, particularly during the homework review. If you provide a meal, be sure to have teens raise their hands to ask for more servings or drinks, reinforce appropriate table manners, and provide coaching for inappropriate eating behavior.

Opening Remarks

- Begin by welcoming the group.
- Introduce self and coach(es).
- Go around the room and have everyone say:
  - Their name
  - Their age and grade
  - Where they go to school
- Start giving points right away for following directions and participation:
  - List the name of each teen on the board and use hatch marks next to names to indicate points.
- If the teens ask about the points, tell them you will explain the points later.

Rules for the Group

- Present the rules for the group (write the rules on the board).
- For each rule ask: "Why is this a good rule to have?"

Rules

1. Listen to the other group members (no talking when others are speaking)
2. Follow directions
3. Raise your hand
4. Be respectful (no teasing or making fun of others, no swearing)
5. No touching (no hitting, kicking, pushing, hugging, etc.)

Overview of PEERS

Reason for the Group

Explain the following:

- Tell the teens that the name of the group is PEERS.
- Ask them: *What is a peer?*
  - Answer: Someone else your age, a friend, a classmate, a colleague.
- PEERS is a social skills group to help teens make and keep friends.
- We will be meeting once a week for 90 minutes for the next 14 weeks.
- There will be a teen group and a parent group that meet in separate rooms at the same time.

■ Parents will be told what the teens are talking about in the group.

■ Parents will be talking to teens and helping them with the skills they learn in PEERS.

■ At the end of the 14 weeks, we will have a graduation party and ceremony.

Structure of the Sessions

Explain the structure for each session:

■ The session begins with a review of the homework (approximately 20 to 30 minutes).
  - You will be given homework assignments each week to practice the skills you learn in PEERS.
  - These are FUN assignments—so do not worry.
  - Your parents may or may not be helping you with these assignments—it depends on what you prefer.
  - But you must discuss your homework with your parents.
  - Your parents will be reviewing the homework at the beginning of each session, so they need to know what you did.
    • [Get all of the teens to agree to discuss their homework assignments with their parents each week before moving on with the lesson.]
■ Then we go over the lesson for the day (approximately 30 minutes).
■ We practice the skills in the session in the context of:
  - Socialization activities
  - Indoor games
  - Outdoor games and sports
■ We end by going back to the parent room and briefly going over the buzz-words from the lesson and the homework for the week (approximately 10 to 20 minutes).
  - Explain: *Buzzwords are words or terms that we use to describe some type of social skill. We use them so we can have a common language when we're talking about the rules or steps of social etiquette.*

Earning Points

■ Explain that teens will receive points for the following:
  - Following the rules (e.g., listening, being respectful, following directions)
  - Completing homework assignments
  - Participating in the lesson
  - Practicing newly learned skills in the session
■ Points are calculated at the end of every session for the group and the individual.
■ Group points are earned for a graduation party at the end of the intervention:
  - The more points earned, the bigger and better the party.

■ Individual points are earned for graduation prizes:
  – The more points earned, the better the prizes.
  – The individuals with the most points get to choose from the prizes first.
  – The prizes may include:
    • Basketballs, footballs, volleyballs, soccer balls, baseball equipment, Frisbees
    • Board games, card games
      ■ [Note: Prizes are intended to be interactive and promote social engagement with peers.]
■ Ask the question: *So if you earn a point, does this mean you're helping your-self, you're helping the group, or both?*
  – Answer: Both

Discussion Questions

Explain: *The name of this group is PEERS. And peers are sometimes also friends or potential friends. The purpose of this group is for us to learn to make and keep friends. Which means it's important for us all to agree on what makes a good friend.*

[Ask the group the following questions and allow them to briefly discuss. Use this as a brainstorming activity, in which you write their good responses on the board. Try to fit the answers the teens provide into the language described in the "Characteristics of Good Friendships" section below until all bullet points are covered.]

■ *What is a friend?*
■ *How do you know when you have a friend?*
■ *What do friends have in common?*
■ *What is a best friend?*

Characteristics of Good Friendships

After the teens brainstorm, briefly review the basic characteristics of good friendships:

■ Common Interests
  – Similar interests, likes, hobbies (e.g., you have things in common)
■ Self-disclosure/Share Secrets
  – Feel comfortable sharing private thoughts, feelings, stories (e.g., you feel comfortable sharing your secrets)
■ Understanding
  – Mutual understanding (e.g., you understand one another)
■ Conflict Resolution
  – Can solve potential arguments and conflicts without hurting the friend-ship (e.g., if you argue or disagree, you can make up and still be friends)

▪ Mutual/Shared/Equal
  - A shared friendship; reciprocal in nature (e.g., you are equals, you both share the friendship, no one dominates the other person)
▪ Affection/Care
  - A friendship based on fondness, warmth, and caring for one another (e.g., you both care about the other person)
▪ Commitment/Loyalty/Trust
  - A friendship based on loyalty, allegiance, and trust (e.g., you are loyal to each other, you trust each other)

Didactic Lesson: Rules for Trading Information

Explain: *Each week in PEERS, we focus on a different social skill. Today we're going to be talking about how to have a conversation with someone. One of the most important parts of teen friendships is the ability to carry on a conversation. Having a conversation involves trading information, which is the natural exchange of information that occurs between two people when they're getting to know one another. The most important goal of trading information is to find common interests so that you can find out if there are things you might enjoy talking about or doing together.*

Present the rules for **trading information** (our first buzzword):

1. **Ask the other person about himself or herself** (e.g., his or her interests, hobbies, weekend activities).
   a. Say: *One of the first rules for trading information is to ask the other person about himself or herself. You might ask them about their interests, their hobbies, or what they like to do on the weekend. Why is it important to ask the person about himself or herself?*
      i. Answer: Because this is how you discover their interests, hobbies, and likes—and if you have **common interests**.
2. After the other person finishes, **answer your own question**.
   a. **Share something related about yourself** (e.g., your interests, likes, hobbies).
   b. Say: *Another rule for trading information is that we need to answer our own questions and share something about ourselves. This includes sharing our own interests, likes, or hobbies. Why is it important to answer your own question?*
      i. Answer: Because they may not know to ask you the same question and in order to trade information, you have to also share things about yourself.
3. **Find common interests**
   a. Identify things you can talk about.
   b. Identify activities you can do together.

    c. Pay attention to what he or she does not like to do—so you can avoid doing these things.

    d. Say: *The most important goal of trading information is to find common interests. We need to find common interests so that we have things to talk about or do together. It's also helpful to pay attention to what people don't like, so we can avoid doing those things when we're together. Why do you think it's so important to find common interests?*

       i. Answer: Because common interests are the foundation of friendships.

4. ***Share the conversation***

    a. Say: *Another rule for trading information is to be sure to share the conversation. Why is it important to share the conversation?*

       i. Answer: This is how we trade information and get to know one another.

    b. This means you give the person a chance to ask you a question or make a comment.

       i. Pause occasionally to let the other person direct the conversation.

       ii. If the person does not say anything—follow up with another question or comment.

5. ***Do not get too personal at first***

    a. Say: *A final rule for trading information is not to get too personal at first. Why is it a bad idea to get too personal when you are first getting to know someone?*

       i. Answer: This may make the other person uncomfortable and they may be less willing to talk to you in the future.

    b. Give examples of getting too personal. (For example: *What kind of grades do you get?*)

       i. Avoid having teens give examples as this may encourage silliness.

    c. Ask: *Once you've gotten to know someone well, then is it okay to get more personal?*

       i. Answer: Yes, if you are good friends.

■ You may also need to assess to make sure the person is interested in the conversation.
- Are they participating in the conversation (e.g., talking to you, asking questions)?
- Are they making eye contact?
- Are they trying to walk away?
- What is their body language saying (e.g., facing toward you)?

■ If they do not seem interested in talking to you, then you may need to **move on** and find someone else to talk to.

Role-Play Exercise

■ The teen group leader should demonstrate ***trading information*** with a coach using an ***appropriate*** role play.
  – Say: *Now we're going to show you an example of how to appropriately trade information. Watch this conversation and when we've finished, tell us what we did **right***.

> ***Teen group leader (facing the coach and making good eye contact)*:** Hey (insert name)! How are you doing?
> ***Coach*:** I'm fine. How are you (insert name)?
> ***Teen group leader*:** I'm great. So how was your weekend?
> ***Coach*:** It was good. I went to the movies with some friends.
> ***Teen group leader*:** That sounds fun. What did you see?
> ***Coach*:** We saw that new sci-fi movie everyone's been talking about.
> ***Teen group leader*:** How cool! I've been wanting to see that. Was it good?
> ***Coach*:** Yeah, it was really good. I might see it again. Do you like sci-fi movies?
> ***Teen group leader*:** Yeah, I love them! I like reading sci-fi books, too. How about you?
> ***Coach*:** Definitely. I read them all the time.
> ***Teen group leader*:** Me, too. So, which one is your favorite?

  – Say: *Okay, so time-out on that. Who can tell me what we did RIGHT in that conversation?*
    • Answer: You traded information by asking each other questions and answering your own questions, you found common interests, did not get too personal, and shared the conversation.
  – Ask: *Did it seem like we wanted to talk to each other?*
    • Answer: Yes.
  – Ask: *How could you tell?*
    • Answer: Because you were making good eye contact, you were each talking to each other and answering each other's questions, you were facing each other, and not trying to walk away.

Behavioral Rehearsal

■ Say: *Now that we know the rules for trading information, we're going to have each of you practice trading information with the person sitting next to you. Remember, the goal is to find a common interest.*
■ Have teens practice trading information with the person sitting next to them:
  – The teen group leader should assign the pairs, and move teens around if the dyad is inappropriate.
  – If there are an uneven number of teens create a triad.
■ Group leader and coaches should help facilitate the exercise when necessary:

- Examples: *You could ask each other about your school or hobbies. You could talk about your favorite books, movies, or television programs. You could find out what the other person likes to do on the weekend.*
■ Group leader and coaches may need to troubleshoot if problems arise:
  - Examples: *Remember not to get too personal at first. Be sure to share the conversation. You may need to answer your own question.*
■ Spend about 2 to 3 minutes on this exercise.
■ Then, briefly have teens identify whether they were able to find a common interest by saying: *It's time to wrap up your conversations. I heard lots of good trading information. Let's go around the room and find out what common interests you found.*
■ Praise teens for their efforts.

Homework Assignments

■ Briefly explain the homework for the week by saying: *We are going to continue to have you practice trading information this week. Remember that I mentioned that each week you would have some homework assignments related to the lessons you are learning in PEERS. Your homework assignment this week is to:*
  - *Practice trading information with your parent and find a common interest.*
  - *Have an in-group phone call with another group member:*
    • *This should be at least 5 to 10 minutes.*
    • *You will need to find a common interest to report to the group.*
■ Group leader and coaches should assign the in-group calls for the week and write this on the "In-Group Phone Call Assignment Log" for future reference:
  - If there are an uneven number of teens, assign someone "double duty."
    • This person will have two in-group phone calls (one as a caller and the other as a receiver).
    • This person will receive extra points for completing the extra call.

Teen Activity: Jeopardy

Note: See the "Teen Activity Guide" for rules.

■ Teens need to complete the ***Jeopardy*** answer sheets before beginning the activity:
  - To save time, it is very helpful to have teens complete these forms while they are waiting in the lobby before the start of the group.
■ Teens need to **trade information** before *Jeopardy* and practice asking questions:
  - Write topics on the board and then break the teens into dyads or triads.

- After the teens have **traded information** with most of the group members for 2 to 3 minutes each, have them reconvene as a group and play the game of *Jeopardy*.
■ Teens compete against themselves to earn points for correct responses to questions from **trading information** exercise:
  - The teen who raises his or her hand first gets to take the first guess.
  - If the teen is wrong, someone else has a chance to answer (the person who raised his or her hand second).
  - The teens get only one guess per question.
  - Do not give teens clues.

■ Encourage the teens to clap for each other during the game.
■ Keep track of the points on the board using a different colored marker.
■ At the end of the game, the person with the most points is the ***Jeopardy Challenge Winner***.

Reunification

■ Announce that teens should join their parents:
  - Be sure that the teens are standing or sitting next to their parents.
  - Be sure to have silence and the full attention of the group before starting with reunification.
■ Say: *Today we learned how to* **trade information**. *Who can tell us what some of the rules are for trading information?* [Have teens generate all of the rules. Be prepared to give prompts if necessary.]
  - ***Ask the other person about themselves*** (e.g., their interests, hobbies)
  - ***Answer your own questions***
    - ***Share something related about yourself*** (e.g., your interests, likes, hobbies)
  - ***Find common interests***
  - ***Share the conversation***
  - ***Do not get too personal at first***
■ Say: *This group did a great job of practicing trading information today. They played a game called Jeopardy where they practiced trading information. Let's give them a round of applause. And tonight's Jeopardy Challenge Winner is (insert name). Let's also give him/her a round of applause.*
■ Go over the homework for the next week (see below):
  - Be sure to read off the in-group call assignment in front of parents.
  - Remind parents to make a note of who is calling who.
■ Individually and separately negotiate with each family where the parent will be during the phone call.

Homework Assignments

1. Parents and teens should practice **trading information** this week.
   a. Parents and teens should go over the rules for **trading information** before practicing.
   b. Find one common interest to share with the group.
2. ***In-Group Call***
   a. Before the Call:
      i. Before you leave the group, parents should arrange for their teen to call another member of the group to practice conversational skills.
      ii. Set up a day and time to make the call.
      iii. Negotiate where the parent will be during the call.
      iv. Go over the rules for **trading information** with the teen before the call.
   b. During the Call:
      i. Teens should **trade information** on this phone call.
      ii. **Find a common interest** to report back to the group.
   c. After the Call:
      i. Parents and teens should discuss the phone call and identify **common interests** and troubleshoot any problems.

Calculate Points

Keep track of the following for each week of the intervention:

■ Calculate the number of points earned by each teen, but do not calculate this in the teen's presence.
■ Add up the total number of points earned by the group:
   – Do not disclose the individual or group total of points.
   – Discourage attempts to compare number of points earned between teens.
■ Remind them that they are working as a team to earn a bigger and better graduation party.

Teen Activity Guide: Session 1

"Jeopardy"

Materials Needed

■ Blackboard and chalk/whiteboard and markers
■ Answer sheets
■ Scissors
■ Pens

Rules

- Teens will compete against themselves in this game of ***trading information***.
- Like the television show, ***Jeopardy***, teens will be given answers by the group leader and asked to respond in the form of a question.
  - Example:
    - ***Teen group leader***: "The answer is Jimmy's favorite sport."
    - ***Teen***: "What is baseball?"
- To promote interest and cooperation, the teen group leader will give out points for correct responses.
- Pass out answer sheets before the ***trading information*** exercise.
- Have teens fill in responses and return to the teen group leader:
  - To save time, it is very helpful to have teens complete these forms while they are waiting in the lobby before the start of the group.
- Have teens practice ***trading information*** in dyads or triads for 2 to 3 minutes each (depending on time) until each teen has ***traded information*** with all group members.
- Group leader will suggest topics for ***trading information*** and write these on the board:
  - Name
  - City where they live
  - Name of school
  - Favorite game
  - Favorite sport
  - Favorite television show
  - Favorite movie
  - Favorite weekend activity
  - Eye color (Note: this is not to be asked, but noticed by using good eye contact when ***trading information***)
- Write categories on the board to help teens:
  - "School" Spirit
    - Answer sheet: Name of school
  - TGIF
    - Answer sheet: Favorite weekend activity
  - "Sports" and Leisure
    - Answer sheet: Favorite sport
  - "Game" Time
    - Answer sheet: Favorite game
  - Movies, Movies, Movies
    - Answer sheet: Favorite movie
  - "TV" Time
    - Answer sheet: Favorite television show
  - "Home" Sweet "Home"

- • Answer sheet: City where they live
  - – The "Eyes" Have It
    - • Answer sheet: Eye color
- ■ While teens are ***trading information***, one of the coaches will:
  - – Cut the answer sheets into individual questions (cut along the lines provided).
  - – Separate the answer sheets according to category and mix the order of the answer sheets.
- ■ The teen group leader and coaches should prompt teens to ask relevant questions to the *Jeopardy* topics when necessary.
- ■ Once the teens have finished ***trading information***, reconvene as a group and begin the *Jeopardy Challenge*.
  - – Begin by having the teen with the most points pick the category.
  - – Notify the group that if they raise their hand before the question has been asked, they are disqualified from answering.
  - – The person who raises his or her hand first gets to take the first guess.
  - – If that person provides the wrong answer, the person who raised his or her hand second has a chance to answer (and so on).
  - – The teens get only one guess per question
  - – Do not give teens clues.
- ■ When reading the items, you may need to point to the person to whom the item relates (while saying their name), because the teens are just becoming acquainted with each other.
- ■ You may need to enforce a time limit if teens take a long time to answer.
- ■ Do not correct the teens if they answer the questions in the incorrect format (i.e., instead of saying "What is baseball?" they say "Baseball").
  - – All that matters is that they remembered the information they obtained through ***trading information***.
- ■ The person who answers the question correctly gets a point and chooses the next category.
- ■ If no one answers correctly, the person about which the last question relates gets to pick the category.
- ■ Encourage the teens to clap for each other during the game.
- ■ Give points for correct responses.
- ■ Keep track of the points on the board using a different colored marker.
- ■ At the end of the game, the person with the most points is the ***Jeopardy Challenge Winner***.
- ■ **Save the answer sheets for the next two sessions.**

"Jeopardy" Answer Sheets

"School" Spirit
 	
The answer is:
The name of _____ 's school.
               (Name)
 	
The question is:
What is _____ ?
     (Name of your school)
	TGIF
	
	The answer is:
	_____ 's favorite weekend activity.
	(Name)
	
	The question is:
	What is _____ ?
	   (Favorite weekend activity)

Sports & Leisure
 	
The answer is:
_____ 's favorite sport.
   (Name)
 	
The question is:
What is _____ ?
     (Favorite sport)
	"Game" Time
	
	The answer is:
	_____ 's favorite game.
	   (Name)
	
	The question is:
	What is _____ ?
	     (Favorite game)

Movies, Movies, Movies
 	
The answer is:
_____ 's favorite movie.
   (Name)
 	
The question is:
What is _____ ?
     (Favorite movie)
	"TV" Time
	
	The answer is:
	_____ 's favorite TV show.
	   (Name)
	
	The question is:
	What is _____ ?
	     (Favorite TV show)

"Home" Sweet "Home"
 	
The answer is:
The name of the city _____ lives in.
                (Name)
 	
The question is:
What is _____ ?
 (Name of the city you live in)
	The "Eyes" Have It
	
	The answer is:
	The color of _____ 's eyes.
	             (Name)
	
	The question is:
	What is _____ ?
	     (Your eye color)

Chapter 4

Session 2
Conversational Skills II— Two-Way Conversations

Parent Session Therapist Guide

Guiding Principles of the Parent Session

The structure of the session helps keep parents on track, which is absolutely necessary to keep the session productive and the group leader in charge. The sequence of homework review, then Parent Handout, then homework assignments is pretty straightforward, and parents will catch onto the routine quickly. For parents who missed the previous session, it is important to avoid giving "extra time" during the group, or assigning a special phone call to someone missing a session, as this is unfair to those who attend regularly. This special treatment also gives the message that it is not important to attend regularly. Similarly, if a spouse "filled in" during the previous session, do not count on the spouse conveying enough of the session content to be sufficient to completing the assignments. Instead, give the handout of the missed session to the returning parent and use the homework review with other parents as a way of informing them of what they missed.

This session introduces conversational techniques. The first task for anyone first meeting someone with whom they would like to be friends is to search for common-ground activities (Frankel & Myatt, 2003). The primary focus for this session is teaching teens how to share a conversation and teaching parents how to monitor their teen's conversations. This is one skill that will be crucial for beginning and maintaining a friendship.

Becoming friends is a continuous process (cf., Frankel & Myatt, 2003). However, from a pragmatic point of view, it is easier to understand this process as occurring in discrete stages. The first stage is turning a stranger into a friendly acquaintance. The next stage is the beginning of closer friendships. The third stage is turning these closer friendships into best friendships. Each stage calls for different conversational constraints.

Teens should regulate how intimate their exchanges are depending upon the phase of their relationships (cf., Altman & Taylor, 1973). Effective regulation involves greater disclosure only with repeated contact and receptivity by the partner. At first meetings, teens need to focus on information exchange of superficial aspects describing what they like and dislike. They need to avoid evaluating each other, especially in a negative light, and avoid telling each other what to do.

The group leader starts immediately with the homework review. The group leader should redirect any off-topic parent conversations by starting off with a statement like: *The last homework assignment was to call another member of the group. Let's start off with successes. Can I see a show of hands on who was able to make the call?* The initial focus on successes is crucial. It helps to set the expectation that homework is to be completed. A noncompliant parent (one who did not get his or her teen to the phone at the appointed time) will hear how several other parents were able to complete the assignment.

The most important homework to review was the in-session phone call, so this should go first. Make sure that you get responses from all the homework completers. Avoid just going around the room (e.g., from left to right). Be ready to redirect parents who do not listen to your focus on homework completers (i.e., "Let's hear about homework successes first."). Then focus the noncompliant parents with the statement: *For those who weren't able to do this assignment, let's figure out how to get it done next week.* Listening to the reasons why they could not get it done is only productive if the debriefing is short and ends with a solution to the barrier. Responses like: *I'm sorry I was just too busy this week,* do not fulfill these requirements. An expanded recount of how busy the parent was or how overscheduled the teen was also does not meet requirements. In response to such excuses, focus may be placed on how necessary the homework is for a productive outcome for the intervention. Another problem that might present at this point is the parent not listening to the call. A parent may say the call was done but perhaps left the monitoring to the spouse who did not attend the session. Some parents will state that they simply did not monitor the call whatsoever. Do not count this as a complete success unless this was negotiated with the teen in the previous session, because this was the parents' missed opportunity to have their teen practice conversational skills in their presence. Instead, use this information as an opportunity to improve upon homework completion in the coming week. Before the family leaves the session, make sure the parent and teen arrange the next call for a time when both can be present.

Another problem that may occur is that some parents will be "script writers" (where the whole phone call is written out in advance using a script). It is clear that using a script does not involve having a two-way conversation with another teen, undermining the main purpose of the call. Discourage the parent from using a script next time. The group leader can say: *This is your opportunity to have your teen learn how to have more spontaneous conversations.* The group leaders can support this by saying to the teen during the end of session reunification that if the phone call was conducted using a script, then it does not follow the rules for a two-way conversation (i.e., listening to the other person) so it will not count as homework.

Approaches to Challenging Parent Behaviors That Appear in This Session

1. *The parent who asks irrelevant questions of the group, ignoring the group leader during the presentation of the Parent Handout.* Redirect this parent by stating that you have a lot to get done and will need to move on.
2. *The parent who is ignoring the group leader and conversing with the parent next to him or her.* Do not try to talk over this parent. Try pausing for a couple of seconds looking at the parents conversing to see if they will stop. Usually the listener will turn toward you and that will end the interaction. If this does not work, you can say: *Can I have everyone's attention please?* wait for silence, and then continue with the session.
3. *The parent who says his or her teen does not need part of the instruction being given* (e.g., he or she does fine on get-togethers, he or she just does not have friends in school). This parent may be ambivalent about whether he or she wants to be in group and may be trying to take charge of the group or make the group leader work to keep him or her in the group. Remember if this parent had brought this ambivalence up during screening or intake, you could have discouraged them from entering the group (most likely he or she did not address this concern and you are hearing it for the first time now). It is important not to try to convince the parent that his or her teen needs the group or to give any group time to this. The other group members may be polite but will not benefit or wish you to continue with this exchange. You can offer to schedule a time outside of the group to discuss a more appropriate referral.
4. *The latecomer.* Some parents will occasionally come late and some will do this habitually. Either way, at the time the parent enters late, their arrival should not cause a disruption in the material presented. If they come during homework review, have the parent wait until the end (because you do not know if they completed the homework assignment) to recount their homework. If they come in the middle of the Parent Handout review, you can pass them a handout without directly addressing their tardiness. Do

not encourage excuses for lateness, as it takes valuable time away from the session. Chronic lateness should be addressed with the parent outside of the session, having the parent wait after session and speaking to the parent away from his or her teen. You can remind the parent of the portions of the session they missed and how it will decrease the benefits his or her teen might reap from the classes.

Homework Review

1. **In-Group Call**
   a. Make sure teen **traded information** on this phone call.
   b. Have parents identify a **common interest** discovered through **trading information**.
   c. Troubleshoot any problems that may have arisen.
2. Parents practice **trading information** with his or her teen.
   a. Ask if any parents practiced **trading information** with his or her teen.
   b. Have parents identify a **common interest** discovered through **trading information**.
   c. Troubleshoot any problems that may have arisen.

Didactic Lesson: Sources of Friends / Two-Way Conversations

- Distribute the Parent Handout.
- Explain: *The goal of trading information during a conversation is to find common interests. However, it is difficult to find common interests or people to talk to about these interests if we don't know what we're interested in. One of the most important jobs you as parents will have during this group is to help your teen find activities where they can pursue their interests and meet other people that are interested in the same things.*
- Go around the room and have parents identify:
  - Their teen's interests.
  - Activities that their teen could participate in to pursue these interests.
  - Current or past activities that their teen has participated in.
  - Refer parents to suggestions in the table in the Parent Handout.
  - Allow other parents to provide suggestions.
- Go around the room and have parents take turns reading the Parent Handout:
  - Do not have parents read the handout if you suspect that one or more parents are language or reading impaired.
- Sections in **bold print** come directly from the Parent Handout.

Sources of Friends

Teen Interests	Related Activities
Computers	Join a computer club, attend computer camp, take computer classes, start a Web site with friends
Video games, computer games	Join a gaming club, play video games with friends, go to video arcades with friends
Chess	Join a chess club, play chess with friends, attend chess camp
Movies	Join a movie club, go to movies with friends, watch DVDs with friends, join audiovisual club
Television	Watch favorite television shows with friends, join audiovisual club
Comic books	Attend comic book conventions, share/trade/read comic books with friends, go to comic book stores with friends, take art classes
Sports	Join a team (varsity, junior varsity, intramural, extramural), play sports at recreation center, join a junior league team, watch sporting events on TV with friends, go to sporting events with friends (e.g., high school, college, professional games), attend a sports camp
Cars	Go to car shows with friends, take auto shop, look at car magazines with friends
Music	Go to concerts with friends, listen to music with friends, watch music videos with friends, read/share music magazines with friends, join the school band/orchestra, take music classes, start a band with friends
Science	Join a science club, attend science camp, go to science museum with friends, take science classes
Photography	Join photography club, volunteer for the yearbook staff, take photojournalism classes, take pictures with friends, start a photo Web site with friends

Rules for Having a Two-Way Conversation

- Explain: *Today your teens will be learning how to have a two-way conversation with peers. Having a two-way conversation is one in which both people participate equally. There are very specific rules for having a two-way conversation, which your teens will be practicing.*
- Go around the room and have parents take turns reading from the Parent Handout:
  - **Trade information** (review from last session)
  - **Answer your own questions** (review from last session)
  - **Find a common interest** (review from last session)
  - **Share the conversation** (review from last session)
  - **Do not get too personal at first** (review from last session)
  - **Ask open-ended questions**

- Questions should be open-ended so the person can give extended responses:
    - *Open-ended question*: "What kind of movies do you like?"
    - *Answer*: "I like action movies, like…"
- Repeated questions that are closed only allow the person to give brief responses (e.g., "yes/no") and end up sounding like an interview:
    - *Closed question*: "What is your favorite movie?"
    - *Answer*: "Lord of the Rings."
- **Ask follow-up questions**
    - **Follow-up questions** are those we ask on a specific topic to keep the conversation going.
    - Example: **Follow-up questions** to what kind of movies one likes include "Have you seen any good movies lately?" or "Are you going to see the new (insert actor's name) movie?"
- **Do not be a conversation hog**
    - Do not monopolize the conversation.
    - Do not brag about yourself.
    - Try not to interrupt.
    - Let the other person talk.
    - Ask the person what they like.
- **Do not be an interviewer**
    - Do not ask question after question.
    - Ask the other person questions and then share things about yourself.
    - Make sure all of your questions and comments are related to the topic.
- **Do not be repetitive**
    - Do not talk about the same thing over and over.
    - Try talking about a few different topics.
- **Listen to your friend**
    - This means that if you ask a question, listen to the answer.
    - You are supposed to know the answer once you have asked the question.
    - You should not ask the same question again.
    - When you listen it shows that you are interested in your friend.
- **Do not criticize or tease**
    - This includes not making fun of what the other person says.
    - Do not pass judgment on what the person has to say.
- **Be serious**
    - Do not act silly when you are *first* getting to know someone.
    - You might make the other person uncomfortable.
    - They might not understand your sense of humor and they might think you are making fun of them.
    - Do not tell "dirty" jokes, swear, or act rudely.
- **Use good volume control**
    - Do not speak too quietly or too loudly.
    - Parents may need to give feedback to teens on this.

- *Have good body boundaries*
  - Do not stand too close or too far away when talking to someone.
  - Parents may need to give feedback to teens on this.
- *Make eye contact*
  - Girls: Look the person in the eyes; smile when appropriate.
  - Boys: Do not stare too much; make occasional eye contact.

Homework Assignments

The parent group leader should go over the homework assignment and trouble-shoot any potential problems with parents

1. *Sources of Friends*
   a. **Parents should identify and investigate at least one new extracurricular activity for their teen based on his or her teen's interests. (Do not involve your teen at this point.)**
2. **Parents practice *trading information* and having a *two-way conversation* with his or her teen.**
   a. **Begin by going over the rules for having a *two-way conversation* with their teen.**
   b. ***Find a common interest*.**
3. *In-Group Call*
   a. **Before the Call:**
      i. **Before you leave the group, parents should arrange for their teen to call another member of the group to practice conversational skills.**
         a. The treatment team will assign the calls.
      ii. **Set up a day and time to make the call.**
      iii. **Negotiate where the parent will be during the call and the parent's role if the assignment is not followed.**
   b. **During the Call:**
      i. **Teens should *trade information* and have a *two-way conversation* on this phone call.**
      ii. ***Find a common interest* to report back to the group.**
   c. **After the Call:**
      i. **Parents and teens should discuss the phone call and identify *common interests*.**

Parent Handout 2: Conversational Skills II—Two-Way Conversations

Sources of Friends

Teen Interests	Related Activities
Computers	Join a computer club, attend computer camp, take computer classes, start a Web site with friends
Video games, computer games	Join a gaming club, play video games with friends, go to video arcades with friends
Chess	Join a chess club, play chess with friends, attend chess camp
Movies	Join a movie club, go to movies with friends, watch DVDs with friends, join audiovisual club
Television	Watch favorite television shows with friends, join audiovisual club
Comic books	Attend comic book conventions, share/trade/read comic books with friends, go to comic book stores with friends, take art classes
Sports	Join a team (varsity, junior varsity, intramural, extramural), play sports at recreation center, join a junior league team, watch sporting events on TV with friends, go to sporting events with friends (e.g., high school, college, professional games), attend a sports camp
Cars	Go to car shows with friends, take auto shop, look at car magazines with friends
Music	Go to concerts with friends, listen to music with friends, watch music videos with friends, read/share music magazines with friends, join the school band/orchestra, take music classes, start a band with friends
Science	Join a science club, attend science camp, go to science museum with friends, take science classes
Photography	Join photography club, volunteer for the yearbook staff, take photojournalism classes, take pictures with friends, start a photo Web site with friends

Rules for Having a Two-Way Conversation

- ■ *Trade information*
- ■ *Answer your own questions*
- ■ *Find a common interest*
- ■ *Share the conversation*
- ■ *Do not get too personal at first*
- ■ *Ask open-ended questions*
- ■ *Ask follow-up questions*

■ *Do not be a conversation hog*
■ *Do not be an interviewer*
■ *Do not be repetitive*
■ *Listen to your friend*
■ *Do not criticize or tease*
■ *Be serious*
■ *Use good volume control*
■ *Have good body boundaries*
■ *Make eye contact*

Homework Assignments

1. ***Sources of Friends***
   a. Parents should identify and investigate at least one new extracurricular activity for their teen based on their teen's interests. (Do not involve the teen at this point.)
2. Parents practice ***trading information*** and having a ***two-way conversation*** with their teen.
   a. Begin by going over the rules for having a ***two-way conversation*** with their teen
   b. ***Find a common interest***
3. ***In-Group Call***
   a. Before the Call:
      i. Before you leave the group, parents should arrange for their teen to call another member of the group to practice conversational skills.
      ii. Set up a day and time to make the call.
      iii. Negotiate where the parent will be during the call and the parent's role if the assignment is not followed.
   b. During the Call:
      i. Teens should ***trade information*** and have a ***two-way conversation*** on this phone call.
      ii. ***Find a common interest*** to report back to the group.
   c. After the Call:
      i. Parents and teens should discuss the phone call and identify ***common interests***.

Teen Therapist Guide—Session 2: Conversational Skills II—Two-Way Conversations

Guiding Principles of the Teen Session

The focus of this didactic lesson is on the rules for having a two-way conversation. It will be critical to engage the teens in this session and win over any teens that may be ambivalent about the treatment at this point. This session involves a number of role-play demonstrations that will afford a wonderful opportunity to engage and entertain the teens. Perhaps the best method of engaging the teens in the treatment is to have them generate the rules for the lesson. Use a Socratic method of instruction in combination with the use of a series of role plays demonstrating *inappropriate* methods of conversation. This method of showing bad examples (i.e., what not to do) may be counterintuitive to the therapist but has been found to be highly effective in encouraging teens to generate rules of social etiquette, thereby making them more likely to believe what you are teaching them. Inappropriate role plays should be introduced by saying: *Watch this and tell me what I'm doing **wrong**.* At the end of the role play, ask the question: *So what was I doing **wrong** in that conversation?* The demonstrations should be overdramatized and obvious to the teens, which they will find amusing and easy to decode. Of course, following the presentation of the didactic lesson should be the demonstration of a role play of *appropriate* methods of conversation. *Appropriate* role plays of good social behavior are also critical to success in the program, in that they will demonstrate the skills that the teens should actually be following. The *appropriate* role plays are often demonstrated at the end of the didactic lesson, preceded by the question: *Watch this and tell me what I'm doing **right*** and followed by the question: *So what was I doing **right** in that conversation?*

The social errors demonstrated in the inappropriate role plays should be quite obvious to the teens and somewhat over-the-top (for instructive as well as entertainment value). However, for groups of older teens, you may want to be less dramatic with your demonstrations, as they may think you are talking down to them. The inappropriate role plays are often very humorous and will help to engage the teens in the group. Some teens will use this as an opportunity to act silly and make jokes. It is important that the group leader remain serious when eliciting feedback from the teens about what went wrong in the role play, as to avoid losing control of the group. If a teen provides an inappropriate comment about the role play in an effort to make a joke and be the "class clown," rather than engaging in a debate about why this was an inappropriate response, the group leader should open this comment up to response by the group by asking in a general way why the suggestion might be inappropriate. For example, if a teen made the comment that a particular role play was inappropriate because the group leader should have told the coach to *mind her own business*, rather than getting into a debate, it is more advisable to generally say to the group: *Why would it be a bad idea to tell someone to "mind their own business*"? This manner of handling inappropriate behavior from teens is far more effective in defusing the situation and makes it far less likely that other teens will follow in this inappropriate behavior. The goal is not to embarrass the teen, which is why it is important for the group leader to remain serious and respectful, but rather to provide just enough peer pressure to make the behavior less reinforcing. Once this has been done, it is critical to move on to a more appropriate topic immediately.

Some of the rules for having a two-way conversation do not involve role-play demonstrations. In these cases, it is helpful to begin by presenting the rule and immediately asking: *Why is it important to* (state the rule)? This is a very effective method of rule generating in that teens are being asked to generate a rationale for the rule, thereby making it more likely that they will believe what they are being taught. Teens are more likely to believe what you have to teach them if they and their group members imagine that they are generating the ideas themselves.

Finally, because most people have various types of learning styles, it will be helpful to present the material in each lesson in multiple formats. This should not only include verbal instruction and behavioral demonstration, but also writing the buzzwords (***bolded and italicized***) on the board. It is highly recommended that each lesson be captured through an outline of the rules and steps of the particular skill by writing the key elements of instruction on the board for the teens to review throughout the session. These buzzwords should be visually accessible to the teens during behavioral rehearsal exercises and should not be erased until the end of the session.

Rule Review

[Only go over session rules again if the teens are having difficulty following them.]

1. Listen to the other group members (no talking when others are speaking)
2. Follow directions
3. Raise your hand
4. Be respectful (no teasing or making fun of others)
5. No touching (no hitting, kicking, pushing, hugging, etc.)

Homework Review

- Start with successful homework completion first. If you have time, you can inquire as to why others were unable to complete the assignment and try to troubleshoot how they might get it done for the coming week.
- When reviewing homework, be sure to use buzzwords (e.g., ***trading information*** and ***common interests***).
- Spend the majority of the homework review on the in-group phone call, as this is the most important assignment for this session.

Note: Give points for homework *parts*—not just one point per assignment.

1. Practice ***trading information*** with parents.
   a. Say: *One of your assignments this week was to practice trading informa-tion with a parent. Raise your hand if you practiced trading information with one of your parents this week.*
      i. Begin by calling on teens who completed the assignment.
      ii. Ask:
         1. *Who did you practice trading information with (mom, dad, etc.)?*
         2. *What did you talk about?*
         3. *Did you trade information?*
         4. *Did you find a common interest?*
   a. When they identify ***common interests***, ask: *What could you do with that information if you were ever to hang out with your parent?*
   b. If you have time, check in with teens who did not complete the assign-ment and troubleshoot how they might get it done this week.
2. ***In-Group Call***
   a. Say: *The other assignment you had this week was to have a phone conver-sation with someone in the group in order to practice trading information and finding common interests. Raise your hand if you did the in-group call.*
      i. Begin by calling on the teens who completed the call.
      ii. Ask:
         1. *Who did you talk to?*
         2. *Who called who?*
         3. *Did you trade information?*
         4. *Did you find a common interest?*
            a. When they identify *common interests*, ask: *What could you do with that information if you were ever to hang out?*
         5. Avoid general questions like: *How did it go?*
      iii. Have the other person who participated in the call give his or her account immediately after, but not at the same time.
         1. Do not allow teens to talk about mistakes the other person made.
      iv. Troubleshoot any problems that may have arisen.
      v. If you have time, check in with teens who did not complete the assignment and troubleshoot how they might get it done this week.

Discussion Questions

■ Begin by saying: *Today we are going to continue our discussion about con-versational skills. In particular, we are going to talk about how to have a two-way conversation with someone. Before we get into the rules of having a two-way conversation, it might be helpful to brainstorm what kinds of things teens like to talk about.*

- Ask the question: *What do teenagers talk about?*
- Have the group brainstorm common topics of conversation for teens.
- Mention the topics below if the group does not think of them on their own.

Common Conversational Topics for Boys and Girls

People at school/school gossip/events at school	Problems with school, teachers, school administration, parents, family, friends
Dating	Cars/motorcycles/bikes
Parties and get-togethers	Movies, television, celebrities
Weekend activities	School sports, teams, and clubs
Professional sports	Clothes and fashion
Music and musical artists	Makeup and hair
Video games/computer games	Comic books/anime/art

Didactic Lesson: Rules for Having a Two-Way Conversation

- Explain: *So now that we have some ideas about **what** to talk about, we need to figure out **how** to talk to our friends. When you are first getting to know someone it is important to share the conversation. We can do this by having a two-way conversation.*
- Present the rules for having a ***two-way conversation***.

1. ***Trade information*** (review from last session)
   a. Say: *One of the rules for having a two-way conversation is to trade information. Why is it important to trade information in a conversation?*
      i. Answer: So you can get to know one another.
   b. Ask: *What is the most important goal of trading information?*
      i. Answer: To ***find common interests***.
   c. Ask: *Why is it important to find common interests?*
      i. Answer: Because it gives you something to talk about or something to do together.

2. ***Answer your own question*** (review from last session)
   a. Say: *Another rule for having a two-way conversation is to answer your own question. Why is it important to answer your own questions?*
      i. Answer: Because sometimes people do not know to ask a question in return and it is important to ***share something related about yourself***.

3. ***Share the conversation*** (review from last session)
   a. Say: *Another rule for having a two-way conversation is to share the conversation. Why is it important to share the conversation?*

i. Answer: Because then everyone has an equal opportunity to speak and it is fun for everyone.

4. ***Do not get too personal at first*** (review from last session)

a. Say: *Another rule for having a two-way conversation is not to get too personal at first. Why is it a bad idea to get too personal when you're first getting to know someone?*

i. Answer: Because it may make the other person feel uncomfortable and if they do not understand your sense of humor, they may think you are making fun of them.

5. ***Ask open-ended questions***

a. Explain: *Another rule for having a two-way conversation is to ask open-ended questions. Open-ended questions are ones where the person's response can be extended and can lead to more conversation. Closed questions are ones that only require a brief response. This doesn't mean you can't ask closed questions, but you should try to vary your conversations with both so it doesn't sound like you're interviewing the other person.*

i. Open-ended question: "What kind of movies do you like?"

ii. Answer: "I like action movies, like…"

b. Do not ***only*** ask closed questions in which the person gives a brief response (e.g., "yes/no" answers).

i. Closed question: "What is your favorite movie?"

ii. Answer: "Lord of the Rings."

iii. Ask: *Why is it a bad idea to **only** ever ask closed questions?*

1. Answer: Because they do not keep the conversation going.

iv. Ask: *Why is it a good idea to try to ask open-ended questions?*

1. Answer: Because it elicits extended responses and keeps the conversation going.

c. Go around the room and have each teen generate an open-ended question from the stem of a closed question.

i. Example: *If the closed question was: "What is your favorite movie"; what would the open-ended question be?*

1. Answer: "What kind of movies do you like?"

ii. Example: *If the closed question was: "What is your favorite television show"; what would the open-ended question be?*

1. Answer: "What kind of TV shows do you like?"

iii. Example: *If the closed question was: "What is your favorite band"; what would the open-ended question be?*

1. Answer: "What kind of music do you like?"

6. ***Ask follow-up questions***

a. Explain: *Another rule for having a two-way conversation is to ask follow-up questions. Follow-up questions are questions we ask on a specific topic to keep the conversation going. For example, if you asked someone what kind of movies he or she likes and that person tells you he or she likes comedies, good follow-up questions might be "Have you seen any good comedies lately?" or "Are you going to see the new (insert comedic actor's name) movie?"*

b. Go around the room and have each teen come up with three follow-up questions to the following topics of conversation:

i. *What kinds of TV shows do you like?*
ii. *What kinds of movies do you like?*
iii. *What kinds of music do you like?*
iv. *What kinds of books do you like?*
v. *What kinds of food do you like?*
vi. *What sports do you like?*
vii. *What games do you like?*
viii. *What video games do you like?*
ix. *What do you like to do on the weekends?*
x. *What classes are you taking?*

7. ***Do not be a conversation hog***

a. The teen group leader and coach should do an *inappropriate* role play with the group leader being a **conversation hog**.

i. Begin by saying: *Watch this and tell me what I'm doing **wrong***.
ii. Example of an *inappropriate* role play:

Teen group leader: "Hi (insert name). What have you been up to?"

Coach: "Not much. Just going to school and hanging out. What about you?"

Teen group leader: "Well, I had a really fun weekend. I went to the movies with my parents and we saw the new (insert actor's name) movie."

Coach: "Oh, I heard that was good…."

Teen group leader: (interrupts) "…yeah, it was. And then we went out to eat at my favorite restaurant and I ate a whole pizza on my own. And then the next day I went to the mall with my cousin and we went to this really cool arcade and played video games all day…."

Coach: "Oh, you like video games…."

Teen group leader: (interrupts) "…yeah, and then we went home and watched some movies and I didn't go to sleep until really late and I'm so tired today. I thought I'd fall asleep in science class…."

Coach: (looks bored)

Teen group leader: "…and tomorrow I have a test in my history class and I haven't even started to study, so I'm going to have to stay up really late again….."

Coach: (looking around, appears bored)

iii. End by saying: *Okay, so time out on that. So what did I do **wrong** in that conversation?*

1. Answer: The group leader was **hogging the conversation**.

b. Explain: *One of the rules for having a two-way conversation is don't be a conversation hog.*

i. Do not monopolize the conversation.
ii. Do not brag about yourself.

    iii. Try not to interrupt.

    iv. Let the other person talk.

    v. Ask the person what he or she likes.

8. ***Do not be an interviewer***

    a. The teen group leader and coach should do an ***inappropriate*** role play with the leader being an ***interviewer***.

       i. Begin by saying:, *Watch this and tell me what I'm doing **wrong**.*

       ii. Example of an ***inappropriate*** role play:

Teen group leader: "Hi (insert name). How are you doing?"

Coach: "Fine. How are you?"

Teen group leader: "I'm good. Hey, I was wondering, what kind of movies do you like?"

Coach: "Oh, I like action adventure movies and comedies. What about you?"

Teen group leader: "Yeah, and what's your favorite movie?"

Coach: "I guess my favorite is (insert current movie). What's your favorite?"

Teen group leader: "Yeah, that was good. What about TV shows? What kind of TV shows do you watch?"

Coach: "I like sit-coms. What about you?"

Teen group leader: "Well, what's your favorite TV show?"

Coach: "I guess (insert current TV sit-com) is my favorite." (looks bored)

Teen group leader: "So what kind of music do you like?"

Coach: "I guess I like (insert genre of music)." (looking around, appears bored)

      iii. End by saying: *Okay, time-out on that. So what did I do **wrong** in that conversation?*

        1. Answer: The group leader was being an ***interviewer***.

      iv. Explain: *One of the rules for having a two-way conversation is don't be an interviewer.*

        1. Do not ask question after question.

        2. Ask the other person questions and then share things about yourself.

        3. Make sure all of your questions and comments are related to the topic.

9. ***Do not be repetitive***

    a. Say: *Another rule for having a two-way conversation is not to be repetitive. That means don't talk about the same thing over and over. What is the problem with talking about the same thing over and over?*

       i. Answer: It is boring for the other person.

    b. Ask: *Just because you find a common interest with someone, does that mean that is the only thing you should talk about?*

       i. Answer: No—you can talk about a variety of things.

    c. Explain the following:

       i. Do not be repetitive.

       ii. Try talking about a few different topics.

10. ***Listen to your friend***

a. Ask: *Another rule for having a two-way conversation relates to listening. If you ask your friend a question, do you think you should listen to the answer?*
   i. Answer: Yes.
b. Ask: *What is the problem with not listening to the answer?*
   i. Answer: Your friend will think you do not care about what he or she has to say.
c. Explain the following:
   i. If you ask a question—listen to the answer.
      1. You are supposed to know the answer once you have asked the question.
      2. You should not ask the same question again.
      3. When you listen it shows that you are interested in your friend.

11. ***Do not criticize or tease***
   a. Ask: *Our next rule for having a two-way conversation is not to criticize or tease the person you're talking to. What is wrong with criticizing or teasing other people?*
      i. Answer: It makes them feel bad.
   b. Ask: *Will people want to be your friend if you criticize them?*
      i. Answer: No—they may avoid you.
   c. Ask: *What is wrong with teasing or making fun of other people?*
      i. Answer: It makes them feel bad.
   d. Ask: *Will people want to be your friend if you tease or make fun of them?*
      i. Answer: Probably not.
   e. Explain the following:
      i. You should not criticize or make fun of other people.
         1. Even if you think you are being funny, it may hurt their feelings.
         2. This is especially true when you are *first* getting to know someone and that person does not yet know your sense of humor.
         3. Boys in particular like to tease each other, but this is very risky behavior for making and keeping friends.

12. ***Be serious*** when you are first getting to know someone.
   a. Say: *Another rule for having a two-way conversation is that you should be serious when you're first getting to know someone. What is the problem with acting silly when you're first getting to know someone?*
      i. Answer: They may think you are strange, they may not understand your humor, they may think you are making fun of them.
   b. Explain the following:
      i. Do not act silly when you are *first* getting to know someone.
         1. You might make the other person uncomfortable.
         2. They might not understand your sense of humor and they might think you are making fun of them.
      ii. Do not tell "dirty" jokes, swear, or act rudely.
         1. This can easily put people off.

13. ***Use good volume control***
   a. The teen group leader and coach should do an ***inappropriate*** role play with the leader speaking too quietly.
      i. Begin by saying: *Watch this and tell me what I'm doing **wrong**.*
      ii. Example of an ***inappropriate*** role play:

Teen group leader: (whispering) "Hi (insert name). How's it going?"
Coach: (straining to hear) "What?"
Teen group leader: (whispering) "How's it going?"
Coach: (looking confused) "Oh, fine thanks."
Teen group leader: (whispering) "So what have you been up to?"
Coach: (straining to hear, moving closer) "What?"
Teen group leader: (whispering) "What have you been up to?"
Coach: (looking around, appears bored) "Oh, not much."

      iii. End by saying: *Okay, time-out on that. So what did I do **wrong** in that conversation?*
         1. Answer: The group leader was speaking too softly.
   b. Explain the following:
      i. Do not speak too quietly because the person may not hear you.
      ii. If the person cannot hear you, he or she may avoid speaking to you in the future.
   c. The teen group leader and coach should do another ***inappropriate*** role play with the leader speaking too loudly.
      i. Begin by saying: *Now watch this and tell me what I'm doing **wrong**.*
      ii. Example of an ***inappropriate*** role play:

Teen group leader: (speaking very loudly) "Hi (insert name). How's it going?"
Coach: (startled, moves back) "Oh, it's going good."
Teen group leader: (speaking very loudly) "What have you been up to?"
Coach: (looking annoyed, moving farther away) "Oh, not much."
Teen group leader: (speaking very loudly) "So what did you do over the weekend?"
Coach: (looking around, trying to escape) "Not much."

      iii. End by saying: *Okay, time-out on that. So, what did I do **wrong** in that conversation?*
         1. Answer: The group leader was speaking too loudly.
      iv. Explain the following:
         1. Do not speak too loudly or the person may get annoyed or bothered by you.
         2. If the person is annoyed or bothered, they may avoid speaking to you in the future.

14. ***Have good body boundaries***
   a. The teen group leader and coach should do an ***inappropriate*** role play with the leader standing too close to the coach.
      i. Begin by saying: *Now watch this and tell me what I'm doing **wrong**.*
      ii. Example of an ***inappropriate*** role play:

Teen group leader: (standing too close) "Hi (insert name). How are you doing?"

Coach: (startled, moves back) "Oh, I'm fine."

Teen group leader: (Moves forward) "What have you been up to?"

Coach: (looking annoyed, moving farther back) "Not much."

Teen group leader: (moves forward again) "So how's school going?"

Coach: (looking around, trying to escape) "Fine."

  iii. End by saying: *Okay, time-out on that. So what did I do **wrong** in that conversation?*

    1. Answer: The group leader was standing too close.

  iv. Explain the following:

    1. Standing too close to someone is likely to make them feel uncomfortable.

    2. They may not want to talk to you again.

    3. They may avoid you.

    4. The general rule is to stand about an arm's length away (but do not measure first!).

  b. The teen group leader and coach should do an *inappropriate* role play with the leader standing too far away.

  i. Begin by saying: *Now watch this and tell me what I'm doing **wrong**.*

  ii. Example of an *inappropriate* role play:

Teen group leader: (standing across the room) "Hi (insert name). How are you doing?"

Coach: (straining to hear and looking confused) "Oh, hi (insert name)."

Teen group leader: (still standing across the room) "How are you doing?"

Coach: (looking confused) "Fine."

Teen group leader: (still standing across the room) "So what have you been up to?"

Coach: (looking confused, looking around the room, trying to escape) "Not much."

  iii. End by saying: *Okay, time-out on that. So what did I do **wrong** in that conversation?*

    1. Answer: The group leader was too far away.

  iv. Explain the following:

    1. Standing too far away is awkward in a conversation and may feel like your conversation is too public.

    2. The person may think you are strange for trying to have a conversation when you are standing so far away.

    3. Saying hello across the hall in school is fine, but do not try to get into a lengthy conversation.

    4. Again, the general rule is to stand about an arm's length away.

15. ***Make eye contact***

  a. Say: *Our final rule for having a two-way conversation is to have good eye contact. That means looking at the person when you're talking to them. Why is it important to look at someone when you're talking to them?*

      i. Answer: So they will know you are talking to them, so they will know you are interested in them.

   b. Explain the following:

      i. Make more eye contact when you are *first* getting to know someone.

         1. This tells them that you are interested in them.

     ii. Girls: Look the person in the eyes; smile when appropriate.

   iii. Boys: Do not stare too much; make occasional eye contact.

   iv. Girls generally make more eye contact than boys, but everyone should make more eye contact when they are *first* getting to know someone.

Role Play

- The teen group leader and a coach should demonstrate an *appropriate* role play using all of the steps for having a *two-way conversation*.

- Begin by saying: *Now that we know the rules for having a two-way conversation, watch this and tell us what we're doing right.*

  – Example of an *appropriate* role play:

    Teen group leader: (standing about an arm's length away, maintaining good eye contact, using appropriate volume) "Hi (insert name). How's it going?"

    Coach: "Oh, it's going good. How are you?"

    Teen group leader: "I'm fine. So what have you been up to lately?"

    Coach: "Oh, not much. Just studying a lot, but I'm going to the movies this weekend."

    Teen group leader: "Oh, yeah. So what are you going to see?"

    Coach: "I think I'm going to see (insert current sci-fi movie). What are you doing this weekend?"

    Teen group leader: "I was thinking about going to the movies, too, but I already saw (insert current sci-fi movie)."

    Coach: "Oh, yeah. Was it good?"

    Teen group leader: "Yeah, it was really good. Do you like sci-fi movies?"

    Coach: "Yeah. They're my favorite kind. What about you?"

    Teen group leader: "They're my favorite, too!"

    Coach: "Cool. What's your favorite movie?"

  – End by saying: *Okay, time-out on that. So what did we do right in that conversation?*

    • Answer: The group leader and coach followed all of the rules for having a two-way conversation [be sure to have teens review all the rules in the context of the role play].

Behavioral Rehearsal

- Say: *Now that we know the rules for having a two-way conversation, we're going to have each of you practice with the person sitting next to you. Remember, the goal is to find a common interest.*
- Have teens practice having a two-way conversation with the person sitting next to them.
    - The teen group leader should assign the pairs, and move teens around if the dyad is inappropriate.
    - If there are an uneven number of teens, create one triad.
- Group leader and coaches should help facilitate the exercise when necessary:
    - Examples of prompts: *You could ask each other about your school or hobbies. You could talk about your favorite books, movies, or television programs. You could find out what the other person likes to do on the weekend.*
    - Group leader and coaches may need to troubleshoot if problems arise:
        - Examples of prompts: *Remember not to get too personal at first. Be sure to share the conversation. You may need to answer your own question. Don't be an interviewer. Don't be a conversation hog. Remember to ask follow-up questions.*
- Spend about 2 to 3 minutes on this exercise.
- Then briefly have teens identify whether they were able to find a common interest by saying: "It's time to wrap up your conversations. I heard lots of good trading information. Let's go around the room and find out what common interests you found."
- Praise teens for their efforts.

Homework Assignments

- Briefly explain the homework for the week by saying: *We are going to continue to have you practice having two-way conversations this week. Your homework assignment this week is to:*
    - *Practice having a two-way conversation with your parent and find a common interest.*
    - *Have an in-group phone call with another group member.*
        - *This should be at least 5 to 10 minutes.*
        - *You will need to find a common interest to report to the group.*
- Group leader and coaches should assign the in-group phone calls for the week and write this on the "In-Group Phone Call Assignment Log" for future reference.
    - If there are an uneven number of teens, assign someone "double duty."
        - This person will have two in-group phone calls (one as a caller and the other as a receiver).
        - This person will receive extra points for completing the extra call.

Teen Activity: Jeopardy

Note: See the "Teen Activity Guide" for rules.

- Teens need to complete the **Jeopardy** answer sheets before beginning the activity if they haven't already):
  - To save time, it is very helpful to have teens complete these forms while they are waiting in the lobby before the start of the group.
- Teens need to **trade information** before Jeopardy and practice asking questions:
  - Write topics on the board and then break the teens into dyads or triads.
  - After the teens have **traded information** with most of the group members for 2 to 3 minutes each, have them reconvene as a group and play the game of **Jeopardy.**
- Teens compete against themselves to earn points for correct responses to questions from **trading information** exercise:
  - The teen who raises his or her hand first gets to take the first guess.
  - If the teen is wrong, someone else has a chance to answer (the person who raised his or her hand second).
  - The teens get only one guess per question.
  - Do not give teens clues.
- Encourage the teens to clap for each other during the game.
- Keep track of the points on the board using a different colored marker.
- At the end of the game, the person with the most points is the **Jeopardy Challenge Winner.**

Reunification

- Announce that teens should join their parents:
  - Be sure that the teens are standing or sitting next to their parents.
  - Be sure to have silence and the full attention of the group.
- Say: *Today we worked on having a two-way conversation. Who can tell us what some of the rules for having a two-way conversation are?* [Have teens generate all of the rules. Be prepared to give prompts if necessary.]
  - **Trade information**
  - **Answer your own questions**
  - **Find common interests**
  - **Share the conversation**
  - **Do not get too personal at first**
  - **Ask open-ended questions**
  - **Ask follow-up questions**
  - **Do not be a conversation hog**
  - **Do not be an interviewer**
  - **Do not be repetitive**

- *Listen to your friend*
- *Do not criticize or tease*
- *Be serious*
- *Use good volume control*
- *Have good body boundaries*
- *Make eye contact*

■ Say: *This group did a great job of practicing two-way conversations today. Let's give them a round of applause. The group also played a game called* **Jeopardy** *where they practiced trading information. Tonight's* **Jeopardy** *Challenge Winner is* (insert name). *Let's give him/her a round of applause.*

■ Go over the homework for the next week (see below):
  - Be sure to read off the in-group phone call assignment in front of parents.
  - Remind parents to make a note of who is calling whom.

■ Individually and separately negotiate with each family where the parent will be during the phone call.

Homework Assignments

1. Parents and teens should practice **trading information** and having a **two-way conversation**.
   a. Parents should go over the rules for having **two-way conversations** with his or her teen.
   b. **Find a common interest.**
2. **In-Group Call**
   a. Before the Call:
      i. Before you leave the group, parents should arrange for their teen to call another member of the group to practice conversational skills.
      ii. Set up a day and time to make the call.
      iii. Negotiate where the parent will be during the call and the parent's role if the assignment is not followed.
   b. During the Call:
      i. Teens should **trade information** and have a **two-way conversation** on this phone call.
      ii. **Find a common interest** to report back to the group.
   c. After the Call:
      i. Parents and teens should discuss the phone call and identify **common interests**.

Calculate Points

Keep track of the following for each week of the intervention:

■ Calculate the number of points earned by each teen.
■ Add up the total number of points earned by the group.

- Do not calculate the points in the presence of the teens.
  - Do not disclose the individual or group total of points.
  - Discourage attempts to compare number of points earned between teens.
- Remind them that they are working as a team to earn a bigger and better graduation party.

Teen Activity Guide: Session 2

"Jeopardy"

Materials Needed

- Blackboard and chalk/whiteboard and markers
- Answer sheets
- Scissors
- Pens

Rules

- Teens will compete against themselves in this game of ***trading information***.
- Like the television show, ***Jeopardy,*** teens will be given answers by the group leader and asked to respond in the form of a question.
  - Example:
    - *Teen group leader*: "The answer is Jimmy's favorite sport."
    - *Teen*: "What is baseball?"
- To promote interest and cooperation, the teen group leader will give out points for correct responses.
- Pass out answer sheets before the ***trading information*** exercise (if you haven't already).
- Have teens fill in responses and return to the teen group leader.
  - To save time, it is very helpful to have teens complete these forms while they are waiting in the lobby before the start of the group.
- Have teens practice ***trading information*** in dyads or triads for 2 to 3 minutes each (depending on time) until each teen has ***traded information*** with all group members.
- Group leader will suggest topics for ***trading information*** and write these on the board:
  - Name
  - City where they live
  - Name of school
  - Favorite game
  - Favorite sport

- Favorite television show
- Favorite movie
- Favorite weekend activity
- Eye color (Note: This is *not* to be asked, but noticed by using good eye contact when *trading information*.)

■ Write categories on the board to help teens:
  - "School" Spirit
    • Answer sheet: Name of school
  - TGIF
    • Answer sheet: Favorite weekend activity
  - "Sports" and Leisure
    • Answer sheet: Favorite sport
  - "Game" Time
    • Answer sheet: Favorite game
  - Movies, Movies, Movies
    • Answer sheet: Favorite movie
  - "TV" Time
    • Answer sheet: Favorite television show
  - "Home" Sweet "Home"
    • Answer sheet: City where they live
  - The "Eyes" Have It
    • Answer sheet: Eye color

■ While teens are *trading information*, one of the coaches will:
  - Cut the answer sheets into individual questions (cut along the lines provided).
  - Separate the answer sheets according to category and mix the order of the answer sheets.

■ The teen group leader and coaches should prompt teens to ask relevant questions to the *Jeopardy* topics when necessary.

■ Once the teens have finished *trading information*, reconvene as a group and begin the *Jeopardy Challenge*.
  - Begin by having the teen with the most points pick the category.
  - Notify the group that if they raise their hand before the question has been asked, they are disqualified from answering.
  - The person who raises his or her hand first gets to take the first guess.
  - If that person provides the wrong answer, the person who raised his or her hand second has a chance to answer (and so on).
  - The teens get only one guess per question.
  - Do not give teens clues.

■ When reading the items, you may need to point to the person to whom the item relates (while saying their name), because the teens are just becoming acquainted with each other.

■ You may need to enforce a time limit if teens take a long time to answer.

■ Do not correct the teens if they answer the questions in the incorrect format (i.e., instead of saying "What is baseball?" they say "Baseball").

- All that matters is that they remembered the information they obtained through **trading information**.

■ The person who answers the question correctly gets a point and chooses the next category.

■ If no one answers correctly, the person about which the last question relates gets to pick the category.

■ Encourage the teens to clap for each other during the game.

■ Give points for correct responses.

■ Keep track of the points on the board using a different colored marker.

■ At the end of the game, the person with the most points is the **Jeopardy Challenge Winner.**

■ **Save the answer sheets for the next session**.

"Jeopardy" Answer Sheets

"School" Spirit
 	
The answer is:
The name of _____ 's school.
                (Name)
 	
The question is:
What is _____ ?
       (Name of your school)
	TGIF
	
	The answer is:
	_____ 's favorite weekend activity.
	     (Name)
	
	The question is:
	What is _____ ?
	   (Favorite weekend activity)

Sports & Leisure
 	
The answer is:
_____ 's favorite sport.
     (Name)
 	
The question is:
What is _____ ?
     (Favorite sport)
	"Game" Time
	
	The answer is:
	_____ 's favorite game.
	     (Name)
	
	The question is:
	What is _____ ?
	     (Favorite game)

Movies, Movies, Movies
 	
The answer is:
_____ 's favorite movie.
     (Name)
 	
The question is:
What is _____ ?
     (Favorite movie)
	"TV" Time
	
	The answer is:
	_____ 's favorite TV show.
	     (Name)
	
	The question is:
	What is _____ ?
	     (Favorite TV show)

"Home" Sweet "Home"
 	
The answer is:
The name of the city _____ lives in.
             (Name)
 	
The question is:
What is _____ ?
  (Name of the city you live in)
	The "Eyes" Have It
	
	The answer is:
	The color of _____ 's eyes.
	           (Name)
	
	The question is:
	What is _____ ?
	     (Your eye color)

Chapter 5

Session 3
Conversational Skills III—Electronic Communication

Parent Session Therapist Guide

Guiding Principles of the Parent Session

Recent research indicates that information technology (e.g., Internet, cell phone, portable music player, and so forth) is an integral part of teen culture (cf., Thurlow & McKay, 2003). Despite this, the telephone continues to be the main form of communication between teens (via phone calls or text messaging). More than 70% of teens use e-mail and instant messaging to contact friends. The popularity of online games, Internet social networking sites, and music downloads is also increasing dramatically among teens. The focus of the teen session and portions of the parent session will be on how to effectively navigate these forms of electronic communication.

In the homework review, the major focus should be on the parents' search for extracurricular activities. Desperate parents will try to find shortcuts, such as football players taking their teen under their wing (i.e., mentorship), "accepting" teens who are different, and after-school activities such as homework clubs (i.e., where the purpose is for the teen to complete homework assignments, not socialize). These are not acceptable extracurricular activities, as the goal is for parents to help find friends, not mentors or tutors. The focus should be on finding places where the teens fit in. The session handout listing teen "crowds" or "peer groups" is often a surprise to parents. They often have not thought about crowds, but consideration of these potential peer groups is essential to figuring out how their teens will best fit in. A review of techniques the parent group leader can use to assist parents in improving homework compliance is listed below in Box 5.1.

BOX 5.1   HONING THE GROUP LEADER'S SKILLS AT GETTING HOMEWORK COMPLIANCE

1. During the homework review, ask for successes first and redirect parents who report on anything else.
2. Be specific about how to comply for the next homework assignment. For example, do not just say: *Keep looking for extracurricular activities*, but ask each parent: *What will you do this week to find extracurricular activities?* Do not throw out ideas to the group; instead, go around to individual parents and get a commitment from each of them on their specific plan.
3. Ask each parent: *What difficulties do you anticipate?* If you do not have a strategy for the parent to try, open it up to the group by asking: *Who can suggest something that might work?* If you get more than one good suggestion from the group, pick the best suggestion for the parent to try first.
4. Avoid general discussion. Keep all points specific to each parent's teen and relevant to the homework item being discussed.

Homework Review

1. Parents practice **trading information** and having a **two-way conversation** with his or her teen.
   a. Ask for a show of hands from parents who practiced **trading information** with their teen.
   b. Have parents identify a **common interest** discovered through **trading information**.
   c. Troubleshoot any problems that may have arisen.
2. **In-Group Call**
   a. Make sure teen **traded information** on this phone call.
   b. Have parents identify a **common interest** discovered through **trading information**.
   c. Troubleshoot any problems that may have arisen:
      i. A common problem here is the teen that has too long a conversation. For example, one conversation between two teens in a group went 90 minutes and consequently ended badly with the teens becoming bored with one another. Rarely can another teen with social problems converse this long with someone they have only just met. The phone calls should be anticipated to last 10 to 15 minutes on average.
3. **Sources of Friends**
   a. As always, start with successful homework assignments (i.e., anyone who found an extracurricular activity for his or her teen) and redirect parents who are talking about anything off-topic. Usually the latter are attempts to distract

from homework noncompliance. Common diversionary tactics for homework noncompliance even include the parent talking about how well his or her teen is allegedly doing in the program. Other diversions include talking about how their teen is sick, overburdened with schoolwork, and so forth.

b. If a teen does not feel comfortable trying new activities by himself or herself, then help the parent figure out how he or she might go along with the teen and not really be a part of the new activity (but hold off on making this arrangement until it can be negotiated with the teen).

c. Some parents will report that the teen has no interests and "always stays by himself or herself." Interpret this with the parent as the teen not being ready right now, but follow up by asking: *If he or she were ready, what would he or she enjoy doing?*

d. Wait until after the Parent Handout review to have parents who have yet to identify at least one new extracurricular activity, what they will investigate for their teen based on their teen's interests. The Parent Handout is often helpful in this regard.

Didactic Lesson: Choosing Appropriate Friends / Electronic Communication

■ Distribute the Parent Handout.

■ Explain: *Today we are talking about choosing appropriate friends. Teens sometimes need help with choosing appropriate friends. Having a friend is a choice. We don't have to be friends with everybody. You will want to help your teen choose appropriate friends. In doing this, the first thing we need to talk about is your teen's reputation and where he or she might appropriately fit in at school. In every school, there are different "groups" or "crowds" of kids. What are some of the groups of kids?*

■ Go around the room and have parents take turns reading the Parent Handout and have parents brainstorm the different groups of kids.

■ Sections in **bold print** come directly from the Parent Handout.

Different Peer Groups or Crowds

Jocks	Brains/smart kids	Stoners/burners/druggies
Cheerleaders	Chess club kids	Rockers
Popular kids	Gamers/video game geeks	Hip-hop group
Student council kids	Nerds	Detention club/slackers
Drama club kids	Math geeks	Wannabe gangbangers/taggers
Choir/chorus	Computer geeks	Musicians (rock bands)
Pep squad	Band kids/band geeks	Skaters
Partiers	Science geeks	Surfers
Preppies	Math geeks	Hippies/granolas
Artists	Goths	ROTC
Comic book geeks/anime geeks	Emos	Ethnic/cultural/religious groups

- Have parents identify how to tell which group a teen is in:
  - Clothing, hair, appearance
  - Interests
  - Who they hang out with
  - After-school activities
- Explain: *Some kids try to fit in with the wrong group. This can result in rejection by peers. As parents, it is important to think about which group your teen is trying to fit in with and consider whether this is the best fit for your teen. If your teen is trying to fit in with the wrong crowd, it is important to know this in order to help him or her find a crowd in which he or she is likely to be accepted.*
- Go around the room and have parents identify:
  - Which group they think their teen **attempts** to fit in with.
  - Which group they think their teen would **best** fit in with.
  - If the parents are unsure, remind them that this is their homework for this week.
- It is important for parents to come to grips with the peer group that their teens will feel happiest fitting into. For teens with autism spectrum disorders, a good question to consider is whether they can fit in with mainstream peers or will they be happiest and most accepted by fitting in with other teens with autism spectrum disorders. It is also important to consider whether the teen has a negative reputation right now at school. If so, then school should be avoided as a source for meeting new friends until they are able to change their reputation or find a crowd that will be more accepting.
- Explain: *Next week your teens will be learning about the different groups or crowds in school and how to choose appropriate friends. This week your teens are learning about how to use electronic communication appropriately. That includes things like making phone calls, sending e-mail, text messaging, instant messaging, and using the Internet. Electronic communication is a very popular method of communicating for teens, so they need to know what the rules are for using electronics to talk with friends.*
- Go around the room and have parents take turns reading the Parent Handout.
- Sections in **bold print** come directly from the Parent Handout.

Rules for Starting and Ending a Phone Call

- **Starting the conversation**
  - **Ask for the person you are calling by name**
    - Example: "Hi. May I please speak to Lance?"
  - **Say who you are**
    - Example: "Hi Lance. This is Janet."
  - **Ask if the person you are calling can talk**
  - **Give a *cover story* for why you are calling**

- A *cover story* is a reason for calling.
    - Example: "I was just calling to see how you're doing."
    - Example: "I was calling to see if I could get the homework assignment from you."
■ **Ending the conversation**
  - **Wait for a longer pause (i.e., transitional moment)**
    - Some parents will be stuck on where their teens were functioning before peers. Parents may wrongly think that the teen will not be able to interpret or accept the pause as the end of the conversation. Encourage parents by saying: *Let's see if your teen can do it now. Let's have a backup plan for how you would intervene if your teen can't do it.*
  - **Give a *cover story* for why you have to hang up**
    - A *cover story* is a reason for ending the call.
      - Example: "I have to go now. I have to eat dinner."
      - Example: "I have to go finish my homework."
    - **Parents can often help with providing *cover stories*.**
  - **Tell the person it was nice talking to him or her**
  - **Tell the person you will talk to or see him or her later**
  - **Say good-bye**

Cover Story Examples

Reasons You Are Calling	*Reasons You Have to Hang Up*
"Just calling to see how you're doing."	"I have to get going."
"Just calling to hear what's up with you."	"I better let you go."
"I'm calling to get the homework."	"I need to finish my homework."
"I haven't talked to you in a while."	"I have to eat dinner now."
"I was wondering what you're up to."	"My mom needs to use the phone."

Rules for Leaving a Voice-Mail Message

■ **Say your name**:
  - "Hi this is Jennifer."
■ **Say whom you are calling for**:
  - "I'm calling for Ruth."
■ **Say when you are calling**:
  - "It's about 6 o'clock on Thursday night."
■ **Give a *cover story* for calling**:
  - "I was just calling to see what you've been up to."
■ **Leave your phone number**:
  - "Give me a call at xxx-xxxx."
■ **Say good-bye**:

- "Talk to you soon. Bye."
■ Tell the parents that they may want to practice starting and ending a phone call with their teen and practice leaving voice-mail messages.
  - Using *cover stories* is essential.
  - This practice is particularly helpful just prior to making the call.
■ Have parents identify any potential difficulties their teen may have with starting and ending phone calls or leaving messages.
■ Troubleshoot these problems with the help of the other parents.

Rules for Phone Calls / Text Messages / Instant Messages / E-mail

■ **Use *cover stories* for text messaging, instant messaging (IM), and e-mail for people you do not know well.**
  - **You do not need *cover stories* for contacting friends you are close to.**
  - **If you are contacting someone for the first time, it is best to have a *cover story*.**
    • Examples:
      ■ "Thought I'd check out your Facebook page."
      ■ "Wondering what you've been up to."
      ■ "Just calling to see what you're doing this weekend."
      ■ "Wanted to know if you're going to the game."
■ **Avoid *cold calling*:**
  - **Do not call someone who has not given you his or her phone number, e-mail, or screen name.**
  - **Giving out a phone number, e-mail address, or screen name is giving someone permission to contact you.**
    • Just because a teen has access to someone's contact information (e.g., a school directory, online directory) does not give him or her permission to contact that person.
  - **Ask for the person's contact information before calling.**
  - **This will give you permission to contact them.**
    • Examples:
      ■ "We should hang out some time. Why don't I get your number."
      ■ "Are you on Facebook/MySpace? Maybe I'll look you up." (Then pay attention to their response to assess their interest.)
■ **If you try to "friend" someone on Facebook, MySpace, or some other Internet social networking site, you should actually know them first.**
  • "Friending" someone refers to adding them to your list of contacts on your home page.
  • You should know someone first before you ask to "friend them."
■ **Use the *two-message rule*:**
  • **Do not leave more than two messages in a row with no response.**
    ■ This can be annoying for the other person and may result in further rejection.

- Exception to the *two-message rule*: When you try to "friend" someone on Facebook, MySpace, or some other Internet social networking site, the person has the choice of "accepting" or "ignoring" the request.
- If someone ignores your first request, do not make another attempt.
  - *Move on* and find someone else to "friend" who knows you and seems interested in you.

■ *Do not get too personal*:
  - Avoid getting too personal over electronic communication (even if you know the person well).
  - Many people may have access to this form of communication (particularly on Internet social networking sites).
  - You may embarrass the other person by getting too personal.

Rules for Using the Internet

■ Explain that many teens use the Internet for social interactions:
  - Internet chat rooms
  - MySpace.com
  - Facebook.com
■ **Teens should *not* use the Internet to make *new* friends:**
  - **Teens should never give personal information to a stranger online.**
  - **Teens should never agree to meet with a stranger from the Internet.**
  - **Teens should not accept invitations to be "friends" with strangers on Facebook, MySpace, or other online social networking sites.**
  - **Parents should help teens set up privacy settings on *Facebook*, *MySpace*, and other social networking sites so that people who do not know the teen cannot access his or her account.**
■ **The Internet is best used to develop stronger friendships with *pre-existing* friends.**
  - **It can be used to *trade information* and plan *get-togethers*.**
■ **Parents should monitor their teen's social networking pages discreetly to ensure that their teen is being safe and responsible.**
  - **This will also give parents a glimpse at which friends are appropriate.**
■ **Teens should avoid *cyberbullying*.**
  - **Do not make fun of others.**
  - **If someone is *cyberbullying* your teen, it can be helpful to have a friend get involved to defend your teen.**
  - **If *cyberbullying* occurs and physical threats are made, your teen should notify an adult.**
    - **Parents may need to get the school involved.**
    - **Parents may need to contact the Webmaster.**

Homework Assignments

The parent group leader should go over the homework assignment and troubleshoot any potential problems with parents.

1. ***Sources of friends* (do not involve your teen at this point)**
   a. **Parents should identify and investigate at least one new extracurricular activity for their teen based on their teen's interests.**
   b. **Parents should identify:**
      i. **Which group they think their teen *attempts* to fit in with.**
      ii. **Which group they think their teen would *best* fit in with.**
2. **Parents practice having a phone call with their teen using *cover stories***
   a. **Go over the rules for making phone calls, including using *cover stories*.**
   b. ***Trade information* and *find a common interest*.**
3. ***In-Group Call***
   a. Before the Call:
      i. Before you leave the group, parents should arrange for their teen to call another member of the group to practice conversational skills.
      ii. Set up a day and time to make the call.
      iii. Negotiate where the parent will be during the call and what the parent role will be.
      iv. Parent and teen may need to practice beginning and ending the phone call.
   b. During the Call:
      i. **Teens should *trade information* on this phone call.**
      ii. ***Find a common interest* to report back to the group.**
      iii. **Follow the rules for beginning and ending a phone call, including using *cover stories*.**
   c. After the Call:
      i. Parents and teens should discuss the phone call and identify:
         1. ***Common interests***
         2. ***Cover stories***
         3. How the phone call began and ended
      ii. Parents should help the teen troubleshoot any problems that may have arisen.
4. ***Bring a personal item***
   a. **Bring a favorite item to share with the group (e.g., CD, magazine, game, book, pictures)**—group leader negotiates this with each teen and parent.
   b. **Be prepared to *trade information* about the item one-on-one with someone else in the group.**

Parent Handout 3: Conversational Skills III—Electronic Communication

Different Peer Groups or Crowds

Jocks	Brains/smart kids	Stoners/burners/druggies
Cheerleaders	Chess club kids	Rockers
Popular kids	Gamers/video game geeks	Hip-hop group
Student council kids	Nerds	Detention club/slackers
Drama club kids	Math geeks	Wannabe gangbangers/taggers
Choir/chorus	Computer geeks	Musicians (rock bands)
Pep squad	Band kids/band geeks	Skaters
Partiers	Science geeks	Surfers
Preppies	Math geeks	Hippies/granolas
Artists	Goths	ROTC
Comic book geeks/anime geeks	Emos	Ethnic/cultural/religious groups

Rules for Starting and Ending a Phone Call

- Starting the conversation:
  - Ask for the person you are calling by name.
  - Say who you are.
  - Ask if the person you are calling can talk.
  - Give a **cover story** for why you are calling.
- Ending the conversation:
  - Wait for a longer pause (i.e., transitional moment).
  - Give a **cover story** for why you have to hang up.
    - Parents can often help with providing **cover stories.**
  - Tell the person it was nice talking to him or her.
  - Tell the person you will talk to or see him or her later.
  - Say good-bye.

Cover Story Examples

Reasons You Are Calling	Reasons You Have to Hang Up
"Just calling to see how you're doing."	"I have to get going."
"Just calling to hear what's up with you."	"I better let you go."
"I'm calling to get the homework."	"I need to finish my homework."
"I haven't talked to you in a while."	"I have to eat dinner now."
"I was wondering what you're up to."	"My mom needs to use the phone."

Rules for Leaving a Voice-Mail Message

- Say your name.
- Say whom you are calling for.
- Say when you are calling.
- Give a **cover story** for calling.
- Leave your phone number.
- Say good-bye.

Rules for Phone Calls / Text Messages / Instant Messages / E-mail

- Use **cover stories** for text messaging, instant messaging (IM), and e-mail for people you do not know well.
  - You do not need **cover stories** for contacting friends you are close to.
  - If you are contacting someone for the first time, it is best to have a **cover story**.
- Avoid **cold calling**:
  - Do not call someone who has not given you his or her phone number, e-mail, or screen name.
  - Giving out a phone number, e-mail address, or screen name is giving someone permission to contact you.
  - Ask for the person's contact information before calling:
    - This will give you permission to contact them.
  - If you try to "friend" someone on Facebook, MySpace, or some other Internet social networking site, you should actually know them first.
- Use the **two-message rule**:
  - Do not leave more than two messages in a row with no response.
  - Exception to the **two-message rule**: When you try to "friend" someone on Facebook, MySpace, or some other Internet social networking site, the person has the choice of "accepting" or "ignoring" the request.
    - If someone ignores your first request, do not make another attempt.
- Do not get too personal.

Rules for Using the Internet

- Teens should *not* use the Internet to make *new* friends.
  - Teens should never give personal information to a stranger online.
  - Teens should never agree to meet with a stranger from the Internet.
  - Teens should not accept invitations to be "friends" with strangers on Facebook, MySpace, or other online social networking sites.
  - Parents should help teens set up privacy settings on Facebook, MySpace, and other social networking sites so that people who do not know them cannot access their account.
- The Internet is best used to develop stronger friendships with *preexisting* friends.
  - It can be used to ***trade information*** and plan ***get-togethers***.
- Parents should monitor their teen's social networking pages discreetly to ensure that their teen is being safe and responsible.
  - This will also give parents a glimpse at which friends are appropriate.
- Teens should avoid ***cyberbullying***:
  - Do not make fun of others.
  - If someone is ***cyberbullying*** your teen, it can be helpful to have a friend get involved to defend your teen.
  - If ***cyberbullying*** occurs and physical threats are made, your teen should notify an adult:
    - Parents may need to get the school involved.
    - Parents may need to contact the Webmaster.

Homework Assignments

1. ***Sources of friends*** (do not involve your teen at this point)
   a. Parents should identify and investigate at least one new extracurricular activity for their teen based on their teen's interests.
   b. Parents should identify:
      i. Which group they think their teen *attempts* to fit in with.
      ii. Which group they think their teen would *best* fit in with.
2. Parents practice having a phone call with their teen using ***cover stories***
   a. Go over the rules for making phone calls, including using ***cover stories***.
   b. ***Trade information*** and ***find a common interest***.
3. **In-Group Call**
   a. Teens should ***trade information*** on this phone call.
   b. ***Find a common interest*** to report back to the group.
   c. Follow the rules for beginning and ending a phone call, including using ***cover stories***.
4. **Bring a personal item**

   a. Bring a favorite item to share with the group (e.g., CD, magazine, game, book, pictures).

   b. Be prepared to ***trade information*** about the item one-on-one with someone else in the group.

Teen Therapist Guide—Session 3: Conversational Skills III—Electronic Communication

Guiding Principles of the Teen Session

It seems with every succeeding generation that teens learn to use more sophisticated electronic communication at younger ages. The purpose of this session is to help teens learn the appropriate uses of electronic forms of communication with peers. For some teens, the first portion of the didactic on using the telephone will already be included in their repertoire. The challenge will be to keep their interest until you move into more sophisticated forms of electronic communication. The role-play demonstration will be helpful in this respect. It can also be helpful to point out to the teens that although some of them may already know these skills, it is very easy to forget one or two of the steps. It is also helpful to have teens think of a time when someone forgot one of the steps and how it affected the conversation. For example, you might say: *I know it seems obvious that you should identify yourself when calling someone on the phone, but how many of you have had someone call you on the phone who didn't identify himself or herself and you had no idea who you were talking to? It seems obvious and yet people often forget!*

During the online safety portion of the didactic, it is common for one or two group members to challenge the point that the Internet should not be used for teens to make new friends. With the rising popularity of Web sites like MySpace and Facebook, teens often use the Internet to communicate with strangers, as well as friends. Even though the latter is perfectly appropriate, the former can be dangerous for teenagers. As described in previous sessions, the best way to handle this objection is to ask the group: *What is the problem with making new friends on the Internet?* The other teens will quickly offer that it can be dangerous and will often even launch into stories from the news about predators targeting children online. Once this point has sufficiently been made, remind teens that the Internet can actually be very helpful in strengthening current friendships and developing friendships with preexisting acquaintances.

At the time of writing this manual, cyberbullying was still a relatively new phenomenon but was already becoming widespread. Consequently, certain group members may have already experienced situations in which they have been bullied online. In these cases, this material may be emotionally charged. The group leader will want to avoid allowing teens to talk about specific ways in which they have been bullied online in order to minimize the negative effects of these disclosures. Instead, you will want to focus on ways to handle cyberbullying. You may redirect personal disclosures from teens by saying: *I'm sure we could go on and on sharing stories of how we or people we know have been cyberbullied. But instead, I want to focus on what we can do in these situations to make it less likely that we will be bullied again.* By focusing on the strategies for handling cyberbullying, you can minimize the negative effects of these types of personal disclosures. If the teen appears to be particularly affected by this topic, the group leader may want to speak with the teen and his or her parents at the end of the session to identify additional strategies (e.g., involving the parent, notifying the school, and so forth).

Rule Review

[Only go over session rules again if the teens are having difficulty following them.]

1. Listen to the other group members (no talking when others are speaking)
2. Follow directions
3. Raise your hand
4. Be respectful (no teasing or making fun of others)
5. No touching (no hitting, kicking, pushing, hugging, etc.)

Homework Review

Note: Give points for homework *parts*—not just one point per assignment.

1. Practice ***trading information*** with parents:
   a. Say: *One of your assignments this week was to practice trading information and having a two-way conversation with your parent. Raise your hand if you practiced trading information with one of your parents this week.*
      i. Begin by calling on teens who completed the assignment.
      ii. Ask:
         1. *Who did you practice having a two-way conversation with* (mom, dad, etc.)?
         2. *Did you trade information?*
         3. *Did you find a common interest?*
            a. When they identify common interests, ask: *What could you do with that information if you were ever to hang out with your parent?*
   b. If you have time, check in with teens who did not complete the assignment and troubleshoot how they might get it done this week.
2. ***In-Group Call***
   a. Say: *The other assignment you had this week was to practice having a two-way conversation on the phone with another group member. Raise your hand if you did the in-group call.*
      i. Begin by calling on the teens who completed the call.
      ii. Ask:
         1. *Who did you talk to?*
         2. *Who called who?*
         3. *Did you trade information?*

4. *Did you find a common interest?*
   a. When they identify common interests, ask: *What could you do with that information if you were ever to hang out?*
     iii. Avoid general questions like: *How did it go?*
   b. Have the other person who participated in the call give his or her account immediately after, but not at the same time.
     i. Do not allow teens to talk about mistakes the other person made.
   c. Troubleshoot any problems that may have arisen.
   d. If you have time, check in with teens who did not complete the assignment and troubleshoot how they might get it done this week.

Didactic Lesson: Electronic Communication

Explain: *Today we're going to be talking about electronic communication. That includes things like making phone calls, sending e-mail, text messaging, instant messaging, and using the Internet. Electronic communication is a very popular method of communicating for teens, so we need to know what the rules are for using electronics to talk with friends.*

Rules for Starting and Ending a Phone Call

Say: *One of the most popular ways for teens to communicate is on the phone. But it can often be difficult to know how to begin and end these conversations. There are very specific steps for starting and ending phone calls.*

1. Starting the phone call:
   a. The teen group leader and coach should do an *inappropriate* role play of an incorrect beginning to a phone call.
     i. Begin by saying: *Watch this and tell me what I'm doing **wrong**.*
     ii. Example of an *inappropriate* role play:

Teen group leader: (pretend to hold a phone to your ear) "Ring, ring."

Coach: (pretend to pick up the phone) "Hello?"

Teen group leader: "Hey. What are you doing?"

Coach: (sounds confused) "Umm, watching TV."

Teen group leader: "Oh, what are you watching?"

Coach: (sounds confused) "Some reality show."

Teen group leader: "Oh, I like reality shows."

Coach: (sounds annoyed) "Great."

Teen group leader: "So what are you doing this weekend?"

Coach: (sounds annoyed) "Umm….I gotta go."

  iii. End by saying: *Okay, time-out on that. So what did I do **wrong** in that phone call?*

1. Answer: The group leader did not give his or her name, ask for the person he or she was calling for, ask if the person could talk, or give a cover story for calling.

b. Present the rules for starting a phone call.

 i. Ask for the person you are calling by name.

 1. Example: "Hi. May I please speak to Jennifer?"

 ii. Say who you are.

 1. Example: "Hi Jennifer. This is Blair."

 iii. Ask the person if he or she can talk.

 1. Example: "Can you talk right now?"

 iv. Give a **cover story** for why you are calling.

 1. Examples:

 a. "I was just calling to see how you're doing."

 b. "I was calling to see if I could get the homework assignment from you."

 2. Have the teens come up with different examples of **cover stories** (see "Cover Story Example" table).

c. The teen group leader and coach should do an **appropriate** role play of a correct beginning to a phone call.

 i. Begin by saying: *So now that we know the rules for starting a phone call, watch this and tell me what I'm doing **right***.

 ii. Example of an **appropriate** role play:

Teen group leader: (pretend to hold a phone to your ear) "Ring, ring."

Coach: (pretend to pick up the phone) "Hello?"

Teen group leader: "Hi. Can I speak to Jennifer?"

Coach: "This is Jennifer."

Teen group leader: "Hi Jennifer. This is Blair."

Coach: "Oh, hi Blair."

Teen group leader: "Hey, can you talk right now?"

Coach: "Sure."

Teen group leader: "So I was just calling to see how you've been doing."

Coach: "Oh, I'm good. How are you?"

Teen group leader: "I'm fine. How's school going?"

Coach: "It's good. We have a school dance this weekend."

Teen group leader: "Oh that sounds fun. Are you going?"

Coach: "I was thinking about it."

 iii. End by saying: *Okay, time-out on that. So what did I do **right** in that phone call?*

 1. Answer: The group leader gave his or her name, asked for the person he or she was calling for, asked if the person could talk, and gave a cover story for calling.

2. Ending the phone call:

a. The teen group leader and coach should do an **inappropriate** role play of an incorrect ending to a phone call.

    i. Begin by saying: *Now that we know how to start a phone call, let's talk about how to end a phone call. Watch this and tell me what I'm doing* **wrong**.

    ii. Example of an ***inappropriate*** role play:

Teen group leader: (pick up where you left off) "So who's going to the dance?"

Coach: "I'm not sure. I haven't decided if I'm going to go. I don't really like to dance, but I like music."

Teen group leader: "Oh yeah, me too. What kind of music do you like?"

Coach: "I kind of like everything. What about you?"

Teen group leader: "Yeah, me too. Okay, bye."

    iii. End by saying: *Okay, time-out on that. So what did I do* **wrong** *in that phone call?*

        1. Answer: The group leader did not wait for a pause, give a reason for getting off the phone, say it was nice talking to the person, say he or she would talk to that person later, or say good-bye.

  b. Present the rules for ending a phone call.

    i. Wait for a bit of a pause (i.e., transitional moment).

    ii. Give a ***cover story*** for why you have to hang up.

        1. "I have to go now. I have to eat dinner."

        2. "I have to go finish my homework."

        3. Have the group come up with different examples of ***cover stories*** (see "Cover Story Examples" table).

    iii. Tell the person it was nice talking to him or her.

    iv. Tell the person you will talk to or see him or her later.

    v. Say good-bye.

Cover Story Examples

Reasons You Are Calling	*Reasons You Have to Hang Up*
"Just calling to see how you're doing."	"I have to get going."
"Just calling to hear what's up with you."	"I better let you go."
"I'm calling to get the homework."	"I need to finish my homework."
"I haven't talked to you in a while."	"I have to eat dinner now."
"I was wondering what you're up to."	"My mom needs to use the phone."

  c. The teen group leader and coach should do an ***appropriate*** role play of a correct ending to a phone call.

    i. Begin by saying: *Now that we know the rules for ending a phone call, watch this and tell me what I'm doing* **right**.

    ii. Example of an ***appropriate*** role play:

Teen group leader: (pick-up where you left off) "So who's going to the dance?"

Coach: "I'm not sure. I haven't decided if I'm going to go. I don't really like to dance, but I like music."

Teen group leader: "Oh yeah, me too. What kind of music do you like?"

Coach: "I kind of like everything. What about you?"

Teen group leader: "Yeah, me too." (pause) "Well my mom needs to use the phone, so I should probably get going."

Coach: "Okay."

Teen group leader: "But it was good talking to you."

Coach: "You too. Thanks for calling."

Teen group leader: "I'll talk to you later."

Coach: "Sounds good."

Teen group leader: "Take care."

Coach: "You, too."

Teen group leader: "Bye!"

Coach: "Bye!"

      iii. End by saying: *Okay, time-out on that. So what did I do **right** in that phone call?*

         1. Answer: The group leader waited for a pause, gave a cover story for getting off the phone, said it was nice talking to the person, said he or she would talk to the person later, and said good-bye.

   3. Leaving a message:

     a. The teen group leader and coach should do an *inappropriate* role play of an incorrect voice-mail message.

       i. Begin by saying: *So now we know how to start and end phone calls, but sometimes when we call our friends they don't pick up and we have to leave voice mail. Watch this and tell me what I'm doing **wrong**.*

       ii. Example of an *inappropriate* role play:

Teen group leader: (pretend to hold a phone to your ear) "Ring, ring."

Coach: (voice-mail message) "Hi, this is Jennifer. I can't get to the phone right now. Please leave a message. Beep."

Teen group leader: "Umm, it's me. Why aren't you home? I'm just sitting around doing nothing. Call me later."

       iii. End by saying: *Okay, time-out on that. So what did I do **wrong** on that voice mail?*

         1. Answer: The group leader did not say who he or she was calling for, say who he or she was, when he or she was calling, give a reason for calling, leave a phone number, or say good-bye.

     b. Present the rules for leaving a voice-mail message:

       i. Say your name.

         1. "Hi this is Blair."

       ii. Say who you are calling for:

         1. "I'm calling for Jennifer."

       iii. Say when you are calling:

         1. "It's about 6 o'clock on Thursday night."

       iv. Give a ***cover story*** for calling:

         1. "I was just calling to see what you've been up to."

      v. Leave your phone number:
         1. "Give me a call at xxx-xxxx."
     vi. Say good-bye:
        1. "Talk to you soon. Bye."
  c. The teen group leader and coach should do an *appropriate* role play of a correct voice-mail message.
    i. Begin by saying: *So now that we know the steps for leaving a voice mail, watch this and tell me what I'm doing **right**.*
    ii. Example of an *appropriate* role play:

Teen group leader: (pretend to hold a phone to your ear) "Ring, ring."

Coach: (voice-mail message) "Hi, this is Jennifer. I can't get to the phone right now. Please leave a message. Beep."

Teen group leader: "Hi this is Blair. I'm calling for Jennifer. It's about 6 o'clock on Thursday evening. I was just calling to see what you've been up to. Give me a call at xxx-xxxx. Talk to you soon. Bye."

    iii. End by saying: *Okay, time-out on that. So what did I do **right** on that voice mail?*
       1. Answer: The group leader said who he or she was calling for, said who he or she was, what time he or she was calling, gave a reason for calling, left a phone number, and said good-bye.

Rules for Phone Calls / Text Messages / Instant Messages / E-mail

Explain: *Now that we have some rules around making phone calls, it's also important for us to understand the rules for things like text messaging, instant messaging, and e-mail. Some of the rules are similar, so they should be easy to remember.*

  1. Use ***cover stories*** for text messaging, instant messaging, and e-mail for people you do not know well.
    a. Say: *First, just like with phone calls, we need to use cover stories when we're text messaging, instant messaging, or e-mailing for people we don't know well. Why would it be important to use cover stories with people we don't know well?*
      i. Answer: Because otherwise they will wonder why you are calling them.
    b. Ask: *Do we always need to use cover stories for text messaging, instant messaging, and e-mailing our close friends?*
      i. Answer: No, but it does not hurt to use cover stories even with close friends.
    c. Have teens generate some examples.
      i. Examples:
        1. "Thought I'd check out your Facebook page."
        2. "Wondering what you've been up to."

3. "Just calling to see what you're doing this weekend."
4. "Wanted to know if you're going to the game."

2. Avoid ***cold calling***:
   a. Say: *Another rule for text messaging, instant messaging, and e-mailing people you don't know well is to avoid cold calling. Does anyone know what cold calling is?*
      i. Answer: Cold calling is contacting someone who has not given you his or her phone number, e-mail, or screen name.
         1. Giving out a phone number, e-mail address, or screen name is giving someone permission to contact you.
   b. Just because you may have access to someone's contact information in a school directory or online directory does not give you permission to contact that person.
      i. This includes inviting someone to be your friend on Facebook, MySpace, or other Internet social networking sites.
         1. You need to know the person if you try to friend them, and it is best to get that person's permission first.
         2. Ask: "What might someone think of you if you cold called them, with no permission to call?"
            a. Answer: They might think you are strange, weird, a "stalker."
         3. Ask: "Do you think they'll want to be friends with you?"
            a. Answer: Probably not.
         4. Say: *Instead, you need to ask for the person's contact information before calling. This will give you permission to contact them. That means if you want to get someone's phone number you could say: "We should hang out some time. Why don't I get your number." Or if you want to friend someone on Facebook you could say: "Are you on Facebook? Maybe I'll look you up." Then you need to pay attention to their response to see if they're interested.*

3. Use the ***two-message rule***:
   a. Explain: *Just like with phone calls, sometimes we might text message, IM, or e-mail someone and we don't get a hold of them. About how many times in a row should we leave a voice-mail message for someone without him or her responding before we stop calling?*
      i. Answer: About two times.
   b. Ask the question: *What is wrong with leaving more messages than that?*
      i. Answer: The other person may be busy; may not want to talk to you;
   c. Ask the question: *About how many times in a row should we text or instant message someone without them responding before we give up?*
      i. Answer: About two times.
   d. Ask the question: *What is wrong with messaging more than that?*
      i. Answer: The other person may be busy; may not want to talk to you; may get annoyed with your messages.

e. Ask the question: *About how many times in a row should we e-mail some-one without him or her responding before we stop trying?*
   i. Answer: About two times.

f. Ask the question: *What is wrong with leaving more e-mail than that?*
   i. Answer: The person is going to likely get annoyed; think you are weird; probably will not want to be your friend; and you may even get a bad reputation as a "stalker."

g. Explain: *There's one exception to the two-message rule. That's if we're try-ing to "friend" someone on Facebook or MySpace or some other Internet site. When we try to "friend" someone, they have the option to "accept" or "ignore" our request. If someone ignores your request, what should you do?*
   i. Answer: **Move on** and find someone else to "friend" who knows you and seems interested in you; do not try with the same person twice.

4. ***Do not get too personal***:

a. Say: *Another important rule for electronic communication is to avoid getting too personal. This is true even if you know the person well. Why would it be a bad idea to get too personal over e-mail, text messaging, instant messaging, Facebook, or MySpace?*
   i. Answer: Many people may have access to this form of communication (particularly on Internet social networking sites); you may embarrass the other person by getting too personal; you should avoid discussing things that you don't want others to know.

Rules for Using the Internet

Explain: *We all know that the Internet has become a very popular way for teens to socialize, and many of you are probably online and even use social network-ing sites like MySpace or Facebook. But just like with any kind of communication, there are rules about how to be safe when you are online.*

1. Teens should ***not*** use the Internet to make ***new*** friends.
   a. Ask: *Why is it a bad idea for teens to make new friends on the Internet?*
      i. Answer: Because it is dangerous; the person could be a predator.
   b. Explain the following:
      i. Never give your personal information to a stranger online.
      ii. Never agree to meet with a stranger from the Internet.
      iii. Do not accept invitations to be "friends" with strangers on Facebook or MySpace.
      iv. Use privacy settings on Facebook and MySpace so that people who do not know you cannot access your account.

2. The Internet is best used to develop stronger friendships with ***preexisting*** friends:

   a. Ask: *Is it okay to use the Internet to develop stronger friendships with people we already know?*

      i. Answer: Yes.

   b. Ask: *Is it okay to use the Internet to reconnect with friends we haven't talked to in awhile?*

      i. Answer: Yes.

   c. Explain: *The Internet is very useful for trading information with preexisting friends and for planning get-togethers, but we shouldn't use it to make new friends.*

3. Avoid **cyberbullying**:

   a. Ask: *Who has heard of cyberbullying and who can explain to the group what cyberbullying means?*

      i. Answer: Teasing, bullying, or threatening someone on the Internet.

   b. Ask: *What is the problem with cyberbullying?*

      i. Answer: It is mean; it hurts people's feelings; it gives you a bad reputation; people do not want to be friends with you.

   c. Explain: *It is never acceptable to tease or make fun of others online, or otherwise. If someone is cyberbullying you, it can be helpful to have friends get involved to defend you. Why is this helpful?*

      i. Answer: People who bully often pick on kids who are defenseless; having your friends "have your back" will protect you against cyberbullying.

   d. Say: *If someone is cyberbullying you and physical threats are made, you should notify an adult. Your parents may need to get the school involved or contact the Webmaster.*

Behavioral Rehearsal

- Have the teens practice having a **two-way conversation** on the phone.
- Be sure teens follow the rules for starting and ending a phone conversation.
- Give teens 2 to 3 minutes to practice.
- Assign a "caller" and a "receiver":
  - Have the caller start the call.
  - Have the receiver end the call (with a prompt from the group leader).
- Debrief at the end of the exercise:
  - Have the caller identify how he or she started the conversation.
    - Identify **cover stories** for making the call.
  - Ask them if they **traded information**.
  - Have teens identify any **common interests**.
  - Find out how the receiver ended the conversation.
    - Identify **cover stories** for ending the call.

Homework Assignments

- Briefly explain the homework for the week by saying: *We are going to continue to have you practice having two-way conversations and beginning and ending phone calls this week. Your homework assignment this week is to:*
  - *Practice beginning and ending a phone call and having a two-way conversation with your parent and find a common interest.*
  - *Have an in-group phone call with another group member.*
    - *This should be at least 5 to 10 minutes.*
    - *Use the steps for beginning and ending phone calls.*
    - *You will need to trade information and find a common interest to report to the group.*
  - *You will need to bring some personal item to trade information about next week (e.g., CD, magazine, game, book, pictures).*
- The group leader and coaches should assign the in-group phone calls for the week and write this on the "In-Group Phone Call Assignment Log" for future reference.
  - If there are an uneven number of teens, assign someone "double duty."
    - This person will have two in-group phone calls (one as a caller and the other as a receiver).
    - This person will receive extra points for completing the extra call.

Teen Activity: Jeopardy

Note: See the "Teen Activity Guide" for rules.

- Teens need to complete the ***Jeopardy*** answer sheets before beginning the activity (if they haven't already).
  - To save time, it is very helpful to have teens complete these forms while they are waiting in the lobby before the start of the group.
- Teens need to ***trade information*** before *Jeopardy* and practice asking questions:
  - Write topics on the board and then break the teens into dyads or triads.
  - After the teens have ***traded information*** with most of the group members for 2 to 3 minutes each, have them reconvene as a group and play the game of *Jeopardy*.
- Teens compete against themselves to earn points for correct responses to questions from ***trading information*** exercise.
  - The teen who raises his or her hand first gets to take the first guess.
  - If the teen is wrong, someone else has a chance to answer (the person who raised his or her hand second).
  - The teens get only one guess per question.
  - Do not give teens clues.
- Encourage the teens to clap for each other during the game.

■ Keep track of the points on the board using a different colored marker.
■ At the end of the game, the person with the most points is the ***Jeopardy Challenge Winner***.

Reunification

■ Announce that teens should join their parents:
  – Be sure that the teens are standing or sitting next to their parents.
  – Be sure to have silence and the full attention of the group.
■ Say: *One of the things we worked on today was having a phone conversation. Who can tell us how we begin and end a phone conversation?* [Have teens generate all of the steps. Be prepared to give prompts if necessary.]
  – Ask for the person you are calling by name.
  – Say who you are.
  – Ask the person you are calling if he or she can talk.
  – Give a ***cover story*** for why you are calling.
    • Have teens give examples of good cover stories for making a call.
■ Ask: *What are the steps for ending a phone call?*
  – Wait for a brief pause (i.e., transitional moment).
  – Give a ***cover story*** for why you have to hang up.
    • Have teens give examples of good cover stories for ending a call.
  – Tell the person it was nice talking to him or her.
  – Tell the person you will talk to or see him or her later.
  – Say good-bye.
■ Ask: *What are the steps for leaving a voice mail?*
  – Say your name.
  – Say who you are calling for.
  – Say when you are calling.
  – Give a ***cover story*** for calling.
  – Leave your phone number.
  – Say good-bye.
■ Ask: *What are the rules for phone calls, e-mailing, text messaging, instant messaging, and online social networking sites?*
  – ***Use the two-message rule.***
  – ***Avoid cold calling.***
  – ***Use cover stories.***
  – ***Do not get too personal.***
■ Explain when using the Internet:
  – Do not try to make *new* friends.
  – Work on developing closer friendships with *preexisting* friends.
  – Avoid ***cyberbullying.***
    • If someone threatens you online, get help from an adult.
■ Say: *This group did a great job of practicing phone calls and having two-way conversations today. Let's give them a round of applause.*

■ Go over the homework for the next week (see below):
  - Be sure to read off the in-group phone call assignment in front of parents.
  - Remind parents to make a note of who is calling whom.
■ Individually and separately negotiate with each family:
  - Where the parent will be during the phone call.
  - What personal item will be brought next week.

Homework Assignments

1. ***Sources of friends*** [Do not announce this assignment during reunification.] (Parents do not involve their teen at this point.)
   a. Parents should identify and investigate at least one new extracurricular activity for their teen based on their teen's interests.
   b. Parents should identify:
      i. Which group they think their teen ***attempts*** to fit in with.
      ii. Which group they think their teen would ***best*** fit in with.
2. Parents and teens practice having a phone call using ***cover stories***:
   a. Go over the rules for making phone calls, including using ***cover stories***.
   b. ***Trade information*** and ***find a common interest***.
3. ***In-Group Call***
   a. Before the Call:
      i. Before you leave the group, parents should arrange for their teen to call another member of the group to practice conversational skills.
      ii. Set up a day and time to make the call.
      iii. Negotiate where the parent will be during the call and what the parent role will be.
   b. During the Call:
      i. Teens should ***trade information*** on this phone call.
      ii. ***Find a common interest*** to report back to the group.
      iii. Follow the rules for beginning and ending a phone call, including using ***cover stories***.
   c. After the Call:
      i. Parents and teens should discuss the phone call and identify:
         1. ***Common interests***
         2. ***Cover stories***
         3. How the phone call began and ended
      ii. Parents should help teens troubleshoot any problems that may have arisen.
4. ***Bring a Personal Item***
   a. Bring a favorite item to share with the group (e.g., CD, magazine, game, book, pictures)—group leader negotiates this with each teen and parent.
   b. Be prepared to ***trade information*** about the item one-on-one with someone else in the group.

Calculate Points

Keep track of the following for each week of the intervention:

- Calculate the number of points earned by each teen.
- Add up the total number of points earned by the group.
- Do not calculate the points in the presence of the teens.
  - Do not disclose the individual or group total of points.
  - Discourage attempts to compare number of points earned between teens.
- Remind them that they are working as a team to earn a bigger and better graduation party.

Teen Activity Guide: Session 3

"Jeopardy"

Materials Needed

- Blackboard and chalk/whiteboard and markers
- Answer sheets
- Scissors
- Pens

Rules

- Teens will compete against themselves in this game of ***trading information***.
- Like the television show, *Jeopardy,* teens will be given answers by the group leader and asked to respond in the form of a question.
  - Example:
    - *Teen group leader*: "The answer is Jimmy's favorite sport."
    - *Teen*: "What is baseball?"
- To promote interest and cooperation, the teen group leader will give out points for correct responses.
- Pass out answer sheets before the ***trading information*** exercise (if you haven't already).
- Have teens fill in responses and return to the teen group leader.
  - To save time, it is very helpful to have teens complete these forms while they are waiting in the lobby before the start of the group.
- Have teens practice ***trading information*** in dyads/triads for 1 to 2 minutes each (depending on time) until each teen has ***traded information*** with all group members.
- Group leader will suggest topics for ***trading information*** and write these on the board:

- Name
- City where they live
- Name of school
- Favorite game
- Favorite sport
- Favorite television show
- Favorite movie
- Favorite weekend activity
- Eye color (Note: This is **not** to be asked, but noticed by using good eye contact when **trading information**.)

■ Write categories on the board to help teens:
  - "School" Spirit
    • Answer sheet: Name of school
  - TGIF
    • Answer sheet: Favorite weekend activity
  - "Sports" and Leisure
    • Answer sheet: Favorite sport
  - "Game" Time
    • Answer sheet: Favorite game
  - Movies, Movies, Movies
    • Answer sheet: Favorite movie
  - "TV" Time
    • Answer sheet: Favorite television show
  - "Home" Sweet "Home"
    • Answer sheet: City where they live
  - The "Eyes" Have It
    • Answer sheet: Eye color

■ While teens are **trading information**, one of the coaches will:
  - Cut the answer sheets into individual questions (cut along the lines provided).
  - Separate the answer sheets according to category and mix the order of the answer sheets.

■ The teen group leader and coaches should prompt teens to ask relevant questions to the *Jeopardy* topics when necessary.

■ Once the teens have finished **trading information**, reconvene as a group and begin the **Jeopardy Challenge**.
  - Begin by having the teen with the most points pick the category.
  - Notify the group that if anyone raises his or her hand before the question has been asked, he or she is disqualified from answering.
  - The person who raises his or her hand first gets to take the first guess.
  - If he or she provides the wrong answer, the person who raised his or her hand second has a chance to answer (and so on).
  - The teens get only one guess per question.
  - Do not give teens clues.

- When reading the items, you may need to point to the person to whom the item relates (while saying their name), because the teens are just becoming acquainted with each other.
- You may need to enforce a time limit if teens take a long time to answer.
- Do not correct the teens if they answer the questions in the incorrect format (i.e., instead of saying "What is baseball?" they say "Baseball").
  - All that matters is that they remembered the information they obtained through *trading information*.
- The person who answers the question correctly gets a point and chooses the next category.
- If no one answers correctly, the person about which the last question relates gets to pick the category.
- Encourage the teens to clap for each other during the game.
- Give points for correct responses.
- Keep track of the points on the board using a different colored marker.
- At the end of the game, the person with the most points is the *Jeopardy Challenge Winner*.

"Jeopardy" Answer Sheets

"School" Spirit The answer is: The name of _____ 's school. (Name) The question is: What is _____ ? (Name of your school)	**TGIF** The answer is: _____ 's favorite weekend activity. (Name) The question is: What is _____ ? (Favorite weekend activity)
Sports & Leisure The answer is: _____ 's favorite sport. (Name) The question is: What is _____ ? (Favorite sport)	**"Game" Time** The answer is: _____ 's favorite game. (Name) The question is: What is _____ ? (Favorite game)
Movies, Movies, Movies The answer is: _____ 's favorite movie. (Name) The question is: What is _____ ? (Favorite movie)	**"TV" Time** The answer is: _____ 's favorite TV show. (Name) The question is: What is _____ ? (Favorite TV show)
"Home" Sweet "Home" The answer is: The name of the city _____ lives in. (Name) The question is: What is _____ ? (Name of the city you live in)	**The "Eyes" Have It** The answer is: The color of _____ 's eyes. (Name) The question is: What is _____ ? (Your eye color)

Chapter 6

Session 4
Choosing Appropriate Friends

Parent Session Therapist Guide

Guiding Principles of the Parent Session

The main homework focus should continue to be on identifying extracurricular activities. This may not be an issue for some teens who already have activities from which they can draw new friends. Expect some parent resistance on this assignment for the teens who do not belong to such activities. Some parents may present activities that fall far short, hoping not to be challenged. Parents may also present activities the teen has been attending without benefit of generating closer friendships. For instance, a teen may love to attend a youth group, but would not consider asking any of the members for their phone number. Just because a teen loves the youth group does not mean it fits the parameters of the homework assignment. Now is a good time to find *new* activities because the teen will be more motivated, in order to complete the homework assignment for PEERS. The group leader may need to help the parent by judging when an extracurricular activity is not productive by sharing this with the parent and getting them motivated to find better alternatives. At the end of the discussion of the extracurricular activities, summarize all of the good ideas. Ask each parent to state what he or she will do to follow-up in the coming week.

Part of the focus of this session is finally involving the teen in the process of joining a new extracurricular activity. Many teens may be reluctant to do so. If this has been approached adequately by the parent, then it will go more smoothly. If the teen has a functional extracurricular activity already and parents say they have good friend options, they do not need to look for new activities.

The out-of-group phone call is assigned for the first time in this session, so this will also be a new experience for the now trained teen to try the new skills being taught. There may be some anxiety or resistance by the teen to identify a person to call outside of the group. The parents may be helpful in identifying appropriate options for this phone call, and the teen group leader can be helpful in negotiating getting the call done. Parents and teens should not leave the session until they have identified at least one person the teen will attempt to call.

Homework Review

1. Parents practice having a phone call with their teen using ***cover stories***:
   a. Ask if parents went over the rules for making phone calls, including using ***cover stories***.
   b. Ask if parents practiced ***trading information*** with their teen.
   c. Have parents identify a ***common interest*** discovered through ***trading information***.
   d. Troubleshoot any problems that may have arisen.
2. ***In-Group Call***
   a. Make sure the teen ***traded information*** on this phone call.
   b. Have parents identify:
      i. A ***common interest*** discovered through ***trading information*** on the phone call.
      ii. The ***cover stories*** their teen used on the phone call.
      iii. How their teen began and ended the phone call.
3. ***Sources of Friends***
   a. Have parents identify at least one new extracurricular activity that they investigated for their teen based on their teen's interests.
   b. Have parents identify:
      i. Which group they think their teen ***attempts*** to fit in with.
      ii. Which group they think their teen would ***best*** fit in with.
4. ***Bring a Personal Item***
   a. Identify the favorite item the teen brought to share with the group (e.g., CD, magazine, game, book, pictures).
   b. Only give credit for appropriate items.

Didactic Lesson: Sources of Friends

- Distribute the Parent Handout.
- Say: *Today we are continuing our discussion about choosing appropriate friends. Remember that teens sometimes need help with choosing appropriate friends. You will want to help your teen make good choices. Last week we talked about your teen's reputation and where he or she might appropriately fit in at school. This week we're going to talk about the importance of having a*

crowd or a clique and how you can help your teen develop friendships within the appropriate peer group.

Importance of Having a Crowd or Clique

- Having a crowd or clique protects teens from individual teasing.
  - Bullies are less likely to individually pick on teens who are in groups.
  - Teens appear stronger and more protected when they are affiliated with a group.
- When a teen who belongs to a group experiences teasing:
  - They feel a sense of support from other group members.
  - They bond with the other group members.
  - They experience in-group solidarity.
- Between-group rivalry is common and normal.
  - Teens bond over between-group rivalry.
    - Example: The jocks may dislike the geeks and the geeks may dislike the jocks.
      - Each group may complain about the other.
      - Group members bond over the experience.
- Discuss how teens can identify if they are *accepted* by a group.
  - The other teens in the group:
    - Give you their phone numbers, e-mail addresses, screen names.
    - Call, e-mail, or text you just to talk.
    - Invite you to do things.
    - Accept your invitations to do things.
    - Add you to their Facebook or MySpace pages.
    - Seek you out to do things.
- Discuss how teens can identify if they are ***not accepted*** by a group.
  - The other teens in the group:
    - Laugh or make fun of you.
    - Do not give you their phone numbers, e-mail addresses, screen names.
    - Do not call you.
    - Do not take your phone calls.
    - Do not accept your invitations to do things.
    - Put off your invitations to do things (e.g., they say things like, "Yeah, let's do that sometime" but never follow through).
    - Do not accept your invitation to "friend you" on Facebook or MySpace.
    - Do not invite you to do things.
- Go around the room and have parents identify whether their teen seems to be accepted or rejected by the group he or she is attempting to fit in with.
  - Have the parents give examples of how they can tell the teen is accepted or rejected.

- If the teen appears to be rejected, have the parent identify a different group the teen might be accepted by.
■ Explain: *As parents, one of the ways you can help your teen is by finding sources for friendships. The best sources of friends come from extracurricular activities, clubs, or sports because presumably the group members all share some collective common interest. Once you've helped your teen find sources for friends, you will need to help your teen decide which friends are appropriate.*
■ Go around the room and have parents take turns reading the Parent Handout.
■ Sections in **bold print** come directly from the Parent Handout.

Sources for Friendships

■ **Encourage your teen to make friends with other teens at school:**
  - **Before or after school**
  - **Between classes**
  - **During lunch**
■ **Help your teen develop hobbies or pursue special interests at school which could potentially include others (*get a list of clubs from the school by calling the school or going to the school's Web site*):**
  - **Chess club**
  - **Computer club**
  - **Science club**
  - **Video game club**
  - **Anime club**
■ **Encourage your teen to participate in extracurricular activities at school:**
  - **Sports teams**
  - **Yearbook**
  - **School play (e.g., stage crew, set design, acting, etc.)**
  - **Band/orchestra**
  - **Community service projects**
  - **After-school programs**
■ **Encourage your teen to pursue recreational activities and leisure activities in the community, particularly if your teen has a bad reputation at school:**
  - **Boy scouts**
  - **Girl Scouts**
  - **YMCA/YWCA**
  - **4-H**
  - **Community youth sports leagues**
  - **Sports classes (swimming, tennis, golf, etc.)**
  - **Teen activities through parks and recreation centers**
  - **Drama clubs**
  - **Dance classes**

- **Art classes**
- **Music classes**
- **Computer classes**
- **Martial arts classes**
- **Community clubs**
- **Hobby stores (e.g., Warhammer for making models)**
- **Church/temple/mosque**:
  - **Youth groups**
  - **Choir**
  - **Bible study, Hebrew school, etc.**
- **Teen book clubs (public library, Borders, Barnes & Noble)**

■ **Take your teen to places where he or she can be around other teens (be sure to check out these places in advance to make sure there is no gang activity)**:
  - **Recreational centers**
  - **Local parks (for basketball, etc.)**
  - **Community pool**
  - **Private gym**
  - **Sports club/golf club**
  - **Public library (during teen activities)**

■ Explain that it is important that teens be involved in activities that regularly expose them to other teens.
  - We suggest that teens be enrolled in *one or two extracurricular activities* at a time.
  - When one activity ends, another should begin.

■ Remind parents that this week they are going to begin to *discuss* and *decide* on extracurricular activities with their teen based on their teen's interests.
  - Parents should also *begin to enroll* teens in these activities.
  - Some parents will need to make this mandatory for their teens, others will just need to strongly suggest.
  - When presenting new activities, ask your teen, "Which one do you want to join?" rather than "Do you want to join?"
    - Provide different choices.
    - Participating in activities should not be negotiable.

■ Choosing which activities to join is negotiable.

Homework Assignments

■ Explain: *Today your teens have been talking about the different crowds or groups in school, just like you all did last week. Your teens will think about the groups they try to fit in with at school and which groups they actually fit in best with at school. One of your jobs this week is to continue this discussion with your teen and help him or her choose an appropriate group to try to make friends. Your teen's job this week is to choose someone from this identified group and practice trading information. You will also be discussing possible extracurricular activities with your teen this week and deciding on which activities to enroll your teen in.*

■ The parent group leader should go over the homework assignment and troubleshoot any potential problems with parents.

1. ***Sources of Friends***
   a. **Teens should find a new group that they do not normally hang out with and *trade information* with someone in that group.**
      i. **Try to find a *common interest*.**
      ii. **Parents should assist teens in thinking of appropriate groups.**
   b. **Parents should *discuss* and *decide* on extracurricular activities with their teen based on their teen's interests and *begin to enroll* in these activities.**
      i. **Criteria for a good extracurricular activity:**
         1. **Meets weekly or bimonthly.**
         2. **Age range of other teens includes the social age of your teen.**
         3. **Activity includes informal time so that your teen can informally interact with other participants.**
         4. **Activity starts within the next couple of weeks.**
         5. **You are able to help facilitate your teen's involvement.**
2. ***In-Group Call***
   a. **Before the Call:**
      i. **Before you leave the group, parents should arrange for their teen to call another member of the group to practice conversational skills.**
      ii. **Set up a day and time to make the call.**
      iii. **Negotiate where the parent will be during the call and what the parent role will be.**
      iv. **Parent and teen may need to practice beginning and ending the phone call.**
   b. **During the Call:**
      i. **Teens should *trade information* on this phone call.**
      ii. ***Find a common interest* to report back to the group.**
      iii. **Follow the rules for beginning and ending a phone call, including using *cover stories*.**
   c. **After the Call:**
      i. **Parents and teens should discuss the phone call and identify:**
         1. ***Common interests***
         2. ***Cover stories***
         3. **How the phone call began and ended**
      ii. **Parents should help their teen troubleshoot any problems that may have arisen.**

3. ***Out-of-Group Call***
   a. **Before the Call**:
      i. **Parents arrange with their teen to call someone outside of the group to practice conversational skills.**
      ii. **Choose someone that the teen *feels comfortable* talking with.**
      iii. **Negotiate where the parent will be during the call.**
   b. **During the Call**:
      i. **Teens should *trade information* on this phone call.**
      ii. **Find a *common interest* to report back to the group.**
      iii. **Follow the rules for a *two-way conversation*.**
      iv. **Use the rules for starting and ending a conversation, including using *cover stories*.**
   c. **After the Call**:
      i. **Parents and teens should discuss the call and identify *common interests*.**
      ii. **Parents should help the teen troubleshoot any problems that may have arisen.**
4. ***Bring a Personal Item***
   a. **Bring a favorite item to share with the group (e.g., CD, magazine, game, book, pictures).**
   b. **Be prepared to *trade information* about the item one-on-one with someone else in the group.**

■ Go around the room and have each parent identify someone his or her teen could call *outside of the group* this week to practice ***trading information***.
   – Choose someone that the teen will feel comfortable talking with.
   – To begin, the teen can choose someone who is a best friend or a cousin of the same age.
   – The most important thing is that the teen make the call.
   – Eventually we will want to expand the teen's peer network, so the teen may want to start getting phone numbers from potential new friends.
■ Go around the room and have parents identify the personal item that their teen could bring to share with another group member.

Parent Handout 4: Choosing Appropriate Friends

Sources for Friendships

- Encourage your teen to make friends with other teens at school:
  - Before or after school
  - Between classes
  - During lunch
- Help your teen develop hobbies or pursue special interests at school which could potentially include others (*get a list of clubs from the school by calling the school or going to the school's Web site*):
  - Chess club
  - Computer club
  - Science club
  - Video game club
  - Anime club
- Encourage your teen to participate in extracurricular activities at school:
  - Sports teams
  - Yearbook
  - School play (e.g., stage crew, set design, acting, etc.)
  - Band/orchestra
  - Community service projects
  - After-school programs
- Encourage your teen to pursue recreational activities and leisure activities in the community, particularly if your teen has a bad reputation at school:
  - Boy Scouts
  - Girl Scouts
  - YMCA/YWCA
  - 4-H
  - Community youth sports leagues
  - Sports classes (swimming, tennis, golf, etc.)
  - Teen activities through parks and recreation centers
  - Drama clubs
  - Dance classes
  - Art classes
  - Music classes
  - Computer classes
  - Martial arts classes
  - Community clubs
  - Hobby stores (e.g., Warhammer for making models)
  - Church/temple/mosque:
    - Youth groups
    - Choir
    - Bible study, Hebrew school, etc.

– Teen book clubs (public library, Borders, Barnes & Noble)
■ Take your teen to places where he or she can be around other teens (be sure to check out these places in advance to make sure there is no gang activity):
  – Recreational centers
  – Local parks (for basketball, etc.)
  – Community pool
  – Private gym
  – Sports club/golf club
  – Public library (during teen activities)

Homework Assignments

1. ***Sources of Friends***
   a. Teens should find a new group that they do not normally hang out with and ***trade information*** with someone in that group.
      i. Try to find a ***common interest***.
      ii. Parents should assist teens in thinking of appropriate groups.
   b. Parents should ***discuss*** and ***decide*** on extracurricular activities with their teen based on their teen's interests and ***begin to enroll*** in these activities.
      i. Criteria for a good extracurricular activity:
         1. Meets weekly or bimonthly.
         2. Age range of other teens includes the social age of your teen.
         3. Activity includes informal time so that your teen can informally interact with other participants.
         4. Activity starts within the next couple of weeks.
         5. You are able to help facilitate your teen's involvement.
2. ***In-Group Call***
   a. Before the Call:
      i. Before you leave the group, parents should arrange for their teen to call another member of the group to practice conversational skills.
      ii. Set up a day and time to make the call.
      iii. Negotiate where the parent will be during the call and what the parent role will be.
      iv. Parent and teen may need to practice beginning and ending the phone call.
   b. During the Call:
      i. Teens should ***trade information*** on this phone call.
      ii. ***Find a common interest*** to report back to the group.
      iii. Follow the rules for beginning and ending a phone call, including using ***cover stories***.
   c. After the Call:
      i. Parents and teens should discuss the phone call and identify:
         1. ***Common interests***
         2. ***Cover stories***

3. How the phone call began and ended

   ii. Parents should help teens troubleshoot any problems that may have arisen.

3. ***Out-of-Group Call***

   a. Before the Call:

      i. Parents arrange with your teen to call someone outside of the group to practice conversational skills.

      ii. Choose someone that your teen *feels comfortable* talking with.

      iii. Negotiate where the parent will be during the call.

   b. During the Call:

      i. Teens should ***trade information*** on this phone call.

      ii. Find a ***common interest*** to report back to the group.

      iii. Follow the rules for a ***two-way conversation***.

      iv. Use the rules for starting and ending a conversation, including using ***cover stories***.

   c. After the Call:

      i. Parents and teens should discuss the call and identify ***common interests***.

      ii. Parents should help their teen troubleshoot any problems that may have arisen.

4. ***Bring a Personal Item***

   a. Bring a favorite item to share with the group (e.g., CD, magazine, game, book, pictures).

   b. Be prepared to ***trade information*** about the item one-on-one with someone else in the group.

Teen Therapist Guide—Session 4: Choosing Appropriate Friends

Guiding Principles of the Teen Session

Teens find themselves embedded in a multilevel system of peer affiliations. At the lowest level is the best friendship network, also known as a clique, which may have between two and six individuals. At the highest level is the school peer group, usually composed of all other teens at the same grade level. These levels are present even in elementary school (Frankel & Myatt, 2003). Beginning in middle school, an intermediate level, the crowd, makes its first appearance and becomes very important in defining the teen's social world (Hartup, 1993). Being associated with a crowd, or a group (the terms are used interchangeably), is an important component of an adolescent's reputation and school standing. Between-group rivalry is common, and may promote bonding and in-group solidarity between members of a crowd. Identifying with the appropriate crowd may provide protection from teasing or bullying. Group identification is helpful in promoting new friendships as it points the teen to a source of potential friends with similar interests and likes.

Problems with group identification may characterize many teens referred for social skills training. Typically, they have failed to identify with a crowd and are socially isolated, or they have repeatedly attempted to make friends with teens from an inappropriate crowd. Socially isolated teens often end up either completely withdrawn from peer social networks (i.e., the loners) or on the periphery of one or more inappropriate peer groups, (i.e., the floaters).

By helping teens to understand the function and social meaning of crowds, the instruction in this session assists them in identifying appropriate sources of friends. Teens are taught that it is not enough to simply have a preference for an activity; to be accepted into a crowd like the jocks or the computer geeks, one has to have a minimum proficiency at sports or computer science, respectively.

Teens will be looking to the teen group leader as an expert in these matters, as most of the teens presenting for treatment will have heard of these crowds, but will not have given much thought to their functionality. Thus, it is important for the teen group leader to have a good understanding of these groups prior to the didactic.

Some teens will incorrectly state that they would fit in with the popular kids or the jocks. The most important part of the session is for the teen group leader to gently dissuade the teen from attempting to fit in with inappropriate crowds, while identifying more appropriate options based on the teen's interests. Session content has teens identify body language and behavior indicative of acceptance or rejection. If this content leads to the admission of previous rejection, the group leader will need to follow up by assisting the teen with finding a more appropriate group.

Some teens may come to treatment with such a negative reputation that choosing a crowd from within their school may not be a viable option. In these cases, finding an extracurricular activity outside of the school setting will be essential to identifying sources of potential friends. Parents will be an integral part of this process.

Rule Review

Note: Only go over session rules again if the teens are having difficulty following them.

1. Listen to the other group members (no talking when others are speaking)
2. Follow directions
3. Raise your hand
4. Be respectful (no teasing or making fun of others)
5. No touching (no hitting, kicking, pushing, hugging, etc.)

Homework Review

Note: Give points for homework *parts*—not just one point per assignment.

1. ***Bring a Personal Item***
   a. Identify the favorite item the teen brought to share with the group (e.g., CD, magazine, game, book, pictures).
   b. Only give credit for appropriate items.
   c. To avoid distractions, have a coach put the item away until the teen session activity.
2. Practice having a phone call using ***cover stories*** with a parent.
   a. Say: *One of your assignments last week was to practice having a phone call using cover stories with your parent. Raise your hand if you practiced having a phone call with one of your parents this week.*
      i. Begin by calling on teens who completed the assignment:
      ii. Ask:
         1. *Who did you practice your phone call with* (mom, dad, etc.)?
         2. *How did you begin the call?*
            a. *Did you use a cover story for calling?*
         3. *Did you trade information?*
         4. *Did you find a common interest?*
            a. When they identify common interests, ask: *What could you do with that information if you were ever to hang out with your parent?*
         5. *How did you end the call?*
            a. *Did you use a cover story for ending the call?*
3. ***In-Group Call***
   a. Say: *Another assignment this week was to practice beginning and ending phone calls with another member of the group. Raise your hand if you did the in-group call.*

      i. Begin by calling on the teens who completed the call.

     ii. Ask:

        1. *Who did you talk to?*

        2. *Who called who?*

        3. *How did the conversation begin?*

          a. *Did you use a cover story for calling?*

        4. *Did you trade information?*

        5. *Did you find a common interest?*

          a. When they identify common interests, ask: *What could you do with that information if you were ever to hang out?*

        6. *How did the conversation end?*

          a. *Did you use a cover story for ending the call?*

    iii. Avoid general questions like: *How did it go?*

  b. Have the other person who participated in the call give his or her account immediately after, but not at the same time.

     i. Do not allow teens to talk about mistakes the other person made.

  c. Troubleshoot any problems that may have arisen.

     i. If the teen gives an incorrect response, ask: *What could you say differently next time?* or *How do you think you should have ended the call?*

  d. Check in with teens who did not complete the assignment and troubleshoot how they might get it done this week.

Didactic Lesson: Choosing Appropriate Friends

- Explain: *Today we are talking about choosing appropriate friends. Having a friend is a **choice** and it is important that we **choose** our friends wisely. There are good choices and bad choices for choosing potential friends.*

- Present each of the ***good*** suggestions below for choosing friends by saying: *Do you want to try to choose someone who….?* (while shaking your head yes):
  - …*is nice and friendly to you?*
  - …*is interested in you?*
  - …*likes the same things as you?*
  - …*is a similar age as you?*
  - …*is not likely to get you into trouble?*

- Follow each point by saying: *Why is that a good idea?*

- Present each of the ***bad*** suggestions below for choosing friends by saying: *Do you want to try to choose someone who….?* (while shaking your head no)
  - …*is mean to you?*
  - …*is going to make fun of you?*
  - …*is way more popular than you and hangs out with people who may not be nice to you?*
  - …*is much smarter than you and whom you don't have much in common with?*
  - …*has a bad reputation and is likely to get you into trouble?*

■ Follow each point by saying: *Why is that a bad idea?*

Identifying Different Crowds

■ Explain: *Now that we've talked about some guidelines for choosing friends, we need to talk about your reputation and where you might appropriately fit in at school. In every school, there are different "groups" or "crowds" of kids. Within these crowds, there are usually cliques, or small groups of best friends. In order to develop close friendships with other people, it can be helpful to find a crowd that you might fit in with. What are some of the groups or crowds of kids?*

■ Go around the room and have teens brainstorm the different groups of kids.

Jocks	Brains/smart kids	Stoners/burners/druggies
Cheerleaders	Chess club kids	Rockers
Popular kids	Gamers/video game geeks	Hip-hop group
Student council kids	Nerds	Detention club/slackers
Drama club kids	Math geeks	Wannabe gangbangers/taggers
Choir/chorus	Computer geeks	Musicians (rock bands)
Pep squad	Band kids/band geeks	Skaters
Partiers	Science geeks	Surfers
Preppies	Math geeks	Hippies/granolas
Artists	Goths	ROTC
Comic book geeks/anime geeks	Emos	Ethnic/cultural/religious groups

■ When the teens begin to identify the different types of geeks, it will be important to present the following information:
   – The term "geek" refers to someone that has interest and exceptional skill in a certain area.
      • Examples:
         ■ Computer geeks are interested in computers and are very good with computers.
         ■ Video game geeks (more commonly referred to as "gamers") enjoy video games and are very good at them.
         ■ Band geeks enjoy playing a musical instrument and play in the school band.

- Science geeks enjoy science and are gifted in this area, often belonging to a science club.
- Math geeks enjoy math and have exceptional abilities in this area.
- Comic book geeks (anime geeks) are really interested in comics and have exceptional knowledge in this area.
  - It is not simply enough just to enjoy a particular activity in order to be a geek; you also have to be good at it or know a lot about it.
    - For example, in order to truly be a computer geek, you not only need to have a love of computers, but you have to be proficient in your use of them.
  - It has become very cool to be a geek, because it means that you are really good at something.
    - For example, we often hear the complimentary terms of "geek chic" or the "geek squad" in reference to being a geek.
- [**Note**: The teen group leader should make a good sales pitch for being a geek, because many of the teens in the group will be able to appropriately fit in with geeks. If the teen group leader helps to normalize and even promote the affiliation of being a geek, many if not most of the teens will identify themselves with one or more of these groups.]

Importance of Having a Crowd or a Group

Explain the following without using a Socratic presentation.

- Having a crowd or a group protects teens from individual teasing:
  - Bullies are less likely to individually pick on teens who are in groups.
  - Teens appear stronger and more protected when they are affiliated with a group.
- When a teen experiences teasing within a group:
  - They feel a sense of support from other group members.
  - They bond with the other group members.
  - They experience in-group solidarity.
- Between-group rivalry is common and normal:
  - Teens bond over between-group rivalry.
    - Example: The jocks may dislike the geeks and the geeks may dislike the jocks.
      - Each group may complain about the other.
    - Group members bond over the experience.

Identifying Which Group You Fit in With

- Have teens identify how one can tell which group a teen is in.
  - Say: *We know that there are many different groups or crowds in school. How can you tell which group someone belongs to?*

- Answers:
  - Clothing, hair, appearance
  - Interests—peer groups are usually based on **common interests**
  - Who they hang out with
  - After-school activities
■ Have teens identify how they can tell when they are **accepted** by a group.
  - Ask: *How can you tell when you're accepted by a group?*
  - Answers:
    - The other kids in the group:
      - Give you their phone numbers, e-mail addresses, screen names.
      - Call, e-mail, or text you just to talk.
      - Invite you to do things.
      - Accept your invitations to do things.
      - Add you to their Facebook, MySpace pages.
      - Seek you out to do things.
■ Have teens identify how they can tell when they are **not accepted** by a group.
  - Ask: *How can you tell when you're not accepted by a group?*
  - Answers:
    - The other kids in the group:
      - Laugh at or make fun of you.
      - Do not give you their phone numbers, e-mail addresses.
      - Do not call you.
      - Do not take your phone calls.
      - Do not accept your invitations to do things.
      - Put off your invitations to do things (e.g., they say things like, "Yeah, let's do that sometime" but never follow through).
      - Do not accept your invitation to "friend you" on Facebook or MySpace.
      - Do not invite you to do things.
■ Have teens identify where these groups hang out.
  - Ask: *How can you find these groups at school?*
  - Answers:
    - The computer geeks hang out in the computer lab.
    - The gamers are playing video games and often wear gaming T-shirts.
    - The bookworms hang out in the library and can often be found reading.
    - The artists hang out in the art room and take art classes.
    - The band geeks play in the band and carry around their musical instruments.
    - The jocks play sports and often wear athletic clothing and letterman's jackets.
■ Have teens identify two to three groups in which they might best fit in with.
  - Say: *We've spent a lot of time the last few weeks trading information about the things you like to do. Based on your interests, think about which group you might best fit in with. We're going to go around the room and I want*

everyone to think of two to three groups that they might fit in with based on your interests.

- Ask the teens if they have tried to hang out with this crowd before.
    - If they say yes, ask them if they think they are accepted by this group.
- If they say they are accepted, have the teens give examples of how they know they are accepted:
- Teen group leader should assess whether this teen is accepted or rejected by the group.
- Provide feedback to teens who appear to be rejected by helping them identify a new group that might be more appropriate.
    - Challenge teens who choose an antisocial group.
        - Example: For a teen who identifies the "slackers" as an appropriate group for him or her, open this up to the group by asking, "What's the problem with choosing to join the slacker group?"
    - Do not allow teens to choose "floaters" (i.e., teens who float from one group to another) or "loners," as neither is a true crowd.
    - Make sure to write down the groups the teens identified to present to parents during reunification.
    - Ask teens what they can do if they are not accepted by a group.
        - Answer: Find a new group that is accepting of you.

Homework Assignments

- Briefly explain the homework for the week by saying: *We are going to continue to have you practice your conversational skills this week by making phone calls and having conversations with other teens. Your homework assignment this week is to:*
    - *Practice trading information over the next week with someone from one of the groups you identified that you might fit in with.*
        - *Find a common interest to report back to the group.*
    - *Begin to enroll in extracurricular activities based on your interests.*
        - *Your parents will be providing you with a list of ideas and you will get to negotiate your choice with them.*
    - *Have an in-group phone call with another group member:*
        - *This should be at least 5 to 10 minutes.*
        - *Use the steps for beginning and ending phone calls.*
        - *You will need to trade information and find a common interest to report to the group.*
    - *Make an out-of-group phone call to someone not in PEERS:*
        - *This should be at least 5 to 10 minutes.*
        - *Pick a friend that you would be comfortable trading information with.*
        - *Find a common interest to report to the group.*
    - *You will also need to bring some personal item to trade information about next week (e.g., CD, magazine, game, book, pictures).*

- Group leader and coaches should assign the in-group phone calls for the week and write this on the "In-Group Phone Call Assignment Log" for future reference.
  - If there are an uneven number of teens, assign someone "double duty."
    - This person will have two in-group phone calls (one as a caller and the other as a receiver).
    - This person will receive extra points for completing the extra call.

Teen Activity—Trading Information: Personal Items

Note: See the "Teen Activity Guide" for rules.

- Teens break up into dyads and trade information about their personal items.
- Have a selection of magazines for teens who did not bring items to share.
- Girls should be paired with girls, and boys should be paired with boys when possible.
- If there are an uneven number of teens, create one triad.
- Teens receive points for ***trading information***.
- If a teen did not bring a personal item, the teen still has to participate by asking questions and ***trading information***.

Reunification

- Announce that teens should join their parents:
  - Be sure that the teens are standing or sitting next to their parents.
  - Be sure to have silence and the full attention of the group.
- Say: *Today we talked about choosing appropriate friends. We also talked about the different groups or crowds in school and where we might best fit in. We even went around the room and had each teen identify two to three crowds that he or she might fit in with, based on shared interests. Let's go around the room now and have teens share which groups they identified. Parents should be making a note of these options.*
  - Have teens identify these groups.
  - Coaches should have notes from the session about which appropriate groups were selected in case the teens forget.
- Say: *The teens also practiced trading information with their personal items today and they did a great job. Let's give them a round of applause.*
- Go over the homework for the next week (see below):
  - Be sure to read off the in-group phone call assignment in front of parents.
  - Remind parents to make a note of who is calling whom.
- Individually and separately negotiate with each family:
  - Which peer group the teen will attempt to trade information with.

– What extracurricular activity the teen will enroll in.

– Who the teen will call for the out-of-group phone call.

– What personal item will be brought next week.

Homework Assignments

1. ***Sources of Friends***
   a. Teens should find a new group that they do not normally hang out with and ***trade information*** with someone in that group.
      i. Try to find a ***common interest***.
      ii. Parents should assist teens in thinking of appropriate groups.
   b. Parents should *discuss* and *decide* on extracurricular activities with their teen based on their teen's interests and ***begin to enroll*** in these activities.
      i. Criteria for a good extracurricular activity:
         1. Meets weekly or bimonthly.
         2. Age range of other teens includes the social age of your teen.
         3. Activity includes informal time so that teens can informally interact with other participants.
         4. Activity starts within the next couple of weeks.
         5. Parents are able to help facilitate your teen's involvement.

2. ***In-Group Call***
   a. Before the Call:
      i. Before you leave the group, parents should arrange for their teen to call another member of the group to practice conversational skills.
      ii. Set up a day and time to make the call.
      iii. Negotiate where the parent will be during the call and what the parent role will be.
      iv. Parent and teen may need to practice beginning and ending the phone call.
   b. During the Call:
      i. Teens should ***trade information*** on this phone call.
      ii. ***Find a common interest*** to report back to the group.
      iii. Follow the rules for beginning and ending a phone call, including using ***cover stories***.
   c. After the Call:
      i. Parents and teens should discuss the phone call and identify:
         1. ***Common interests***
         2. ***Cover stories***
         3. How the phone call began and ended
      ii. Parents should help teen troubleshoot any problems that may have arisen.

3. ***Out-of-Group Call***
   a. Before the Call:

     i. Parents arrange with your teen to call someone outside of the group to practice conversational skills.

     ii. Choose someone that your teen *feels comfortable* talking with.

     iii. Negotiate where the parent will be during the call.

  b. During the Call:

     i. Teens should **trade information** on this phone call.

     ii. Find a **common interest** to report back to the group.

     iii. Follow the rules for a **two-way conversation**.

     iv. Use the rules for starting and ending a conversation, including using **cover stories**.

  c. After the Call:

     i. Parents and teens should discuss the call and identify **common interests**.

     ii. Parents should help teen troubleshoot any problems that may have arisen.

4. ***Bring a Personal Item***

  a. Bring a favorite item to share with the group (e.g., CD, magazine, game, book, pictures).

  b. Be prepared to **trade information** about the item one-on-one with someone else in the group.

Calculate Points

Keep track of the following for each week of the intervention:

■ Calculate the number of points earned by each teen.

■ Add up the total number of points earned by the group.

■ Do not calculate the points in the presence of the teens.

  – Do not disclose the individual or group total of points.

  – Discourage attempts to compare the number of points earned between teens.

■ Remind them that they are working as a team to earn a bigger and better graduation party.

Teen Activity Guide: Session 4

"Trading Information: Personal Items"

Materials Needed

■ Teens bring personal items

■ CD players and headphones for music (optional)

■ In the event that a teen forgets to bring a personal item, have magazines available to share:

- Computer magazines
- Anime magazines
- Teen magazines
- Sports magazines

Rules

- Break teens up into dyads.
- Have teens practice ***trading information*** about their personal items.
- Encourage teens to identify ***common interests*** through ***trading information***.
- Prompt teens to ask questions when appropriate.
- Rotate teens approximately every 5 minutes:
  - Match girls with girls and boys with boys, whenever possible.
  - It may be necessary to create triads if there are an uneven number of girls or boys.
- Give points for trading information.
- Debrief during the final 5 minutes of the teen session:
  - Go around the room and have teens recall what they learned about their partners through ***trading information***.
  - Have teens identify ***common interests***.
- Give points for accurate recall of information.

Chapter 7

Session 5
Appropriate Use of Humor

Parent Session Therapist Guide

Guiding Principles of the Parent Session

This week the focus of the lesson is on humor. Humor is perhaps one of the more outstanding and obvious social deficits for many people with autism spectrum disorder (ASD). Teens with ASD often have substantial deficits in understanding punch lines to jokes (Emerich, Creaghead, Grether, Murray, & Grasha, 2003). Van Bourgondien and Mesibov (1987) reported that adults with high-functioning autism tended to tell jokes that were at the level of preschoolers, although 16% could tell jokes at the level of teenagers. Even given deficits in this area, many teens with ASD like to tell jokes. This, coupled with insensitivity to feedback from others after joke-telling, are the reasons for inclusion of this treatment module.

The content of this session highlights the advantages of the parent-assisted approach. Giving a general handout about humor to teens would probably not be effective. The informed parent is more likely to encounter a specific example of inappropriate "humor" and intervene during a "teachable moment" in a way that is specific enough for teens to understand. The handout gives parents and teens a common vernacular from which to judge the teen's humor. The group lesson ensures that the teen will give the parents' feedback due consideration.

Reports of the out-of-group phone call will be an important part of the homework review, as the teen and parent may have misjudged the friendship potential of the teen that was called. Rudeness, not returning two calls, and lack of interest are all signs of the wrong choice in friend. The parent and teen group leader should delicately point this out so that the teen can move on to more productive friendships.

Homework Review

- Spend *less* time on the in-group phone call and personal item.
- Spend the *majority* of the homework review on sources of friends and the out-of-group phone call.

1. ***Sources of Friends***
   a. Have parents identify the extracurricular activities they decided on with their teen based on their teen's interests.
      i. Find out if the parents enrolled their teen in this activity.
   b. Identify whether teens practiced **trading information** with a new group of teens.
      i. Find out which group they **traded information** with.
      ii. Find out if they found a **common interest**.
2. ***Out-of-Group Call***
   a. Make sure teen **traded information** on this phone call.
   b. Have parents identify:
      i. A **common interest** discovered through **trading information** on the call.
      ii. The **cover stories** their teen used on the phone call.
      iii. How their teen began and ended the phone call.
   c. Troubleshoot any problems that may have arisen.
      i. If parents report homework difficulty, ask: *Has anyone else had a similar problem? How did you handle it?*
      ii. Allow the other parents to provide suggestions before having the group leader give advice on handling the problem.
3. ***In-Group Call***
   a. Make sure the teen **traded information** on this phone call.
   b. Have parents identify:
      i. A **common interest** discovered through **trading information** on the call.
      ii. The **cover stories** their teen used on the phone call.
      iii. How their teen began and ended the phone call.
4. ***Bring a Personal Item***
   a. Very briefly identify the favorite item the teen brought to share with the group (e.g., CD, magazine, game, book, pictures).
   b. Only give credit for appropriate items.

Didactic Lesson: Appropriate Use of Humor

- Distribute the Parent Handout.
- Explain: *Today your teens will be learning about the rules for using appropriate humor. Humor is one important way that people communicate with each other. The problem is that sometimes teens do not use humor appropriately and they end up pushing people away. It's important to understand the rules about using*

humor when trying to make and keep friends. Over the next couple of weeks, you will be asked to assist your teen by paying attention to their humor feedback. If you have observed that your teen has a tendency to be silly or tell jokes that no one else seems to think are funny, it will be especially important for you to use this opportunity to give your teen feedback about his or her humor.

- Go around the room and have parents take turns reading the Parent Handout.
- Sections in **bold print** come directly from the Parent Handout.

Rules About Using Humor

- ***Be serious when you are first getting to know someone***:
  - **They may not understand your sense of humor**:
    - **They may think you are making fun of them.**
    - **They may think you are weird.**
  - Once you have gotten to know them better, it is fine to be less serious.
- ***Do not repeat jokes***:
  - **Never tell the same joke more than once in front of the same person.**
  - **Avoid repeating jokes that people have already heard.**
    - This is true even if the majority of people in the group have not heard the joke.
      - An exception would be if someone who has heard the joke asks you to tell it.
    - **A joke is not funny if you have already heard it**:
      - It makes the joke-teller look like he or she does not have any other material.
- **Humor should be *age-appropriate***:
  - **Teens should avoid immature joke-telling**:
    - Knock-knock jokes
    - Silly humor
- ***Avoid "insult jokes"***:
  - **Do not tell jokes at other people's expense**:
    - You might hurt their feelings.
    - It makes you look insensitive.
    - People will not want to be friends with you.
  - **Do not tell racial, ethnic, or religious jokes**:
    - Many people find these jokes offensive (even if they are not from the targeted group).
      - Even if the person you are telling the joke to is not offended, someone overhearing the joke may be upset.
      - Telling offensive jokes is a fast way to get a bad reputation and ensure that people will not want to be your friend.
- ***Avoid "inside jokes" with people who will not get them***:

- *Inside jokes* are those that only a few people would understand, are specific to a context, and are only shared by a particular circle of friends.
- Do not tell *inside jokes* to people who would not understand the context, unless you are willing to explain it to them.
  • Note that jokes that have to be explained are generally not funny to the receiver.

■ *Avoid "dirty jokes"*:
- *Dirty jokes* are generally sexual in nature.
  • They are not age-appropriate for teenagers.
- *Dirty jokes* often make other people uncomfortable and may give the teen a bad reputation.

■ *Think about whether it is the right time to be telling jokes*:
- Right times: Parties, get-togethers
- Wrong times: During class, when the teacher is talking, during passing period (when people are in a hurry)

■ *Pay attention to your humor feedback*:
- If you are going to try to be a *joke-teller*, pay attention to whether the other person thinks you are funny.
  • Signs that they *do not* think you are funny:
    ■ They do not laugh.
    ■ They give a *courtesy laugh*:
      • A *courtesy laugh* is one where someone laughs to be polite, but does not actually think you are funny.
- They look confused.
- They insult you or the joke (e.g., roll their eyes, make a sarcastic comment).
- They walk away.
- They *laugh at you*.
- It is important to notice whether they are *laughing at you* or *laughing with you*:
  • In order to do this, you must *watch* the other person for his or her reaction.
    ■ Simply listening to whether they laugh will not give you enough feedback.

Humor Feedback

Laughing at You	Laughing With You
Laugh and roll their eyes	Laugh and smile at the punch line
Look at someone else and then laugh	Compliment your joke or sense of humor
Laugh before the joke is over	They say: "That's a good one" and smile

| Long pause before they laugh | They say: "I'll have to remember that one." |
| They sarcastically say: "You're funny" and roll their eyes | They say: "You're funny" and smile |

- Best indicators that someone is *laughing at you*:
  - Rolling eyes
  - Sarcastic comments
- **Remember that not everyone needs to be a *joke-teller*:**
  - **You can also be a *joke-receiver*.**
    - **It is more important that you be able to laugh *with* your friends, than that you *make* your friends laugh.**
    - **Being a *joke-teller* is *very* difficult:**
      - **Very few people are good *joke-tellers*.**
      - **Most people are better at being *joke-receivers*.**
- ***Joke-receivers* may still tell the occasional joke, but they do not frequently and actively try to be funny.**

What to Do With Humor Feedback

- **If your *humor feedback* is that people are *laughing at you*:**
  - ***Be more serious***
  - **Avoid being a *joke-teller***
  - **Try being a *joke-receiver***
- **If your *humor feedback* is that people are *laughing with you*:**
  - ***Be serious when you are first getting to know someone.***
  - ***Do not repeat jokes.***
  - ***Only use age-appropriate jokes.***
  - ***Avoid insult jokes.***
  - ***Avoid inside jokes with people who will not get them.***
  - ***Avoid dirty jokes.***
  - ***Think about whether it is the right time to be telling jokes.***
  - ***Pay attention to your humor feedback.***

Homework Assignments

The parent group leader should go over the homework assignment and troubleshoot any potential problems with parents.

1. ***Humor Feedback***
   a. **Teen should pay attention to *humor feedback*.**
      i. **Teen should notice whether people are *laughing at you, laughing with you,* or not laughing at all.**
      ii. **Teen should discuss *humor feedback* with parent.**

1. **Teen and parent should decide if teen is more of a *joke-teller* or a *joke-receiver*.**
2. ***Sources of Friends***
   a. **Teens should find a new group that they do not normally hang out with and *trade information* with someone in that group.**
      i. Try to find a ***common interest***.
      ii. Parents should assist teens in thinking of appropriate groups.
   b. **Parents should *discuss* and *decide* on extracurricular activities with their teen based on their teen's interests and begin to enroll in these activities** (if they have not already).
3. ***In-Group Call***
   a. **Before the Call**:
      i. **Before you leave the group, parents should arrange for their teen to call another member of the group to practice conversational skills.**
      ii. **Set up a day and time to make the call.**
      iii. **Negotiate where the parent will be during the call and what the parent role will be.**
      iv. **Parent and teen may need to practice beginning and ending the phone call.**
   b. **During the Call**:
      i. **Teens should *trade information* on this phone call.**
      ii. ***Find a common interest* to report back to the group.**
      iii. **Follow the rules for beginning and ending a phone call, including using *cover stories*.**
   c. **After the Call**:
      i. **Parents and teens should discuss the phone call and identify**:
         1. ***Common interests***
         2. ***Cover stories***
         3. **How the phone call began and ended**
      ii. **Parents should help teen troubleshoot any problems that may have arisen.**
4. ***Out-of-Group Call***
   a. **Before the Call**:
      i. **Parents arrange with teen to call someone outside of the group to practice conversational skills.**
      ii. **Choose someone that your teen feels comfortable talking with.**
      iii. **Negotiate where the parent will be during the call.**
   b. **During the Call**:
      i. **Teens should *trade information* on this phone call.**
      ii. ***Find a common interest* to report back to the group.**
      iii. **Follow the rules for a *two-way conversation*.**
      iv. **Use the rules for starting and ending a conversation, including using *cover stories*.**

c. **After the Call**:
   i. **Parents and teens should discuss the call and identify *common interests*.**
   ii. **Parents should help teen troubleshoot any problems that may have arisen.**

5. ***Bring a Personal Item***
   a. **Bring a favorite item to share with the group (e.g., CD, magazine, game, book, pictures).**
   b. **Be prepared to *trade information* about the item one-on-one with someone else in the group.**

Parent Handout 5: Appropriate Use of Humor

Rules About Using Humor

- **Be serious when you are first getting to know someone**:
  - They may not understand your sense of humor:
    - They may think you are making fun of them.
    - They may think you are weird.
- **Do not repeat jokes**:
  - Never tell the same joke more than once in front of the same person.
  - Avoid repeating jokes that people have already heard.
    - A joke is not funny if you have already heard it.
- Humor should be **age-appropriate**:
  - Teens should avoid immature joke-telling.
- **Avoid "insult jokes"**:
  - Do not tell jokes at other people's expense.
  - Do not tell racial, ethnic, or religious jokes.
- **Avoid "inside jokes" with people who will not get them**:
  - **Inside jokes** are those that only a few people would understand, are specific to a context, and are shared only by a particular circle of friends.
  - Do not tell **inside jokes** to people who would not understand the context, unless you are willing to explain it to them.
- **Avoid "dirty jokes"**:
  - **Dirty jokes** are generally sexual in nature.
  - **Dirty jokes** often make other people uncomfortable and may give the teen a bad reputation.
- **Think about whether it is the right time to be telling jokes**.
- **Pay attention to your humor feedback**.
  - If you are going to try to be a **joke-teller**, pay attention to whether the other person thinks you are funny.
    - Signs that they **do not** think you are funny:
      - They do not laugh.
      - They give a **courtesy laugh**:
        - A **courtesy laugh** is one where someone laughs to be polite, but does not actually think you are funny.
      - They look confused.
      - They insult you or the joke (e.g., roll their eyes, make a sarcastic comment).
      - They walk away.
      - They **laugh at you**.
  - It is important to notice whether they are **laughing at you** or **laughing with you**.
    - In order to do this, you must **watch** the other person for his or her reaction.

■ Simply listening to whether they laugh will not give you enough feedback.

Humor Feedback

Laughing at You	Laughing With You
Laugh and roll their eyes	Laugh and smile at the punch line
Look at someone else and then laugh	Compliment your joke or sense of humor
Laugh before the joke is over	They say: "That's a good one" and smile
Long pause before they laugh	They say: "I'll have to remember that one"
They sarcastically say: "You're funny" and roll their eyes	They say: "You're funny" and smile

■ Remember that not everyone needs to be a *joke-teller*.
  – You can also be a *joke-receiver*:
    • It is more important that you be able to laugh *with* your friends, than that you *make* your friends laugh.
    • Being a *joke-teller* is *very* difficult:
      ■ Very few people are good *joke-tellers*.
      ■ Most people are better at being *joke-receivers*.
■ *Joke-receivers* may still tell the occasional joke, but they do not frequently and actively try to be funny.

What to Do With Humor Feedback

■ If your *humor feedback* is that people are *laughing at you*:
  – *Be more serious.*
  – Avoid being a *joke-teller*.
  – Try being a *joke-receiver*.
■ If your *humor feedback* is that people are *laughing with you*:
  – *Be serious when you are first getting to know someone.*
  – *Do not repeat jokes.*
  – *Only use age-appropriate jokes.*
  – *Avoid insult jokes.*
  – *Avoid inside jokes with people who will not get them.*
  – *Avoid dirty jokes.*
  – *Think about whether it is the right time to be telling jokes.*
  – Pay attention to your *humor feedback*.

Homework Assignments

1. ***Humor Feedback***
   a. Teen should pay attention to ***humor feedback***.
      i. Teen should notice whether people are ***laughing at you***, ***laughing with you***, or not laughing at all.
      ii. Teen should discuss ***humor feedback*** with parent.
         1. Teen and parent should decide if teen is more of a ***joke-teller*** or a ***joke-receiver***.
2. ***Sources of Friends***
   a. Teens should find a new group that they do not normally hang out with and ***trade information*** with someone in that group.
   b. Parents should ***discuss*** and ***decide*** on extracurricular activities with their teen based on their teen's interests and ***begin to enroll*** in these activities.
3. ***In-Group Call***
   a. Before the Call:
      i. Before you leave the group, parents should arrange for their teen to call another member of the group to practice conversational skills.
      ii. Set up a day and time to make the call.
      iii. Negotiate where the parent will be during the call and what the parent role will be.
      iv. Parent and teen may need to practice beginning and ending the phone call.
   b. During the Call:
      i. Teens should ***trade information*** on this phone call.
      ii. ***Find a common interest*** to report back to the group.
      iii. Follow the rules for beginning and ending a phone call, including using ***cover stories***.
   c. After the Call:
      i. Parents and teens should discuss the phone call and identify:
         1. ***Common interests***
         2. ***Cover stories***
         3. How the phone call began and ended
      ii. Parents should help the teen troubleshoot any problems that may have arisen.
4. ***Out-of-Group Call***
   a. Before the Call:
      i. Parents arrange with your teen to call someone outside of the group to practice conversational skills.
      ii. Choose someone that your teen *feels comfortable* talking with.
      iii. Negotiate where the parent will be during the call.
   b. During the Call:
      i. Teens should ***trade information*** on this phone call.
      ii. Find a ***common interest*** to report back to the group.

          iii. Follow the rules for a ***two-way conversation***.

          iv. Use the rules for starting and ending a conversation, including using ***cover stories***.

    c. After the Call:

          i. Parents and teens should discuss the call and identify ***common interests***.

          ii. Parents should help the teen troubleshoot any problems that may have arisen.

5. ***Bring a Personal Item***

    a. Bring a favorite item to share with the group (e.g., CD, magazine, game, book, pictures).

    b. Be prepared to ***trade information*** about the item one-on-one with someone else in the group.

Teen Therapist Guide—Session 5: Appropriate Use of Humor

Guiding Principles of the Teen Session

For some of the teens in the group, learning to use humor appropriately will be of paramount importance to developing friendships, particularly for teens with autism spectrum disorders, who often engage in silly or immature humor or the telling of jokes that no one else seems to understand. Many teens who are socially rejected are often oblivious to the negative humor feedback they receive. This causes them to be further rejected and may even result in a bad reputation among peers. Teens who regularly engage in inappropriate use of humor are often seen as strange or weird by their peers, which may ultimately lead to teasing and bullying, if not simply peer rejection. Therefore, paying attention to one's humor feedback and learning to use humor appropriately will be critical for a select group of rejected teens. For some teens, failing to develop this one core skill may be the difference between success and failure in the PEERS program. In other words, even if a teen was able to successfully master all of the other skills outlined in the PEERS curriculum, and if they continued to persist with inappropriate use of humor, it is likely that they would continue to experience rejection from peers.

Perhaps the greatest challenge for the teen group leader in this session will involve addressing the reemergence of symptoms of the "too cool for school" syndrome. Some teens may hold onto their identity as a joke-teller despite repeated social failures. Teens may claim that they are joke-tellers, as this role may be seen as having a higher social standing, and may initially feel reluctant to identify themselves as joke-receivers, wrongly believing that this position may make them inferior. This issue is defused in two ways: First, the role of the joke-receiver is presented and normalized as a helpful social role that most people fulfill (including the group leader and coaches), and very few people are successful joke-tellers. This will help teens "save face." Second, part of the homework assignment involves paying attention to humor feedback, which will afford a good opportunity to challenge any wrongful notions about joke-telling. Parents will also be integral to pointing out humor feedback from peers and giving it themselves during teachable moments.

Rule Review

Note: Only go over session rules again if the teens are having difficulty following them.

1. Listen to the other group members (no talking when others are speaking)
2. Follow directions
3. Raise your hand
4. Be respectful (no teasing or making fun of others)
5. No touching (no hitting, kicking, pushing, hugging, etc.)

Homework Review

Note: Give points for homework *parts*—not just one point per assignment.

1. ***Bring a Personal Item***
   a. Briefly identify the favorite item the teen brought to share with the group (e.g., CD, magazine, game, book, pictures).
   b. Only give credit for appropriate items.
   c. To avoid distractions, have a coach put the item away until the teen session activity.

2. ***Sources of Friends***
   a. Identify whether teens practiced ***trading information*** with a new group of teens.
      i. Say: *Last week we talked about the different groups or crowds at school and where you might best fit in. One of your assignments this week was to trade information with someone from one of these groups. Raise your hand if you traded information with someone from an appropriate group.*
         1. Briefly ask:
            a. *Which groups did you identify that you might fit in with?*
            b. *Did you trade information with someone from one of those groups?*
            c. *Which group did you choose?*
            d. *Did you find a common interest?*
      ii. Say: *Another assignment was that you and your parents were supposed to identify an extracurricular activity for you to join where you might meet other teens with common interests and then begin to enroll in those activities. Raise your hand if you found an extracurricular activity.*
         1. Briefly ask:
            a. *Which extracurricular activity did you choose?*
            b. *Did you enroll in the activity?*
            c. *Are there other teens your age in the group?*
            d. *Does this seem like a good place for you to make potential new friends?*

3. ***Out-of-Group Call***
   a. Say: *Another assignment this week was to trade information on a phone call with someone not in PEERS. Raise your hand if you did the out-of-group call.*
      i. Begin by calling on the teens who completed the call.
      ii. Ask:
         1. *Who did you talk to?*
         2. *How did the conversation begin?*
         3. *Did you trade information?*

    4. *Did you find a common interest?*
       a. When they identify common interests, ask: *What could you do with that information if you were ever to hang out?*
    5. *How did the conversation end?*
  iii. Avoid general questions like "How did it go?"
 b. Troubleshoot any problems that may have arisen.
  i. If the teen gives an incorrect response, ask: *What could you say differently next time?* or *How do you think you should have ended the call?*
 c. If you have time, check in with teens who did not complete the assignment and troubleshoot how they might get it done this week.

4. *In-Group Call*

 a. Say: *Your last assignment this week was to trade information on a phone call with another member of our group. Raise your hand if you did the in-group call.*
  i. Begin by calling on the teens who completed the call.
  ii. Briefly ask:
    1. *Who did you talk to?*
    2. *Who called who?*
    3. *Did you trade information?*
    4. *Did you find a common interest?*
       a. When they identify common interests, ask: *What could you do with that information if you were ever to hang out?*
  iii. Avoid general questions like "How did it go?"
  iv. Have the other person who participated in the call give his or her account immediately after, but not at the same time.
    1. Do not allow teens to talk about mistakes the other person made.
 b. Troubleshoot any problems that may have arisen.
  i. If the teen gives an incorrect response, ask: *What could you say differently next time?* or *How do you think you should have ended the call?*
 c. If you have time, check in with teens who did not complete the assignment and troubleshoot how they might get it done this week.

Didactic Lesson: Rules About Using Humor

Explain: *Tonight we're going to be talking about appropriate use of humor. Humor is one important way that people communicate with each other. The problem is that sometimes people do not use humor appropriately and they end up pushing people away. It's important to understand the rules about using humor when trying to make and keep friends.*

■ **Be serious when you are first getting to know someone**:
  – Say: *The first rule for appropriate use of humor is to be serious when you're first getting to know someone. Why is it important that we be more serious when we're first getting to know someone?*

- Answer: They may not understand your sense of humor.
    - They may think you are making fun of them.
    - They may think you are weird.
  - Ask: *Is it okay to be less serious once you've gotten to know the person?*
    - Answer: Yes.
- ***Do not repeat jokes***:
  - Never tell the same joke more than once in front of the same person.
  - Avoid repeating jokes that people have already heard.
  - Say: *Another rule for appropriate use of humor is not to repeat jokes to people that have already heard them. Why would we want to avoid repeating jokes?*
    - Answer: A joke is not funny if you have already heard it.
    - This is true even if the majority of people in the group have not heard the joke:
      - An exception would be if someone who has heard the joke asks you to tell it.
      - It makes the joke-teller look like he or she does not have any other material.
- Humor should be ***age-appropriate***:
  - Teens should avoid immature joke-telling:
    - Knock-knock jokes
    - Silly humor
  - Say: *It's also important that humor should be age-appropriate. That means teenagers shouldn't be telling knock-knock jokes or really silly jokes that a five-year-old might tell. Why should humor be age-appropriate?*
    - Answer: Because your friends will not think it is funny if your jokes are too immature.
- ***Avoid "insult jokes"***:
  - Do not tell jokes at other people's expense.
  - Say: *Another rule for appropriate use of humor is avoiding insult jokes. These are jokes that make fun of another person. What would be the problem with telling jokes where you make fun of another person?*
    - Answer: You might hurt their feelings.
  - Do not tell racial, ethnic, or religious jokes.
    - Say: *This also includes jokes that make fun of someone's ethnicity, race, or religion, for example. Why would we want to avoid telling insult jokes that make fun of someone's ethnicity, race, or religion?*
      - Answer: Many people find these jokes offensive (even if they are not from the targeted group); it makes you look insensitive; people will not want to be friends with you.
        - Even if the person that you are telling the joke to is not offended, someone overhearing the joke may be upset.
  - Telling ***insult jokes*** is a fast way to get a bad reputation and ensure that people will not want to be your friend.

■ *Avoid "inside jokes" with people who will not get them*:
- Say: *Another rule for appropriate use of humor is to avoid inside jokes with people who won't get them. Inside jokes are those that only a few people would understand. They're usually specific to a context and only shared by a particular circle of friends. What's the problem with telling inside jokes to people not in on the joke?*
  • Answer: The people not in on the joke will feel left out.
- Explain: *So don't tell inside jokes to people who wouldn't understand the context, unless you are willing to explain it to them. But remember that jokes that have to be explained are generally not funny to the receiver.*

■ *Avoid "dirty jokes"*:
- Say: *Another important rule about humor is to avoid telling dirty jokes. Dirty jokes are ones that make fun of sex or someone's body parts or bodily functions, and they're not considered age-appropriate for teenagers. What's the problem with telling dirty jokes?*
  • Answer: **Dirty jokes** often make other people uncomfortable and may give the teen a bad reputation.

■ *Think about whether it is the right time to be telling jokes*:
- Say: *It's also important that we consider whether it's the right time or the wrong time to be telling jokes. Why is it important to think about the timing when we tell a joke?*
  • Answer: Because jokes are not funny if they are told at the wrong time.
    ■ Right times: Parties, get-togethers.
    ■ Wrong times: During class, when the teacher is talking, during passing period (when people are in a hurry).

■ *Pay attention to your humor feedback*:
- If you are going to try to be a **joke-teller**, pay attention to whether the other person thinks you are funny.
- Say: *Telling jokes is really hard to do and most people shouldn't even attempt it; but if you do tell a joke, you need to pay attention to your humor feedback. Humor feedback is the reaction someone gives you after you've told a joke. Why would it be important to pay attention to your humor feedback?*
  • Answer: Because if people do not think you are funny, then maybe you should not be trying to tell jokes; when you try to tell jokes and no one thinks you are funny, you may end up pushing people away; they may think you are weird or strange and not want to be your friend.
- Say: *When you're paying attention to your humor feedback, one of the things you need to notice is whether the other person thinks you're funny.*
- Signs that they don't think you're funny include:
  • They don't laugh.
  • They give a **courtesy laugh**:

- A ***courtesy laugh*** is one where someone laughs to be polite, but doesn't actually think you're funny.
    - They look confused.
    - They insult you or the joke (e.g., roll their eyes, make a sarcastic comment).
    - They walk away.
    - They ***laugh at you*** (not your joke).
  - Say: *One of the best ways to pay attention to humor feedback is to notice whether the person is laughing at you or laughing with you. In order to do this, you must watch the other person for his or her reaction. Simply listening to whether they laugh will not give you enough feedback.*
- Ask: *How you can tell if someone is laughing at you or laughing with you?* (See the table below.)

Laughing at You	*Laughing With You*
Laugh and roll their eyes	Laugh and smile at the punch line
Look at someone else and then laugh	Compliment your joke or sense of humor
Laugh before the joke is over	They say: "That's a good one" and smile
Long pause before they laugh	They say: "I'll have to remember that one"
They sarcastically say: "You're funny" and roll their eyes	They say: "You're funny" and smile

- Best indicators that someone is ***laughing at you***:
  - Rolling eyes
  - Sarcastic comments
- Say: *Remember that not everyone needs to be a joke-teller. You can also be a joke-receiver. In the end, it's more important that you be able to laugh with your friends, than that you **make** your friends laugh.*
  - Being a ***joke-teller*** is ***very*** difficult:
    - Very few people are good ***joke-tellers***.
    - Most people are better at being ***joke-receivers***.
  - ***Joke-receivers*** may still tell the occasional joke, but they do not frequently and actively try to be funny.
  - [It is useful for the group leader to divulge that he or she is a ***joke-receiver***, to point out that very few people are successful ***joke-tellers*** and that most teens will be more successful ***joke-receivers***. Point out that being a ***joke-receiver*** is equally fun, as the role still involves laughter and fun times with friends.]
- Say: *Some people are not comfortable with humor at all and prefer not to be around people who tell jokes. In this case, they're neither a joke-teller nor a joke-receiver; but it's important to remember that people will sometimes want*

to tell jokes and we should still be polite and even give a courtesy laugh when appropriate. Why would it be important to still give a courtesy laugh?
- Answer: Because it is polite and we would not want to make the person feel embarrassed.

■ Say: *So if you're someone who is not comfortable with humor, remember that friendship is a choice and you don't have to be friends with people who are joke-tellers if that makes you uncomfortable.*

What to Do With Humor Feedback

Explain the following:

■ If your ***humor feedback*** is that people are ***laughing at you***:
- ***Be more serious***.
- Avoid being a ***joke-teller***.
- Try being a ***joke-receiver***.
■ If your ***humor feedback*** is that people are ***laughing with you***:
- ***Do not repeat jokes***.
- ***Use age-appropriate jokes***.
- ***Avoid insult jokes***.
- ***Avoid inside jokes***.
- ***Avoid dirty jokes***.
- ***Think about whether it is the right time to be telling jokes***.
- ***Pay attention to your humor feedback***.
■ Go around the room and have each teen identify if he or she is more of a ***joke-teller*** or a ***joke-receiver***:
- Praise those who claim to be ***joke-receivers***.
- Any teen claiming to be a ***joke-teller*** should be asked to support this claim by describing his or her ***humor feedback*** and providing details about how people tend to laugh with them, rather than laugh at them.
  • Remind them that is it very difficult to be a ***joke-teller*** and you expect them to pay very close attention to their ***humor feedback***.
  • Let them know that their parents will also be giving them feedback.
■ Let teens know that we will be checking in with them next week to report on their ***humor feedback***.

Behavioral Rehearsal

■ Go around the room and have each teen practice paying attention to his or her humor feedback.
- Say: *Now we're going to practice paying attention to our humor feedback. Remember that the most important way to pay attention to humor feedback is to **watch** the other person's reaction. Listening for whether they*

laughed or not is not enough, because they could be rolling their eyes or making a face.

– Have each teen say the same knock-knock joke to the group leader on two different occasions.

- Say: *We're going to go around the room and each of you is going to say the same knock-knock joke twice. This joke is not meant to be funny; in fact it's a good example of humor that is not age-appropriate for you. The reason we're using it is because it's simple, but long enough to give you time to pay attention to your humor feedback.*
- Be sure that each teen uses the same joke or the group may get out of control.

■ Example:

Teen: "Knock knock."

Group leader: "Who's there?"

Teen: "Banana."

Group leader: "Banana who?"

Teen: "Knock knock."

Group leader: "Who's there?"

Teen: "Banana."

Group leader: "Banana who?"

Teen: "Knock knock."

Group leader: "Who's there?"

Teen: "Orange."

Group leader: "Orange who?"

Teen: "Orange you glad I didn't say banana?"

- Teens will be telling this joke to the group leader while the rest of the group watches:
  ■ Encourage all of the teens to be watching the group leader's reaction to the joke.
- The group leader should randomly alternate between demonstrating ***laughing at you*** (e.g., laughing but then rolling eyes or making a face) and ***laughing with you*** (e.g., laughing and smiling) throughout the exercise.
- On the first occasion the teen should have his or her eyes ***closed*** when he or she tells the joke and is paying attention to his or her humor feedback.
  ■ When the joke is finished and the group leader has given a reaction, have the teen interpret the ***humor feedback***:
    • Say: *Okay, now open your eyes. Tell us if you think that was laughing at you or laughing with you.*
  ■ Allow the teen to take a guess and then have the rest of the teens (who had their eyes open) interpret the ***humor feedback***.
  ■ The group leader will tell them if they were correct or incorrect.

- On the second occasion the teen should have his or her eyes *open* and looking at the group leader when he or she tells the joke and is paying attention to his or her ***humor feedback***.
    - When the joke is finished and the group leader has given a reaction, have the teen interpret the ***humor feedback***:
        - Say: *Okay, so tell us if you think that was laughing at you or laughing with you.*
    - Allow the teen to take a guess and then have the rest of the teens also interpret the ***humor feedback***.
    - The group leader will tell them if they were correct or incorrect.
    - Then ask the teen which way was easier to interpret the ***humor feedback***:
    - Ask: *Which way was easier to notice the humor feedback: eyes opened or eyes closed?*
        - Answer: Eyes open.
- During this exercise, it will be more difficult for the teens to interpret their ***humor feedback*** when their eyes are closed:
    - Some teens may try to make a joke or be oppositional and say that it is easier with eyes closed.
    - Do not engage in a debate with the teen; instead, open it up to the group and say: *What do we think everyone? Is it generally easier to notice humor feedback with eyes open or eyes closed?*
    - The group will most likely say "eyes open" and this will apply sufficient peer pressure, so that the opposing teen will back down.
- The purpose of this demonstration is to show the teens that they need to *watch* the other person for their reaction by making eye contact.
    - When you do not *watch* the other person's reaction, you may miss out on the ***humor feedback***.

Homework Assignments

- Briefly explain the homework for the week by saying: *We are going to continue to have you practice your conversational skills this week by making phone calls and having conversations with other teens. Your homework assignment this week is to:*
    - *Practice **trading information** over the next week with someone from one of the groups you identified that you might fit in with.*
        - ***Find a common interest** to report back to the group.*
    - *Begin to enroll in extracurricular activities based on your interests.*
        - *Your parents will be providing you with a list of ideas and you will get to negotiate your choice with them.*
    - *Have an in-group phone call with another group member:*
        - *This should be at least 5 to 10 minutes.*
        - *Use the steps for beginning and ending phone calls.*

- *You will need to trade information and find a common interest to report to the group.*
  - *Make an out-of-group phone call to someone not in PEERS:*
    - *This should be at least 5 to 10 minutes.*
    - *Pick a friend that you would be comfortable trading information with.*
    - *Find a common interest to report to the group.*
  - *You will also need to bring some personal item to trade information about next week (e.g., CD, magazine, game, book, pictures).*
  - *Pay attention to your humor feedback if you tell any jokes this week:*
    - *Notice if people are laughing at you or laughing with you.*
    - *Decide if you're more of a joke-teller or a joke-receiver.*
- Group leader and coaches should assign the in-group calls for the week and write this on the "In-Group Phone Call Assignment Log" for future reference.
  - If there are an uneven number of teens, assign someone "double duty."
    - This person will have two in-group phone calls (one as a caller and the other as a receiver).
    - This person will receive extra points for completing the extra call.

Teen Activity—Trading Information: Personal Items

Note: See the "Teen Activity Guide" for rules.

- Teens break up into dyads and trade information about their personal items.
- Have a selection of magazines for teens who did not bring items to share.
- Girls should be paired with girls, and boys should be paired with boys when possible.
- If there are an uneven number of teens, create one triad.
- Teens receive points for **trading information**.
- If a teen did not bring a personal item, the teen still has to participate by asking questions and **trading information**.

Reunification With Parents

- Announce that teens should join their parents:
  - Be sure that the teens are standing or sitting next to their parents.
  - Be sure to have silence and the full attention of the group.
- Say: *Today we talked about the appropriate use of humor in conversations and worked on paying attention to our humor feedback. Who can tell us what some of the rules for appropriate humor are?* [Have teens generate all of the rules. Be prepared to give prompts if necessary.]
  - **Be serious when you are first getting to know someone**.
  - **Do not repeat jokes**.
  - **Humor should be age-appropriate**.
  - **Avoid insult jokes**.

- *Avoid inside jokes*.
- *Avoid dirty jokes*.
- *Think about whether it is the right time to be telling jokes*.
- *Pay attention to your humor feedback*.
  - Notice if people are **laughing at you** or **laughing with you** or not laughing at all.
- Not everyone needs to be a **joke-teller**.
  - It is just as much fun to be a **joke-receiver**.
  - Say: *Today we also worked on trading information with our personal items and this group did a great job of trading information. Let's give them a round of applause.*

■ Go over the homework for the next week (see below):
- Be sure to read off the in-group phone call assignment in front of parents.
- Remind parents to make a note of who is calling who.

■ Individually and separately negotiate with each family:
- Which peer group the teen will attempt to trade information with.
- What extracurricular activity they will enroll in.
- Who the teen will call for the out-of-group phone call.
- What personal item will be brought next week.

Homework Assignments

1. **Humor Feedback**
   a. Teen should pay attention to **humor feedback**:
      i. Teen should notice whether people are **laughing at you**, **laughing with you**, or not laughing at all.
      ii. Discuss **humor feedback** with parent.
         1. Teen and parent should decide if teen is more of a **joke-teller** or a **joke-receiver**.
2. **Sources of Friends**
   a. Teens should find a new group that they do not normally hang out with and **trade information** with someone in that group.
   b. Parents should *discuss* and *decide* on extracurricular activities with their teen based on their teen's interests and *begin to enroll* in these activities.
3. **In-Group Call**
   a. Before the Call:
      i. Before you leave the group, parents should arrange for their teen to call another member of the group to practice conversational skills.
      ii. Set up a day and time to make the call.
      iii. Negotiate where the parent will be during the call and what the parent role will be.

      iv. Parent and teen may need to practice beginning and ending the phone call.
  b. During the Call:
      i. Teens should ***trade information*** on this phone call.
      ii. ***Find a common interest*** to report back to the group.
      iii. Follow the rules for beginning and ending a phone call, including using ***cover stories***.
  c. After the Call:
      i. Parents and teens should discuss the phone call and identify:
         1. ***Common interests***
         2. ***Cover stories***
         3. How the phone call began and ended
      ii. Parents should help their teen troubleshoot any problems that may have arisen.

4. ***Out-of-Group Call***
  a. Before the Call:
      i. Parents arrange with your teen to call someone outside of the group to practice conversational skills.
      ii. Choose someone that your teen *feels comfortable* talking with.
      iii. Negotiate where the parent will be during the call.
  b. During the Call:
      i. Teens should ***trade information*** on this phone call.
      ii. Find a ***common interest*** to report back to the group.
      iii. Follow the rules for a ***two-way conversation***.
      iv. Use the rules for starting and ending a conversation, including using ***cover stories***.
  c. After the Call:
      i. Parents and teens should discuss the call and identify ***common interests***.
      ii. Parents should help their teen troubleshoot any problems that may have arisen.

5. ***Bring a Personal Item***
  a. Bring a favorite item to share with the group (e.g., CD, magazine, game, book, pictures).
  b. Be prepared to ***trade information*** about the item one-on-one with someone else in the group.

Calculate Points

Keep track of the following for each week of the intervention:

- Calculate the number of points earned by each teen.
- Add up the total number of points earned by the group.
- Do not calculate the points in the presence of the teens.

- Do not disclose the individual or group total of points.
- Discourage attempts to compare number of points earned between teens.
■ Remind them that they are working as a team to earn a bigger and better graduation party.

Teen Activity Guide: Session 4

"Trading Information: Personal Items"

Materials Needed

■ Teens bring personal items
■ CD players and headphones for music (optional)
■ In the event that a teen forgets to bring a personal item, have magazines available to share:
  - Computer magazines
  - Anime magazines
  - Teen magazines
  - Sports magazines

Rules

■ Break teens up into dyads.
■ Have teens practice **trading information** about their personal items.
■ Encourage teens to identify **common interests** through **trading information**.
■ Prompt teens to ask questions when appropriate.
■ Rotate teens approximately every 5 minutes:
  - Match girls with girls and boys with boys, whenever possible.
  - It may be necessary to create triads if there are an uneven number of girls or boys.
■ Give points for **trading information**.
■ Debrief during the final 5 minutes of the teen session.
  - Go around the room and have teens recall what they learned about their partners through **trading information**.
  - Have teens identify **common interests**.
■ Give points for accurate recall of information.

Chapter 8

Session 6
Peer Entry I—Entering a Conversation

Parent Session Therapist Guide

Guiding Principles of the Parent Session

Much of what we know about how teens make and keep friends comes from the research based upon younger children (Frankel & Myatt, 2003). We have successfully extrapolated these findings to apply to teens. By extrapolation, successful entries into a group of teens in conversation may begin with low-risk tactics such as waiting and listening until positive feedback from the conversing peers permits entry (cf., Dodge, Schlundt, Schocken, & Delugach 1983; Garvey, 1984). Unsuccessful entry attempts might include disrupting an ongoing conversation by asking for information or disagreeing (Coie & Kupersmidt, 1983).

The focus for this session is having the teen slip into a conversation with the most appropriate "crowd" for him or her. Helping parents and teens pick the crowd the teen intends to join is important to help establish potentially successful friendships, but more immediately, successful entry into conversations. Most of the important work will be in the teen group for this session, because teens usually slip into conversations out of sight of the parents. The parents need to be alert to encourage the best crowd for the teen to try to join and where to find this crowd. If the out-of-group phone call does not turn out well, it may raise the possibility that the teen has a negative reputation or is trying to join an inappropriate crowd (e.g., one that is not likely to accept him or her). The parent and teen group leaders should be ready to point this out to both the parent and teen and help change the choice in crowd.

Homework Review

- Unless parents are presenting a new extracurricular activity, spend *less* time on:
  - Sources of friends
  - In-group call
  - Personal items
- Spend the *majority* of the homework review on the out-of-group call and humor feedback.

1. ***Out-of-Group Call***
   a. Make sure the teen ***traded information*** on this phone call.
   b. Have parents identify:
      i. A ***common interest*** discovered through ***trading information*** on the call.
      ii. The ***cover stories*** their teen used on the phone call.
      iii. How their teen began and ended the phone call.

2. ***Humor Feedback***
   a. Have parents identify:
      i. Whether teens practiced interpreting their ***humor feedback*** with family and friends.
      ii. Whether teens noticed if people were ***laughing at them***, ***laughing with them***, or not laughing at all.
      iii. Whether the teen decided if he or she was more of a ***joke-teller*** or a ***joke-receiver***.

3. ***Sources of Friends***
   a. Have parents identify the extracurricular activities they decided on with their teen based on their teen's interests.
      i. Find out if the parents enrolled their teen in this activity.
   b. Identify whether teens practiced ***trading information*** with a new group of teens.
      i. Find out which group they ***traded information*** with.
      ii. Find out if they found a ***common interest***.

4. ***In-Group Call***
   a. [Very brief review—two sentences from each parent.]
   b. Have parents identify:
      i. If the phone call was made.
      ii. A ***common interest*** discovered through ***trading information*** on the call.
   c. Troubleshoot any problems that may have arisen.
      i. If parents report homework difficulty, ask: "Has anyone else had a similar problem? How did you handle it?"
      ii. Allow the other parents to provide suggestions before having the group leader give advice on handling the problem.

5. ***Bring a Personal Item***
   a. Identify the favorite item the teen brought to share with the group (e.g., CD, magazine, game, book, pictures).
   b. Only give credit for appropriate items.

Didactic Lesson: Peer Entry

■ Distribute the Parent Handout.
■ Explain: *Now that your teens have had lots of practice trading information and have identified at least one group they think they might fit in with, we are going to begin to teach your teens how to join conversations with other teens that they are trying to get to know better. We call this type of peer entry, "slipping into conversations"—because your teen will be casually slipping into other teens' conversations. Here is what your teen will be expected to do.*
■ Go around the room and have parents take turns reading the Parent Handout.
■ Sections in **bold print** come directly from the Parent Handout.

Steps for Slipping Into a Conversation

1. ***Watch/Listen***
   a. **Watch and listen to the conversation before you try to join:**
      i. **You need to know what they are talking about before you join.**
      ii. **You need to know whether you have something to contribute to the conversation.**
      iii. **If you try to join a conversation without knowing what the people are talking about, you will only interrupt the conversation.**
   b. **Watch to see if you know one of the people:**
      i. **Joining a conversation is easier if you know at least one of the people.**
      ii. **They are more likely to accept you into the conversation.**
   c. **Move closer (not *too* close) to watch the activity/conversation to find out if you want to join.**
   d. **Listen to make sure they are talking nicely:**
      i. **If they are not being nice to each other, try a different group.**
   e. **Listen to make sure they are not talking above your head (i.e., too sophisticated).**
   f. **Find a *common interest* from the conversation.**
   g. **Show interest in the group:**
      i. **Laugh or smile faintly and when relevant.**
      ii. **Shake head when agreeing.**
   h. **Try to make *periodic* eye contact.**
      i. **Do not stare—that would seem like eavesdropping.**

2. ***Wait***
   a. **Wait for one of three things**:
      i. **Wait for a brief pause or break in the conversation.**
      ii. **If there is not a pause, wait for the right time (e.g., a transitional moment), where you are not interrupting too much.**
      iii. **Wait for some sign of receptiveness from the group (e.g., they look over at you and smile).**
3. ***Join***
   a. **Have a reason for joining the conversation (e.g., contributing to it).**
   b. **Move closer (arm's length away), but not too close.**
   c. **Make a comment, ask a question, or bring over an item that is related to the conversation.**
   d. ***Do not get too personal.***
   e. **Assess receptiveness of the person or group**:
      i. **Are they making eye contact with you?**
      ii. **Are comments being directed to you from the group?**
      iii. **Are group members turned more toward you (i.e., they "*open the circle*")?**
   f. **Use gaze aversion (this protects you against possible rejection)**:
      i. **Do not stare.**
      ii. **Look at the group occasionally; look away the rest of the time.**
   g. ***Do not be a conversation hog*—you should listen more than you talk at first.**
   h. **If they ignore you or do not want you to join in the conversation—*move on*.**

■ Go around the room and have each parent identify any potential problems with their teen slipping into a conversation with an *appropriate* crowd.
   – Say: *Now that we've gone over the appropriate way to slip into a conversation, which of these areas (if any) do you think your teen tends to struggle with?*
■ Troubleshoot these problems with the help of the group.
   – In general, parents can effectively help their teens with slipping in by discussing their teens' efforts in the following manner:
      • Ask teen if he or she had a chance to ***slip into a conversation*** recently.
      • Have teen give a blow-by-blow description of the interaction.
      • Praise the teen for something he or she did well.
      • ***Offer suggestions*** about things the teen could have done differently.
         ■ Suggestions can often be given with statements that start with, "How about if…."
         ■ Example: "How about if next time when you slip in, you wait for a pause before you join?"
      • Do not overtly tell your teen that he or she did something wrong.

■ This may discourage them or make them feel embarrassed:
  • Example: "You didn't **slip in** the right way!"
  – Allow parents to come up with other suggestions for handling potential problems with **slipping in** by saying: *Does anyone have any other suggestions?*

Homework Assignments

The parent group leader should go over the homework assignment and troubleshoot any potential problems with parents.

1. **Teens should practice *slipping into a conversation* between at least two teens they feel comfortable with:**
   a. **Before slipping in:**
      i. **Think of a place where the teen is likely to be accepted (i.e., low-risk place) and they do not have a bad reputation.**
      ii. **Parent and teen may want to rehearse the steps for *slipping into a conversation* prior to the attempt.**
   b. **During slipping in:**
      i. **Follow the steps for *slipping into a conversation*.**
   c. **After slipping in:**
      i. **Parents and teens should discuss how the teen *slipped into the conversation*.**
      ii. **Parents should help teen troubleshoot any problems that may have arisen.**
   d. For teens who are particularly socially anxious and reluctant to complete this assignment, it may be helpful to have teens practice just the first step of peer entry (i.e., watch/listen), while establishing proximity and interest in the group. In subsequent sessions, the teen may be encouraged to add additional steps as he or she feels more comfortable.
2. ***In-Group Call*** (notify parents this will be the last in-group phone assignment)
   a. **Before the call:**
      i. **Before you leave the group, parents should arrange for their teen to call another member of the group to practice conversational skills.**
      ii. **Set up a day and time to make the call.**
      iii. **Negotiate where the parent will be during the call and what the parent role will be.**
      iv. **Parent and teen may need to practice beginning and ending the phone call.**
   b. **During the call:**
      i. **Teens should *trade information* on this phone call.**
      ii. ***Find a common interest* to report back to the group.**

       iii. **Follow the rules for beginning and ending a phone call, including using *cover stories*.**

  c. **After the call:**

     i. **Parents and teens should discuss the phone call and identify:**

       1. ***Common interests***

       2. ***Cover stories***

       3. **How the phone call began and ended**

     ii. **Parents should help teen troubleshoot any problems that may have arisen.**

3. ***Out-of-Group Call***

  a. **Before the call:**

     i. **Parents arrange with your teen to call someone outside of the group to practice conversational skills.**

     ii. **Choose someone that your teen would like to get to know better.**

     iii. **Negotiate where the parent will be during the call.**

  b. **During the call:**

     i. **Teens should *trade information* on this phone call.**

     ii. **Find a *common interest* to report back to the group.**

     iii. **Follow the rules for a *two-way conversation*.**

     iv. **Use the rules for starting and ending a conversation, including using *cover stories*.**

  c. **After the call:**

     i. **Parents and teens should discuss the call and identify *common interests*.**

     ii. **Parents should help teen troubleshoot any problems that may have arisen.**

4. ***Humor Feedback***

  a. **Teens practice interpreting *humor feedback* with family and friends.**

  b. **Teen should pay attention to *humor feedback*:**

     i. **Teen should notice whether people are *laughing at him or her*, *laughing with him or her*, or not laughing at all.**

     ii. **Teen should discuss *humor feedback* with parent.**

       1. **Teen and parent should decide if teen is a *joke-teller* or a *joke-receiver*.**

5. ***Bring a Personal Item***

  a. **Bring a favorite item to share with the group (e.g., CD, magazine, game, book, pictures).**

  b. **Be prepared to *trade information* about the item one-on-one with someone else in the group.**

Parent Handout 6: Peer Entry I—Entering a Conversation

Steps for Slipping Into a Conversation

1. ***Watch / Listen***
   a. Watch and listen to the conversation before you try to join:
      i. You need to know what they are talking about before you join.
      ii. You need to know whether you have something to contribute to the conversation.
      iii. If you try to join a conversation without knowing what the people are talking about, you will only interrupt the conversation.
   b. Watch to see if you know one of the people:
      i. Joining a conversation is easier if you know at least one of the people.
      ii. They are more likely to accept you into the conversation.
   c. Move closer (not *too* close) to watch the activity/conversation to find out if you want to join.
   d. Listen to make sure they are talking nicely:
      i. If they are not being nice to each other, try a different group.
   e. Listen to make sure they are not talking above your head (i.e., too sophisticated).
   f. Find a ***common interest*** from the conversation.
   g. Show interest in the group:
      i. Laugh or smile faintly and when relevant.
      ii. Shake head when agreeing.
   h. Try to make *periodic* eye contact:
      i. Do not stare—that would seem like eavesdropping.
2. ***Wait***
   a. Wait for one of three things:
      i. Wait for a brief pause or break in the conversation.
      ii. If there is not a pause, wait for the right time (e.g., a transitional moment), where you are not interrupting too much.
      iii. Wait for some sign of receptiveness from the group (e.g., they look over at you and smile).
3. ***Join***
   a. Have a reason for joining the conversation (e.g., contributing to it).
   b. Move closer (arm's length away), but not too close.
   c. Make a comment, ask a question, or bring over an item that is related to the conversation.
   d. ***Do not get too personal***.
   e. Assess receptiveness of the person or group:
      i. Are they making eye contact with you?
      ii. Are comments being directed to you from the group?

    iii. Are group members turned more toward you (i.e., they **open the circle**)?

  f. Use gaze aversion (this protects you against possible rejection):

    i. Do not stare.

    ii. Look at the group occasionally; look away the rest of the time.

  g. **Do not be a conversation hog**—you should listen more than you talk at first.

  h. If they ignore you or do not want you to join in the conversation—**move on**.

Homework Assignments

1. Teens should practice **slipping into a conversation** between at least two teens they feel comfortable with.

  a. Before **slipping in**:

    i. Think of a place where the teen is likely to be accepted (i.e., low-risk place) and does not have a bad reputation.

    ii. Parent and teen may want to rehearse the steps for **slipping into a conversation** prior to the attempt.

  b. During **slipping in**:

    i. Follow the steps for **slipping into a conversation**.

  c. After **slipping in**:

    i. Parents and teens should discuss how the teen **slipped into the conversation**.

    ii. Parents should help teen troubleshoot any problems that may have arisen.

2. **In-Group Call**

  a. Before the call:

    i. Before you leave the group, parents should arrange for their teen to call another member of the group to practice conversational skills.

    ii. Set up a day and time to make the call.

    iii. Negotiate where the parent will be during the call and what the parent role will be.

    iv. Parent and teen may need to practice beginning and ending the phone call.

  b. During the call:

    i. Teens should **trade information** on this phone call.

    ii. **Find a common interest** to report back to the group.

    iii. Follow the rules for beginning and ending a phone call, including using **cover stories**.

  c. After the call:

    i. Parents and teens should discuss the phone call and identify:

      1. **Common interests**

      2. **Cover stories**

3. How the phone call began and ended

 ii. Parents should help teen troubleshoot any problems that may have arisen.

3. ***Out-of-Group Call***

 a. **Before the call:**

  i. **Parents arrange with your teen to call someone outside of the group to practice conversational skills.**

  ii. **Choose someone that your teen would like to get to know better.**

  iii. **Negotiate where the parent will be during the call.**

 b. **During the call:**

  i. **Teens should *trade information* on this phone call.**

  ii. **Find a *common interest* to report back to the group.**

  iii. **Follow the rules for a *two-way conversation*.**

  iv. **Use the rules for starting and ending a conversation, including using *cover stories*.**

 c. **After the call:**

  i. **Parents and teens should discuss the call and identify *common interests*.**

  ii. **Parents should help teen troubleshoot any problems that may have arisen.**

4. ***Humor Feedback***

 a. Teens practice interpreting ***humor feedback*** with family and friends.

 b. Teen should pay attention to ***humor feedback***:

  i. Teen should notice whether people are ***laughing at him or her***, ***laughing with him or her***, or not laughing at all.

  ii. Teen should discuss ***humor feedback*** with parent.

   1. Teen and parent should decide if teen is a ***joke-teller*** or a ***joke-receiver***.

5. ***Bring a Personal Item***

 a. Bring a favorite item to share with the group (e.g., CD, magazine, game, book, pictures).

 b. Be prepared to ***trade information*** about the item one-on-one with someone else in the group.

Teen Therapist Guide—Session 6: Peer Entry I—Entering a Conversation

Guiding Principles of the Teen Session

This is a pivotal session for teens in that they are now being taught skills to help them approach new potential friends. Until this point, teens have been working on improving their communication skills and identifying appropriate friends. They should now have the prerequisite skills for developing new friendships.

Teens will be taught the basic steps of peer entry (that is, how to slip into conversations with peers). When teaching peer entry, it is helpful to break down this complex social behavior into discrete steps. Teens will find it easier to understand when they are taught the three main steps of slipping into a conversation: watch/listen, wait, and join.

A critical aspect of success with peer entry skills will be identifying the appropriate crowd or group with which to slip into conversation. This point cannot be understated and will likely be the most common error the teens will make. If teens choose to slip into conversation with peers who are likely to reject them (the wrong crowd or places where they have a negative reputation), this will only serve to make the teen feel defeated and may increase his or her social anxiety and avoidant behavior. Group leaders and parents will need to be very specific with teens in having them identify which crowd or group they plan to enter conversation with. If there are serious questions about whether the teen will be accepted by this group, it may be advisable to have the teen choose a different crowd or group for the time being that is less likely to reject them.

Rule Review

Note: Only go over session rules again if the teens are having difficulty following them.

- ■ Have teens identify the rules for the group.
- ■ Give them points for remembering:
  1. Listen to the other group members (no talking when others are speaking)
  2. Follow directions
  3. Raise your hand
  4. Be respectful (no teasing or making fun of others)
  5. No touching (no hitting, kicking, pushing, hugging, etc.)

Homework Review

Note: Give points for homework *parts*—not just one point per assignment.

1. ***Bring a Personal Item***
   a. Briefly identify the favorite item the teen brought to share with the group (e.g., CD, magazine, game, book, pictures).
   b. Only give credit for appropriate items.
   c. To avoid distractions, have a coach put the item away until the teen session activity.

2. ***Humor Feedback***
   a. Say: *Last week we talked about appropriate use of humor. One of your assignments this week was to pay attention to your humor feedback. Raise your hand if you paid attention to your humor feedback this week.*
      i. Briefly ask:
         1. *Did you try to tell a joke this week?* (this was not an assignment)
         2. If yes: *Did it seem like the people were laughing at you or laughing with you?*
         3. *How could you tell?*
         4. *Do you think you're more of a joke-teller or a joke-receiver?*
            a. Praise those who claim to be ***joke-receivers***.
            b. Any teen claiming to be a ***joke-teller*** should be asked to support this claim by describing his or her ***humor feedback*** and providing details about how people tend to laugh with them, rather than laugh at them.
      ii. Remind them that it is very difficult to be a ***joke-teller*** and you expect them to pay very close attention to their ***humor feedback***.

3. ***Out-of-Group Call***
   a. Say: *You also had an assignment to trade information on a phone call with someone not in PEERS this week. Raise your hand if you did the out-of-group call.*
      i. Begin by calling on the teens who completed the call.
      ii. Ask:
         1. *Who did you talk to?*
         2. *How did the conversation begin?*
         3. *Did you trade information?*
         4. *Did you find a common interest?*
            a. When they identify common interests, ask: *What could you do with that information if you were ever to hang out?*
         5. *How did the conversation end?*
      iii. Avoid general questions like: *How did it go?*
   b. Troubleshoot any problems that may have arisen.
      i. If the teen gives an incorrect response, ask: *What could you say differently next time?* or *How do you think you should have ended the call?*
   c. If you have time, check in with teens who did not complete the assignment and troubleshoot how they might get it done this week.

4. ***In-Group Call***
   a. Say: *Another assignment this week was to trade information on a phone call with another member of our group. Raise your hand if you did the in-group call.*
      i. Begin by calling on the teens who completed the call.
      ii. Briefly ask:
         1. *Who did you talk to?*
         2. *Who called who?*
         3. *Did you trade information?*
         4. *Did you find a common interest?*
            a. When they identify ***common interests***, ask: *What could you do with that information if you were ever to hang out?*
      iii. Avoid general questions like "How did it go?"
      iv. Do not allow teens to talk about mistakes the other person made.
      v. Have the other person who participated in the call give his or her account immediately after, but not at the same time.
   b. Troubleshoot any problems that may have arisen.
      i. If the teen gives an incorrect response, ask: *What could you say differently next time?* or *How do you think you should have ended the call?*

5. ***Sources of Friends***
   a. Say: *A couple of weeks ago we talked about the different groups or crowds at school and where you might best fit in. One of your assignments this week was to trade information with someone from one of these groups. Raise your hand if you traded information with someone from an appropriate group.*
      i. Briefly ask:
         1. *Which groups did you identify that you might fit in with?*
         2. *Did you trade information with someone from one of those groups?*
         3. *Which group did you choose?*
         4. *Did you find a common interest?*
   b. Say: *Another assignment was that you and your parents were supposed to identify an extracurricular activity for you to join where you might meet other teens with common interests and then begin to enroll in those activities. Raise your hand if you found an extracurricular activity.*
      i. Briefly ask:
         1. *Which extracurricular activity did you choose?*
         2. *Did you enroll in the activity?*
         3. *Are there other teens your age in the group?*
         4. *Does this seem like a good place for you to make potential new friends?*

Didactic Lesson: Slipping Into Conversations

Good Times and Places to Make Friends

- ■ Explain: *Two weeks ago we talked about the different groups or crowds of kids at school and which group you might best fit in with. Now that we've figured out which group you might best fit in with, we need to think about* **when** *and* **where** *to make new friends. There are good times and bad times to make friends and there are good places and bad places to make friends.*
- ■ Go around the room and have the teens come up with **good** places and times to make friends.
  - Ask: *What are some good places or times to make friends?* (See the table below.)
  - Make suggestions and troubleshoot as necessary.
- ■ Go around the room and have the teens come up with **bad** places and times to make friends.
  - Ask: *What are some bad places or times to make friends?* (See the table below.)
- ■ Make suggestions and troubleshoot as necessary.

Good Places / Times to Make Friends	*Bad Places / Times to Make Friends*
Before or after school	In detention
Between classes	In the principal's office
During lunch	Juvenile detention
After-school activities	When people are standing around watching a fight
School bus	In class when the teacher is talking
Sports activities/teams	In the bathroom
Recreational centers	In the middle of playing a sporting game (people are focused on playing the game)
Community pool	During study hall
Public library activities	During quiet time
With a mutual friend	During a religious sermon
Youth groups	Street corner
Clubs	
Boy Scouts/Girl Scouts	
YMCA/YWCA	

Good Choices for Friends

- Explain: *Now that we have identified some good times and places to make friends, let's think about who you should be trying to make friends with and where we might find these teens. We've talked about the different groups of teens you might fit in with. Let's go around the room and have each person identify which group they think they might fit in with and how you could identify the kids in these groups.*
- Go around the room and have teens identify:
  - The groups they might best fit in with.
  - Where they might find the kids from the group they are likely to fit in with.
    - Example: Computer geeks may be in the computer lab at school.
  - How they can identify the kids from the group they might fit in with.
    - Example: Gamers might be playing video games; might wear gamer T-shirts.
- Make suggestions and troubleshoot as necessary.

Steps for Slipping Into a Conversation

- Explain: *Now that we have some ideas about **where** we might find teens that we fit in with, we need to talk about **how** to get to know these teens better. One way you can meet **new** friends is by joining the conversations of teens that you are trying to get to know better. We call this "slipping into a conversation." It's called "slipping in" because it should be done slowly and casually, with very little disruption to the people whose conversation you're joining. Once you slip into a conversation, you can begin to trade information and find common interests.*
- Make it clear that these are **not** the steps for slipping into a group of teens you know well.
  - With friends we know well we can just walk up and say hello.
  - These are the steps for slipping into a group of teens you are trying to get to know better.
  - These steps should mainly be used for entering conversations where the teen knows at least one person or knows members of the group somewhat.
    - Exception: If the teen is on vacation or at a gathering where no one knows one another, then they can try these steps.
- Present the steps for slipping into a conversation.
1. ***Watch / Listen***
   a. Watch and listen to the conversation before you try to join.
      i. Say: *The first step for slipping into a conversation is to watch and listen to the conversation. What do you think we're watching and listening for?*
         1. Answer: You need to know what they're talking about before you join; you need to know whether you have something to contribute

to the conversation; if you try to join a conversation without knowing what the people are talking about, you will only interrupt the conversation.

b. Watch to see if you know one of the people.
    i. Say: *You also need to watch and make sure that you know at least one of the people in the conversation. Why is that important to do?*
        1. Answer: Joining a conversation is easier if you know at least one of the people; they are more likely to accept you into the conversation.

c. Move closer to watch the activity/conversation to find out if you want to join.
    i. Say: *In order to watch and listen, you'll need to move a bit closer to hear what they're saying. It's important not to get too close though. Why would it be a bad idea to move too close to the group before joining?*
        1. Answer: Because they'll think you're eavesdropping (you actually are); they may think you're weird; they will be less likely to accept you into the conversation.

d. Listen to make sure they're talking nicely.
    i. Say: *You'll also want to listen to make sure they're talking nicely to each other. Why is that important to do?*
        1. Answer: If they are not being nice to each other, then they're not likely to be nice to you.
    ii. Explain: *You should avoid conversations where teens are teasing or making fun of each other. Instead, try a different group.*

e. Listen to make sure they are not talking above your head (i.e., too sophisticated).
    i. Say: *We also need to listen to make sure they're not talking about things we don't understand. Why is that important to do?*
        1. Answer: Because you cannot contribute to the conversation if you do not understand what they are talking about; you will only slow the conversation down by asking questions; you will be interrupting the natural flow of the conversation.

f. **Find a common interest** from the conversation.
    i. Say: *The best conversations to join are those where we share a common interest. Why would it be good to join conversation where we have a common interest?*
        1. Answer: Because it is easier to talk about things you understand and like; if we are trying to make friends with new people it helps to have things in common; friendships are based on common interests.

g. Show interest in the group.
    i. Say: *While you're watching and listening to the conversation, if the group notices you it can be good to show that you're interested in what they're saying. You might laugh or smile faintly when it's relevant, or*

shake your head when agreeing. Why would it be good to show interest in the group?

    1. Answer: Because you are establishing your interest in what they are talking about; you are showing agreement with what they are saying; they are more likely to accept you into the conversation.

h. Try to make *periodic* eye contact.

    i. Say: *It's also a good idea to make occasional eye contact with the group. But you **don't** want to **stare**! That would seem like eavesdropping and they would be less likely to accept you into the conversation. Instead, you can look over at the group once in a while. Why would that be a good idea?*

        1. Answer: Because it shows that you are interested in them and what they are talking about.

2. **Wait**

a. Say: *The next step for slipping into a conversation between people we only know so-so is to wait. What do you think we're waiting for?*

    i. Answer: We're waiting for one of three things.

        1. Wait for a brief pause or break in the conversation.

        2. If there is not a pause, wait for the right time (e.g., a transitional moment), where you are not interrupting too much.

        3. Wait for some sign of receptiveness from the group (e.g., they look over at you and smile).

b. Ask: *Is there ever a perfect pause?*

    i. Answer: Very rarely.

c. Say: *You just need to try not to interrupt the conversation too much. The best time to join is usually when someone has just finished speaking. If the group notices you before this and they seem interested in you, then that would also be a good time to join.*

3. **Join**

a. Say: *The final step for slipping into a conversation between people we only know so-so is to actually join the conversation.*

b. Have a reason for joining the conversation (e.g., contributing to it).

    i. Say: *But it's important that we have a reason for joining the conversation. We shouldn't try to join a conversation where we have nothing to contribute. Why is it important to have something to contribute to the conversation?*

        1. Answer: It makes it easier to join; if you do not have anything to contribute then you are only interrupting the conversation and slowing it down.

c. Move closer (about an arm's length away), but not *too* close.

    i. Say: *Just before we join the conversation, it's important to move closer. An arm's length away is usually about right. But you should be careful not to get too close. Why would it be a bad idea to get too close?*

1. Answer: You would be invading their space; they might think you're weird.
    ii. Demonstrate an arm's length away.
    iii. Remind the teens not to measure the space before joining (you can make a joke of this).
d. Join by ***making a comment*** or ***asking a question*** or bringing over an item that is related to the conversation—and ***stay on topic***.
    i. Say: *The next part is to join by making a comment or asking a question that shows that you know what they're talking about. You can also bring over an item that's relevant to the conversation. The important thing is to stay on topic! Why is it so important to stay on topic?*
       1. Answer: Because otherwise you are interrupting the conversation and changing the subject; they will be less willing to accept you in the conversation.
e. ***Do not get too personal***
    i. Say: *Once we've joined the conversation it will be important not to get too personal. Why is it important not to get too personal?*
       1. Answer: Because if you get too personal, you may make them feel uncomfortable and they will not want to talk to you.
f. ***Do not be a conversation hog***
    i. Say: *Once we've joined the conversation it will also be important not to be a conversation hog. This means we should actually talk less and listen more when we're first joining a conversation. It's like we're the visitor in their conversation. Why would it be a bad idea to be a conversation hog?*
       1. Answer: Because you would be interrupting the flow of their conversation; you would be making the conversation about you instead of about what they were talking about.

Note: Only present ***gaze aversion*** to high-functioning teens who you suspect will be able to master the skill. If presented to certain teens, they may appear "shifty" and awkward.

g. Use ***gaze aversion*** (this protects you against possible rejection).
    i. [***Gaze aversion*** is a method of establishing interest in a group, while protecting yourself from possible rejection by not completely focusing your attention on the group. ***Gaze aversion*** is often naturally used when someone is attempting to join a conversation, but has not been completely accepted by the group. The person attempting peer entry makes periodic eye contact with the group, but also casually looks around away from the group, thereby dividing his or her attention and not making the group members or themselves uncomfortable.]
    ii. Say: *One way we can protect ourselves from possible rejection when we're slipping into conversations is to use what we call gaze aversion. This involves looking at the people we are talking to occasionally, but*

not completely focusing on them. Instead, we might look around the room occasionally, showing that our interest is not fully captured yet.

   iii. Demonstrate ***gaze aversion***:
     1. Do not stare.
     2. Look at the group occasionally; look away the rest of the time.
   iv. Demonstrate looking "shifty":
     1. Show how this is different than gaze aversion.
     2. [The difficulty with ***gaze aversion*** is in not appearing "shifty" with one's fleeting eye contact. This skill may be even more difficult for socially awkward teens. In that case, its use should be avoided.]

  h. Assess receptiveness of the group.
   i. Say: *Finally, we will want to pay attention to whether or not we're accepted into the conversation. How can you tell if you're accepted into a conversation?*
     1. Answer:
       a. The group makes eye contact with you.
       b. The group directs comments or questions to you.
       c. Group members turn more toward you; they ***open the circle***.
         i. [When people converse in small groups, they tend to form a circle. When you are accepted into a conversation, the group ***opens the circle***, thereby allowing you space to join. When you are not accepted into a conversation, the group tends to ***close the circle***, or turn their backs to you, thereby pushing you out of the conversation.]
   iii. Say: *If the group ignores you or closes the circle on you, should you keep talking and try to force them to talk to you?*
     1. Answer: No.
   iv. Say: *Instead, you should just move on. Try to find another conversation to join with a different group of people, but don't give up trying to slip in.*

Role Play

■ Have the teen group leader demonstrate an ***inappropriate*** role play with two coaches in which the teen group leader attempts to ***inappropriately slip into a conversation***.
  – Begin by saying: *Now we're going to do a little role play where I will try to slip into a conversation. Watch this and then tell me what I'm doing wrong.*
  – Demonstrate barging into a conversation between two coaches without watching or listening first, asking them what they are talking about, and then completely changing the topic.
  – [Note: If there is only one coach, you can select the highest functioning teen in the group and ask him or her to assist with the role play. Be sure

to give the teen an overview of what you plan to do before the role play demonstration. This is best done before the teen session begins. The teen will often feel flattered to be included in the exercise. When using teens, it is best to let them naturally trade information with the coach, rather than trying to provide them with a script.]

■ Example of an *inappropriate* role play:

Teen group leader: (standing several feet from the two coaches)

Coach 1: "Hi (insert name). How was your weekend?"

Coach 2: "It was good. How was yours?"

Coach 1: "It was pretty good. What did you do?"

Coach 2: "Oh, I did a little homework and watched some movies."

Coach 1: "Yeah, what movies did you watch?"

Coach 2: "I watched a couple of (insert comedic actor's name) movies. Have you ever seen any of his movies?"

Coach 1: "Sure. I love his movies. They're so funny…"

Teen group leader: (Walks over abruptly, stands too close) "Hey guys. What are you talking about?"

Coach 1: (startled) "We were talking about our weekends. (Turning away from the group leader, closing the circle) So anyway, you were saying that you watched some movies…"

Teen group leader: (interrupts) "So I had a good weekend. I went to that new water park. Have you guys been there?"

Coach 2: (looking annoyed) "Umm…no. (Turning away from the group leader, closing the circle) So, yeah, I watched some movies and did a little homework. What did you do?"

Coach 1: "Oh, I went to the mall with a couple of friends…"

Teen group leader: (interrupts) "So you guys should go to this new water park. It's really cool!"

Coaches 1 and 2: (looking annoyed, ignoring comments)

– End by saying: *Okay, so time out on that. So what did I do **wrong** in trying to slip into that conversation?*

  • Answer: Teen group leader did not follow the rules: watch/listen, wait, join.

– Ask: *Did it seem like they wanted to talk to me?*

  • Answer: No.

– Ask: *How could you tell?*

  • Answer: They closed the circle; ignored comments; looked annoyed.

– Ask: *What should I have done when I realized they didn't want to talk to me?*

  • Answer: Do not try to force them to talk; **move on**.

■ The teen group leader should then demonstrate an *appropriate* role play with two coaches (or a coach and a teen) in which the teen group leader *appropriately* **slips into a conversation**.

– Say: *Now let's try this again, and this time I will follow the steps for slipping in. Watch this and then tell me what I'm doing* **right**.

– Demonstrate following the steps for **_slipping in_**: watch/listen, wait, join.

– Example of an **_appropriate_** role play:

Teen group leader: (standing several feet from the two coaches)

Coach 1: "Hi (insert name). How was your weekend?"

Coach 2: "It was good. How was yours?"

Coach 1: "It was pretty good. What did you do?"

Coach 2: "Oh, I did a little homework and watched some movies."

Teen group leader: (looking over at the coaches periodically)

Coach 1: "Yeah, what movies did you watch?"

Coach 2: "I watched a couple of (insert comedic actor's name) movies. Have you ever seen any of his movies?"

Coach 1: "Sure. I love his movies. They're so funny! Do you like comedies?"

Teen group leader: (walks a little closer, making periodic eye contact)

Coach 2: "Yeah. I love comedies! What about you?"

Coach 1: "Sure. Those are my favorite kinds of movies!"

Coach 2: "So have you seen (insert name of current comedic movie) then?"

Coach 1: "Yeah! I just saw it!"

Coach 2: "Me too. It was great!"

Teen group leader: (waits for a brief pause) "So you guys saw (insert name of the movie mentioned) too?"

Coaches 1 and 2: (looking over, opening the circle) "Yeah. Did you see it?"

Teen group leader: "Yeah. It was so funny! I love (insert actor's name) movies!"

Coach 2: "Me too! I never get tired of watching them. (looking at the teen group leader) Which one is your favorite?"

– End by saying: *Okay, so time out on that. So what did I do right in trying to slip into that conversation?*

  • Answer: Teen group leader followed the rules: watch/listen, wait, join.

– Ask: *Did it seem like they wanted to talk to me?*

  • Answer: Yes.

– Ask: *How could you tell?*

  • Answer: They opened the circle; answered the question; made good eye contact; asked the teen group leader questions.

Homework Assignments

■ Briefly explain the homework for the week by saying: *This week we're going to have each of you practice slipping into conversation with people you only know so-so, but would like to get to know better. Ideally, these should be people from the group you identified where you think you might fit in. We are also going to have you continue to practice your conversational skills this week by making phone calls. So, your homework assignment this week is to:*

- *Slip into a conversation following the steps we have outlined.*
- *Have an in-group phone call with another group member:*
  - *This should be at least 5 to 10 minutes.*
  - *Use the steps for beginning and ending phone calls.*
  - *You will need to trade information and find a common interest to report to the group.*
- *Make an out-of-group phone call to someone not in PEERS:*
  - *This should be at least 5 to 10 minutes.*
  - *Pick a friend that you would be comfortable trading information with.*
  - *Find a common interest to report to the group.*
- *Bring some personal item to trade information about next week (e.g., CD, magazine, game, book, pictures).*
- *Pay attention to your humor feedback if you tell any jokes this week:*
  - *Notice if people are laughing at you or laugh with you.*
  - *Decide if you're more of a joke-teller or a joke-receiver.*

■ Group leader and coaches should assign the in-group calls for the week and write this on the "In-Group Phone Call Assignment Log" for future reference.
  - If there are an uneven number of teens, assign someone "double duty."
    - This person will have two in-group phone calls (one as a caller and the other as a receiver).
  - This person will receive extra points for completing the extra call.

Teen Activity: Slipping Into Conversations

Note: See the "Teen Activity Guide" for rules.

■ Teens break up into small groups (no less than three teens) and **trade information** about their personal items.
■ Have a selection of magazines for teens who did not bring items to share.
■ Girls should be paired with girls, and boys should be paired with boys when possible.
■ Notify teens that they will be practicing **slipping into a conversation** while **trading information** about their personal items.
■ Have each teen practice **slipping into a conversation** between the other members.
  - Tell the other group member that he or she must allow the person to enter the conversation.
    - Do not allow group members to reject attempts at **slipping in**.
  - Have the teen verbally go over the steps for **slipping in** with the teen group leader or the coach before they make the attempt to join the conversation.
  - The teen group leader and coach should provide immediate performance feedback after the **slipping in** attempt:
    - Give the teen praise for what they did correctly.
    - **Offer suggestions** for doing something differently when necessary.

- Have the teens redo any inappropriate attempts to *slip in*.
- The teen group leader will want to take special notice of "shiftiness" among group members practicing *gaze aversion* and provide performance feedback appropriately.
  - For some teens, the skill of *gaze aversion* may be overly challenging, in which case the teen may be better off focusing on the other substeps within peer entry and limiting their use of *gaze aversion*.
- Each teen should practice *slipping in* at least once during the session.
- Teens will receive points for these practice attempts.
- Encourage teens to applaud for one another after each attempt is complete.
- Teens who refuse or are reluctant to practice this skill are likely to be experiencing significant social anxiety, and perhaps even phobic avoidance.
  - Socially anxious teens with autism spectrum disorders often experience significant anxiety around this lesson. In such cases, it may be helpful to have teens practice just the first step of peer entry (i.e., watch/listen), while establishing proximity and interest in the group.
  - In subsequent sessions, the teen may be encouraged to add additional steps as he or she feels more comfortable.

Reunification With Parents

- Announce that teens should join their parents:
  - Be sure that the teens are standing or sitting next to their parents.
  - Be sure to have silence and the full attention of the group.
- Say: *Today we worked on slipping into a conversation. Who can tell us what the steps for slipping into a conversation are?* [Have teens generate all of the steps. Be prepared to give prompts if necessary.]

Watch

- Watch and listen to the conversation before you try to join.
- Watch to see if you know one of the people.
- Move closer to watch the activity/conversation to find out if you want to join.
- Listen to make sure they are talking nicely.
- Listen to make sure they are not talking above your head (i.e., too sophisticated).
- *Find a common interest* from the conversation.
- Show interest in the group.
- Try to make *periodic* eye contact.

Wait

- Wait for the right time (e.g., a pause or a break in the conversation).
- If there is not a perfect pause, just try not to interrupt too much.
- Wait for some sign of receptiveness before completely joining.

Join

- Have a reason for joining the conversation (e.g., contributing to it).
- Move closer.
- ***Make a comment***, ***ask a question***, or bring over an item that is related to the conversation and stay on topic.
- ***Do not get too personal***.
- ***Do not be a conversation hog***—you should listen more than you talk at first.
- Use ***gaze aversion*** [if appropriate for these teens].
- Assess receptiveness of the person or group.

- If they ignore you or do not want you to join in the conversation—***move on***.
- Say: *Today we practiced slipping into conversation and this group did a great job of trading information. Let's give them a round of applause.*
- Go over the homework for the next week (see below):
  - Be sure to read off the in-group call assignment in front of parents.
  - Remind parents to make a note of who is calling whom.
  - Announce that this will be the last in-group phone assignment.
- Individually and separately negotiate with each family:
  - Where the teens will attempt to slip in and with which peer group.
  - Who the teen will call for the out-of-group phone call.
  - What personal item will be brought next week.

Homework Assignments

1. Practice ***slipping into a conversation*** between at least two teens you feel comfortable with.
   a. Before ***slipping in***:
      i. Think of a place where you are likely to be accepted (i.e., low-risk place) and you do not have a bad reputation.
      ii. Parent and teen may want to rehearse the steps for ***slipping into a conversation*** prior to the attempt.
   b. During ***slipping in***:
      i. Follow the steps for slipping into a conversation.
   c. After ***slipping in***:
      i. Parents and teens should discuss how the teen ***slipped into the conversation***.
      ii. Parents should help teen troubleshoot any problems that may have arisen.
   d. [For teens who are particularly socially anxious and reluctant to complete this assignment, it may be helpful to have teens practice just the first step of peer entry (i.e., watch/listen), while establishing proximity and interest in the group. In subsequent sessions, the teen may be encouraged to add additional steps as he or she feels more comfortable.]

2. ***In-Group Call***
   a. Before the call:
      i. Before you leave the group, parents should arrange for their teen to call another member of the group to practice conversational skills.
      ii. Sct up a day and time to make the call.
      iii. Negotiate where the parent will be during the call and what the parent role will be.
      iv. Parent and teen may need to practice beginning and ending the phone call.
   b. During the call:
      i. Teens should ***trade information*** on this phone call.
      ii. ***Find a common interest*** to report back to the group.
      iii. Follow the rules for beginning and ending a phone call—including using ***cover stories***.
   c. After the call:
      i. Parents and teens should discuss the phone call and identify:
         1. ***Common interests***
         2. ***Cover stories***
         3. How the phone call began and ended
      ii. Parents should help the teen troubleshoot any problems that may have arisen.

3. ***Out-of-Group Call***
   a. Before the call:
      i. Parents arrange with their teen to call someone outside of the group to practice conversational skills.
      ii. Choose someone that the teen would like to get to know better.
      iii. Negotiate where the parent will be during the call.
   b. During the call:
      i. Teens should ***trade information*** on this phone call.
      ii. Find a ***common interest*** to report back to the group.
      iii. Follow the rules for a ***two-way conversation***.
      iv. Use the rules for starting and ending a conversation—including using ***cover stories***.
   c. After the call:
      i. Parents and teens should discuss the call and identify ***common interests***.
      ii. Parents should help teen troubleshoot any problems that may have arisen.

4. ***Humor Feedback***
   a. Teens practice interpreting ***humor feedback*** with family and friends.
   b. Teen should pay attention to ***humor feedback***.
      i. Teen should notice whether people are ***laughing at you***, ***laughing with you***, or not laughing at all.
      ii. Teen should discuss ***humor feedback*** with parent.

      1. Teen and parent should decide if teen is a ***joke-teller*** or a ***joke-receiver***.

5. ***Bring a Personal Item***

    a. Bring a favorite item to share with the group (e.g., CD, magazine, game, book, pictures).

    b. Be prepared to ***trade information*** about the item one-on-one with someone else in the group.

Calculate Points

Keep track of the following for each week of the intervention.

- Calculate the number of points earned by each teen.
- Add up the total number of points earned by the group.
- Do not calculate the points in the presence of the teens.
  - Do not disclose the individual or group total of points.
  - Discourage attempts to compare number of points earned between teens.
- Remind them that they are working as a team to earn a bigger and better graduation party.

Teen Activity Guide: Session 6

"Slipping Into Conversations"

Materials Needed

- Teens bring personal items
- CD players and headphones for music (optional)
- In the event that a teen forgets to bring a personal item, have magazines available to share:
  - Computer magazines
  - Anime magazines
  - Teen magazines
  - Sports magazines

Rules

- Break teens up into small groups (no less than three teens per group).
  - Match girls with girls and boys with boys, whenever possible.
- Have teens practice ***trading information*** about their personal items while taking turns ***slipping into conversations***.
- Encourage teens to identify ***common interests*** through ***trading information***.

■ Prompt teens to ask questions when appropriate.
■ For teens practicing **slipping into conversations**:
  – Group leader and coaches should separate the teen from the group and have him or her identify the steps for **slipping in** (they may need to look at the board at first).
  – Then have the teen practice using these steps by **slipping into conversations** with their peers in which the others will be **trading information** about their personal items.
  – Remind the other teens that they should accept everyone into these conversations.
  – Teens may need you to provide prompting for specific steps, such as:
    • *What was the first step for slipping in? Do you know what they're talking about? Do you know anything about that subject? If you have something to contribute to the conversation, then you may want to try joining.*
    • *What is the second step for slipping in? What are you waiting for* [answer: a pause]? *If there's not a good pause, you may need to just go ahead and join by trying not to interrupt too much.*
    • *What is the last step for slipping in? How do you join? You could ask a question or make a comment about what they are saying. Be sure to stay on topic.*
■ In the event that a teen incorrectly attempts to **slip in**, call a "time-out" and use this teachable moment to gently point out the error, while providing feedback on how to more appropriately attempt to **slip in**.
  – Have the teen try again until he or she is successful.
■ Once the teen has successfully **slipped in**, call a "time-out" and have the other teens applaud.
  – Teen group leader should briefly point out the steps that the teen followed for **slipping in**.
■ Rotate teens after each has successfully **slipped in** (each teen should practice at least once).
■ Give points for following the steps for **slipping in**.

Chapter 9

Session 7
Peer Entry II—Exiting a Conversation

Parent Session Therapist Guide

Guiding Principles of the Parent Session

The parent group leader should review the out-of-group call first. This is because the parent was present for this assignment, presumably, unlike the slipping-in assignment, and can report on what happened. As usual, ask for successful homework completion first. Next, review the slipping-in homework assignment with parents by first introducing the steps for slipping in, as a nice review. Briefly summarize slipping-in successes before helping parents whose teens were not successful.

The didactic lesson for this session helps teens recover from an unsuccessful entry into a conversation. Sometimes teens with autism spectrum disorders (ASD) are puzzled when they try to enter a conversation and their entry attempt does not go as planned (or as they were taught) because they were turned down. Although this could happen to anyone, for a socially awkward teen (especially those with autism spectrum disorders), it adds to their confusion when peers do not respond as expected. This session teaches teens important social cues to which they should attend in order to determine if they were accepted into the conversation. It also teaches them how to extricate themselves if they were not accepted in a way that minimizes the negative social impact of their unsuccessful entry attempt. Unfortunately, peer exit strategies can only be taught after the teens are taught how to slip into conversations. If the teen has confined his or her entry attempt to just watching and listening to the conversation, it is relatively easy for the teen to extricate himself or herself when the group is not receptive to the teen's entry. It is only after the teen has begun to contribute to the conversation and has been turned down, that knowing how to slip out is more complicated.

Hopefully, most or all of the teens have attempted to slip into a conversation as part of the previous homework assignment. If they followed the instructions from this assignment, they would have attempted to enter a group that is likely to be receptive and accepting of their peer entry attempt, making it less likely that they will need to utilize peer exit strategies.

Homework Review

1. ***Out-of-Group Call***
   a. Make sure teen ***traded information*** on this phone call.
   b. Have parents identify:
      i. A ***common interest*** discovered through ***trading information*** on the call.
      ii. The ***cover stories*** their teen used on the phone call.
      iii. How their teen began and ended the phone call.
   c. Troubleshoot any problems that may have arisen:
      i. If parents report homework difficulty, ask: *Has anyone else had a similar problem? How did you handle it?*
      ii. Allow the other parents to provide suggestions before having the group leader give advice on handling the problem.
2. ***Slipping Into a Conversation***
   a. Say: *Last week we went over the steps for slipping into conversations with people we know only so-so. These steps included watching and listening to the conversation, then waiting for a pause, and then joining the conversation by making a comment or asking a question that was on topic. One of your teen's assignments this week was to practice slipping into a conversation with a group they were likely to be accepted by. Raise your hand if your teen was successful slipping into a conversation this week.*
   b. Begin by calling on parents whose teens completed the assignment.
   c. Have parents identify:
      i. Where their teen ***slipped in***.
      ii. If the teen was familiar with someone in the group.
      iii. If the teen followed the steps for ***slipping into a conversation***.
   d. Troubleshoot any problems that may have arisen.
3. ***Humor Feedback***
   a. Have parents identify:
      i. Whether teens practiced interpreting their ***humor feedback*** with family and friends.
      ii. Whether teens noticed if people were ***laughing at them***, ***laughing with them***, or not laughing at all.
      iii. Whether the teen decided if he or she was more of a ***joke-teller*** or a ***joke-receiver***.
4. ***In-Group Call***
   a. [Very brief review—two sentences from each parent.]

   b. Have parents identify:
      i. If the phone call was made.
      ii. A ***common interest*** discovered through ***trading information*** on the call.
   c. Troubleshoot any problems that may have arisen.
5. ***Bring a Personal Item***
   a. Identify the favorite item the teen brought to share with the group (e.g., CD, magazine, game, book, pictures).
   b. Only give credit for appropriate items.

Didactic Lesson: Exiting Conversations

- Distribute the Parent Handout.
- Explain: *Last week the teens learned how to slip into a conversation and they practiced this in the session and during their homework assignment. This week the teens are learning how to slip out of a conversation. Slipping out is what we do when our attempts to enter a conversation fail. The teens will be practicing slipping in and slipping out of conversations in their session today. The teens are also learning that not being welcomed into a conversation is a very common experience and shouldn't been taken too personally. In fact, teens will be informed that approximately 50% of attempts to enter a conversation are unsuccessful. In order for you to help your teen handle unsuccessful slipping-in attempts, it is important for you each to know the rules for slipping out. There are many reasons why teens get turned down when trying to join conversations. It's important for parents to be able to talk to their teens about these interactions and help them understand the reasons why they might have been turned down and what to do differently next time.*
- Go around the room and have parents take turns reading the Parent Handout.
- Sections in **bold print** come directly from the Parent Handout.

Reasons for Being Turned Down	*What to Do Differently Next Time*
They want to talk privately	Try again later
They are talking at a different level	Try a different group
They do not want to make new friends	Try a different group
They are stuck up	Try a different group
They are in a clique	Try a different group
You might have a bad reputation with them	Lay low and try again much later
They did not understand that you were trying to join in	Try again later, following the rules
You violated one of the rules for slipping in	Try again later, following the rules
You got too personal	Try a different group, following the rules

Slipping Out of a Conversation

■ *Check the signs for interest.*
  – **Look for signs they are not interested in having a conversation with you**:
    • Very little eye contact
    • Group members' bodies are turned away from you (they **closed the circle**)
    • Rolling their eyes
    • Sighing at you
    • No positive comments directed at you from anyone in the group
    • Ignoring your comments, questions, entry attempts
    • Verbal aggression directed at you from the group
    • Making fun of what you said
    • Laughing at you (inappropriately)
    • Physical aggression directed at you from the group
  – **If the group does not seem interested in having a conversation with you—then *move on* (see steps below).**
  – **Remember that 50% of attempts to join conversations are not successful**:
    • **Do not take it personally**
    • **Do not give up trying in the future**
  – **If you accept this gracefully then maybe they will let you into the conversation next time.**

1. *Keep your cool.*
2. *Look away*—casually stop eye contact.
3. *Turn away*—casually and slowly turn your body away.
4. *Walk away*—casually and calmly walk away.

If you were initially accepted in the conversation, but then appear to be excluded:

■ **Have a *brief cover story* for leaving before you exit the conversation**:
  – **This is necessary if you have participated in three or more conversational exchanges.**
  – **A *brief cover story* is necessary because you have already joined the conversation and leaving would be abrupt.**
  – ***Cover stories* must be *very brief* and *not specific***:
    • **This is because the group is no longer interested in you and probably does not care where you are going anyway.**
  – **Examples of *cover stories***:
    • ***Well, I have to get to class.***
    • ***Well, gotta go.***
    • ***I'd better go.***

- *Take care.*
- *See you later.*

■ **In this case, you would want to keep your cool, but you would not follow the additional steps of looking away, turning away, and walking away.**

Homework Assignments

■ Explain: *One of the homework assignments for this week is to practice slipping into a conversation where you know at least one of the people so-so and where you do not have a bad reputation.*

■ The parent group leader should go over the homework assignment and troubleshoot any potential problems with parents.

1. **Practice *slipping into a conversation* between at least two teens.**
   a. **Before slipping in:**
      i. **Try to choose a conversation where you know at least one but not all of the people.**
      ii. **Try a place where you are likely to be accepted (i.e., low-risk place) and you do not have a bad reputation. You may need to find a new place.**
      iii. **Parent and teen may want to rehearse the steps for *slipping in*.**
   b. **During *slipping in*:**
      i. **Follow the steps for slipping into a conversation.**
      ii. **If you are not accepted—use the steps for slipping out.**
   c. **After *slipping in*:**
      i. **Parents and teens should discuss how the teen *slipped into the conversation* and *slipped out* (if applicable).**
      ii. **Parents should help teen troubleshoot any problems that may have arisen.**

2. ***Out-of-Group Call***
   a. **Before the call:**
      i. **Parents arrange with their teen to call someone outside of the group to practice conversational skills.**
      ii. **Negotiate where the parent will be during the call.**
   b. **During the call:**
      i. **Teens should *trade information* on this phone call.**
      ii. **Find a *common interest* to report back to the group.**
      iii. **Follow the rules for a *two-way conversation*.**
      iv. **Use the rules for starting and ending a conversation, including using *cover stories*.**
   c. **After the call:**
      i. **Parents and teens should discuss the phone call and identify *common interests*.**

      ii. **Parents should help teen troubleshoot any problems that may have arisen.**

3. ***Bring an Inside Game***

    a. **Bring an inside game to share with the group (e.g., age-appropriate board game, card game, etc.):**

      i. **No solitary games.**

    b. **Do not bring something that you are:**

      i. **Unwilling to share with group members.**

      ii. **Worried about breaking or losing.**

■ Go around the room and have each parent identify potential places where their teen might *slip in* this week where they are likely to be accepted:

  – They may need to choose a new place.

■ Focus particular attention on parents whose teens were turned down in the last *slipping-in* homework assignment:

  – Discuss reasons they may have been turned down.

  – Discuss what they can do differently:

    • Choose peers from crowds that are likely to let them join the conversation.

    • Choose places where they do not have a bad reputation.

Parent Handout 7: Peer Entry II—Exiting a Conversation

Reasons for Being Turned Down	*What to Do Differently Next Time*
They want to talk privately	Try again later
They are talking at a different level	Try a different group
They do not want to make new friends	Try a different group
They are stuck up	Try a different group
They are in a clique	Try a different group
You might have a bad reputation with them	Lay low and try again much later
They did not understand that you were trying to join in	Try again later, following the rules
You violated one of the rules for slipping in	Try again later, following the rules
You got too personal	Try a different group, following the rules

Rules for Slipping Out of a Conversation

- ■ **Check the signs for interest**:
  - – Look for signs they are not interested in having a conversation with you.
  - – If the group does not seem interested in having a conversation with you—then ***move on*** (see steps below).
  - – Remember that 50% of attempts to join conversations are not successful:
    - • Do not take it personally.
    - • Do not give up trying in the future.
  - – If you accept this gracefully then maybe they will let you into the conversation next time.

1. ***Keep your cool***.
2. ***Look away***—casually stop eye contact.
3. ***Turn away***—casually and slowly turn your body away.
4. ***Walk away***—casually and calmly walk away.

If you were initially accepted in the conversation, but then appear to be excluded:
  - – Have a ***brief cover story*** for leaving before you exit the conversation.
    - • This is necessary if you participated in three or more conversational exchanges.
    - • A ***brief cover story*** is necessary because you already joined the conversation and leaving would be abrupt.
    - • ***Cover stories*** must be ***very brief*** and ***not specific***.
    - • This is because the group is no longer interested in you and probably does not care where you are going anyway.
  - – Examples of ***cover stories***:

- *Well, I have to get to class.*
- *Well, gotta go.*
- *I'd better go.*
- *Take care.*
- *See you later.*

- In this case, you would want to **keep your cool**, but you would not follow the additional steps of **looking away**, **turning away**, and **walking away**.

Homework Assignments

1. Practice **slipping into a conversation** between at least two teens.
   a. Before **slipping in**:
      i. Try to choose a conversation where you know at least one but not all of the people.
      ii. Try a place where you are likely to be accepted (i.e., low-risk place) and you do not have a bad reputation. You may need to find a new place.
      iii. Parent and teen may want to rehearse the steps for **slipping in**.
   b. During **slipping in**:
      i. Follow the steps for **slipping into a conversation**.
      ii. If you are not accepted—use the steps for **slipping out**.
   c. After **slipping in**:
      i. Parents and teens should discuss how the teen **slipped into** the conversation and **slipped out** (if applicable).
      ii. Parents should help teens troubleshoot any problems that may have arisen.
2. **Out-of-Group Call**
   a. Before the call:
      i. Parents arrange with their teen to call someone outside of the group to practice conversational skills.
      ii. Negotiate where the parent will be during the call.
   b. During the call:
      i. Teens should **trade information** on this phone call.
      ii. Find a **common interest** to report back to the group.
      iii. Follow the rules for a **two-way conversation**.
      iv. Use the rules for starting and ending a conversation, including using **cover stories**.
   c. After the call:
      i. Parents and teens should discuss the phone call and identify **common interests**.
      ii. Parents should help teen troubleshoot any problems that may have arisen.
3. **Bring an Inside Game**

a. Bring an inside game to share with the group (e.g., age-appropriate board game, card game, etc.):
    i. No solitary games.
b. Do not bring something that you are:
    i. Unwilling to share with group members.
    ii. Worried about breaking or losing.

Teen Therapist Guide—Session 7: Peer Entry II—Exiting a Conversation

Guiding Principles of the Teen Session

This session focuses on how to appropriately handle rejection during peer entry attempts and will be critical for teens struggling with bad reputations. In the previous session, teens were taught to notice the basic signs that a group is not interested in speaking with them (for example, no eye contact, turned away, not speaking to you) and were instructed to "move on" in such cases. This session will equip teens with more concrete strategies for handling peer rejection during conversational entry.

The most common reason for teen peer entry attempts to be turned down is that the teen has a bad reputation among his or her peers or the teen chose the wrong group of peers with whom to slip into a conversation. In the event that the teen has a bad reputation, it will be important to work with the parents on identifying other peer networks. This will involve the parents investigating extra-curricular activities and clubs outside of the school setting in which the teen is not known, and the teen group leader will need to work with the teen on identifying a more accepting peer group to practice peer entry skills with in the following week.

Whatever the cause of the peer entry being turned down, teens will need to be reassured that this is common (even for adults) and that they do not need to take it too personally. It can be very helpful for the group leaders and parents to normalize this experience by telling the teens that even they experience being turned down from entering a conversation. If these efforts are successful in normalizing the experience for the teens, they will be more willing to attempt to enter conversations in the future.

Rule Review

Note: Only go over session rules again if the teens are having difficulty following them.

- ■ Have teens identify the rules for the group.
- ■ Give them points for remembering:
1. Listen to the other group members (no talking when others are speaking)
2. Follow directions
3. Raise your hand
4. Be respectful (no teasing or making fun of others)
5. No touching (no hitting, kicking, pushing, hugging, etc.)

Homework Review

Note: Give points for homework *parts*—not just one point per assignment.

1. ***Bring a Personal Item***
   a. Briefly identify the favorite item the teen brought to share with the group (e.g., CD, magazine, game, book, pictures).
   b. Only give credit for appropriate items.
   c. To avoid distractions, have a coach put the item away until the teen session activity.

2. ***Slipping Into a Conversation***
   a. Say: *Last week we went over the steps for slipping into conversations with people we know only so-so. These steps included watching and listening to the conversation, then waiting for a pause, and then joining the conversation by making a comment or asking a question that was on topic. One of your assignments this week was to practice slipping into a conversation with a group that you were likely to be accepted by. Raise your hand if you practiced slipping into a conversation this week.*
      i. Begin by calling on the teens who completed the assignment.
      ii. Briefly ask:
         1. *Where did you slip in?*
         2. *Which group did you choose to slip in with?*
         3. *Did you know at least one of the people?*
         4. *How did you slip in?*
            a. Be sure they followed the steps for slipping in.
            b. If they did not follow the steps ask: *What could you do differently next time?*
      iii. Troubleshoot any problems that may have arisen.

3. ***Humor Feedback***
   a. Say: *Another one of your assignments this week was to pay attention to your humor feedback. Raise your hand if you paid attention to your humor feedback this week.*
      i. Briefly ask:
         1. *Did you try to tell a joke this week?* (not an assignment)
         2. *If yes: Did it seem like the people were laughing at you or laughing with you?*
         3. *How could you tell?*
         4. *Do you think you're more of a joke-teller or a joke-receiver?*
            a. Praise those who claim to be ***joke-receivers***.
            b. Any teen claiming to be a ***joke-teller*** should be asked to support this claim by describing his or her ***humor feedback*** and providing details about how people tend to laugh with him or her, rather than laugh at him or her.

ii. Remind them that is it very difficult to be a ***joke-teller*** and you expect them to pay very close attention to their ***humor feedback***.

4. ***In-Group Call***

a. Say: *Another assignment this week was to trade information on a phone call with another member of our group. Raise your hand if you did the in-group call.*

i. Begin by calling on the teens who completed the call.

ii. Briefly ask:

1. *Who did you talk to?*
2. *Who called who?*
3. *Did you trade information?*
4. *Did you find a common interest?*

a. When they identify common interests, ask: *What could you do with that information if you were ever to hang out?*

iii. Avoid general questions like: "How did it go?"

b. Do not allow teens to talk about mistakes the other person made.

c. Have the other person who participated in the call give his or her account immediately after, but not at the same time.

d. Troubleshoot any problems that may have arisen.

5. ***Out-of-Group Call***

a. Say: *You also had an assignment to trade information on a phone call with someone not in PEERS this week. Raise your hand if you did the out-of-group call.*

i. Begin by calling on the teens who completed the call.

ii. Ask:

1. *Who did you talk to?*
2. *Did you trade information?*
3. *Did you find a common interest?*

a. When they identify common interests, ask: *What could you do with that information if you were ever to hang out?*

iii. Avoid general questions like "How did it go?"

b. Troubleshoot any problems that may have arisen.

c. If you have time, check in with teens who did not complete the assignment and troubleshoot how they might get it done this week.

Didactic Lesson: Slipping Out of Conversations

■ Say: *Last week we talked about the rules for slipping into a conversation. This week we're going to talk about what to do if the people you are trying to talk to don't let you into their conversation. We call this slipping out of a conversation. Even when you follow all of the steps for slipping in, sometimes people will still not want to talk to you. For example, if someone were to try to join 10 different conversations, on average how many times out of 10 do you think they will get turned down?*

- Go around the room and have everyone take a guess.
- Answer: Five out of ten times you will not be accepted into the conversation.
■ Stress that it is not a big deal:
- Do not take it personally.
- Explain that it happens to everyone (including the group leader and the teens' parents).
- Do not let this stop you from trying to **slip into conversations** in the future.
■ Explain: *There are many reasons for being turned down when you're trying to slip into a conversation. Even though you won't be invited to join half of the time, it's important to think about why you might have been turned down and what you can do differently next time.*
■ Using the Socratic method, have teens come up with reasons for being turned down and what they can do differently next time. (See the table below.)
- Ask the question: *What are some reasons why you might be turned down?*
■ Follow up each answer with: *What could you do differently next time?*

Reasons for Being Turned Down	*What to Do Differently Next Time*
They want to talk privately	Try again later
They are talking at a different level	Try a different group
They do not want to make new friends	Try a different group
They are stuck up	Try a different group
They are in a clique	Try a different group
You might have a bad reputation with them	Lay low and try again much later
They did not understand that you were trying to join in	Try again later, following the rules
You violated one of the rules for slipping in	Try again later, following the rules
You got too personal	Try a different group, following the rules

Rules for Slipping Out of a Conversation

■ Explain: *Since we know that it's common for people to not let us join their conversations, we need to know what to do in these situations. We call this slipping out of a conversation. Just like with slipping into conversations, there are very specific steps we need to follow for slipping out of conversations.*
■ **Check the signs for interest**.
- Say: *The first thing we need to do is to check the signs if they're interested in talking to us. How can you tell if someone doesn't want to talk to you?*

- Answers:
  - ■ Very little eye contact
  - ■ Rolling their eyes
  - ■ Sighing at you
  - ■ No positive comments directed at you from anyone in the group
  - ■ Ignoring your comments or questions
  - ■ Group members turned away from you (e.g., **closed the circle**)
  - ■ Verbal aggression directed at you from the group
  - ■ Making fun of what you said
  - ■ Laughing at you (inappropriately)
  - ■ Physical aggression directed at you from the group
- – If the group does not seem interested in having a conversation with you—then **move on**.
- – Explain that 50% of attempts to join conversations are not successful.
- – Do not take it personally.
- – Do not give up trying in the future.
- ■ If you accept this gracefully then maybe they will let you into the conversation next time.

Steps for Slipping Out of a Conversation

1. **Keep Your Cool**
   a. Say: *The first step for slipping out of a conversation is to keep your cool. This means don't get upset or try to force them to talk to you.* **Why is it important for you to keep your cool?**
      i. Answer: Because if you lose your cool and get upset, they're going to think you're weird; they will be less likely to want to talk to you in the future; they will likely tell other teens about your reaction, which may result in giving you a bad reputation.

2. **Look Away**
   a. Say: *The next step for slipping out of a conversation is to look away. This means you shouldn't stare. Instead, you should casually stop eye contact and look in a different direction. What does it tell the group when you start to look away?*
      i. Answer: That your attention is now somewhere else; you are not interested in what they are talking about anymore.
   b. Explain: *We want to be careful not to draw too much attention to ourselves when we look away. That means choosing something to look at that doesn't involve looking over your shoulder or turning your whole head and body around. What would be wrong with turning your whole head and body around to look away?* (Demonstrate turning in the opposite direction.)

  i. Answer: This would look strange and would draw attention to your behavior; the group might think the behavior was weird and might laugh or make fun of you.

3. ***Turn Away***
   a. Say: *After we've kept our cool and looked away, the next step for slipping out of a conversation is to turn away. This means that you casually and slowly turn your body in a different direction. What does it tell the group when you turn away?*
      i. Answer: That you are about to walk away; that you lost interest in what they are saying; that you are preparing to leave.
   b. Explain: *It's also important to turn your body away in the direction that you're already looking. What would be the problem with turning your body in a different direction from where you were looking?* (Demonstrate looking in one direction and turning your body in another.)
      i. Answer: This would also look strange and would draw attention to your behavior; the group would surely think this odd behavior; they would likely think you were weird.

4. ***Walk Away***
   a. Say: *The last step for slipping out of a conversation is to walk away. This doesn't mean storming off or walking away quickly. Instead, you will want to casually and calmly walk away. Why would it be important to casually and calmly walk away, rather than walk off quickly?*
      i. Answer: Because if you remain casual and calm, you don't appear to be upset or bothered by the group not letting you into their conversation; by casually slipping out of the conversation, they will likely not even notice you have gone, which is what you want; you don't want to call attention to yourself when exiting a conversation when you have not been accepted.
   b. Explain: *It's also important that we walk away in the direction that we're looking and facing. What would be the problem with walking in a different direction from where you were looking and facing?* (Demonstrate walking in a separate direction from where you were looking and facing.)
      i. Answer: This would look very odd and would certainly draw attention to you; strange behavior such as this might result in you getting a bad reputation.

Role Play

- Have the teen group leader demonstrate an *inappropriate* role play with two coaches in which the teen group leader attempts to *inappropriately **slip into a conversation*** and then *inappropriately **slip out of the conversation***.
  - [Note: If there is only one coach, you can select the highest functioning teen in the group and ask him or her to assist with the role play. Be sure

to give the teen an overview of what you plan to do before the role-play demonstration. This is best done before the teen session begins. The teen will often feel flattered to be included in the exercise. When using teens, it is best to let them naturally trade information with the coach, rather than trying to provide them with a script.]

– Begin by saying: *Now that you all know the steps for slipping in and slipping out of a conversation, we're going to do a little role play. Watch this and then tell me what I'm doing wrong.*

– Demonstrate barging into a conversation between two coaches (or a coach and a teen) without following the steps for slipping in, then trying to force the group to talk to you, and then storming off when rejected.

  • Example of an *inappropriate* role play:

   Teen group leader: (standing several feet away)

   Coach 1: "Hi (insert name). How've you been doing?"

   Coach 2: "I've been pretty good. How about you?"

   Coach 1: "I'm good. Hey, didn't you tell me you like comic books? Did you go to that big comic book convention last weekend?"

   Coach 2: "Yeah, I went on Saturday! It was great! Did you go?"

   Teen group leader: (walks over abruptly, stands too close) "Hey guys. What are you talking about?"

   Coach 2: (startled) "We were talking about the comic book convention. (turning away from the group leader, closing the circle) So anyway, did you go…"

   Teen group leader: (interrupts) "So what are you guys doing this weekend?"

   Coach 1: (looking annoyed) "Umm…I don't know. (turning away from the group leader, closing the circle) So anyway, no I couldn't go, but I was thinking about going to the next one…"

   Coach 2: "Well, if you do, let me know 'cause I want to go again…"

   Teen group leader: (interrupts) "So you guys are going to the comic book convention? I really want to go to that too!"

   Coaches 1 and 2: (looking annoyed, ignoring comments)

   Teen group leader: "What's your problem? I was just trying to talk to you guys. You don't have to be so rude!" (storms off)

   Coaches 1 and 2: (look at each other and laugh)

  • End by saying: *Okay, so time out on that. So what did I do* **wrong** *in trying to slip into that conversation?*

   ■ Answer: Teen group leader did not follow the rules for slipping in (watch/listen, wait, join).

  • Ask: *Did it seem like they wanted to talk to me?*

   ■ Answer: No.

  • Ask: *How could you tell?*

   ■ Answer: They closed the circle; ignored comments; looked annoyed.

- Ask: *What should I have done when I realized they didn't want to talk to me?*
  - ■ Answer: Shouldn't have tried to force them to talk; should have slipped out of the conversation.
- Ask: *What did I do wrong in trying to slip out of that conversation?*
  - ■ Answer: Did not pay attention to the signs of disinterest; did not follow the rules for slipping out (keep your cool, look away, turn away, walk away).

■ The teen group leader should then demonstrate an *appropriate* role play with two coaches (or a coach and a teen) in which the teen group leader *appropriately slips into a conversation* and then *slips out of* the conversation.

- Say: *Now let's try this again. Watch this and then tell me what I'm doing right.*
- Demonstrate slipping into a conversation between two coaches that follows the rules for slipping in, but still results in rejection that is followed by an appropriate demonstration of slipping out (i.e., keep your cool, look away, turn away, walk away).
  - Example of an *appropriate* role play:

    Teen group leader: (standing several feet from the two coaches)
    Coach 1: "Hi (insert name). How've you been doing?"
    Coach 2: "I've been pretty good. How about you?"
    Coach 1: "I'm good. Hey, didn't you tell me you like comic books? Did you go to that big comic book convention last weekend?"
    Teen group leader: (moves a little closer, makes periodic eye contact, starting to show interest)
    Coach 2: "Yeah, I went on Saturday! It was great! Did you go?"
    Coach 1: "No, I didn't go, but I was thinking about going to the next one."
    Coach 2: "Well, if you do, let me know 'cause I want to go again."
    Coach 1: "That would be fun! We should do that!"
    Teen group leader: (moves closer) "So you guys are going to a comic book convention?"
    Coaches 1 and 2: (ignore comments)
    Coach 1: "So when is the next one?"
    Teen group leader: (begins to look away)
    Coach 2: "I'm not sure, but I think it's next month."
    Teen group leader: (slowly turns away)
    Coach 1: "We should figure out when it is and get tickets."
    Teen group leader: (casually walks away)
    Coaches 1 and 2: (don't appear to notice that the teen group leader has left)
  - End by saying: *Okay, so time out on that. So what did I do right in trying to slip out of that conversation?*

■ Answer: The teen group leader followed the rules for slipping out (kept cool, turned away, walked away).

Slipping Out of a Conversation You Already Joined

■ Explain: *In some cases, we may have been partially accepted into a conversation, but then something happens to shut us out from the conversation. For example, you may have slipped into a conversation and initially the group spoke to you; but then you notice that they've closed the circle, are ignoring your comments, and are no longer talking to you or looking at you. If you have already joined a conversation, leaving without saying anything would seem awkward. In this case, do the following:*

■ Have a *brief **cover story*** before you exit the conversation:
  – This is necessary if you participated in three or more conversational exchanges.
  – A *brief **cover story*** is necessary because you already joined the conversation and leaving would be abrupt.
  – ***Cover stories*** must be *very brief* and *not specific*:
    • This is because the group is no longer interested in you and probably does not care where you are going anyway.
  – Have teens come up with possible ***cover stories*** for ***slipping out of a conversation***.
  – Examples of ***cover stories***:
    • *Well, I have to get to class.*
    • *Well, gotta go.*
    • *I'd better go.*
    • *Take care.*
    • *See you later.*

■ In this case, you would want to ***keep your cool***, but you would not follow the additional steps of ***looking away***, ***turning away***, and ***walking away***.

Role Play

■ The teen group leader should then demonstrate an *appropriate* role play with two coaches (or a coach and a teen) in which the teen group leader *appropriately **slips into a conversation***, is initially accepted into the conversation, but is then shut out of the conversation and has to ***slip out***.
  – Say: *Now that you know the rules for slipping out of a conversation using cover stories, we're going to do another little role play. Watch this and then tell me what I'm doing **right**.*
  – Demonstrate slipping into a conversation between two coaches that follows the rules for slipping in and initially involves acceptance into the conversation, but then results in rejection that is followed by an appropriate demonstration of slipping out using cover stories.

- Example of an *appropriate* role play:
  Teen group leader: (standing several feet from the two coaches)
  Coach 1: "Hi (insert name). How've you been doing?"
  Coach 2: "I've been pretty good. How about you?"
  Coach 1: "I'm good. Hey, didn't you tell me you like comic books? Did you go to that big comic book convention last weekend?"
  Teen group leader: (moves a little closer, makes periodic eye contact, starting to show interest)
  Coach 2: "Yeah, I went on Saturday! It was great! Did you go?"
  Coach 1: "No, I didn't go, but I was thinking about going to the next one."
  Coach 2: "Well, if you do, let me know 'cause I want to go again."
  Coach 1: "That would be fun! We should do that!"
  Teen group leader: (moves closer) "So you guys are going to a comic book convention?"
  Coach 2: (looks over, turns toward group leader) "Yeah."
  Teen group leader: "I love comic books!"
  Coach 2: "That's cool."
  Teen group leader: "So where was the last convention?"
  Coach 2: "It was downtown." (looks away, turns away, starts to close the circle)
  Coach 1: (turned away from group leader) "So when is the next one?"
  Teen group leader: (begins to look away)
  Coach 2: "I'm not sure, but I think its next month."
  Coach 1: "We should figure out when it is and get tickets."
  Teen group leader: "Well, see you later."
  Coaches 1 and 2: (casually look over) "Yeah. See ya."
- End by saying: *Okay, so time out on that. So what did I do right in trying to slip out of that conversation?*
  - Answer: Teen group leader followed the rules for slipping out using a cover story (keep your cool, give a brief cover story for leaving).
- Ask: *In this situation, would it have been awkward to slip out using the steps of looking away, turning away, and walking away?*
  - Answer: Yes, because you were initially accepted into the conversation.

Homework Assignments

- Briefly explain the homework for the week by saying: *This week we're going to continue to have each of you practice slipping into conversations with people you only know so-so, and if necessary, we want you to practice slipping out. We are also going to have you continue to practice your conversational skills this week by making phone calls. So, your homework assignment this week is to:*

- *Slip into a conversation following the steps we've outlined.*
  - *Slip out if the group doesn't seem interested in talking to you.*
- *Make an out-of-group phone call to someone not in PEERS:*
  - *This should be at least 5 to 10 minutes.*
  - *Pick a friend that you would be comfortable trading information with*
  - *Find a common interest to report to the group.*
- *Bring an inside game to share with the group (e.g., age appropriate board game, card game, etc.):*
  - *No solitary games.*
- ■ Announce that there will be no more in-group phone call assignments.

Teen Activity: Slipping In and Out of Conversations

Note: See the "Teen Activity Guide" for rules.

- ■ Notify teens that they will be practicing ***slipping into a conversation*** and ***slipping out of a conversation*** while ***trading information*** about their personal items.
  - Have teens separate into groups of approximately three to four teens.
  - Girls should be paired with girls, and boys should be paired with boys when possible.
- ■ Have a selection of magazines for teens who did not bring items to share.
- ■ Teens receive points for ***slipping into*** and ***slipping out of conversations***.
- ■ Have each teen practice ***slipping into a conversation*** between the other members and ***slipping out of this conversation***.
  - Tell the other group member that he or she must allow the person to enter the conversation.
    - Do not allow group members to reject attempts at ***slipping in***.
  - Have the teen verbally go over the steps for ***slipping in*** before he or she makes the attempt to join the conversation.
  - Once the teen has successfully ***slipped into the conversation***, pull the teen out and say: *That was great! Now pretend that they said no. Why might they have said no?*
    - Have the teen generate some ideas and ask the teen what he or she could do differently in the future.
    - Have the teen verbally go over the steps for ***slipping out*** before he or she makes the attempt to exit the conversation.
  - Then have the teen demonstrate how he or she would ***slip out of the conversation***.
  - The teen group leader and coach should provide immediate performance feedback after the ***slipping in*** and ***slipping out*** attempts:
    - Give the teen praise for what he or she did correctly.
    - ***Offer suggestions*** for doing something differently when necessary.
    - Have the teens redo any inappropriate attempts to ***slip in*** or ***slip out***.

    – Each teen should attempt to ***slip in*** and ***slip out*** at least once.
■ Encourage teens to applaud for one another after each attempt is complete.

Reunification With Parents

■ Announce that teens should join their parents:
    – Be sure that the teens are standing or sitting next to their parents.
    – Be sure to have silence and the full attention of the group.
■ Say: *Today we worked on what to do when we try to slip into a conversation and the group doesn't want to talk to us. We call this slipping out of a conversation. Who can tell us one of the steps for slipping out of a conversation?* [Have teens generate all of the rules. Be prepared to give prompts if necessary.]
    – ***Check signs for interest***
    – ***Keep your cool***
    – ***Look away***
    – ***Turn away***
    – ***Walk away***
    – Use a ***cover story*** for leaving if you were initially in the conversation.
■ Say: *Today we practiced slipping in and slipping out of conversations and this group did a great job. Let's give them a round of applause.*
■ Go over the homework for the next week (see below).
■ Individually and separately negotiate the following with each family:
    – Where the teens will attempt to slip in and with which peer group.
    – Who the teen will call for the out-of-group phone call.
    – What inside game will be brought next week.

Homework Assignments

1. Practice ***slipping into a conversation*** between at least two teens.
    a. Before ***slipping in***:
        i. Try to choose a conversation where you know at least one but not all of the people.
        ii. Try a place where you are likely to be accepted (i.e., low-risk place) and you do not have a bad reputation. You may need to find a new place.
        iii. Parent and teen may want to rehearse the steps for ***slipping in***.
    b. During ***slipping in***:
        i. Follow the steps for slipping into a conversation.
        ii. If you are not accepted—use the steps for slipping out.
    c. After ***slipping in***:
        i. Parents and teens should discuss how the teen ***slipped into the conversation*** and ***slipped out*** (if applicable).

      ii. Parents should help their teen troubleshoot any problems that may have arisen.

2. ***Out-of-Group Call***
   a. Before the call:
      i. Parents arrange with your teen to call someone outside of the group to practice conversational skills.
      ii. Negotiate where the parent will be during the call.
   b. During the call:
      i. Teens should ***trade information*** on this phone call.
      ii. Find a ***common interest*** to report back to the group.
      iii. Follow the rules for a ***two-way conversation***.
      iv. Use the rules for starting and ending a conversation, including using ***cover stories***.
   c. After the call:
      i. Parents and teens should discuss the phone call and identify ***common interests***.
      ii. Parents should help their teen troubleshoot any problems that may have arisen.

3. ***Bring an Inside Game***
   a. Bring an inside game to share with the group (e.g., age-appropriate board game, card game, etc.):
      i. No solitary games.
   b. Do not bring something that you are:
      i. Unwilling to share with group members.
      ii. Worried about breaking or losing.

Calculate Points

Keep track of the following for each week of the intervention:

- Calculate the number of points earned by each teen.
- Add up the total number of points earned by the group.
- Do not calculate the points in the presence of the teens:
  - Do not disclose the individual or group total of points.
  - Discourage attempts to compare number of points earned between teens.
- Remind them that they are working as a team to earn a bigger and better graduation party.

Teen Activity Guide: Session 7

"Slipping In and Out of Conversations"

Materials Needed

- Teens bring personal items
- CD players and headphones for music (optional)
- In the event that a teen forgets to bring a personal item, have magazines available to share:
  - Computer magazines
  - Anime magazines
  - Teen magazines
  - Sports magazines

Rules

- Break teens up into small groups (no less than three teens per group):
  - Match girls with girls and boys with boys, whenever possible.
- Have teens practice ***trading information*** about their personal items while taking turns ***slipping into conversations*** and ***slipping out of conversations***.
- Encourage teens to identify ***common interests*** through ***trading information***.
- Prompt teens to ask questions when appropriate.
- For teens practicing ***slipping into conversations***:
  - Group leader and coaches should separate the teen from the group and have him or her identify the steps for ***slipping in***.
  - Then have the teen practice using these steps by ***slipping into conversations*** with their peers in which the others will be ***trading information*** about their personal items.
  - Remind the other teens that they should accept everyone into these conversations.
    - Teens may need you to prompt them for specific steps.
- Once the teen has successfully ***slipped into the conversation***, pull them out and say: *That was great! Now pretend that they said no. Why might they have said no?*
  - Have the teen generate some ideas and ask the teen what he or she could do differently in the future.
  - Have the teen verbally go over the steps for ***slipping out*** before he or she makes the attempt to exit the conversation (the teen may need to look at the board at first).
- Then have the teen demonstrate how he or she would ***slip out of the conversation***.

- – The teen group leader and coach should provide immediate performance feedback after the ***slipping-in*** and ***slipping-out*** attempts.
  - – In the event that a teen incorrectly attempts to ***slip in*** or ***slip out***, call a "time-out" and use this teachable moment to gently point out the error, while providing feedback on how to more appropriately attempt to ***slip in*** or ***slip out***.
  - – Have the teen try again until he or she is successful in following the steps.
- ■ Once the teen has successfully ***slipped out***, call a "time-out" and have the other teens applaud.
  - – The teen group leader should briefly point out the steps that the teen followed for ***slipping in*** and ***slipping out***.
- ■ Rotate teens after each has successfully ***slipped in*** and ***slipped out*** (each teen should practice at least once).
- ■ Give points for ***slipping in*** and ***slipping out of conversations***.

Chapter 10

Session 8
Get-Togethers

Parent Session Therapist Guide

Guiding Principles of the Parent Session

Parents will be reporting on their teen's attempts at slipping into conversations. The parents will have little to do with this homework (except by encouraging compliance by debriefing with their teen). Continue to ask for successes first. Give considerable attention to the unsuccessful attempts in which teens were not successful entering a conversation, because this was the focus of the previous session and will provide a good context in which to discuss slipping out of conversations.

The content of this session focuses upon get-togethers for the first time. Much of our knowledge about get-togethers comes from observations of play dates of children. Frankel and Myatt (2003) were among the first to include in-home get-togethers and good host etiquette within social skills training curricula. Research with younger children indicates that the best way to form a best friendship is through organizing and frequently carrying out successful play dates for two children who like each other. The same applies to adolescents through organizing get-togethers. The most effective means of having successful play dates for younger children is for parents and children to collaborate in having them (Frankel, 1996). Getting together after school is correlated with more social contacts at school (Frankel, Gorospe, Chang, & Sugar, 2009). Thus, it is important for teens with autism spectrum disorders (ASD) to have get-togethers with peers in order to develop closer friendships and develop more positive peer interactions. The degree to which parents will be involved in these get-togethers, however, will need to be individually negotiated with each family.

Parents must take the major responsibility for this homework assignment. This means the group leader has to maintain pressure on parents to get this to happen. However, this does not mean that parents will be calling other teens or the parents of other teens to arrange the get-together, as this would be developmentally inappropriate. Instead, parents are expected to be responsible for assisting their teen in organizing the get-together. In presenting the details of how each parent should attempt this homework with their teen, the group leader should make the best deal possible as to potential guests for each family. The goal is to make sure a get-together happens, even if it is not with a peer who satisfies the "gold standard."

The group leader should also consider how overprotective each parent is and whether parental involvement needs to be decreased. For example, "helicopter parents" feel the need to hover close to their teens regardless of necessity. This type of parenting is prevalent among parents of developmentally delayed teens. In many cases, the group leader may be able to actively dissuade these parents from intruding. One suggestion is to limit intrusiveness by having the parent confine his or her involvement to bringing treats into the room where the get-together is taking place. In some cases, the helicopter parent cannot stay out of the get-together when not needed. This should be broached in subsequent homework debriefings and actively discouraged by the group leader, or this intrusiveness will limit the autonomy and friendships of their teen. Some of the better adapted teens have coped with the helicopter parent by refusing to have get-togethers at their home. In this case, the group leader should respect this preference and support get-togethers outside the teen's home.

Homework Review

1. ***Slipping into or slipping out of a conversation***.
   a. Have parents identify:
      i. Where their teen ***slipped in***.
      ii. If the teen was familiar with someone in the group.
      iii. If the teen followed the steps for ***slipping into a conversation***.
      iv. If the teen had to follow the steps for ***slipping out of the conversation***.
   b. Troubleshoot any problems that may have arisen (examples below).
      i. The teen did not attempt the assignment at all. In this case, it is important to get more information about the problem.
         1. Did the teen have an opportunity to try ***slipping in***, but was too nervous? If so, perhaps an easier situation can be targeted to try next time (e.g., ***slipping into conversation*** with better-known and accepting acquaintances).
         2. Did the teen not have an opportunity to ***slip in*** at all? This is where having an extracurricular activity would be helpful.

ii. The teen attempted the assignment but had to ***slip out of the conversation*** and did this successfully. This may still be a success, as the teen used the previous session content to guide his or her behavior. However, the group leader should explore whether the teen or parent has misjudged the targeted peers. Was this the wrong group to try to join? Does it indicate a more pervading negative reputation in the setting? If so, then ***slipping into conversations*** in another setting is warranted and the previous setting and peers should be avoided. The group leader should point this out to the parent.

iii. The parent reported that the teen attempted the assignment, had to ***slip out of the conversation,*** and did not use the peer exit strategies. On the one hand the teen tried to do the assignment, and this should be acknowledged. On the other hand, the teen probably picked the wrong group to join or did not join correctly, and clearly did not exit properly. As in the above example, explore whether this was the wrong group to try to join and focus on alternative groups to try to join in future.

2. ***Out-of-Group Call***
   a. *Briefly* have parents identify:
      i. How the conversation began and what ***cover story*** was used.
      ii. A ***common interest*** discovered through ***trading information***.
      iii. How the conversation ended and what ***cover story*** was used.
   b. Identify whether this is a good person for a get-together this week.
   c. Troubleshoot any problems that may have arisen.

3. ***Bring an Inside Game***
   a. Have parents identify the inside game their teen brought to share with the group (e.g., age-appropriate board game, card game, etc.).
   b. Only give credit for appropriate items.

Didactic Lesson: Get-Togethers

■ Distribute the Parent Handout.
■ Explain: *Now that your teens have been practicing slipping in and trading information during their out-of-group phone calls, our plan is to develop their friendships even further. The best way to foster a close friendship is by being involved in regular get-togethers. A get-together is when your teen has a friend over to your home to visit. Get-togethers can also take place outside of your home or in the community. In this session, your teens will be learning the rules for having get-togethers and will be practicing these skills in the group. After this session, the major responsibility you will each have is to help your teen organize a get-together with a friend. During this get-together, you will be monitoring your teen's activities. Therefore, it would be best if these get-togethers take place in your home, if possible. We will be giving you*

suggestions for how best to monitor get-togethers when they are at your home and for troubleshooting any potential problems.

What Parents Should Expect During the Get-Togethers

- ■ ***Get-togethers*** should be activity-based:
  - – Activities give the ***get-together*** a ***cover story***.
  - – Activities lessen the pressure of keeping a conversation going.
- ■ Initial ***get-togethers*** should only last about 2 hours (depending on the activity):
  - – As the teens become better friends, the ***get-togethers*** can be longer.
  - – If the planned activity involves a movie or sporting event, the time for the get-together will naturally be longer.
- ■ At least 50% of the time should be spent conversing and ***trading information***:
  - – This is an opportunity for your teen to begin to develop a closer friend-ship with his or her guest.
  - – If the teens are not conversing, they will not be getting to know one another better and will be unable to discover other ***common interests***.
- ■ Many teens (especially boys) will want to play computer or video games or watch TV or movies.
  - – Remind your teen prior to the ***get-together*** that at least 50% of the time should be spent trading information.
    - • Parents will need to limit the amount of time spent playing elec-tronic games.
    - • If your teen has planned to watch a movie or TV show, be sure that the teen spends at least 50% of his or her time trading information before or after the show.
- ■ Sharing a meal or planning other activities can be helpful.
- ■ Go around the room and have parents take turns reading the Parent Handout.
  - – Sections in **bold print** come directly from the Parent Handout.

Suggestions for Activity-Based Get-Togethers

- ■ Explain: *Get-togethers are best when they are activity-based. This is because it lessens the pressure of conversing on a wide variety of topics. Often conver-sations during activity-based get-togethers are focused on the activity itself, which can be a good starting point. Eventually, teens should be able to con-verse on topics other than the activity.*
- ■ Ask: *What are some things that teens like to do during get-togethers?*
- ■ Have parents brainstorm and then provide suggestions from the table in the Parent Handout if parents do not come up with ideas on their own.
- ■ The parent group leader should troubleshoot any potential problems.

Mealtime Activities	Sports Done in Pairs
Barbecue	Swimming
Ordering pizza	Skateboarding
Going to a restaurant	Shooting baskets
Cooking a meal	Bike riding
Picnic	Roller skating
Baking	Tennis

Group Sports	Public Activities
Basketball	Going to the movies
Baseball	Bowling
Soccer	Video arcade*
Touch football	Gaming centers*
Volleyball	Laser tag
Badminton	Going to the mall*
	Teen dance clubs*
	Comic book conventions
	Comic book stores
	Gaming stores
	Going to concerts*

Indoor Activities	Outdoor Activities
Listening to music	Going to the local amusement parks*
Renting movies	Miniature golf parks*
Watching TV	Water parks*
Playing board/card games	Go-carting*
Computer/video games	State fair*
Surfing the Internet (YouTube)	County fair*
Online networking sites (MySpace, Facebook)	Batting cages
	Golf range
Looking at magazines	Dog park
Playing Ping-Pong	Hanging out at the park*
Playing pool	Going to the beach, lake, river, etc.
Playing air hockey	Teen activity centers*
Playing darts	Ski resorts (skiing, snowboarding)
	Beach resorts (surfing, windsurfing, swimming, sailing)

*Be sure to check out these places in advance to make sure there is no gang activity or increased potential for getting into trouble.

Parents' Jobs for Having Good Get-Togethers

- ■ Explain: *There are a number of things that parents can do to improve the success of their teen's get-together.*
- ■ **Provide a safe and comfortable environment in your home.**
  - – **Allow your teen's friends to hang out at your home with some privacy.**
  - – **Check on conversations by offering snacks, junk food.**
    - • **You unobtrusively observe.**
    - • **Do not intrude on conversations unless it is to offer snacks.**
    - • **Hint: Make several trips with the food at various times in order to unobtrusively monitor the *get-together*.**
  - – **Do not allow siblings to join the *get-together*.**
  - – **Help your teen organize an activity that would be of *common interest* to your teen and his or her friends.**
- ■ **Remind your teen prior to the *get-together* that at least 50% of the time should be spent *trading information*.**
- ■ **Try to limit first-time *get-togethers* to no more than 2 hours (depending on the activity) to lessen the pressure on your teen.**
  - – **It is better to have your teen's friend leave wanting more than to have them tire of one another.**
- ■ **Help your teen by providing a *cover story* at the end of the *get-together* (e.g., "It's time to say good-bye to your friend...we need to eat dinner").**

Rules for Having a Good Get-Together

- ■ Explain: *Now we are briefly going to go over the rules your teen should follow when having a get-together. These are the steps that your teens are going to be learning and practicing today in their session. It is important for you to be familiar with these steps so that you can make sure they are following the rules when they have their get-togethers this week and in the future. If you notice that your teen is disobeying one of the rules, you can prompt him or her by calling him or her out of the room and discreetly using the buzzwords. For example, if your teen is ignoring his or her friend to take a call from someone else, you could ask the teen to join you in the other room for a moment and quietly and calmly suggest the teen **be loyal to his or her friend**.*

Teens' Jobs for Having Good Get-Togethers

Before the Get-Together

- ■ **Decide beforehand, with your friend, what you are going to do and who is going to be there (that is, *Who, What, Where, When*).**
- ■ **Have some activities ready:**

- DVDs, videos
- Video games, computer games
- Board games, card games
- Sports equipment

■ Put away any personal items you do not want to share or let other people see.

■ Make sure your room is presentable.

At the Beginning of the Get-Together

■ Greet your guest.

■ Invite your guest in (move out of the doorway so he or she can enter).

■ Introduce your guest to anyone he or she does not know.

■ Give your guest a tour if this is the first time he or she has been to your home (e.g., your bedroom, bathroom, living room).

■ Offer your guest something to drink and eat.

■ Ask your guest what he or she wants to do (even if you already decided with him or her in advance).

During the Get-Together

■ At your home, the guest gets to pick the activity:
  - This is because it is your job to make sure the guest has a good time.
  - The only exception is if your guest wants to do something dangerous or inappropriate.

■ When you are the guest, take the host's lead about what to do (not everyone knows that the guest gets to pick the activity).

■ *Praise* your friend(s).

■ *Compliment* your friend(s).

■ *Be a good sport*.

■ *Be loyal to your friend(s)*:
  - Do not argue with, criticize, or make fun of your friend(s).
  - If someone else makes fun of your friend, stick up for your friend.
  - Do not ignore one friend to talk to another friend.
    • If someone unexpectedly calls, texts, or stops by during your *get-together*:
      ■ Do not invite that person over.
      ■ Do not ignore your friend to talk with that person.
      ■ Tell that person you are busy and that you will get back to him or her later.
    • No text messaging, e-mailing, or instant messaging (unless it is your friend's idea).

■ *Suggest a change* if you are bored or tired of an activity:

– If you are bored, say: "How about when we're done with this we play something else?"
– If your friend does not want to do what you suggest, let your friend pick the next activity.

▪ **At least 50% of the time should be spent conversing and *trading information*.**

End of the Get-Together

▪ **Give a *cover story* for leaving or ending the *get-together* (e.g., "I have to go soon" or "I have homework to do").**
    – **Parents can provide a *cover story* for why the *get-together* has to end.**
▪ **Start to walk your friend to the door.**
▪ **Thank your friend for getting together.**
▪ **If you had a good time, tell your friend.**
▪ **Say good-bye and you will see him or her later.**

▪ Go around the room and have parents identify a couple of potential friends for their teen's ***get-together***. Ideally these friends should come from successful ***out-of-group calls***.
▪ Have parents identify some activities their teen might enjoy during their ***get-together***.
▪ Allow group discussion so that parents can collaborate on ideas.
▪ Encourage parents to help their teen arrange this ***get-together*** as soon as possible, so they do not run out of time (e.g., do not wait until Friday for a Saturday ***get-together***).

Homework Assignments

The parent group leader should go over the homework assignment and trouble-shoot any potential problems with parents.

1. **Teens are to have a friend over for a *get-together*.**
    a. **Make an *out-of-group* call to set up the *get-together*:**
        i. ***Trade information* to find *common interests*.**
        ii. **Decide what you are going to do during your *get-together*.**
    b. **Parents monitor the *get-together* from a *distance*.**
    c. **The *get-together* should be activity-based.**
    d. **First *get-togethers* with a particular teen should be limited to approximately 2 hours (depending on the activity).**
2. **Practice *slipping into a conversation* between at least two teens:**
    a. **Try to choose a conversation where you know at least one of the people.**

b. Try a place where you are likely to be accepted (i.e., low-risk place) and you do not have a bad reputation. You may need to find a new place.

c. Parents and teens should discuss how the teen *slipped into the conversation* and *slipped out* (if applicable) .

d. Parents should help their teen troubleshoot any problems that may have arisen.

3. Bring an inside game.
   a. Bring an inside game to share with the group (e.g., age-appropriate board or card game):
      i. No solitary games.
   b. Do not bring something that you are:
      i. Unwilling to share with group members.
      ii. Worried about breaking or losing.

Parent Handout 8: Get-Togethers

Suggestions for Activity-Based Get-Togethers	
Mealtime Activities Barbecue Ordering pizza Going to a restaurant Cooking a meal Picnic Baking	*Sports Done in Pairs* Swimming Skateboarding Shooting baskets Bike riding Roller skating Tennis
Group Sports Basketball Baseball Soccer Touch football Volleyball Badminton	*Public Activities* Going to the movies Bowling Video arcade* Gaming centers* Laser tag Going to the mall* Teen dance clubs* Comic book conventions Comic book stores Gaming stores Going to concerts*
Indoor Activities Listening to music Renting movies Watching TV Playing board/card games Computer/video games Surfing the Internet (YouTube) Online networking sites (MySpace, Facebook) Looking at magazines Playing Ping-Pong Playing pool Playing air hockey Playing darts	*Outdoor Activities* Going to the local amusement parks* Miniature golf parks* Water parks* Go-carting* State fair* County fair* Batting cages Golf range Dog park Hanging out at the park* Going to the beach, lake, river, etc. Teen activity centers* Ski resorts (skiing, snowboarding) Beach resorts (surfing, windsurfing, swimming, sailing)
*Be sure to check out these places in advance to make sure there is no gang activity or increased potential for getting into trouble.	

Parents' Jobs for Having Good Get-Togethers

■ Provide a safe and comfortable environment in your home.
- Allow your teen's friends to hang out at your home with some privacy.
- Check on conversations by offering snacks, junk food.
  - ■ You unobtrusively observe.
  - ■ Do not intrude on conversations unless it is to offer snacks.

> ■ Hint: Make several trips with the food at various times in order to unobtrusively monitor the **get-together**.
> - Do not allow siblings to join the **get-together**.
> - Help your teen organize an activity that would be of **common inter-est** to your teen and his or her friends.

- Remind your teen prior to the **get-together** that at least 50% of the time should be spent **trading information**.
- Try to limit first time **get-togethers** to no more than 2 hours (depending on the activity) to lessen the pressure on your teen.
  > - It is better to have your teen's friend leave wanting more than to have them tire of one another.

■ Help your teen by providing a cover story at the end of the get-together (e.g., "It's time to say good-bye to your friend....we need to eat dinner.")

Teens' Jobs for Having Good Get-Togethers
Before the Get-Together

■ Decide beforehand, with your friend, what you are going to do and who is going to be there (that is, **Who, What, Where, When**).

■ Have some activities ready:
- DVDs, videos
- Video games, computer games
- Board games, card games
- Sports equipment

■ Put away any personal items you do not want to share or let other people see.

■ Make sure your room is presentable.

At the Beginning of the Get-Together

■ Greet your guest.

■ Invite your guest in (move out of the doorway so he or she can enter).

■ Introduce your guest to anyone he or she does not know.

■ Give your guest a tour if this is the first time he or she has come to your home (e.g., your bedroom, bathroom, living room).

■ Offer your guest something to drink and eat.

■ Ask your guest what he or she wants to do (even if you already decided with him or her in advance).

During the Get-Together

■ At your home, the guest gets to pick the activity:
- This is because it is your job to make sure the guest has a good time.
- The only exception is if your guest wants to do something dangerous or inappropriate.

■ When you are the guest, take the host's lead about what to do (not everyone knows that the guest gets to pick the activity).

■ **Praise** your friend.

■ ***Compliment*** your friend.
■ ***Be a good sport***.
■ ***Be loyal to your friend***.
  – Do not argue with, criticize, or make fun of your friend.
  – If someone else makes fun of your friend, stick up for him or her.
  – Do not ignore one friend to talk to another friend.
    • If someone unexpectedly calls or stops by during your ***get-together***:
      ■ Do not invite that person over.
      ■ Do not ignore your friend to talk with that person.
      ■ Tell him or her that you are busy and that you will get back to that person later.
    • No text messaging, e-mailing, or instant messaging (unless it is your friend's idea).
■ ***Suggest a change*** if you are bored or tired of an activity:
  – If you are bored, say: "How about when we're done with this we play something else?"
  – If your friend does not want to do what you suggest, let your friend pick the next activity.
■ At least 50% of the time should be spent conversing and ***trading information***.

End of the Get-Together

■ Give a ***cover story*** for leaving or ending the ***get-together*** (e.g., "I have to go soon" or "I have homework to do").
  – Parents can provide a ***cover story*** for why the ***get-together*** has to end.
■ Start to walk your friend to the door.
■ Thank your friend for getting together.
■ If you had a good time, tell your friend.
■ Say good-bye and you will see him or her later.

Homework Assignments

1. Teens are to have a friend over for a ***get-together***.
   a. Make an ***out-of-group*** call to set up the ***get-together***.
      i. ***Trade information*** to find ***common interests***.
      ii. Decide what you are going to do during your ***get-together***.
   b. Parents monitor the ***get-together*** from a *distance*.
   c. The ***get-together*** should be activity-based.
   d. First ***get-togethers*** with a particular teen should be limited to approximately 2 hours (depending on the activity).
2. Practice ***slipping into a conversation*** between at least two teens.
   a. Try to choose a conversation where you know at least one of the people.
   b. Try a place where you are likely to be accepted (i.e., low-risk place) and you do not have a bad reputation. You may need to find a new place.

c. Parents and teens should discuss how the teen ***slipped into the conversation*** and ***slipped out*** (if applicable).

d. Parents should help teen troubleshoot any problems that may have arisen.

3. ***Bring an inside game.***

a. Bring an inside game to share with the group (e.g., age appropriate board/card game):

i. No solitary games.

b. Do not bring something that you are:

i. Unwilling to share with group members.

ii. Worried about breaking or losing.

Teen Therapist Guide—Session 8: Get-Togethers

Guiding Principles of the Teen Session

The focus of this session is on teaching teens how to organize and implement a get-together with potential friends. Socially accepted teens have frequent and successful get-togethers. They turn school acquaintances into close friends by spending time with friends outside of the school setting. Therefore, learning the skills necessary to be successful at get-togethers is particularly important in helping teens to make and keep friends.

The ideal circumstance would be to have teens organize get-togethers in their homes where parents can unobtrusively observe the interaction. This allows parents to monitor and appropriately intervene during get-togethers when necessary. However, as mentioned in the parent section, some teens will be uncomfortable with this option. Two reasons may justify a reluctance to have get-togethers in the home: the presence of "helicopter parents" or embarrassment about the teens' home or family members. In both cases, the group leader should encourage the teen to allow his or her parents to be involved in some small part of the get-together (for example, drop off or pick up teens). At the very least, the teen should be willing to discuss the details of the get-together with the parent. This should be negotiated at the reunification before the get-together is scheduled. It is helpful to remind the teen in the presence of his or her parent that the parent also has to report back on the homework next week.

It is also recommended that get-togethers be activity-based. This lessens the pressure of maintaining conversation throughout the get-together. Research suggests that most 11- to 16-year-olds (77.2%) play video games (Phillips, Rolls, Rouse, & Griffiths, 1995), so this will be a common get-together activity. Other common activities include going to the movies and sharing a meal.

One common problem in this session is the lack of choices for potential guests for a get-together. The "gold standard" is someone with whom the teen wishes to get to know better and who appears to be interested in becoming closer friends with the teen. Options from successful out-of-group call assignments are usually helpful in this regard. In the absence of having someone to fill the gold standard, a close friend or a distant family member around the same age would be acceptable options until someone more appropriate can be identified. The most important part of this assignment is that a get-together actually takes place so that the teen can practice the skills just learned. If such practice does not occur soon after learning, the skills are unlikely to be used at a later time.

Rule Review

Note: Only go over session rules again if the teens are having difficulty following them.

- Have teens identify the rules for the group.
- Give them points for remembering:
  1. Listen to the other group members (no talking when others are speaking)
  2. Follow directions
  3. Raise your hand
  4. Be respectful (no teasing or making fun of others)
  5. No touching (no hitting, kicking, pushing, hugging, etc.)

Homework Review

Note: Give points for homework *parts*—not just one point per assignment.

1. ***Bring an Inside Game***
   a. Identify the inside game the teen brought to share with the group (e.g., age-appropriate board game, card game, etc.).
   b. Only give credit for appropriate items.
   c. To avoid distractions, have a coach put the item away until the teen session activity.

2. ***Slipping Into a Conversation***
   a. Say: *Last week we went over the steps for slipping out of a conversation in which we were not accepted. These steps included keeping your cool, looking away, turning away, and walking away. We also reviewed the steps for slipping into conversations, which includes watching and listening to the conversation, waiting for a pause, and joining the conversation by making a comment or asking a question that was on topic. One of your assignments this week was to practice slipping into a conversation with someone from a group that you were likely to be accepted by. Raise your hand if you practiced slipping into a conversation this week.*
      i. Begin by calling on the teens who completed the assignment.
      ii. Briefly ask:
         1. *Where did you slip in?*
         2. *Which group did you choose to slip in with?*
         3. *Did you know at least one of the people?*
         4. *How did you slip in?*
            a. Be sure they followed the steps for ***slipping in***.
            b. If they did not follow the steps, ask: *What could you do differently next time?*
         5. *Did you need to slip out?*
            a. If so, be sure they followed the steps for ***slipping out***.

> b. If they did not follow the steps, ask: *What could you do differently next time?*
>
> 6. Troubleshoot any problems that may have arisen.

3. ***Out-of-Group Call***

   a. Say: *You also had an assignment to trade information on a phone call with someone not in PEERS this week. Raise your hand if you did the out of group call.*

   i, Begin by calling on the teens who completed the call.

   ii. Ask:

   1. *Who did you talk to?*
   2. *Did you trade information?*
   3. *Did you find a common interest?*
      a. When they identify common interests, ask: *What could you do with that information if you were ever to hang out?*
   4. *Is this someone you might want to have a get-together with?*

   iii. Avoid general questions such as: "How did it go?"

   b. Troubleshoot any problems that may have arisen.

   c. If you have time, check in with teens who did not complete the assignment and troubleshoot how they might get it done this week.

Didactic Lesson: Rules for Having a Good Get-Together

■ Say: *Tonight we're going to be talking about how to have a successful get-together with friends. Having a get-together is a popular way for teens to hang-out with their friends and get to know one another better. A good way to start a close friendship is to have someone you like and want to get to know better over to your home for a get-together. This involves you being the host of the get-together. Who can tell me the difference between a host and a guest?*

  – Answer: The host organizes the get-together; the guest attends the get-together; it is the host's job to make sure the guest has a good time.

■ Say: *In order to make sure that your get-togethers are a success, we will need to be familiar with the rules for having get-togethers.*

Before the Get-Together

■ Decide beforehand with your friend what you are going to do and who is going to be there.

  – Say: *The first part of having a successful get-together involves planning the get-together. This means you will need to decide beforehand, with your friend, what you are going to do and who is going to be there* (parents, siblings, etc.).

■ ***Who*** is going to be there?

- Say: *One part of this involves deciding who is going to be there. Why should everyone invited to a get-together know in advance who is going to be there?*
  - Answer: Because you do not want your friends to be surprised if there are other people at the get-together; certain people may not get along and would not want to be around each other.

■ **What** are you going to do?
  - Say: *Another part of planning the get-together involves figuring out what you're going to do. Why would this be important to do?*
    - Answer: Because get-togethers are easier and more fun if you plan activities; you do not want your friend to get bored; you should have an idea of what you are going to do beforehand.
  - Ask: *What are some activities that teens enjoy doing on get-togethers?*
    - Have teens brainstorm ideas.
    - Refer to the table "Suggestions for Activity-Based Get-Togethers" for suggestions.

■ **Where** are you going to have the **get-together**?
  - Say: *It's also important to figure out where the get-together is going to take place. Why is this important to figure out?*
    - Answer: Because the get-together may never happen if no one knows where to go.

■ **When** are you going to have the **get-together**?
  - Say: *We also need to figure out when the get-together is going to take place. Why is that important to figure out?*
    - Answer: Because if you do not decide in advance when you are going to get together, your schedules may become full and the get-together might never take place.

■ Have some activities ready.
  - Say: *Even though you should have decided beforehand what you are going to do on your get-together, you will also need to have some other activities ready for when your friend comes over* (assuming the get-together is at your home). *Why would it be important to have other things to do?*
    - Answer: Because teens get bored easily and you need to have other options ready; your most important job is to make sure your guest has fun, so having a variety of activities at the ready will be helpful.
  - Ask: *What are some activities that you can have ready for your friends in case you get bored?*
    - Answers:
      - DVDs, videos
      - Video games, computer games
      - Board games, card games
      - Sports equipment

■ Put away any personal items you do not want to share or let people see.

    – Say: *Another important part of preparing for a get-together involves putting away any personal items you don't want to share or let other people see. Why would that be important to do?*

        • Answer: Because there may be things that you do not want your friend to see or touch; you do not want to be rude and tell your friend that he or she cannot touch things; it is easier to put things away in advance so your friend does not even know they are there.

■ Make sure your room is presentable.

    – Say: *Another important part of preparing for a get-together in your home is to make sure your room is cleaned up and presentable. Why would that be important to do?*

■ Answer: Because your friend will want to see your room (even if you do not think he or she needs to see it); if your room is a mess, your friend may think you are a slob and this makes you look bad; cleaning up your room before having company over is also a sign of respect for your guests.

Suggestions for Activity-Based Get-Togethers

Mealtime Activities	*Sports Done in Pairs*
Barbecue	Swimming
Ordering pizza	Skateboarding
Going to a restaurant	Shooting baskets
Cooking a meal	Bike riding
Picnic	Roller skating
Baking	Tennis
Group Sports	*Public Activities*
Basketball	Going to the movies
Baseball	Bowling
Soccer	Video arcade*
Touch football	Gaming centers*
Volleyball	Laser tag
Badminton	Going to the mall*
	Teen dance clubs*
	Comic book conventions
	Comic book stores
	Gaming stores
	Going to concerts*

Indoor Activities	*Outdoor Activities*
Listening to music	**Going to the local amusement parks***
Renting movies	**Miniature golf parks***
Watching TV	**Water parks***
Playing board/card games	**Go-carting***
Computer/video games	**State fair***
Surfing the Internet (YouTube)	**County fair***
Online networking sites (MySpace, Facebook)	**Batting cages**
	Golf range
Looking at magazines	**Dog park**
Playing Ping-Pong	**Hanging out at the park***
Playing pool	**Going to the beach, lake, river, etc.**
Playing air hockey	**Teen activity centers***
Playing darts	**Ski resorts (skiing, snowboarding)**
	Beach resorts (surfing, windsurfing, swimming, sailing)
*Be sure to check out these places in advance to make sure there is no gang activity or increased potential for getting into trouble.	

At the Beginning of the Get-Together

- Explain: *Now that we know the rules for planning a get-together, we need to talk about the steps for beginning a get-together at your home.*
- Greet your guest.
  - Say: *The first step when your guest arrives is to greet them at the door. How do we greet our guest?*
    - Answers:
      - Say hello.
      - Ask your guest how he or she is doing:
        - Girls will often hug each other and show excitement to see one another.
        - Boys may give a gesture of casual acknowledgement (e.g., give a pound—bumping knuckles).
- Invite your guest in.
  - Say: *Next we need to invite the guest in. This involves saying something like, "Come in" and move out of the doorway so he or she can come inside. What happens if we forget to invite your guest in?*
    - Answer: He or she ends up standing at the door waiting; this can be awkward.
- Introduce your guest to anyone your guest does not know.
  - Say: *Once we've invited our guest in, we need to introduce our guest to anyone he or she does not know. Why is this important to do?*
    - Answer: If your guest does not know everyone, he or she is going to feel awkward and left out.

■ Give your guest a tour.
- Say: *If this is the first time your guest has come to your home, show him or her around* (e.g., your bedroom, bathroom, living room…). *Why is this important to do?*
  • Answer: It is your job to make your guest feel welcome; the guest should know where the bathroom is located and be familiar with the surroundings in order to feel welcome.
■ Offer your guest something to drink and eat.
- Say: *Next, you will want to offer your guest something to eat or drink. Why is this a nice thing to do?*
  • Answer: The guest may be hungry or thirsty; it is polite to offer a guest in your home food and beverages.
■ Ask your guest what he or she wants to do.
- Say: *Even though you should have planned with your guest what you're going to do, you should still ask your guest what he or she wants to do when the guest is settled. Why should we ask a guest what he or she wants to do?*
  • Answer: The guest may want to do something different from what you planned; the guest gets to pick the activities; the host should be flexible.

Role Play

■ The teen group leader and a coach should then demonstrate an *appropriate* role play in which the teen group leader begins a *get-together* following all of these steps.
- Example of an *appropriate* role play:

Coach: (knocks on door)

Teen group leader: (opens door) "Hi (insert name)! How are you?"

Coach: "Hi (insert name)! I'm fine. How are you?"

Teen group leader: "Fine, thanks. Come on in." (moves aside so the coach can enter)

Coach: (enters) "Thanks."

Teen group leader: "I don't think you've met everyone before. This is (point to each teen in the group and introduce them by name). Everyone, this is (insert coaches name)."

Coach: "Nice to meet you guys."

Teen group leader: "So I guess you've never been here before. I should show you around real quick. (give an imaginary tour) This is the living room, the kitchen is through there. The bathroom is just around the corner. And this is my bedroom."

Coach: "Cool. Thanks."

Teen group leader: "Can I get you something to eat or drink?"

Coach: "Thanks anyway. I'm okay."

Teen group leader: (looking at the whole group) "So what do you guys want to do?"

    – Say: *Okay, let's time-out on that. So that's how you greet your guest and begin a get-together. Each of you is going to be practicing this tonight by being both a host and a guest. But first, we need to figure out the rest of the rules for having a get-together.*

During the Get-Together

■ Say: *So now that we know how to begin the get-together, we need to know what to do during the get-together. There are some important rules for making sure your get-together is a success.*

■ At your home, the ***guest gets to pick the activity***.

    – Say: *The first rule is that at your home, the guest gets to pick the activities. Why do you think the guest gets to pick the activities?*

        • Answer: Because it is the host's job to make sure the guest has a good time.

    – Explain: *But when you're the guest at someone's home, you may need to take the host's lead about what to do, because not everyone knows that the guest gets to pick the activity. There's one exception to this rule. If our guest wants to do something dangerous or inappropriate, what do you think we should do?*

        • Answer: Do not go along with it; consider whether this is a good choice in a friend.

■ ***Praise*** your friend.

    – Say: *Another rule for having a get-together is that you should praise your friend. That means that if your friend does something well, you should let them know by saying "good job" or something relevant. Why is it a good idea to praise your friend?*

        • Answer: Because it makes your friend feel good.

■ ***Compliment*** your friend.

    – Say: *Another rule for having a get-together is that you should compliment your friend. This is like praise, but means that if you notice something about your friend that you like, you should let them know. Like telling someone you like their outfit or that you think they're good at sports. Why is it a good idea to compliment your friend?*

        • Answer: Because it makes your friend feel good.

■ ***Be a good sport***.

    – Say: *When we're having a get-together and we're playing games or sports, it's important to be a good sport. Why would it be important to be a good sport?*

        • Answer: Because teens do not want to play games and sports with people who do not play nicely; they will be less likely to want to hang out with you and be your friend if you are a poor sport.

- Explain: *Next week we're going to be talking about the rules for being a good sport in more detail. This should help you with your get-togethers.*

■ ***Be loyal to your friend****.*

- Say: *Another rule for having a successful get-together is to be loyal to your friend. This means you shouldn't argue with, criticize, or make fun of your friend. And if someone else makes fun of your friend, you should stick up for him or her. Being loyal to your friend also means that you shouldn't ignore one friend to talk to another friend. Why is this important?*
  - Answer: Because it is your job to make sure your friend is having fun; your friend should feel like he or she has your support and attention.
- Explain: *Being loyal to your guest also means that if someone unexpectedly calls or stops by during your get-together, you shouldn't invite them over. Instead, you should tell them you're busy and that you'll get back to them later. You probably don't want to mention that you're having a get-together. Why would it be a bad idea to tell the other friend that you're having a get-together?*
  - Answer: It may make the other friend feel excluded; it might hurt his or her feelings; the other friend might ask to join the get-together.
- Ask: *Why would it be a bad idea to invite your other friend into your get-together unexpectedly?*
  - Answer: It might make your guest feel like he or she was not good enough; the current guest might feel excluded; it is rude (even if your guest says it is okay for you to invite someone else into the get-together—your guest may simply feel obligated to agree).
- Say: *Being loyal to your guest also means no phone calls, text messaging, e-mailing, or instant messaging, unless it's your guest's idea. Your most important job is to make sure your guest has a good time, so if he or she suggests contacting other people, you should go with the flow. But remember, if your guest only seems interested in messaging or talking with other people during your get-together, he or she may be a poor choice for a friend.*

■ ***Suggest a change*** if you are bored or tired with an activity.

- Say: *Sometimes people get bored when they're having a get-together. You should never tell your friends that you're bored. Instead, you should suggest a change. You can do this by saying, "How about when we're done with this we play something else?" What should we do if our friend doesn't want to play what we suggest for a change?*
  - Answer: Let your friend pick the next activity instead; the guest gets to pick the activities, so the host needs to be flexible; if you are the guest and your friend does not want to do what you suggest, be flexible and go with the flow (if this is a regular occurrence you can consider whether this is a good friend choice).

■ At least 50% of the time should be spent conversing and ***trading information***.

– Say: *The last rule for having a get-together is that you should be spending at least 50% of the time conversing and trading information. Why would this be an important rule?*

■ Answer: Because this is how you get to know one another and find common interests.

End of the Get-Together

■ Say: *Now that we know the rules for what to do during a get-together, we need to talk about how to end the get-together.*

■ Give a ***cover story*** for leaving or ending the get-together.
   – Say: *The first step for ending a get-together is to give a cover story or a reason for ending the get-together. What are some examples of things you might say when you have to end a get-together?*
      • Answers:
         ■ *I have to go soon.*
         ■ *I have to start my homework now.*
         ■ *My mom said it's time for dinner.*
         ■ *I have to go to bed soon.*
   – Say: *Parents can also provide a cover story for why the get-together has to end.*

■ Start walking your friend to the door (if the get-together is at your home).
   – Say: *Then you will need to walk your friend to the door to say good-bye. Why do we need to walk our friend to the door?*
      • Answer: Because it is rude to make your friend find his or her way out.

■ Thank your friend for getting together.
   – Say: *The next step for ending a get-together is to thank your friend for getting together. Why is that important to do?*
      • Answer: Because it makes your friend feel nice; it shows that you appreciate him or her.

■ If you had a good time, tell your friend.
   – Say: *Then, if you had a nice time, you should tell your friend. Why is that a nice thing to do?*
      • Answer: It shows your friend that you enjoy being around him or her; it makes your friend feel good.

■ Say good-bye and you will see him or her later.
   – Say: *Finally, as we're preparing to end the get-together it is important to say good-bye. You might even say "I'll see you later" or "I'll see you at school." As you're saying good-bye. This is also a nice time to try to make future plans to get together.*

Role Play

- The teen group leader and a coach should then demonstrate an *appropriate* role play in which the teen group leader ends a **get-together** following all of these steps.
  - Example of an *appropriate* role play:

    Teen group leader: "Well, my mom told me we're having dinner soon."

    Coach: "Oh, okay."

    Teen group leader: (stands up and starts walking to the door) "Thanks for coming over!"

    Coach: (follows teen group leader to the door) "Thanks for having me over!"

    Teen group leader: "It was really fun!"

    Coach: "Yeah, I had a good time, too."

    Teen group leader: "We should hang out again soon."

    Coach: "That would be cool."

    Teen group leader: (opens the door) "So I guess I'll see you at school tomorrow."

    Coach: "Okay. Sounds good." (walks through the door)

    Teen group leader: "Take care. Bye!"

    Coach: "Bye!"

  - Say: *Okay, let's time out on that. So that's how you end a get-together. Each of you is going to be practicing this tonight by being both a host and a guest.*

Homework Assignments

- Briefly explain the homework for the week by saying: *The main homework assignment this week is for each of you to have a get-together with one or more friends. You may need to make a phone call to set up this get-together. We're also going to continue to have each of you practice slipping into conversations with people you only know so-so, and if necessary we want you to practice slipping out. You will also need to bring an inside game to share with the group next week. So again, your homework assignment this week is to:*
  - *Have a get-together with one or more friends.*
    - *Make an out-of-group phone call to figure out what you are going to do on your get-together.*
  - *Slip into a conversation following the steps we have outlined.*
    - *Slip out of the conversation if the group does not seem interested in talking to you.*
  - *Bring an inside game to share with the group (e.g., age-appropriate board game, card game, etc.).*

Teen Activity: Get-Togethers

Note: See the "Teen Activity Guide" for rules.

■ Notify teens they will be practicing having group get-togethers:
   - Break teens up into small groups and have them practice being a host and a guest.
   - Girls should be paired with girls and boys should be paired with boys, when possible.
   - Assign hosts and guests:
      • Have each teen practice beginning the get-together as a host.
      • Give everyone an opportunity to be a host and a guest.
   - Teens will then play indoor games while practicing having a group ***get-together***.
   - Games are chosen from appropriate ***inside games*** brought by teens and other available games.
   - Teens receive points while playing games for practicing:
      • ***Trading information***
      • ***Praise***
      • ***Compliments***
      • ***Being a good sport***
   - At the end of the session, teens should practice ending the get-together.
      • Assign hosts and guests:
         ■ Have each teen practice ending the get-together as a host.
         ■ Give everyone an opportunity to be a host and a guest.

Reunification

■ Announce that teens should join their parents.
   - Be sure that the teens are standing or sitting next to their parents.
   - Be sure to have silence and the full attention of the group.
   - Say: *Today we worked on having a get-together. You will all be having a get-together this week, so it will be important to remember the rules. Who can tell me one of the rules for having a good get-together?* [Have teens generate all of the rules. Be prepared to give prompts if necessary.]
      • At your home, the ***guest gets to pick the activity***.
      • ***Praise*** your friend.
      • ***Be a good sport***.
      • ***Compliment your friend***.
      • ***Be loyal to your friend***.
      • ***Suggest a change*** if you are bored or tired with an activity.
      • At least 50% of the time should be spent conversing and ***trading information***.

■ Say: *Today we practiced having a get-together and this group did a great job of being good hosts and guests. Let's give them a round of applause.*
■ Go over the homework for the next week (see below).
■ Individually and separately negotiate the following with each family:
  – The location of the get-together, the activity planned, who will be present, as well as the parent role in the get-together.
  – Where the teens will attempt to slip in and with which peer group.
  – What inside game will be brought next week.

Homework Assignments

1. Teens are to have a friend over for a ***get-together***.
   a. Make an ***out-of-group call*** to set up the ***get-together***.
      i. ***Trade information*** to find ***common interests***.
      ii. Decide what you are going to do during your ***get-together***.
   b. Parents monitor the ***get-together*** from a ***distance***.
   c. The ***get-together*** should be activity-based.
   d. First ***get-togethers*** with a particular teen should be limited to approximately 2 hours (depending on the activity).
2. Practice ***slipping into a conversation*** between at least two teens.
   a. Try to choose a conversation where you know at least one of the people.
   b. Try a place where you are likely to be accepted (i.e., low-risk place) and you do not have a bad reputation. You may need to find a new place.
   c. Parents and teens should discuss how the teen ***slipped into the conversation*** and ***slipped out*** (if applicable).
   d. Parents should help teen troubleshoot any problems that may have arisen.
3. ***Bring an inside game***.
   a. Bring an inside game to share with the group (e.g., age-appropriate board game, card game, etc.).
      i. No solitary games.
      ii. Do not bring something that you are unwilling to share with group members or are worried about breaking or losing.

Calculate Points

Keep track of the following for each week of the intervention.

■ Calculate the number of points earned by each teen.
■ Add up the total number of points earned by the group.
■ Do not calculate the points in the presence of the teens:
  – Do not disclose the individual or group total of points.
  – Discourage attempts to compare number of points earned between teens.
■ Remind them that they are working as a team to earn a bigger and better graduation party.

Teen Activity Guide: Session 8

"Get-Togethers"

Materials Needed

- ■ Indoor games brought by teens.
- ■ In the event that a teen forgets to bring an indoor game, have board games available to share:
  - – Cards
  - – Checkers
  - – Chess

Rules

- ■ Notify teens they will be practicing having group ***get-togethers***.
- ■ Break teens up into small groups and have them practice being a host and a guest.
- ■ Girls should be paired with girls and boys should be paired with boys, when possible.
- ■ Assign hosts and guests:
  - – Have each teen practice beginning a ***get-together*** by being a host.
    - • Begin by having the teen verbally go over the steps for beginning a ***get-together***:
      - ■ Greet the guest.
      - ■ Invite the guest in.
      - ■ Give the guest a tour.
      - ■ Introduce the guest to everyone.
      - ■ Offer the guest something to eat or drink.
      - ■ Ask the guest what he or she wants to do.
    - • Have the teen rehearse the steps with the entire group.
    - • Give everyone an opportunity to be a host and a guest.
- ■ Teens will then play indoor games while practicing having a group ***get-together***.
- ■ Games are chosen from appropriate ***inside games*** brought by teens and other available games provided by the treatment team:
  - – Have teens negotiate what they will play.
    - • They may need to compromise by playing one game for half the time and then switching games midway.
    - • Be sure that the guests get to choose the game.
  - – You may need to assist teens in understanding the rules for specific games:
    - • Try to avoid acting as a referee if disagreements occur.
    - • Encourage teens to work out their differences by being good sports.

– You may need to prompt teens to be good sports and praise their partners.
– Teens receive points while playing games for practicing:
– ***Trading information***
– ***Praise***
– ***Compliments***
– ***Being a good sport***

■ At the end of the session, teens should practice ending the get-together.
– Assign hosts and guests:
  • Have each teen practice ending the ***get-together*** as a host.
– Begin by having the teen verbally go over the steps for ending a get-together:
  • Give a ***cover story*** for ending the ***get-together***.
  • Start walking the guest to the door.
  • Thank the guest for coming over.
  • Tell the guest you had a nice time.
  • Say good-bye and you will see him or her later.
– Have the teen rehearse these steps with the entire group.
– Give everyone an opportunity to be a host and a guest.

Chapter 11

Session 9
Good Sportsmanship

Parent Session Therapist Guide

Guiding Principles of the Parent Session

The parent was expected to help the teen get the ball rolling for the first get-together; thus, parents must take the major responsibility for this homework assignment. The group leader has to maintain pressure on parents to get this to happen. Review the get-together assignment first by asking for successful get-togethers, and redirecting parents who want to talk about anything else.

In order to save face, parents will sometimes evade this assignment by spending a lot of time talking about how some other feature of the program or the group leader are wonderful or how the slipping-in assignment went well, but after this, casually mentioning they could not do the get-together. Having a parent who did not complete the get-together assignment go first in the homework review will make the parents who were able to do the homework more hesitant to talk about their successes. Parents may also try to deflect group leader comments by going totally off track to talk about something compelling. For example, parents may start talking about how their teens are bullied, trying to avoid talking about the failure to have a get-together. By allowing parents to get off-track in this manner, you will be taking the "heat off" of parents who did not attempt the homework. Do not allow any of this to happen. Having parents who had successful get-togethers present their homework first will demonstrate that the homework was possible to do and will help focus this part of the session.

Even at this point in the treatment, parents and teens may still misjudge the best crowd or group for the teen. Their get-together requests to several teens from school may be turned down because they did not realize (until the group leader points it out) that their teen had a negative reputation at school or was trying to fit in with the wrong crowd. Correcting the error in choice of the wrong crowd might be as simple as encouraging a teen with autism to seek other peers with similar problems. Some teens may feel more comfortable and accepted by other teens who have similar problems. Stating this to parents gives permission for the teen and parent to pursue this option.

As mentioned in the guiding principles of the last session, the group leader needs to be alert for the "helicopter parent." In recounting get-togethers at the teen's home, the group leader should routinely ask where the parent was throughout the get-together and actively discourage parent intrusiveness, as this is not developmentally appropriate. The group leader should be alert to parents who try to short-circuit the get-together process by arranging a get-together with another parent without involving either teen. This approach is inappropriate for adolescents.

After reviewing successes of the other parents, the best approach for working with parents who did not attempt the assignment should be to avoid prolonged discussions as to why they could not do the assignment last week, but instead figuring out how they are going to get the assignment done next week.

The content of this session is concerned with rules for a good sport. Individuals with social problems have been shown to have different priorities in their social goals when compared to individuals without social problems. Crick and Ladd (1990) found that the former tended to focus more on goals that obtained tangible rewards and less on relationship-enhancing goals in comparison to individuals without social problems. Thus, the focus of this session is to begin to change the social priorities of teens in the group. The rules for a good sport are based heavily upon the rules developed and tested extensively in Frankel and Myatt (2003).

Just discussing the rules with the teen has no evidential basis for promoting generalization. Instead, the parent can enforce the good sport rules during get-togethers that take place in their home. Another good opportunity for enforcing these rules is when the parent plays a game with his or her teen or when siblings play games with each other. Parent coaching is the optimal intervention in this case and involves the parent pulling the teen aside when he or she sees a good sport violation and reminding the teen about appropriate good sportsmanship behavior (i.e., a teachable moment).

Homework Review

1. ***Get-together***.
   a. Identify whether the teen made a phone call to set up the ***get-together***.
   b. Identify whether the ***get-together*** was:
      i. Activity-based.
      ii. Monitored by parents from a *distance*.
      iii. No more than 2 hours (depending on the activity).

    c. Be sure that the teen ***traded information*** with his or her guest and found a ***common interest***.

        i. 50% of the time should have been spent ***trading information***.

2. ***Slipping into or slipping out of a conversation***.

    a. Have parents identify:

        i. Where their teen ***slipped in***.

        ii. If the teen was familiar with someone in the group.

        iii. If the teen followed the steps for ***slipping into the conversation***.

        iv. If the teen had to follow the steps for ***slipping out of the conversation***.

    b. Troubleshoot any problems that may have arisen.

3. ***Bring an inside game***.

    a. Have parents identify the inside game their teen brought to share with the group (e.g., age-appropriate board game, card game, etc.).

    b. Only give credit for appropriate items.

Didactic Lesson: Good Sportsmanship

- Distribute the Parent Handout.
- Explain: *Now that teens have learned the rules for having successful get-togethers and have hopefully had some success in organizing and having a get-together with a friend, it will be important to continue to practice these skills on a regular basis. One of the assignments this week is to organize another get-together. In addition, your teens will be learning the rules for being a good sport in the teen session. In order to prevent discord and ensure that everyone has a good time when playing games and sports, it is critical that teens act like good sports. Because many teens enjoy playing games and sports during get-togethers, this will likely be a helpful tool in ensuring successful get-togethers in the future.*
- Go around the room and have parents take turns reading the Parent Handout.
- Sections in **bold print** come directly from the Parent Handout.

Rules for Good Sportsmanship

- ***Praise your friend***.
  - **Examples of praise during a game**:
    - **"Nice move!"**
    - **"Nice try."**
    - **"Nice shot!"**
    - **"Good job!"**
    - **Give a high-five**
    - **Thumbs up**
    - **Give a pound (bumping closed fists)**

- ■ *Do not referee during a game*:
  - Do not try to call plays or boss the other players around.
  - Teens do not like to hang out with people who boss them around.
- ■ *Do not be a coach*:
  - Unless your friend asks, do not try to "help" by giving advice.
  - Even though you may only be trying to help, it may seem like you are being bossy.
  - Teens do not like to hang out with other teens who tell them what to do.
- ■ *Share and take turns*:
  - Do not be a *ball hog* during a sporting game.
  - *Share the controller* if you are playing a video game.
    - No one will want to play with you if you do not share and take turns; it is not fun for other people.
- ■ *If you get bored, suggest a change*:
  - Do not walk away or say "I'm bored" in the middle of a game.
    - It might hurt the other person's feelings; you might look like a poor sport.
  - If you are bored, say: "How about when we're done with this we play something else?"
- ■ *Do not gloat if you win*:
  - Act like winning was not a big deal.
  - If you gloat, it makes the other person feel bad; he or she may not want to play with you again.
- ■ *Do not sulk or get angry if you lose*:
  - If you sulk or get angry, it makes you look like a poor sport; the other person may not want to play with you again.
- ■ *At the end of a game say "good game"*:
  - This shows that you are a good sport; it makes the other person feel good.

Homework Assignments

The parent group leader should go over the homework assignment and trouble-shoot any potential problems with parents.

1. *Teens are to have a friend over for a get-together.*
   a. Make an *out-of-group* call to set up the *get-together*:
      i. *Trade information* to find *common interests*.
      ii. Decide what you are going to do during your *get-together*.
   b. Parents monitor the *get-together* from a *distance*.
   c. The *get-together* should be activity-based.
   d. Be sure the teen *trades information* with the guest:
      i. 50% of the *get-together* should be spent *trading information*.

    ii. First *get-togethers* with a particular teen should be limited to approximately 2 hours (depending on the activity).

2. *Practice being a good sport.*
   a. This can be done during the *get-together* or any other time during the week when the teen plays games (video games, computer games, board games, card games) or sports.
   b. Parents and teens should discuss how the teen was a *good sport* if the parent was unable to observe.

3. *Practice slipping into a conversation between at least two teens.*
   a. Try to choose a conversation where you know at least one of the people.
   b. Try a place where you are likely to be accepted (i.e., low-risk place) and you do not have a bad reputation. You may need to find a new place.
   c. Parents and teens should discuss how the teen *slipped into the conversation* and *slipped out* (if applicable).

4. *Bring an inside game.*
   a. Bring an inside game to share with the group (e.g., an age-appropriate board game, card game, etc.)
      i. No solitary games.
   b. Do not bring something that you are:
      i. Unwilling to share with group members.
      ii. Worried about breaking or losing.

Parent Handout 9: Good Sportsmanship

Rules for Good Sportsmanship

- ■ *Praise* your friend
  - Examples of praise during a game:
    - "Nice move!"
    - "Nice try."
    - "Nice shot!"
    - "Good job!"
    - Give a high-five
    - Thumbs up
    - Give a pound (bumping closed fists)
- ■ *Do not referee* during a game:
  - Do not try to call plays or boss the other players around.
  - Teens do not like to hang out with people who boss them around.
- ■ *Do not be a coach*:
  - Unless your friend asks, do not try to "help" by giving advice.
  - Even though you may only be trying to help, it may seem like you are being bossy.
  - Teens do not like to hang out with other teens who tell them what to do.
- ■ *Share and take turns*:
  - Do not be a *ball hog* during a sporting game.
  - *Share the controller* if you are playing a video game.
    - No one will want to play with you if you do not share and take turns; it is not fun for other people.
- ■ *If you get bored, suggest a change*:
  - Do not walk away or say "I'm bored" in the middle of a game.
    - It might hurt the other person's feelings; you might look like a poor sport.
  - If you are bored, say: *How about when we're done with this we play something else?*
- ■ *Do not gloat if you win*:
  - Act like winning was not a big deal.
  - If you gloat, it makes the other person feel bad; he or she may not want to play with you again.
- ■ *Do not sulk or get angry if you lose*:
  - If you sulk or get angry, it makes you look like a poor sport; the other person may not want to play with you again.
- ■ *At the end of a game say "good game"*:
  - This shows that you are a good sport; it makes the other person feel good.

Homework Assignments

1. The teen is to have a friend over for a ***get-together***.
   a. Make an ***out-of-group*** call to set up the ***get-together***.
      i. ***Trade information*** to find ***common interests***.
      ii. Decide what you are going to do during your ***get-together***.
   b. Parents monitor the ***get-together*** from a *distance*.
   c. The ***get-together*** should be activity-based.
   d. Be sure the teen ***trades information*** with the guest.
      i. 50% of the ***get-together*** should be spent ***trading information***.
      ii. First ***get-togethers*** with a particular teen should be limited to approximately 2 hours (depending on the activity).
2. ***Practice being a good sport***:
   a. This can be done during the ***get-together*** or any other time during the week when the teen plays games (video games, computer games, board games, card games) or sports.
   b. Parents and teens should discuss how the teen was a ***good sport*** if the parent was unable to observe.
3. Practice ***slipping into a conversation*** between at least two teens.
   a. Try to choose a conversation where you know at least one of the people.
   b. Try a place where you are likely to be accepted (i.e., low-risk place) and you do not have a bad reputation. You may need to find a new place.
   c. Parents and teens should discuss how the teen ***slipped into the conversation*** and ***slipped out*** (if applicable).
4. ***Bring an inside game***.
   a. Bring an inside game to share with the group (e.g., age-appropriate board game, card game, etc.).
      i. No solitary games.
   b. Do not bring something that you are:
      i. Unwilling to share with group members.
      ii. Worried about breaking or losing.

Teen Therapist Guide—Session 9: Good Sportsmanship

Guiding Principles of the Teen Session

In the previous session, teens were taught how to be good hosts during get-togethers with friends. Because common activities during get-togethers and other peer social interactions include the playing of games, video games, and sports (particularly for boys), it is essential that teens know how to interact harmoniously during these activities.

Many teens will be accustomed to thinking of game play and sports in terms of winning being the ultimate goal. They may also want to be liked by others, but frequently set good sportsmanship at a low priority. It will be the group leader's responsibility to challenge these priorities by pointing out that a better goal of games and sports with friends should be to have a good time. The rules of a good sport are well defined so that they can be monitored and corrected by the group leader in session and parents at home.

Rule Review

Note: Only go over session rules again if the teens are having difficulty following them.

- Have teens identify the rules for the group.
- Give them points for remembering.
  1. Listen to the other group members (no talking when others are speaking)
  2. Follow directions
  3. Raise your hand
  4. Be respectful (no teasing or making fun of others)
  5. No touching (no hitting, kicking, pushing, hugging, etc.)

Homework Review

Note: Give points for homework *parts*—not just one point per assignment.

1. ***Bring an inside game***
   a. Identify the inside game the teen brought to share with the group (e.g., age-appropriate board game, card game, etc.).
   b. Only give credit for appropriate items.
   c. To avoid distractions, have a coach put the item away until the teen session activity.
2. ***Get-together***
   a. Say: *Your main homework assignment this week was to have a get-together with a friend. Raise your hand if you had a get-together this week.*
      i. Begin by calling on the teens who completed the assignment.

ii. Briefly ask:
1. *Who did you have a get-together with?*
2. *Where was the get-together?*
3. *Did you make an out-of-group phone call to figure out what you were going to do?*
4. *What did you end up doing?*
5. *Who chose the activities?* [Answer should be the guest.]
6. *Did you trade information at least 50% of the time?*
7. *Did you have a good time?*
8. *Did your friend have a good time?*
9. *Is this someone you might want to have a get-together with again?*

iii. Troubleshoot any problems that may have arisen.

3. ***Slipping into a conversation***

a. Say: *Another one of your assignments this week was to practice slipping into a conversation with someone from a group that you were likely to be accepted by. Raise your hand if you practiced slipping into a conversation this week.*

i. Begin by calling on the teens who completed the assignment.

ii. Briefly ask:
1. *Where did you slip in?*
2. *Which group did you choose to slip in with?*
3. *Did you know at least one of the people?*
4. *How did you slip in?*
   a. Be sure they followed the steps for ***slipping in***.
   b. If they did not follow the steps, ask: *What could you do differently next time?*
5. *Did you need to slip out?*
   a. If so, be sure they followed the steps for ***slipping out***.
   b. If they did not follow the steps, ask: *What could you do differently next time?*
6. Troubleshoot any problems that may have arisen.

Didactic Lesson: Rules for Good Sportsmanship

■ Explain: *Today we are going to talk about good sportsmanship. The most important goal of playing games and sports is that everyone has a good time. So it's important that when we're playing video games, board games, or sports, that we act like a good sport. Why is that important?*
– Answer: It is more fun for everyone; the most important part of a game is that everyone have fun.

■ Ask: *What happens if we are a poor sport when playing games or sports?*
– Answer: Our friends will not want to play with us; we may get a bad reputation.

■ Present the rules for being a good sport.

1. ***Praise your friend***.

a. Say: *One of the most important elements of being a good sport is to give praise. Who can tell me what praise is?*

    i. Answer: Praise is a kind of compliment.

b. Ask: *Why might it be a good idea to praise your friend when you're playing games or sports?*

    i. Answer: It makes your friend feel good.

c. Ask teens for examples of praise during a game:

    i. "Nice move!"

    ii. "Nice try."

    iii. "Great shot!"

    iv. "Good job!"

    v. Give a high-five

    vi. Thumbs up

    vii. Give a pound (bump closed fists)

d. Explain: *Praising a friend by saying "good job" or "nice shot" is a simple way to ensure that your friend has a nice time and that the game remains fun. And remember that the goal of a game is that everyone has fun, not to win at any cost.*

2. **Do not referee** during a game.

a. Say: *Another rule for being a good sport is to avoid refereeing. What is a referee?*

    i. Answer: Someone who calls plays during a game.

b. Ask: *Why is it a bad idea to act like a referee during a game?*

    i. Answer: Teens do not like to hang out with people who boss them around.

3. **Do not be a coach**.

a. Say: *It's also important that when we're trying to be a good sport that we don't coach other players. Some kids try to be helpful and give advice during a game, the way that a coach might. Why would it be a bad idea to act like a coach with your friends?*

    i. Answer: Teens do not like to hang out with other teens who tell them what to do.

b. Explain: *Even though you may only be trying to help, it may seem like you're being bossy. So unless your friend asks* (like if you're teaching them a new game), *don't try to "help" by giving advice. One other exception is if you see your friend struggling with a game that you're good at, you can offer to help by saying something like, "Would you like me to show you how to get to the next level?"* [during a video game], *but if your friend doesn't want your help you need to stop giving advice.*

4. **Share and take turns**.

a. Say: *Another rule of being a good sport is to share and take turns. This is different from being a ball hog or someone who doesn't share the controller. What is a "ball hog?"*

    i. Answer: Someone who does not share the ball or take turns.

b. Ask: *What's the problem with being a "ball hog" or not taking turns during a game?*

   i. Answer: No one will want to play with you; it is not fun for other people.

c. Ask: *What's the problem with hogging the controller when you're playing a video game?*

   i. Answer: No one will want to play with you; it is not fun for other people.

d. Ask: *What should you do instead of hogging the ball or not taking turns?*

   i. Answers:

     1. ***Share and take turns***.
     2. ***Share the controller***.
     3. ***Do not be a ball hog***.

5. ***If you get bored, suggest a change***.

a. Say: *Sometimes people get bored in the middle of a game. We talked about this in relation to your get-togethers last week. What can you do if you get bored in the middle of a game?*

   i. Answer: Suggest playing something else.

b. Ask: *What would be the problem with just walking away or saying "I'm bored" in the middle of a game?*

   i. Answer: It might hurt the other person's feelings; you might look like a poor sport.

c. Ask: *What could you say instead of saying "I'm bored?"*

   i. Answer: You could say: "How about when we're done with this we play something else?"

d. Explain: *So one of the rules for being a good sport is that if you get bored, you should suggest a change.*

6. ***Do not gloat if you win***.

a. Say: *Sometimes when people win a game they get really excited and they gloat. They might jump up and down or cheer for themselves. Why is it a bad idea to gloat if you win a game?*

   i. Answer: It makes the other person feel bad; the other person may not want to play with you again.

b. Ask: *What should you do instead of gloating?*

   i. Answer: Act like winning was not a big deal.

7. ***Do not sulk or get angry if you lose***.

a. Say: *Another rule for being a good sport is to avoid sulking or getting angry if you lose. What is the problem with sulking or getting angry after you lose a game?*

   i. Answer: It makes you look like a poor sport; the other person may not want to play with you again.

8. ***At the end of a game say "good game."***

a. Say: *The final rule for being a good sport relates to what we should do at the end of the game. What should you say and do at the end of a game?*

    i. Answer: Say: "Good game"; give a high-five; give a pound.
  b. Ask: *Why is it important to say "good game" at the end of a game?*
    i. It shows that you are a good sport; it makes the other person feel good.

Homework Assignments

■ Briefly explain the homework for the week by saying: *The main homework assignment this week is for each of you to have another get-together with one or more friends. You may need to make a phone call to set up this get-together. During these get-togethers, we want you to practice being a good sport if you play games or sports. We're also going to continue to have each of you practice slipping into conversations with people you only know so-so, and if necessary we want you to practice slipping out. And you will need to bring an inside game to share with the group next week. So again, your homework assignment this week is to:*
  – *Have a get-together with one or more friends.*
    • *Make an out-of-group call to schedule the get-together.*
    • *Trade information to figure out what you are going to do.*
  – *Practice being a good sport:*
    • *This can be done during get-togethers if applicable.*
    • *Other relevant times include during extracurricular sports activities or during gym class.*
  – *Slip into a conversation following the steps we outlined.*
  – *Slip out of the conversation if the group does not seem interested in talking to you.*
  – *Bring an indoor game to share with the group (e.g., age-appropriate board game, card game, etc.).*

Teen Activity: Get-Togethers and Good Sportsmanship

Note: See the "Teen Activity Guide" for rules.

■ Notify teens they will be practicing having group ***get-togethers***.
  – Break teens up into small groups and have them practice being a host and a guest.
  – Girls should be paired with girls and boys should be paired with boys, when possible.
  – Assign hosts and guests.
    • Have each teen practice beginning the get-together as a host.
    • Give everyone an opportunity to be a host and a guest.
  – Teens will then play indoor games while practicing having a group ***get-together***.

- Games are chosen from appropriate ***inside games*** brought by teens and other available games.
- Teens receive points while playing games for practicing being a ***good sport***:
  - ***Praise***
  - ***Do not referee***
  - ***Do not be a coach***
  - ***Share and take turns***
  - ***If you get bored, suggest a change***
  - ***Do not gloat if you win***
  - ***Do not sulk or get angry if you lose***
  - ***At the end of the game say: "Good game"***
- At the end of the session, teens should practice ending the get-together.
  - Assign hosts and guests:
    - Have each teen practice ending the get-together as a host.
    - Give everyone an opportunity to be a host and a guest.

Reunification

- Announce that teens should join their parents.
  - Be sure that the teens are standing or sitting next to their parents.
  - Be sure to have silence and the full attention of the group.
- Briefly describe what the teens did in the session today.
  - Say: *Today we went over the rules for being a good sport. Who can tell me one of the rules for being a good sport?* [Have teens generate all of the rules. Be prepared to give prompts if necessary.]
    - ***Praise***
    - ***Do not referee***
    - ***Do not be a coach***
    - ***Share and take turns***
    - ***If you get bored, suggest a change***
    - ***Do not gloat if you win***
    - ***Do not sulk or get angry if you lose***
    - ***At the end of the game say: "Good game"***
  - Say: *Today we practiced being good sports while having group get-togethers, and this group did a great job of being good sports. Let's give them a round of applause.*
- Go over the homework for the next week (see below).
- Individually and separately negotiate with each family:
  - The location of the get-together, the activity planned, who will be present, as well as the parent role in the get-together.
  - Where the teens will attempt to slip in and with which peer group.
  - What inside game will be brought next week.

Homework Assignments

1. Teens are to have a friend over for a ***get-together***.
   a. Make an ***out-of-group*** call to set up the ***get-together***.
      i. ***Trade information*** to find ***common interests***.
      ii. Decide what you are going to do during your ***get-together***.
   b. Parents monitor the ***get-together*** from a *distance*.
   c. The ***get-together*** should be activity-based.
   d. Be sure the teen ***trades information*** with the guest.
      i. 50% of the ***get-together*** should be spent ***trading information***.
      ii. First ***get-togethers*** should be limited to approximately 2 hours (depending on the activity).
2. Practice ***being a good sport***:
   a. This can be done during the ***get-together*** or any other time during the week when the teen plays games (video games, computer games, board games, card games) or sports.
   b. Parents and teens should discuss how the teen was a ***good sport*** if the parent was unable to observe.
3. Practice ***slipping into a conversation*** between at least two teens:
   a. Try to choose a conversation where *you know at least one of the people*.
   b. Try a place *where you are likely to be accepted* (i.e., low-risk place) and *you do not have a bad reputation*. You may need to find a new place.
   c. Parents and teens should discuss how the teen ***slipped into the conversation*** and ***slipped out*** (if applicable).
4. ***Bring an inside game***.
   a. Bring an inside game to share with the group (e.g., an age-appropriate board game, card game, etc.).
      i. No solitary games.
      ii. Do not bring something that you are unwilling to share with group members or are worried about breaking or losing.

Calculate Points

Keep track of the following for each week of the intervention.

- Calculate the number of points earned by each teen.
- Add up the total number of points earned by the group.
- Do not calculate the points in the presence of the teens:
  - Do not disclose the individual or group total of points.
  - Discourage attempts to compare number of points earned between teens.
- Remind them that they are working as a team to earn a bigger and better graduation party.

Teen Activity Guide: Session 9

"Get-Togethers and Good Sportsmanship"

Materials Needed

- Indoor games brought by teens
- In the event that a teen forgets to bring an indoor game, have board games available to share:
  - Cards
  - Checkers
  - Chess

Rules

- Notify teens they will be practicing having group **get-togethers**.
- Break teens up into small groups and have them practice being a host and a guest.
- Girls should be paired with girls and boys should be paired with boys, when possible.
- Assign hosts and guests.
  - Have each teen practice beginning a **get-together** by being a host.
    - Begin by having the teen verbally go over the steps for beginning a **get-together**:
      - Greet the guest.
      - Invite the guest in.
      - Give the guest a tour.
      - Introduce the guest to everyone.
      - Offer the guest something to eat or drink.
      - Ask everyone what they want to do.
    - Have the teen rehearse the steps with the entire group.
    - Give everyone an opportunity to be a host and a guest.
- Teens will then play indoor games while practicing having a group **get-together**.
- Games are chosen from appropriate **inside games** brought by teens and other available games provided by the treatment team.
  - Have teens negotiate what they will play.
    - They may need to compromise by playing one game for half the time and then switching games midway.
  - You may need to assist teens in understanding the rules for specific games:
    - Try to avoid acting as a referee if disagreements occur.
    - Encourage teens to work out their differences by being **good sports**.
  - You may need to prompt teens to be **good sports** and **praise** their partners.

■ Teens receive points while playing games for practicing being a ***good sport***:
  - *Praise*
  - *Do not referee*
  - *Do not be a coach*
  - *Share and take turns*
  - *If you get bored, suggest a change*
  - *Do not gloat if you win*
  - *Do not sulk or get angry if you lose*
  - *At the end of the game say: "Good game"*
■ Coaches should state why the teen is receiving a point (e.g., "John gets a point for praising!")
  - Be sure to keep track of points on the "Good Sportsmanship Point Log" (see Appendix G).
  - Speak loudly when giving out points so other teens can hear.
    • The social comparison will encourage other teens to ***praise*** and be ***good sports***.
■ At the end of the session, teens should practice ending the ***get-together***.
  - Assign hosts and guests.
    • Have each teen practice ending the ***get-together*** as a host.
  - Begin by having the teen verbally go over the steps for ending a get-together:
    • Give a ***cover story*** for ending the ***get-together***.
    • Start walking the guests to the door.
    • Thank him or her for coming over.
    • Tell him or her you had a nice time.
    • Say good-bye and you will see him or her later.
  - Have the teen rehearse these steps with the entire group.
  - Give everyone an opportunity to be a host and a guest.

Chapter 12

Session 10
Rejection I—Teasing and Embarrassing Feedback

Parent Session Therapist Guide

Guiding Principles of the Parent Session

Teasing is defined as disparaging remarks directed to another person. Younger children tease primarily by name-calling (Frankel & Myatt, 2003). Older children often tease by disparaging the victim or the victim's family (Frankel, 1996). Teasing may be intented to be humorous, but the humor may be a sarcastic comment made at the expense of the victim. It is frequently done in front of onlookers. Although physical victimization declines between third and sixth grade, teasing is initially higher in frequency than physical victimization and remains constant throughout adolescence (Perry, Kusel, & Perry, 1988). In a longitudinal follow-up study, Hodges & Perry (1999) found that third through seventh graders who were withdrawn, physically weak, and rejected by peers were most likely to be victimized by peers, with each of these factors contributing to the level of victimization.

The dominant motivation reported by perpetrators of teasing is their pleasure at the discomfort of the victim (Warm, 1997). While socially accepted teens tend to employ humor or assertion in response to being teased (Perry, Williard, & Perry, 1990), socially rejected teens tend to get angry, upset, or physically aggressive (cf., Shantz, 1986). Differentiating between teasing and embarrassing feedback is included in this session (cf., Frankel, Sinton, & Wilfley, 2007), as this is a peer response frequently encountered by teens with autism spectrum disorders (ASD).

The purpose of this session is to differentiate teasing from embarrassing feedback and train effective strategies for both. Often the terms *teasing* and *bullying* are used interchangeably. Teasing and bullying will be uniquely defined for parents and teens to avoid confusion: the term *teasing* will refer to verbal attacks; the term *bullying* will refer to physical attacks or threats. The strategies for handling verbal and physical attacks are quite different and the latter will be addressed in the next session.

The content of this session is frequently emotionally charged. Many teens have ineffective responses to being teased. Parents and teens thus feel powerless. In some cases, this may be the first time that parents become aware that their teen is being teased. In other cases, parents may want to bring up negative experiences they have had trying to stop their child from being bullied. In order to adequately handle both forms of victimization, the group leader will need to maintain a focus upon teasing for this session, and have parents wait until the next session to discuss bullying.

As mentioned above, the differences between teasing and embarrassing informational feedback is important. For example, saying "you stink" could be a teasing comment, or it could indicate that better oral hygiene or deodorant are required, or that the teen entered a game where his or her skill level was below that of his or her teammates. The latter two may in fact constitute teasing, but also represent rude and embarrassing ways of telling the teen that there is a problem. Identifying embarrassing feedback should motivate the teen to make needed changes in hygiene, appearance, or modifying off-putting behaviors. The tease-the-tease technique (cf., Frankel & Myatt, 2003) will be taught to the teens as an effective way of handling being verbally teased.

Parents are often of limited help in advising teens how to handle being teased, possibly because most parents do not know how to effectively handle teasing. Alternatively, some parents offer advice to their teens such as "walk away" or "ignore them" in response to teasing. The group leader should clarify to parents that these strategies are usually ineffective.

Homework Review

1. **Get-together**.
   a. Identify whether the teen made a phone call to set up the **get-together**.
   b. Identify whether the **get-together** was:
      i. Activity-based.
      ii. Monitored by parents from a *distance*.
      iii. No more than 2 hours (depending on the activity).
   c. Be sure that the teen **traded information** with his or her guest and found a **common interest**:
      i. 50% of the time should have been spent **trading information**.
2. **Being a good sport**.
   a. Have parents report how the teen practiced **being a good sport**.
      i. Identify the specific ways the teen was a **good sport**.
      ii. This practice may have occurred in the context of the **get-together**.

3. ***Slipping into a conversation.***
    a. Have parents identify:
        i. Where their teen ***slipped in***.
        ii. Whether the teen knew at least one of the people.
        iii. If they followed the steps for ***slipping into a conversation***.
        iv. How they handled rejection, when applicable.
    b. Troubleshoot any problems that may have arisen.
4. ***Bring an inside game.***
    a. Have parents identify the inside game their teen brought to share the group (e.g., age-appropriate board game, card game, etc.).
    b. Only give credit for appropriate items.

Didactic Lesson: Teasing and Embarrassing Feedback

■ Distribute the Parent Handout.

■ Explain: *Today we are going to be talking about teasing and what to do to help your teen when someone teases them. We are not going to be specific about the mean things that kids have said to your teens or how they feel about being teased. Instead, we are going to focus on what we can do to help your teens in situations when they might be teased. We will focus on how to react to teasing as an important way to make it less likely that your teen will be teased in the future. Because most kids tease in order to get a reaction out of the other person, the best way to avoid being teased in the future is to act like what the person said doesn't bother you. We call this technique tease-the-tease. The idea is not to tease the person back; that would be "tease-the-teaser." Instead, we are making fun of what they said or acting like what they said was lame. This will take the power out of the teasing and make it less fun for the teaser. If it's not fun for the teaser, the teaser will be less likely to tease in the future.*

■ Go around the room and have parents take turns reading the Parent Handout.

■ Sections in **bold print** come directly from the Parent Handout.

Tease-the-Tease

■ **Act like what they said does not bother you**:
    – **For boys—*act like you do not care*—like what they said was boring or uninteresting**.
    – **For girls—*have an attitude*—like what they just said was stupid or meaningless; you may roll your eyes at him or her**.

■ **Make fun of what the person said**:
    – ***Do not* make fun of the teaser! This will only get you into trouble**.

■ **Have a *brief* comeback to *tease-the-tease***:
    – **Keep your *tease-the tease* comebacks short**.

- **If you say too much, they will think you care**.
- **Examples:**
  - **"Whatever!"**
  - **"Anyway…."**
  - **"Big deal!"**
  - **"So what!"**
  - **"Who cares?"**
  - **"Yeah, and?"**
  - **"And your point is?"**
  - **"Tell me when you get to the funny part."**
  - **"Am I supposed to care?"**
  - **"Is that supposed to be funny?"**
  - **"And why do I care?"**

■ **Do something that shows you do not care:**
  - **Shrug shoulders, shake your head, and walk away.**
  - **Roll your eyes and walk away.**

■ **Do not walk away without showing the teaser that what he or she said did not bother you:**
  - **You do not want the teaser to think that you are running away.**
  - **The teaser may follow you and keep teasing.**

■ **Do not use *tease-the-tease* with someone who is *physically* aggressive.** (Strategies for handling this form of bullying will be covered in the next session.)
  - **This kind of embarrassment may make the bully want to retaliate with further aggression.**

■ ***Never* use *tease-the-tease* with parents, teachers, or adults.**
  - This will only get the teen in trouble.

■ Explain: *So just to summarize, the best way to ensure that people won't tease your teen is to not make it fun for them. Your teens will do this by acting like what the person said didn't bother them or was kind of lame. But for some of your teens, they've already shown people that they get upset when they're teased. If your teen has gotten upset from teasing in the past, it may take a little while for people to catch on that they're not bothered anymore. In fact, the teasers may try even harder for a while to get the kind of reaction they expect. Be sure to reassure your teens that this is expected, so they shouldn't give up. If they keep using tease-the-tease and don't let on that they're upset, eventually the teaser will give up and move onto someone else.*

■ Explain that teens will practice ***tease-the-tease*** in session:
  - The group leader will use a benign tease. ("Your shoes are ugly!")
  - Teens will each pick three ***tease-the-tease*** comebacks to practice, in case the teasing persists.

■ Tell parents that if their teen is willing, they may practice ***tease-the-tease*** with their teen this week:
  - Parents must let their teen know that they are practicing before they begin.
  - Parents must use a benign tease (e.g., "Your shoes are ugly!")

Handling Embarrassing Feedback

- Explain: *The next thing we need to talk about is the important feedback that sometimes accompanies teasing or sounds like teasing. For example, kids will sometimes say things that are embarrassing and may even be meant to tease your teen, but they may also be giving important information at the same time. This information is sometimes embarrassing and makes your teen feel bad, but it can also give you insight into how people see your teen. This is especially true when a lot of people are giving your teen the same feedback or when your teen is getting the same feedback frequently from a small number of people. As parents, it is your job to help your teen figure out if there is an important message when he or she is given this embarrassing feedback and help your teen decide what he or she can do differently.*
- Have parents take turns reading the table "Handling Embarrassing Feedback" from the Parent Handout.
- Material in **bold print** is directly from the Parent Handout.

Handling Embarrassing Feedback

Examples of Embarrassing Feedback	*What the Teen Can Do Differently*
"You dress funny!"	**Change what you wear; try to follow the clothing norms of the school**
"You smell!"	**Use more deodorant; bathe more; wear less cologne/perfume**
"Your hair is greasy!"	**Wash your hair more often; use less hair gel**
"Is that snow on your shoulder?!" (dandruff)	**Use a dandruff shampoo**
"Your breath stinks!"	**Use breath mints after eating; brush your teeth more; use mouthwash; chew gum**
"You stink at this game!"	**Play with kids who are less skilled**
"Say it, don't spray it!" (spitting when talking)	**Be cautious about spitting when talking (swallow more often when talking)**
"You have food in your teeth!"	**Brush your teeth after meals; chew gum after meals; floss more often**
"Stop shouting!" "You talk too loud!"	**Speak more softly**
"I can't hear you!"	**Speak more loudly**
"You're not funny!"	**Pay attention to your humor feedback; consider being a joke-receiver**

- Go around the room and have parents come up with their own examples of what embarrassing feedback their teen might receive (or be receiving) and what the teen could do differently.

- Example: Many kids are teased about their clothing.
  - Parents should try to notice what other teens are wearing or ask friends or relatives about the same age what teens are wearing. Parents can then help their teen pick out more appropriate clothes in this case, if their teen no longer wishes to be the target of this form of teasing.
  - Allow parents to provide other suggestions.
- Some teens will naturally be reluctant to talk about teasing, so some parents will not know if their teen is being teased.
  - Tell parents that these group assignments are great opportunities for them to talk about teasing with their teens.
  - Other suggestions for finding out about teasing:
    - Talk to teachers or coaches at school.
    - Attend open houses at school to set up dialogues with teachers.
    - Pick up or drop off your teen at school and notice his or her interactions with other teens.
  - Ask a sibling who attends the same school.

Homework Assignments

The parent group leader should go over the homework assignment and trouble-shoot any potential problems with parents.

1. **Teen is to have a friend over for a *get-together*.**
   a. **Make an *out-of-group* call to set up the *get-together*.**
      i. ***Trade information* to find *common interests*.**
      ii. **Decide what you are going to do during the *get-together*.**
   b. **Parents monitor the *get-together* from a *distance*.**
   c. **The *get-together* should be activity-based.**
   d. **Be sure the teen *trades information* with the guest:**
      i. **50% of the *get-together* should be spent *trading information*.**
   e. **First *get-togethers* with a particular teen should be limited to approximately 2 hours (depending on the activity).**
2. **Practice *being a good sport*:**
   a. **This can be done during the *get-together* or any other time during the week when the teen plays games (video games, computer games, board games, card games) or sports.**
   b. **Parents and teens should discuss how the teen was a *good sport*.**
3. ***Bring outside sports equipment*.**
   a. **Bring outside sports equipment to share with the group (e.g., basketball, soccer ball, volleyball, football, Frisbee).**
      i. **No solitary games or equipment.**
   b. **Do not bring something that you are:**
      i. **Unwilling to share with group members.**

    ii. **Worried about breaking or losing.**

4. **Practice *tease-the-tease* if it comes up this week:**

   a. **Parents and teens may want to practice *tease-the-tease* during the week.**

   b. **Parents and teens should discuss how the teen used *tease-the-tease*.**

     i. ***Tease-the-tease* is generally appropriate to use with siblings.**

Parent Handout 10: Rejection I—Teasing and Embarrassing Feedback

Tease-the-Tease

- Act like what they said does not bother you:
  - For boys—***act like you do not care***—like what they said was boring or uninteresting.
  - For girls—***have an attitude***—like what they just said was stupid or meaningless; you may roll your eyes at the teaser.
- Make fun of what the person said:
  - *Do not* make fun of the teaser! This will only get you into trouble.
- Have a *brief* comeback to ***tease-the-tease***:
  - Keep your ***tease-the tease*** comebacks short.
  - If you say too much, they will think you care.
  - Examples:
    - "Whatever!"
    - "Anyway…."
    - "Big deal!"
    - "So what!"
    - "Who cares?"
    - "Yeah, and?"
    - "And your point is?"
    - "Tell me when you get to the funny part."
    - "Am I supposed to care?"
    - "Is that supposed to be funny?"
    - "And why do I care?"
- Do something that shows you do not care:
  - Shrug your shoulders, shake your head, and walk away.
  - Roll your eyes and walk away.
- Do not walk away without showing the teaser that what he or she said did not bother you:
  - You do not want the teaser to think that you are running away.
  - The teaser may follow you and keep teasing.
- Do not use ***tease-the-tease*** with someone who is *physically* aggressive:
  - This kind of embarrassment may make the bully want to retaliate with further aggression.
- *Never* use ***tease-the-tease*** with parents, teachers, or adults.

Handling Embarrassing Feedback

Examples of Embarrassing Feedback	*What the Teen Can Do Differently*
"You dress funny!"	Change what you wear; try to follow the clothing norms of the school
"You smell!"	Use more deodorant; bathe more; wear less cologne/perfume
"Your hair is greasy!"	Wash your hair more often; use less hair gel
"Is that snow on your shoulder?!" (dandruff)	Use a dandruff shampoo
"Your breath stinks!"	Use breath mints after eating; brush your teeth more; use mouthwash; chew gum
"You stink at this game!"	Play with kids who are less skilled
"Say it, don't spray it!" (spitting when talking)	Be cautious about spitting when talking (swallow more often when talking)
"You have food in your teeth!"	Brush your teeth after meals; chew gum after meals; floss more often
"Stop shouting!" "You talk too loud!"	Speak more softly
"I can't hear you!"	Speak more loudly
"You're not funny!"	Pay attention to your humor feedback; consider being a joke-receiver

Homework Assignments

1. The teen is to have a friend over for a ***get-together***.
   a. Make an ***out-of-group*** call to set up the ***get-together***.
      i. ***Trade information*** to find ***common interests***.
      ii. Decide what you are going to do during the ***get-together***.
   b. Parents monitor the ***get-together*** from a *distance*.
   c. The ***get-together*** should be activity-based.
   d. Be sure the teen ***trades information*** with the guest:
      i. 50% of the ***get-together*** should be spent ***trading information***.
   e. First ***get-togethers*** with a particular teen should be limited to approximately 2 hours (depending on the activity).
2. Practice ***being a good sport***.
   a. This can be done during the ***get-together*** or any other time during the week when the teen plays games (video games, computer games, board games, card games) or sports.
   b. Parents and teens should discuss how the teen was a ***good sport***.
3. ***Bring outside sports equipment***.
   a. Bring outside sports equipment to share with the group (e.g., basketball, soccer ball, volleyball, football, Frisbee).

      i. No solitary games or equipment.

   b. Do not bring something that you are:

      i. Unwilling to share with group members.

      ii. Worried about breaking or losing.

4. **Practice *tease-the-tease* if it comes up this week.**

   a. Parents and teens may want to practice ***tease-the-tease*** during the week.

   b. Parents and teens should discuss how the teen used ***tease-the-tease***.

      i. ***Tease-the-tease*** is generally appropriate to use with siblings.

Teen Therapist Guide—Session 10: Rejection I—Teasing and Embarrassing Feedback

Guiding Principles of the Teen Session

The major goal of this session is to give teens new and more effective strategies for handling teasing (that is, verbal aggression from peers). Although teasing and bullying are often very much intertwined, for the purposes of clarity in choosing the appropriate strategies for handling both, the term *teasing* will refer to verbal attacks from peers, whereas the term *bullying* will refer to physical attacks or threats from peers. The strategies for handling verbal and physical attacks are very different. Therefore, it is helpful to give teens ways in which to think of these concepts differently in order to choose the more appropriate coping strategy.

Many of the teens in the group will have a long history of being teased. Consequently, this session may be emotionally charged for many of the teens. The group leader should help to limit the affective response by not allowing teens to talk about the specific ways in which they have been teased or bullied, so that they will be more able to focus on the solutions. By this session, the teens will most likely have developed a cohesive group in which their mutual regard and support for one another will minimize much of the anxiety they may have felt in discussing this topic earlier in the treatment.

One issue that commonly comes up in this session is that teens may claim that they are "never teased" or that "no one teases" at their school. In very rare instances, this may be the case; but more often these comments represent an attempt to "save face" or appear to be above this form of social rejection. It is not important to have teens confess to being teased. It is also important not to make teens who are being teased feel embarrassed about their situation. The group leader should normalize this experience for the other group members by explaining that nearly everyone gets teased from time to time (particularly teens). Although the experience can be painful, it is not unusual.

Conversely, some teens will confess to being teased and will want to go into lengthy stories about the ways in which they have been teased. The group leader should not allow this discussion to go far, as these emotionally charged confessions will make it difficult for teens to focus on the lesson. It is helpful for the group leader to remind teens, "We know that teasing feels really awful and we know that it's fairly common. Remember, we're not going to be talking about the specific ways in which we've been teased. Instead, we're going to focus on what we can do to make it less likely that we'll be teased in the future." This clarification will come as a relief to many teens.

Occasionally one of the teens may confess to teasing other teens or being a bully. The group leader will need to briefly discuss the problems associated with being a teaser or a bully, but avoid a lengthy discussion on this topic in order to deflect the anxiety that such a disclosure may generate in other group members. The group leader might say something like, "Who can tell me what the problem with being a bully is?" (Answer: It is mean; people will not want to be friends with you.) A very brief discussion of why it is bad to be a bully will send the message that this behavior is unacceptable, but avoiding a lengthy discussion will be important to minimize the anxiety this might raise in the other group members and maintain focus upon responses to being teased.

Although it is likely that emotions will be elevated during this didactic lesson, this session should focus on the development of specific strategies for handling teasing that will lead to a lower probability of being teased in the future. When the material is presented as described below, this should be an enjoyable session for the teens.

Rule Review

Note: Only go over session rules again if the teens are having difficulty following them.

- Have teens identify the rules for the group.
- Give them points for remembering:
  1. Listen to the other group members (no talking when others are speaking)
  2. Follow directions
  3. Raise your hand
  4. Be respectful (no teasing or making fun of others)
  5. No touching (no hitting, kicking, pushing, hugging, etc.)

Homework Review

Note: Give points for homework *parts*—not just one point per assignment.

1. ***Bring an inside game***.
   a. Identify the inside game the teen brought to share with the group (e.g., age-appropriate board game, card game, etc.).
   b. Only give credit for appropriate items.
   c. To avoid distractions, have a coach put the item away until the teen session activity.
2. ***Get-together***.
   a. Say: *Your main homework assignment this week was to have a get-together with a friend. Raise your hand if you had a get-together this week.*
      i. Begin by calling on the teens who completed the assignment.
      ii. Briefly ask:
         1. *Who did you have a get-together with?*
         2. *Where was the get-together?*

3. *Did you make an out-of-group phone call to figure out what you were going to do?*
4. *What did you end up doing?*
5. *Who chose the activities?* [Answer should be the guest.]
6. *Did you trade information at least 50% of the time?*
7. *Did you have a good time?*
8. *Did your friend have a good time?*
9. *Is this someone you might want to have a get-together with again?*
    iii. Troubleshoot any problems that may have arisen.
3. ***Being a good sport.***
    a. Say: *Last week we learned the rules for being a good sport. One of your assignments was to practice being a good sport this week. This may have happened during your get-together or even at school during gym class or during your extracurricular activities. Raise your hand if you practiced being a good sport this week.*
        i. Briefly ask:
            1. *Where did you practice being a good sport?*
            2. *What did you do or say to show that you were a good sport?*
        ii. Troubleshoot any problems that may have arisen.
4. ***Slipping into a conversation.***
    a. Say: *Another one of your assignments this week was to practice slipping into a conversation with someone from a group that you were likely to be accepted by. Raise your hand if you practiced slipping into a conversation this week.*
        i. Begin by calling on the teens who completed the assignment.
        ii. Briefly ask:
            1. *Where did you slip in?*
            2. *Which group did you choose to slip in with?*
            3. *Did you know at least one of the people?*
            4. *How did you slip in?*
                a. Be sure they followed the steps for ***slipping in***.
                b. If they did not follow the steps, ask: *What could you do differently next time?*
            5. *Did you need to slip out?*
                a. If so, be sure they followed the steps for ***slipping out***.
                b. If they did not follow the steps, ask: *What could you do differently next time?*
            6. Troubleshoot any problems that may have arisen.

Didactic Lesson: Tease-the-Tease

■ Explain: *Today we are going to be talking about teasing and what to do when someone teases us. We are not going to be talking about specific mean things that people have said to us or how we feel about being teased. We all know it feels bad to be teased. Instead, we are going to focus on what we can do in situations when we might be teased to make it less likely that we'll be teased in the future. One important way to make it less likely that we will be teased relates to how we react when someone is teasing us. In order for us to know how to more appropriately react to teasing, it is helpful to think about why people tease.*

■ [Note: If the teens try to talk about specific ways in which they have been teased, be sure to immediately redirect them by saying: *We're not going to talk about the specific ways in which you've been teased. Instead, we're going to talk about what you can do to make it less likely that you will be teased again.*]

■ Ask: *Why do people tease?*
  – Answers:
    • People who tease are trying to get a reaction out of you.
    • They want you to cry; yell; curse; get embarrassed; blush.
    • They are trying to push your buttons.
    • They are putting on a "show" for other teens.
      ■ They may even say "Watch this!" and get other teens in on the teasing.

■ Ask the questions: When you get upset…
  – *Are you doing what the teaser wants?*
    • Answer: Yes.
  – *Are you putting on a show?*
    • Answer: Yes.
  – *Are you making the teasing fun for the teaser?*
    • Answer: Yes.
  – *Are you more likely to get teased next time?*
    • Answer: Yes.

■ [Note: If a teen confesses to being a bully or a teaser, you will need to curtail this confession as much as possible to maintain focus. Instead of allowing the teen to go into details about episodes of bullying other teens, ask the other group members: *What's the problem with being a bully?* Then end with a brief moral lesson that bullying other teens is not a good way to make friends. The group leader may later want to speak privately with the confessor and his or her parent if the issue feels unresolved.]

■ Say: *A lot of adults will give teens advice about what to do in response to teasing. What do most adults tell teens to do?*
  – Answer: Tell an adult; walk away; ignore him or her.

■ Ask: *Do these strategies usually work?*
  – Answer: Not usually.
  – [Note: Acknowledging that the strategies that teens have been given in the past are ineffective will help the teen group leader gain the trust of the teens insofar as they will be more willing to believe what the group leader tells them about how to respond appropriately to teasing.]

■ Explain: *We're not going to suggest that you ignore the teaser or simply walk away. These strategies don't usually work. Instead, you will need to make the teasing less fun for the teaser. You can do this by acting like what they said didn't bother you. You'll need to say something that shows what they said was kind of lame. We call these responses "tease-the-tease" comebacks because you're sort of making fun of what they said. But we're **not** suggesting that you tease them back; this would be "tease-the-teaser" and would only escalate the interaction and get you in trouble. Before we give you specific tease-the-tease comebacks to use, it's important to understand the rules about using tease-the-tease.*

■ Present the rules for **tease-the-tease**.
- Act like what they said did not bother you.
  • Say: *The main point of tease-the-tease is that you're supposed to act like what the person said doesn't bother you. Even if it hurts your feelings, you will need to pretend that it does not.*
    ■ For Girls—**have an attitude**—act like what the person just said was stupid or meaningless; you may roll your eyes at the teaser.
    ■ For Boys—**act like you do not care**—act like what the person said was boring or uninteresting.
  • Ask: *Why would it be important to act like what they said didn't bother you?*
    ■ Answer: Because this makes the teasing less fun; they will be less likely to want to tease you in the future.

■ Make fun of what they said.
- Say: *A good way to show that what the person said didn't bother you is to act like what they said was kind of lame. This **does not** mean you should tease them or make fun of them. This will only get you into trouble.*
- Ask: *What might happen if you make fun of him or her, too?*
  • Answers: You could get into trouble; you will look like the bad guy; you might hurt their feelings; you might get a bad reputation.

■ Give a *brief* comeback to **tease-the-tease**.
- Say: *The best way to show someone that their teasing didn't bother us and that what they said was kind of lame is to give a brief comeback to tease-the-tease. This involves making fun of what they said, not making fun of them.*
  • Say: *The first rule of the tease-the-tease comeback is that it has to be short. Why is it important to keep our comebacks short?*
    ■ Answer: If you say too much, they will think you care.
  • Say: *The next rule of the tease-the-tease comeback is that it has to give the impression that we don't care or the teasing was lame.*
    ■ Examples: (Write these on the board. Do not allow teens to generate their own comebacks, as they are often inappropriate.)

- "Whatever!"
- "Anyway…."
- "Big deal!"
- "So what!"
- "Who cares?"
- "Yeah, and?"
- "And your point is?"
- "Tell me when you get to the funny part."
- "Am I supposed to care?"
- "Is that supposed to be funny?"
- "And why do I care?"

■ Do something that shows you do not care.
  - Say: *If you're uncomfortable giving a verbal response to teasing, another option is to do something that shows you don't care.*
    • Examples:
      ■ Shrug your shoulders, shake your head, and walk away.
      ■ Roll your eyes and walk away.
      ■ [Note: Some teens with autism spectrum disorders will have trouble rolling their eyes or shrugging their shoulders appropriately. Be sure to have each teen demonstrate how he or she would do this during the behavioral rehearsal, if he or she chooses these gestures as an option. In the event the teen appears awkward, gently let him or her know that these nonverbal gestures are difficult to do and may not be the best option for him or her; the teen would be better off choosing a very brief verbal comeback.]
  - Ask: *What impression will a tease-the-tease comeback give the teaser?*
    • Answer: That you do not care; that you are not bothered by what he or she said.
  - Explain: *It is always better to provide a tease-the-tease comeback, but if you find it difficult to use your words in these situations, one of these nonverbal gestures should be sufficient.*
■ Do not stand there and wait to be teased more.
  - Say: *After you have shown the teaser that what he or she said didn't bother you, it's a good idea to casually look away or slowly walk away. What would be the problem with standing there and looking at the person after you used tease-the-tease?*
    • Answer: It is almost an invitation to tease more (like a challenge); you want to give the impression that what they said was lame and that you cannot be bothered to listen anymore.
■ Do not walk away without showing the teaser that what he or she said did not bother you.

- Say: *It's very important that you don't walk away from the teaser without first showing that what the teaser said didn't bother you. Why is it important to show the teaser that we're not bothered?*
  - Answers:
    - Because the teaser is trying to get a reaction out of you; the teaser is trying to get you to put on a show; if you do not react the way the teaser wants you to, then it is less fun for him or her; if it is not fun, he or she will be less likely to tease you in the future.
    - You do not want the teaser to think that you are running away.
    - The teaser may follow you and keep teasing (almost like a predator chasing its prey).
- Do not use ***tease-the-tease*** with someone who is ***physically*** aggressive.
  - Say: *Another important rule of tease-the-tease is that we shouldn't use this strategy with people who tend to get physically aggressive. This is because the point of tease-the-tease is that you kind of embarrass the teaser by acting like what they said was lame. How do people who bully and get physically aggressive react when they're embarrassed?*
    - Answer: It may make the bully want to retaliate with further aggression.
  - Explain: *Next week we're going to be talking about strategies for handling this form of bullying. We think of bullying as a form of physical aggression from peers, and the ways in which we handle bullying are very different from teasing. We think of teasing as verbal attacks from peers that don't involve physical aggression. We only use tease-the-tease in response to teasing or verbal attacks.*
- *Never* use ***tease-the-tease*** with parents, teachers, or adults.
  - Say: *The last rule for using tease-the-tease is that we should never use it with parents, teachers, or adults. Why would it be a bad idea to use tease-the-tease with adults?*
    - Answer: It is disrespectful; this will only get you in trouble.

Role Play

- The teen group leader and a coach should demonstrate an ***appropriate*** role play in which the teen group leader shows how to use ***tease-the-tease*** following all of these rules.
  - Use the benign tease, "Your shoes are ugly!" for all of the teens.
    - Do not use different teasing comments as this will feel personal to the teens.
  - Example of an ***appropriate*** role play:
    Coach: "Your shoes are ugly!"
    Teen group leader: (rolls eyes) "Yeah, and?" (said with attitude, then looks away)
    Coach: "Seriously, those are some ugly shoes!"

> *Teen group leader:* "Am I supposed to care?" (said with indifference, then looks away)
>
> *Coach:* "Well you should care because those are some nasty looking shoes!"
>
> *Teen group leader:* "Whatever." (shrugs shoulder, shakes head, and casually walks away)
>
> *Coach:* (looks defeated)

- Say: *Okay, let's time-out on that. So that's how we use tease-the-tease. Notice I used a different comeback each time, so the teaser thought I had more comebacks than he or she had teases. Now did I seem upset when (insert coach's name) made fun of my shoes?*
  - Answer: No.
- Ask: *Did I make the teasing fun for (insert coach's name)?*
  - Answer: No.
- Ask: *Do you think (insert coach's name) is going to want to tease me in the future?*
  - Answer: Probably not.
- Explain: *The best way to ensure that people won't tease us is to not make it fun for them. But for some of us, we've already shown people that we get upset when they tease us. If you're someone who has gotten upset from teasing in the past, it may take a little while for people to catch on that you're not bothered anymore. In fact, they may try even harder for a while to get the kind of reaction they expect from you. But don't give up. If you keep using different tease-the-tease comebacks and don't let on that you're upset, eventually they will give up and move onto someone else.*

Behavioral Rehearsal

- Tell the teens that they will be practicing using ***tease-the-tease***.
- Go around the room individually and have each teen identify three ***tease-the-tease*** comebacks he or she plans to use.
  - This should be immediately followed by the behavioral rehearsal (before moving onto the next teen), otherwise the teen may forget what he or she was going to say.
  - Discourage teens' attempts to come up with their own comebacks.
  - If the teen comes up with his or her own response, be sure it fits the parameters of a good response (i.e., brief, simple, gives the impression that the teen does not care).
- The group leader should use the benign tease: "Your shoes are ugly!"
  - Use the same benign tease for each teen—otherwise the teen may take the comment personally.
  - Repeat the tease three times in succession, forcing the teen to use different ***tease-the-tease*** comebacks each time.
  - Teens should reply with an appropriate ***tease-the-tease*** comeback.
  - Give performance feedback as necessary.
  - Be sure each teen has mastered the technique before moving on.

– Do not permit teens to practice with each other by allowing them to tease one another during this exercise.

Handling Embarrassing Feedback

■ Explain: *Sometimes people say things that are embarrassing and may even be meant to tease us, but they may also be giving important information about how we appear to others. This information is called feedback. Feedback is sometimes embarrassing and makes us feel bad, but it can also give us insight into how people see us. This is especially true when a lot of people are giving us the same feedback or even when a few people give us the same feedback repeatedly. Instead of only feeling hurt, we can use the feedback we get from others to help change the way people see us. If we consider what people are trying to tell us when they give us embarrassing feedback, we can sometimes do things differently. Sometimes this will make it less likely that we will be teased in the future.*

■ Go over the examples of embarrassing feedback listed below and have the teens come up with what they could do differently in response to this feedback.
  – For each example of embarrassing feedback say: *Let's say that a lot of people are giving you the feedback [use the specific example below]. What could you do differently in response to this feedback?* (See the table below, "Handling Embarrassing Feedback.")

■ Let teens come up with their own examples and what they could do differently if they are appropriate.

Handling Embarrassing Feedback

Examples of Embarrassing Feedback	*What the Teen Can Do Differently*
"You dress funny!"	Change what you wear; try to follow the clothing norms of the school
"You smell!"	Use more deodorant; bathe more; wear less cologne/perfume
"Your hair is greasy!"	Wash your hair more often; use less hair gel
"Is that snow on your shoulder?!" (dandruff)	Use a dandruff shampoo
"Your breath stinks!"	Use breath mints after eating; brush your teeth more; use mouthwash; chew gum
"You stink at this game!"	Play with kids who are less skilled
"Say it, don't spray it!" (spitting when talking)	Be cautious about spitting when talking (swallow more often when talking)
"You have food in your teeth!"	Brush your teeth after meals; chew gum after meals; floss more often
"Stop shouting!" "You talk too loud!"	Speak more softly
"I can't hear you!"	Speak more loudly
"You're not funny!"	Pay attention to your humor feedback; consider being a joke-receiver

Homework Assignments

- Briefly explain the homework for the week by saying: *The main homework assignment this week is for each of you to have another get-together with one or more friends. You may need to make a phone call to set up this get-together. During these get-togethers, we want you to practice being a good sport if you play games or sports. We know teasing is very common among teenagers, so we expect it to come up for everyone at some point this week. We want you to practice using tease-the-tease comebacks when they come up. Next week we will be outside on the play deck, so you will need to bring some type of outside sports equipment to share with the group. Again, your homework assignment this week is to:*
  - *Have a get-together with one or more friends.*
    - *Make an out-of-group call to schedule the get-together.*
    - *Trade information and figure out what you are going to do.*
  - *Practice being a good sport:*
    - *This can be done during get-togethers if applicable.*
    - *Other relevant times include during extracurricular sports activities or during gym class.*

> – *If you are teased this week, practice using tease-the-tease using the comebacks we identified here.*
> > • *Tease-the-tease is generally appropriate to use with siblings.*
> – *Bring outside sports equipment.*
> > • *You should bring appropriate equipment for outdoor activities with groups or pairs (e.g., basketball, soccer ball, volleyball, Frisbee, handball, football). No solitary equipment is allowed.*

Teen Activity: Get-Togethers and Good Sportsmanship

Note: See the "Teen Activity Guide" for rules.

- Notify teens they will be practicing having group get-togethers:
  - Break teens up into small groups and have them practice being a host and a guest.
  - Girls should be paired with girls and boys should be paired with boys, when possible.
  - Assign hosts and guests:
    - Have each teen practice beginning the get-together as a host.
    - Give everyone an opportunity to be a host and a guest.
  - Teens will then play indoor games while practicing having a group ***get-together***.
  - Games are chosen from appropriate ***inside games*** brought by teens and other available games.
  - Teens receive points while playing games for practicing being a ***good sport***:
    - ***Praise***
    - ***Do not referee***
    - ***Do not be a coach***
    - ***Share and take turns***
    - ***If you get bored, suggest a change***
    - ***Do not gloat if you win***
    - ***Do not sulk or get angry if you lose***
    - ***At the end of the game say: "Good game"***
  - At the end of the session, teens should practice ending the get-together.
    - Assign hosts and guests:
      - Have each teen practice ending the get-together as a host.
      - Give everyone an opportunity to be a host and a guest.

Reunification

- Announce that teens should join their parents.
  - Be sure that the teens are standing or sitting next to their parents.
  - Be sure to have silence and the full attention of the group.

■ Say: *Today we worked on how to handle teasing. We call this strategy tease-the-tease. Who can tell us what one of the rules for tease-the-tease is?* [Have teens generate all of the rules. Be prepared to give prompts if necessary.]
  – Response should be brief, simple, and give the impression that you do not care.
  – Examples:
    • "Whatever!"
    • "Anyway…"
    • "Big deal!"
    • "So what!"
    • "Who cares?"
    • "Yeah, and?"
    • "And your point is?"
    • "Tell me when you get to the funny part."
    • "Am I supposed to care?"
    • "Is that supposed to be funny?"
    • "And why do I care?"
    • Shrug your shoulders, shake your head, and walk away.
    • Roll your eyes and walk away.
■ Say: *Today we practiced handling teasing, and this group did a great job! Let's give them a round of applause.*
■ Go over the homework for the next week (see below).
■ Individually and separately negotiate with each family:
  – The location of the get-together, the activity planned, who will be present, as well as the parent role in the get-together.
  – What outside sports equipment will be brought next week.

Homework Assignments

1. Teen is to have a friend over for a ***get-together***.
   a. Make an ***out-of-group*** call to set up the ***get-together***.
      i. ***Trade information*** to find ***common interests***.
      ii. Decide what you are going to do during your ***get-together***.
   b. Parents monitor the ***get-together*** from a *distance*.
   c. The ***get-together*** should be activity-based.
   d. Be sure the teen ***trades information*** with the guest:
      i. 50% of the ***get-together*** should be spent ***trading information***.
      ii. First ***get-togethers*** with a particular teen should be limited to approximately 2 hours (depending on the activity).
2. Practice ***being a good sport***:
   a. This can be done during the ***get-together*** or any other time during the week when the teen plays games (video games, computer games, board games, card games) or sports.
   b. Parents and teens should discuss how the teen was a ***good sport***.

3. ***Bring outside sports equipment***.
   a. Bring outside sports equipment to share with the group (e.g., basketball, soccer ball, volleyball, football, Frisbee).
      i. No solitary games or equipment.
   b. Do not bring something that you are:
      i. Unwilling to share with group members.
      ii. Worried about breaking or losing.
4. **Practice *tease-the-tease* if it comes up this week**.
   a. Parents and teens may want to practice ***tease-the-tease*** during the week.
   b. Parents and teens should discuss how the teen used ***tease-the-tease***.
      i. ***Tease-the-tease*** is generally appropriate to use with siblings of the same age.

Calculate Points

Keep track of the following for each week of the intervention.

- Calculate the number of points earned by each teen.
- Add up the total number of points earned by the group.
- Do not calculate the points in the presence of the teens:
  - Do not disclose the individual or group total of points.
  - Discourage attempts to compare number of points earned between teens.
- Remind them that they are working as a team to earn a bigger and better graduation party.

Teen Activity Guide: Session 10

"Get-Togethers and Good Sportsmanship"

Materials Needed

- Indoor games brought by teens.
- In the event that a teen forgets to bring an indoor game, have board games available to share:
  - Cards
  - Checkers
  - Chess

Rules

- Notify teens they will be practicing having group ***get-togethers***.
- Break teens up into small groups and have them practice being a host and a guest.

■ Girls should be paired with girls and boys should be paired with boys, when possible.
■ Assign hosts and guests.
  – Have each teen practice beginning a ***get-together*** by being a host.
    • Begin by having the teen verbally go over the steps for beginning a ***get-together***:
      ■ Greet the guest.
      ■ Invite the guest in.
      ■ Give the guest a tour.
      ■ Introduce the guest to everyone.
      ■ Offer the guest something to eat or drink.
      ■ Ask everyone what they want to do.
    • Have the teen rehearse the steps with the entire group.
    • Give everyone an opportunity to be a host and a guest.
■ Teens will then play indoor games while practicing having a group ***get-together***.
■ Games are chosen from appropriate ***inside games*** brought by teens and other available games provided by the treatment team.
  – Have teens negotiate what they will play.
    • They may need to compromise by playing one game for half the time and then switching games midway.
  – You may need to assist teens in understanding the rules for specific games:
    • Try to avoid acting as a referee if disagreements occur.
    • Encourage teens to work out their differences by being ***good sports***.
  – You may need to prompt teens to be ***good sports*** and ***praise*** their partners.
■ Teens receive points while playing games for practicing being a ***good sport***:
  – ***Praise***
  – ***Do not referee***
  – ***Do not be a coach***
  – ***Share and take turns***
  – ***If you get bored, suggest a change***
  – ***Do not gloat if you win***
  – ***Do not sulk or get angry if you lose***
  – ***At the end of the game say: "Good game"***
■ Coaches should state why the teen is receiving a point. (e.g., "John gets a point for praising!")
  – Be sure to keep track of points on the Good Sportsmanship Point Log (see Appendix G).
  – Speak loudly when giving out points so other teens can hear.
    • The social comparison will encourage other teens to ***praise*** and be ***good sports***.
■ At the end of the session, teens should practice ending the ***get-together***.
  – Assign hosts and guests.

- Have each teen practice ending the ***get-together*** as a host.
  - Begin by having the teen verbally go over the steps for ending a get-together:
    - Give a ***cover story*** for ending the ***get-together***.
    - Start walking the guest to the door.
    - Thank him or her for coming over.
    - Tell him or her that you had a nice time.
    - Say good-bye and that you will see him or her later.
  - Have the teen rehearse these steps with the entire group.
  - Give everyone an opportunity to be a host and a guest.

Chapter 13

Session 11
Rejection II—Bullying and Bad Reputations

Parent Session Therapist Guide

Guiding Principles of the Parent Session

The get-together should continue to be the major focus of homework review for this and all remaining sessions. Close behind this should be a debriefing of any teens who had the occasion to use tease-the-tease. Debrief for embarrassing feedback first, and then focus upon teasing. The most common errors teens just learning the tease-the-tease technique make are trying to use too long a comeback and not having enough different comebacks (i.e., giving up too soon).

The didactic lesson for this session focuses on bullying and bad reputations. As many as 75% of children and teens with autism spectrum disorders (ASD) have been bullied, according to maternal reports (Little, 2001). For the purpose of this group, we define bullying as physical aggression or threat. The most common form of bullying is the classic form described by Olweus (1993). This involves unprovoked, systematic intimidation or physical abuse by one or more constant perpetrators upon a weaker victim. It is generally done out of sight (e.g., on the way to and from school, in the school bathrooms). Perpetrators may even be well regarded by teachers and supervisors, or at least not distinguished as troublemakers themselves. Their main motivation appears to be the infliction of pain and suffering. Stories abound from parents and teens about school staff who look the other way and allow this form of bullying to continue. The group leader should advise the parents of teens who report severe bullying, met with indifference by school personnel, to seek legal help. Sometimes the mere involvement of an attorney will motivate indifferent school staff into positive action.

The session content formally uses the discussion of bullying to motivate teens to change a bad reputation. The strategies described in the last session to handle teasing are not effective against physical bullying and can in fact lead to increased aggression in the form of retaliation for embarrassment of the bully. Parents are instructed to help their teen identify which strategies to use with which form of peer rejection (i.e., verbal attacks should be responded to with the tease-the-tease comebacks, and physical attacks should be addressed with strategies for handling bullying).

Negative reputations among peers are stable over time (Coie, Dodge, & Kupersmidt, 1990) and negatively impact a teen's ability to interact appropriately with peers, due to the expectations and attributions of peers. Putallaz and Gottman (1981) found that when rejected children attempted appropriate interactions, they were less likely to receive positive feedback from their peers than if a more liked child made the same attempt.

The content of this session will also provide teens with helpful advice on how to jump-start changing a bad reputation. Part of this advice (i.e., laying low) comes from successful trials with our child program (Frankel & Myatt, 2003). This process, however, is long and arduous for teens and will need to continue well after the termination of the group. Thus, parents will need to stay very much involved in the process to improve the likelihood that the teen is successful in changing his or her reputation. Teens who are unsuccessful at using the described technique can nevertheless let their reputation die down by avoiding attempts to make friends from within the peer group with which they have a negative reputation and by "laying low" for a while.

Homework Review

1. ***Get-together***.
   a. Identify whether the teen made a phone call to set up the ***get-together***.
   b. Identify whether the ***get-together*** was:
      i. Activity-based.
      ii. Monitored by parents from a ***distance***.
      iii. No more than 2 hours (depending on the activity).
   c. Be sure that the teen ***traded information*** with his or her guest and found a ***common interest***:
      i. 50% of the time should have been spent ***trading information***.
2. ***Being a good sport***.
   a. Have parents report how the teen practiced ***being a good sport***:
      i. Identify the specific ways the teen was a ***good sport***.
      ii. This practice may have occurred in the context of the ***get-together***.
3. ***Tease-the-tease***.
   a. Check to see if parents practiced ***tease-the-tease*** with their teen (not an assignment).
   b. Have parents report how ***tease-the-tease*** was used.

    c. ***Tease-the-tease*** may have been used with peers or siblings.

    d. Troubleshoot any problems that may have arisen.

4. ***Bring outside sports equipment.***

    a. Have parents identify the outside sports equipment their teen brought to share with the group (e.g., basketball, soccer ball, volleyball, football, Frisbee).

    b. Only give credit for appropriate items.

Didactic Lesson: Bullying and Bad Reputations

■ Distribute the Parent Handout.

■ Explain: "Today we are talking about how to handle bullying and how to change a bad reputation. We are not going to be talking about the specific mean ways that other teens may have bullied your kids or how your teens feel about being bullied. Instead, we are going to focus on what your teens can do in situations when they might be bullied."

■ Have parent read the guidelines for ***tease-the-tease*** from the Parent Handout.

■ Material in **bold print** is directly from the Parent Handout.

How to Handle Bullying

■ ***Lay Low***
- **Keep a low profile.**
- **Do not draw attention to yourself.**

■ ***Avoid the Bully***
- **Stay out of reach of the bully.**
- **Do not try to talk to the bully.**
- **Do not try to make friends with the bully.**

■ ***Do Not Provoke the Bully***
- **Do not use *tease-the-tease* with a bully:**
  - **This may only get the bully more agitated.**
  - **Parents may need to help teens figure out when to use *tease-the-tease*.**
    - **Use *tease-the-tease* with teasers who are *verbally* abusive.**
    - **Do not use *tease-the-tease* with bullies who are *physically* abusive.**
- **Do not tease the bully.**
- **Do not act silly or make fun of the bully.**
- **Do not tell on the bully and try to get him or her in trouble for minor offenses.**
  - **Only get involved if someone could be seriously injured:**
    - **Do this secretly and out of the awareness of peers so the bully does not retaliate against you.**

■ ***Hang Out With Other People***

- **Avoid being alone**.
- **Bullies like to pick on people when they are alone and unprotected**.

■ *If you are in danger—get help from an adult* (e.g., parent, teacher, principal, dean).

■ Go around the room and have the parents of teens who are struggling with bullying identify a couple of strategies that might work well for their teen, including legal approaches (mentioned above), if necessary.
- Tell parents that they can help their teen handle bullying by encouraging them to use these strategies in the future.

■ Tell parents of teens who report severe bullying, met with indifference by school personnel, to seek legal help. Sometimes the mere involvement of an attorney will motivate indifferent school staff into positive action.

■ Explain: *Now that we have some ideas about how to handle bullying, it's important to think about the bad reputations that often accompany victims of bullying. Changing a bad reputation is difficult to do and usually takes time, but it can be done.*

Explain the following:

■ Bad reputations are often associated with bullying and teasing.
- Bullies sometimes have bad reputations because of their negative behavior.
  • Other times they may be well regarded by adults who are unaware of their bad behavior.
- Teens who are targeted for bullying and teasing sometimes also have bad reputations.

■ Teens have bad reputations for a number of reasons, often because they stand out or are different in some way.

■ Bad reputations are difficult to get rid of and can even follow teens to different schools.

■ Changing a bad reputation is difficult to do and usually takes time, but it can be done.

■ Present steps for how to change a bad reputation.

Tips for Changing a Bad Reputation

■ *Lay Low*
- **Keep a low profile**.
- **Do not draw attention to yourself**.
■ *Follow the Crowd*
- *Try to fit in with the crowd*.
  • **This refers to exhibiting good behaviors that often lead to friendships (e.g., demonstrating similar interests as other teens, behaving in a friendly manner)**.

- *Try not to stand out from the crowd.*
  - **This refers to standing out from others in some unusual way and includes:**
    - **Engaging in behaviors that are considered bad and may get you in trouble (e.g., behaving in an overly emotional or aggressive manner, telling on peers for minor offenses).**
    - **Dressing differently from the mainstream peer group or excessively talking about unusual interests.**
  - These behaviors will often result in a bad reputation.

■ *Change Your Look to Change Your Reputation*
  - **The fastest way to let people know that you are no longer doing things to injure your reputation is to change your look.**
  - **You may need to change your look to fit in with the other teens.**
    - **Find a way of dressing that reflects the kind of person you want to be.**
    - **Avoid daring fashion statements that set you apart from the crowd.**
    - **You may need to change your hairstyle to fit in with other teens.**
  - **By changing your look you are drawing positive attention to yourself (after a period of laying low for a while) and letting others know that there is something new and improved about you.**
    - A "makeover" alone will not change your reputation, so once people start to notice that you are different, you will have to prove it (usually by owning up to your previous reputation).

■ *Own Up to Your Previous Reputation*
  - **Own up to any truths about your previously bad reputation.**
  - **Let people know that you have changed and that you want a chance to prove it.**
  - **In response to someone commenting on your bad reputation you might say: "I know people used to think that about me, but I'm different now."**
    - This shows others that you are not defensive and that perhaps you have changed.
    - If you try to disprove their beliefs about you (e.g., by saying: "You just didn't know me" or "I was never like that") they are less likely to believe that you are different now.

■ *Find a New Group or Crowd*
  - **Your reputation is often determined by your group or crowd (who you hang out with).**
  - **Find friends who do not know or care about your reputation.**
  - Think about which group you might fit in with and try to make friends in that group.
  - You may need to go somewhere new to find potential friends (e.g., clubs, teams, youth groups).

■ Go around the room and have parents of teens who are struggling with a bad reputation think of a couple of strategies for changing their bad reputation.
  – The parent group leader should help identify strategies when appropriate.
■ Other parents may also be enlisted to brainstorm ideas for how the teen might change their bad reputation, based on the suggestions discussed.

Homework Assignments

1. **Teens are to have a friend over for a *get-together*.**
   a. **Make an *out-of-group* call to set up the *get-together*:**
      i. ***Trade information to find common interests*.**
      ii. Decide what you are going to do during the *get-together*.
   b. **Parents monitor the *get-together* from a *distance*.**
   c. **The *get-together* should be activity-based.**
   d. **Teen should practice being a *good sport* when playing games.**
   e. **Be sure the teen *trades information* with the guest:**
      i. **50% of the *get-together* should be spent *trading information*.**
   f. **First *get-togethers* with a particular teen should be limited to approximately 2 hours (depending on the activity).**
2. **Practice *tease-the-tease* if it comes up this week.**
   a. **Parents and teens may want to practice *tease-the-tease* during the week.**
   b. **Parents and teens should discuss how the teen used *tease-the-tease*.**
   c. ***Tease-the-tease* is generally appropriate to use with siblings.**
3. ***Bring outside sports equipment*.**
   a. **Bring outside sports equipment to share with the group (e.g., basketball, soccer ball, volleyball, football, Frisbee).**
      i. **No solitary games or equipment.**
   b. **Do not bring something that you are:**
      i. **Unwilling to share with group members.**
      ii. **Worried about breaking or losing.**
4. **If relevant, practice *handling bullying* or *changing a bad reputation*:**
   a. **Parents and teens should discuss how the teen *handled bullying*.**
   b. **Parents and teens should discuss how the teen might *change a bad reputation*.**

Parent Handout 11: Rejection II—Bullying and Bad Reputations

How to Handle Bullying

- **■ *Lay Low***
  - – Keep a low profile.
  - – Do not draw attention to yourself.
- **■ *Avoid the Bully***
  - – Stay out of reach of the bully.
  - – Do not try to talk to the bully.
  - – Do not try to make friends with the bully.
- **■ *Do Not Provoke the Bully***
  - – Do not use ***tease-the-tease*** with a bully:
    - • This may only get the bully more agitated.
    - • Parents may need to help teens figure out when to use ***tease-the-tease***.
      - ■ Use ***tease-the-tease*** with teasers who are *verbally* abusive.
      - ■ Do not use ***tease-the-tease*** with bullies who are *physically* abusive.
  - – Do not tease the bully.
  - – Do not act silly or make fun of the bully.
  - – Do not tell on the bully and try to get him or her in trouble for minor offenses.
    - • Only get involved if someone could be seriously injured:
      - ■ Do this secretly and out of the awareness of peers so the bully does not retaliate against you.
- **■ *Hang Out With Other People***
  - – Avoid being alone.
  - – Bullies like to pick on people when they are alone and unprotected.
- **■ *If You Are in Danger—Get Help From an Adult*** (e.g., parent, teacher, principal, dean).

Tips for Changing a Bad Reputation

- **■ *Lay Low***
  - – Keep a low profile.
  - – Do not draw attention to yourself.
- **■ *Follow the Crowd***
  - – ***Try to fit in with the crowd***.
    - • This refers to exhibiting good behaviors that often lead to friendships (e.g., demonstrating similar interests as other teens, behaving in a friendly manner).
  - – ***Try not to stand out from the crowd***.
    - • This refers to standing out from others in some unusual way and includes:

- Engaging in behaviors that are considered bad and may get you in trouble (e.g., behaving in an overly emotional or aggressive manner, telling on peers for minor offenses).
- Dressing differently from the mainstream peer group or excessively talking about unusual interests.

■ *Change Your Look to Change Your Reputation*
- The fastest way to let people know that you are no longer doing things to injure your reputation is to change your look.
- You may need to change your look to fit in with the other teens.
  - Find a way of dressing that reflects the kind of person you want to be.
  - Avoid daring fashion statements that set you apart from the crowd.
  - You may need to change your hairstyle to fit in with other teens.
- By changing your look, you are drawing positive attention to yourself (after a period of laying low for a while) and letting others know that there is something new and improved about you.

■ *Own Up to Your Previous Reputation*
- Own up to any truths about your previously bad reputation.
- Let people know that you have changed and that you want a chance to prove it.
- In response to someone commenting on your bad reputation you might say: *I know people used to think that about me, but I'm different now.*

■ *Find a New Group or Crowd*
- Your reputation is often determined by your group or crowd (who you hang out with).
- Find friends that do not know or care about your reputation.

Homework Assignments

1. Teens are to have a friend over for a **get-together**.
   a. Make an **out-of-group** call to set up the **get-together**.
      i. Trade information to find **common interests**.
      ii. Decide what you are going to do during the **get-together**.
   b. Parents monitor the **get-together** from a *distance*.
   c. The **get-together** should be activity-based.
   d. Teen should practice being a **good sport** when playing games.
   e. Be sure the teen **trades information** with the guest.
      i. 50% of the **get-together** should be spent **trading information**.
   f. First get-togethers with a particular teen should be limited to approximately 2 hours (depending on the activity).
2. Practice **tease-the-tease** if it comes up this week.
   a. Parents and teens may want to practice **tease-the-tease** during the week.
   b. Parents and teens should discuss how the teen used **tease-the-tease**.
   c. **Tease-the-tease** is generally appropriate to use with siblings.

3. **Bring outside sports equipment** to share with the group (e.g., basketball, soccer ball, volleyball, football, Frisbee).

    a. No solitary games or equipment.

    b. Do not bring something that you are:

        i. Unwilling to share with group members.

        ii. Worried about breaking or losing.

4. If relevant, practice ***handling bullying*** or ***changing a bad reputation***.

    a. Parents and teens should discuss how the teen ***handled bullying***.

    b. Parents and teens should discuss how the teen might ***change a bad reputation***.

Teen Therapist Guide—Session 11: Rejection II—Bullying and Bad Reputations

Guiding Principles of the Teen Session

The purpose of the didactic lesson in this session is to give teens strategies for handling physical forms of aggression. Because the strategies described to handle teasing are inappropriate for bullying (and may even lead to further aggression), it will be important for the group leader to help teens identify which strategies to use with which form of peer rejection. Teens should be reminded to use tease-the-tease only for people who use forms of verbal attack, and to use the strategies for bullying for people who are physically aggressive. Parents are instructed to do the same and to help teens differentiate when to use each strategy.

A second purpose of this session is to provide ways to change a bad reputation. Changing a reputation is a very difficult task and is a long-term project that will continue well after the termination of this treatment. Thus, parents will need to take an active role in assisting their teens with this process. It is important to note that teens in PEERS who were able to change their bad reputations report using all of the strategies presented in this session (not just a few).

The major focus of the homework review should be on get-togethers and the use of tease-the-tease. Occasionally, teens will report that they used tease-the-tease, but that the teaser continued to tease them. From past experience, the teaser may expect an emotional reaction from the victim and when he or she does not get this, the teaser may tease even more, expecting to ultimately obtain the reaction he or she is looking for. It will be helpful for the group leader to remind teens that the teaser may be expecting them to act the way they have in the past, which is why the teaser is trying harder at the moment. Explain to the teens that if they continue to act like the teasing does not bother them and use the tease-the-tease comebacks, eventually the teaser will give up and move onto someone else.

Rule Review

Note: Only go over session rules again if the teens are having difficulty following them.

- Have teens identify the rules for the group.
- Give them points for remembering:

1. Listen to the other group members (no talking when others are speaking)
2. Follow directions
3. Raise your hand
4. Be respectful (no teasing or making fun of others)
5. No touching (no hitting, kicking, pushing, hugging, etc.)

Homework Review

Note: Give points for homework *parts*—not just one point per assignment.

1. ***Bring outside sports equipment***.
   a. Have teens identify the outside sports equipment they brought to share with the group (e.g., basketball, soccer ball, volleyball, football, Frisbee).
   b. Only give credit for appropriate items.
   c. To avoid distractions, have a coach put the item away until the teen session activity.
2. ***Tease-the-tease***.
   a. Say: *One of your assignments this week was to practice using tease-the-tease. We know that teasing is very common for teenagers, so I would expect that everyone here had an opportunity to use tease-the-tease with either a peer or a sibling or maybe through practice with your parents. Raise your hand if you were able to practice using tease-the-tease this week.*
      i. [Note: This introduction will help teens save face about being teased.]
   b. Have teens report how ***tease-the-tease*** was used.
      i. Do not allow teens to talk about the specific way someone teased them, instead have them focus only on their response.
   c. Troubleshoot any problems that may have arisen.
   d. If any teens did not use ***tease-the-tease*** this week, have them identify and demonstrate using a couple of ***tease-the-tease*** comebacks before moving on.
3. ***Get-together***.
   a. Say: *Your main homework assignment this week was to have a get-together with a friend. Raise your hand if you had a get-together this week.*
      i. Begin by calling on the teens who completed the assignment.
      ii. Briefly ask:
         1. *Who did you have a get-together with?*
         2. *Where was the get-together?*
         3. *Did you make an out-of-group phone call to figure out what you were going to do?*
         4. *What did you end up doing?*
         5. *Who chose the activities?* [Answer should be the guest.]
         6. *Did you trade information at least 50% of the time?*
         7. *Did you have a good time?*
         8. *Did your friend have a good time?*
         9. *Is this someone you might want to have a get-together with again?*
      iii. Troubleshoot any problems that may have arisen.

4. ***Being a good sport.***
   a. Say: *Another one of your assignments this week was to practice being a good sport. This may have happened during your get-together or even at school during gym class or during your extracurricular activities. Raise your hand if you practiced being a good sport this week.*
      i. Briefly ask:
         1. *Where did you practice being a good sport?*
         2. *What did you do or say to show that you were a good sport?*
      ii. Troubleshoot any problems that may have arisen.

Didactic Lesson: Bullying and Bad Reputations

Explain: *Last week we talked about teasing and how to handle situations when we are being verbally teased by peers. We called this response "tease-the-tease." Today we are talking about what to do in situations where using "tease-the-tease" is not enough. Specifically, we're going to be talking about how to handle bullying and how to change a reputation. Just like last week, we are not going to be talking about the specific mean ways that people may have bullied us or how it feels to be bullied. Instead, we are going to focus on what we can do in situations when we might be bullied.*

■ Ask the following questions and let teens come up with different explanations:
   – *What is a bully?*
      • Answer: Someone who gets into fights; threatens or assaults people.
   – *What do bullies do to other kids?*
      • Answers:
         ■ Physically attack them (e.g., hit, push, kick, spit, slap, etc.); get into fights; threaten to beat them up.
         ■ Verbally attack them; tease them; make fun of them; spread rumors about them.
         ■ Financially exploit them; steal from them; extort money.
         ■ Take advantage of them; steal their homework; make them do things for them.
   – *What is the problem with being a bully?*
      • Answer: Bullies often do not have good friends; they get in trouble; they sometimes do poorly in school.
   – *Why is it a bad idea to hang out with a bully?*
      • Answer: You may get in trouble; people may think you are a bully; you may get a bad reputation.
   – *How do you know someone is a bully?*
      • Answer: Sometimes they have a bad reputation.

Handling Bullying

Present rules for how to handle bullying.

1. ***Lay Low***
   a. Say: *One of the rules for handling bullying is to lay low. This means keep a low profile and don't draw attention to yourself. Why would it be a good idea to lay low when you're being bullied?*
      i. Answer: Because if the bully does not notice you, the bully will be less likely to bully you; he or she will likely move on to someone else.

2. ***Avoid the Bully***
   a. Say: *Another rule for handling bullying is to avoid the bully. This means we stay out of reach of the bully. For example, if you know where the bully's locker is, you should avoid walking by it. Or if you know where the bully hangs out at lunch, you shouldn't go in that area. Why would it be a good idea to avoid the bully?*
      i. Answer: Because if the bully cannot find you, then he or she cannot bully you.
   b. Say: *It's also important not to try to talk to the bully or try to make friends with the bully. Some people think they can win over the bully, but this almost never works. Instead, it just draws the attention of the bully. Why would it be a bad idea to try to make friends with the bully?*
      i. Answer: It probably will not work; it will just draw attention to you; he or she will just bully you more.

3. ***Do Not Provoke the Bully***
   a. Say: *Another rule for handling bullying is not to use tease-the-tease with a bully. This is because tease-the-tease often results in embarrassment for the bully and may only get the bully more agitated. We should only use tease-the-tease with people who are **verbally** abusive, **not** people who are **physically** abusive. If you're unsure about which strategies to use, your parents can help you figure it out.*
   b. Ask: *What is the problem with using tease-the-tease with a bully who gets physically abusive?*
      i. Answer: They may get more aggressive as retaliation.
   c. Say: *We also don't want to tease the bully. This would also provoke the bully. What would be the problem with teasing a bully?*
      i. Answer: They may get more aggressive as retaliation.
   d. Say: *We also don't want to act silly or make fun of the bully. What would be the problem with acting silly or making fun of a bully?*
      i. Answer: This would draw attention to you.
   e. Say: *It's also important not to tell on the bully and try to get him or her in trouble for minor offenses. That means if the bully is passing notes in class or breaking some minor rule, we should not tell on him or her. What would be the problem with telling on the bully for some minor offense?*

      i. Answer: The bully may get more aggressive as retaliation.

    f. Explain: *We should only get involved if someone could be seriously injured, like if the bully brought a weapon to school or was threatening to beat someone up. If you do have to tell on the bully, be sure that you do this secretly and out of the awareness of your peers so the bully does not retaliate against you.*

4. ***Hang Out With Other People***

    a. Say: *Another strategy for handling bullying is to hang out with other people. This means you should avoid being alone. Bullies like to pick on people when they are alone and unprotected. Why would it be important to hang out with other people?*

      i. Answer: Because the bully is less likely to pick on you if you have people around who might protect you; if you are alone, you are an easy target.

5. ***If You Are in Danger—Get Help From an Adult***

    a. Say: *Finally, if you think you're in danger, you should get help from an adult like a parent, teacher, principal, or dean. That means if the bully has physically assaulted you (e.g., punched, hit, kicked you) or is threatening to beat you up, you should get help from an adult. Why would it be a good idea to get help from an adult?*

      i. Answer: Because you should not be placed in danger; adults can help to keep you and others safe from the bully.

■ Go around the room and have each teen think of at least one bully in their school (they do not have to admit that they are being bullied by this person) and choose at least *two* strategies he or she could use to handle potential bullying from this person.

  – They must use the strategies outlined in the lesson.

  – It is not important for the teen to admit that he or she is being bullied.

  – Teens will often enjoy sharing the first name of the bully (like they are outing the bully).

    • Teens do not have to mention the first name of the bully if they are uncomfortable.

    • [Note: If there are two or more teens from the same school in the group, the teen group leader should discourage identifying the bullies by first name as this may get back to people at school.]

  – Discourage teens from getting too personal when talking about their experiences with bullying.

  – Encourage the use of the following strategies (both of which are effective):

    • Avoid the bully.

    • Hang out with other people

  – The teen group leader should troubleshoot as necessary.

Bad Reputations

- Explain: *Now that we have some ideas about what to do if we're bullied, it's important to think about why some people get bullied and what happens if you are a bully. We know that some bullies have a bad reputation, but some people who get bullied also have a bad reputation.*
- Ask the following questions and let teens come up with different explanations:
- *What is a bad reputation?*
  - Answer: A low opinion held by the larger peer group about a particular teen; often relates to certain characteristics that do not follow the crowd (e.g., unusual or bad behavior, odd appearance, etc.).
- *Are bullies the only ones with bad reputations?*
  - Answer: No, teens who are teased and bullied often have bad reputations.
- *How do you get a bad reputation?*
  - Answers:
    - Getting in physical fights.
    - Being aggressive toward others (e.g., hitting, kicking, pushing, etc.).
    - Hanging out with teens who get in trouble.
    - Talking back to teachers or adults.
    - Teasing or bullying other teens.
    - Skipping school.
    - Getting bad grades, not doing homework, not listening to teachers.
    - Doing drugs, drinking alcohol, smoking.
    - Stealing, damaging property, breaking the law.
    - Telling on peers, getting peers into trouble with adults.
    - Acting different from other teens:
      - Wearing different clothes.
      - Listening to different music.
      - Having unusual interests.
      - Excessively talking (being a conversation hog).
      - Rarely talking (being a loner).
      - Being the teacher's pet, acting like a know-it-all.
      - Engaging in unusual behaviors (self-injurious behavior; abnormal outbursts/cursing/yelling).
      - Having bad hygiene.
      - Having emotional outbursts, tantrums, crying spells, or rages.

Tips for Changing a Bad Reputation

- Explain: *Changing a bad reputation is difficult to do and usually takes time, but it can be done. There are very specific steps for changing a bad reputation. None of these steps alone should be expected to change how people view you. Instead, they need to be followed in order over time. You will not be able to follow all of these steps while you are in PEERS, but your parents are being taught these same steps and will be ready to help you even when our group is over.*

Present steps for how to change a bad reputation:

1. ***Lay Low***
   a. Say: *The first step for changing a reputation is to lay low. This means you will need to keep a low profile for awhile and not draw attention to yourself. This will give your reputation a chance to die down before you try to join a new peer group. What would be the problem with trying to join a new peer group while you have a bad reputation?*
      i. Answer: The new peer group may not want to associate with you because of your reputation.
2. ***Follow the Crowd***
   a. Say: *The next step for changing a reputation is to follow the crowd. This means that you should try to fit in with the crowd. This involves engaging in behaviors that often lead to friendships. Like finding common interests with other teens and behaving in a friendly manner. This also involves trying not to stand out from the crowd. This means avoiding behaviors that make you stand out from others in some unusual way. That might include engaging in behaviors that get you in trouble, like behaving in an overly emotional or aggressive way, or telling on peers for minor offenses. It might also include dressing differently from other people or excessively talking about unusual interests. All of these things will often result in a bad reputation.*
   b. [Note: Do not engage in a discussion about this step as teens will often want to argue about individuality. While individuality is important, the goal of this group is to try to help teens make and keep friends, which during adolescence also generally involves fitting in.]
3. ***Change Your Look to Change Your Reputation***
   a. Say: *The fastest way to let people know that you're no longer doing things to injure your reputation is to change your look. We call this changing your look to change your rep. In some cases, you may need to change your look to fit in with the other teens. This might involve finding a way of dressing that reflects the kind of person you want to be. If you want to fit in, you may need to avoid daring fashion statements that set you apart from the crowd. You may also need to change your hairstyle to fit in with other teens. What do other teens do when they notice something improved about your appearance?*
      i. Answer: They approach you and start asking questions; they notice something is different about you and usually comment on it.
   b. Explain: *By changing your look you are drawing positive attention to yourself. But this should only be done after a period of laying low for a while. By changing your look, you are letting others know that there is something new and improved about you. But a "makeover" alone will not change your*

reputation, so once people start to notice that you're different you will have to prove it; usually by owning up to your previous reputation. Why would changing your look alone not be enough to change your reputation?"

    i. Answer: Because if you do not own up to your previous reputation and change certain things about yourself that people did not like, no one is going to believe that you are different.

4. ***Own Up to Your Previous Reputation***

    a. Say: *The next step for changing a reputation is to own up to your previous rep. That means you have to acknowledge any truths about your reputation. Once people notice there is something different about you, let them know that you have changed and that you want a chance to prove it. For example, in response to someone commenting on your previously bad reputation you might say: "I know people used to think that about me, but I'm different now." Why would it be important to own up to your previous reputation?*

       i. Answer: Because it shows others that you are not defensive and that you may have changed.

    b. Explain: *If you try to disprove their beliefs about you by saying: "You just didn't know me" or "I was never like that" they are less likely to believe that you're different and your reputation will stay the same.*

5. ***Find a New Group or Crowd***

    a. Say: *The last step for changing a reputation is to find a new group or crowd. Your reputation is often determined by the people you hang out with. Once your reputation has died down a bit, you will want to find friends who don't know or care about your reputation and who you have common interests with. Think about which group you might fit in with and try to make friends in that group. You may need to go somewhere new to find potential friends like new clubs, teams, or youth groups.*

Explain: *Remember that in order to change your reputation, you need to do all of these steps. Just doing one or two will not change your reputation. Also remember that changing a reputation is difficult to do and takes time, but it can be done.*

Homework Assignments

▪ Briefly explain the homework for the week by saying: *The main homework assignment this week is for each of you to have another get-together with one or more friends. You may need to make a phone call to set up this get-together. During these get-togethers, we want you to practice being a good sport if you play games or sports. We also want you to practice using tease-the-tease if it comes up this week. We know teasing is very common among teenagers, so we expect it to come up for everyone at some point this week. We also want you to start using the strategies for handling bullying and changing reputations if relevant. Next week we will be outside on the play deck, so you will need to bring some type of outside sports equipment to share with the group. Again, your homework assignment this week is to:*

- *Have a get-together with one or more friends.*
  - *Make an out-of-group call to schedule the get-together.*
  - *Trade information to figure out what you are going to do.*
  - *Practice being a good sport if relevant.*
- *Practice handling bullying and changing a bad reputation if relevant.*
- *Practice using tease-the-tease with the comebacks we identified in the group.*
- *Bring outside sports equipment.*
  - *Bring appropriate equipment for outdoor activities with groups or pairs (e.g., basketball, soccer ball, volleyball, Frisbee, handball, football).*
  - *No solitary equipment is allowed.*

Teen Activity: Good Sportsmanship and Outdoor Activities

Note: See the "Teen Activity Guide" for rules.

- Teens will be playing outdoor games and sports on the play deck.
- The outdoor game is chosen from appropriate **outdoor sports equipment** brought by teens and from other available outdoor gear provided by the treatment team.
- Allow teens to choose what they play so long as it is not aggressive or dangerous (e.g., touch football instead of tackle football).
- Do not allow any teens to engage in solitary play or isolative behavior.
- Teens receive points while practicing **being a good sport**:
  - **Praise**
  - **Do not referee**
  - **Do not be a coach**
  - **Share and take turns**
  - **If you get bored, suggest a change**
  - **Do not gloat if you win**
  - **Do not sulk or get angry if you lose**
  - **At the end of the game say: "Good game"**
- The teen group leader and coaches should monitor points for good sportsmanship using the "PEERS Good Sportsmanship Point Log" (Appendix G).

Reunification With Parents

- Announce that teens should join their parents.
  - Be sure that the teens are standing or sitting next to their parents.

- Be sure to have silence and the full attention of the group.
■ Say: *Today we talked about how to handle bullying. Who can tell us one of the rules for handling bullying?* [Have the teens generate all of the rules. Be prepared to give prompts if necessary.]
  - *Lay low*
  - *Avoid the bully*
  - *Do not provoke the bully*
    - Only use *tease-the-tease* with bullies who are *verbally* aggressive; not *physically* aggressive.
  - *Hang out with other people*
  - *If you are in danger—get help from an adult*
■ Say: *Today we also talked about changing reputations. Who can tell us the first step for changing a reputation?* [Have the teens generate all of the steps. Be prepared to give prompts if necessary.]
  - *Lay low*:
    - Keep a low profile.
    - Do not draw attention to yourself.
  - *Follow the crowd*:
    - *Try to fit in with the crowd.*
    - *Try not to stand out from the crowd.*
  - *Change your look to change your reputation.*
  - *Own up to your previous reputation.*
  - *Find a new group or crowd.*
■ Say: *Today we also practiced playing outdoor sports, and this group did a great job of being good sports. Let's give them a round of applause.*
■ Go over the homework for the next week (see below) individually, and negotiate with each family:
  - The location of the get-together, the activity planned, who will be present, as well as the parent role in the get-together.
  - What outside sports equipment will be brought next week.

Calculate Points

Keep track of the following for each week of the intervention.

■ Calculate the number of points earned by each teen.
■ Add up the total number of points earned by the group.
■ Do not calculate the points in the presence of the teens:
  - Do not disclose the individual or group total of points.
  - Discourage attempts to compare number of points earned between teens.
■ Remind them that they are working as a team to earn a bigger and better graduation party.

Teen Activity Guide: Session 11

"Good Sportsmanship and Outdoor Activities"

Materials Needed

- Outside sports equipment brought by teens.
- In the event that a teen forgets to bring outdoor sports equipment, have the teens share items or have sports equipment available to use:
  - Soccer ball
  - Basketball
  - Handball
  - Frisbee

Rules

- Have teens negotiate what they will play when they reach the play deck.
  - Give examples of possible games:
    - Basketball
    - Soccer
    - Handball
    - Frisbee
  - If there are enough players, you may have teens play different games.
- Explain the rules for the game:
  - We have a "no contact" rule for all sports—no excessive touching, crowding, stealing.
  - Must pass the ball in soccer and basketball.
  - Warnings will be given for poor sportsmanship.
- Coaches may need to periodically remind teens of the rules for specific games:
  - Try to avoid acting as a referee if disagreements occur.
  - Encourage teens to work out their differences by being ***good sports***.
- You may need to prompt teens to be ***good sports*** and ***praise*** other players.
- Give points for ***good sportsmanship***:
  - ***Praise***
  - ***Do not referee***
  - ***Do not be a coach***
  - ***Share and take turns***
  - ***If you get bored, suggest a change***
  - ***Do not gloat if you win***
  - ***Do not sulk or get angry if you lose***
  - ***At the end of the game say: "Good game"***
- Coaches should state why the teen is receiving a point. (e.g., "John gets a point for praising his teammate!")
  - Be sure to keep track of points on the "Good Sportsmanship Point Log."
  - Speak loudly when giving out points so other teens can hear.
    - The social comparison will encourage other teens to ***praise*** and be ***good sports***.

Chapter 14

Session 12
Handling Disagreements

Parent Session Therapist Guide

Guiding Principles of the Parent Session

Beginning with this session, the teen should have had enough get-togethers for parents to reflect on the quality of the potential friendships of the invited teens. Have parents compare get-togethers in terms of how easy they were for the teen and how comfortable the teen felt on them and about them (ideally, not just comfortable, but more like elated). In many cases, teens with developmental delays (particularly teens with autism) feel more comfortable with other teens with similar delays.

Because the primary focus of the last few sessions of this intervention is on arranging get-togethers with others where there is mutual liking and respect, conflict with others may be decreased. Laursen and Koplas (1995) present evidence that teens are more attentive to affect and resolution of conflict rather than the frequency of conflicts. Negotiation resulted in less angry affect after the conflict was over. This lesson incorporates these findings into teaching teens how to deal with conflict. Simple resolution strategies are taught that the teens may use during conflict with peers.

The didactic in the current session, handling disagreements, may have limited immediate applicability for many teens. As with all other sessions, the maximum effectiveness of the lesson comes with practice between sessions. If there are no peer interactions with conflict, then the teen may not get to try out the skills being taught. Consequently, parents may want to practice the skills at home with their teen using role plays, utilize opportunities for practice during real sibling conflict, and hold onto the handouts for a time when conflict is present in one of their teen's friendships.

Homework Review

1. ***Get-together***.
   a. Identify whether the ***get-together*** was:
      i. Activity-based
      ii. Monitored by parents from a ***distance***.
      iii. No more than 2 hours (depending on the activity).
   b. If applicable, check to see if the teen practiced ***being a good sport***.
   c. Be sure that the teen ***traded information*** with his or her guest and found a ***common interest***:
      i. 50% of the time should have been spent ***trading information***.
2. ***Handling bullying*** and ***bad reputations***.
   a. If applicable, have parents report:
      i. How the teen ***handled bullying***.
      ii. How the teen might change his or her ***bad reputation***.
         1. ***Lay low***.
         2. ***Follow the crowd***:
            a. ***Try to fit in with the crowd***.
            b. ***Try not to stand out from the crowd***.
         3. ***Change your look to change your reputation***.
         4. ***Own up to your previous reputation***.
         5. ***Find a new group or crowd***.
   b. Troubleshoot any problems that may have arisen.
3. ***Tease-the-tease***.
   a. Check to see if parents practiced ***tease-the-tease*** with their teen (not an assignment).
   b. Have parents report how ***tease-the-tease*** was used.
      i. ***Tease-the-tease*** may have been used with peers or siblings.
   c. Troubleshoot any problems that may have arisen.
4. ***Bring outside sports equipment***.
   a. Have parents identify the outside sports equipment their teen brought to share with the group (e.g., basketball, soccer ball, volleyball, football, Frisbee).
   b. Only give credit for appropriate items.

Didactic Lesson: Handling Disagreements

- Distribute the Parent Handout.
- Explain: *Today we're going to be talking about how to handle disagreements and arguments. Disagreements between teens are common and occasional disagreements should not end your teen's friendships. However, it's important*

that we know how our teens should handle disagreements appropriately with their friends to minimize the negative impact.
■ Go around the room and have parents take turns reading the Parent Handout.
■ Sections in **bold print** come directly from the Parent Handout.

Handling Disagreements

1. *Keep your cool*.
   a. **Stay calm**.
   b. **Do not get upset**:
      i. You may need to take deep breaths or count slowly to yourself.
      ii. You may need to take some time to cool down before you talk.
2. *Listen to the other person first*.
   a. **Listen to the other person's side first**.
   b. **This will help you to understand what the disagreement is about**.
   c. **Listening is an important part of communication and helps us to understand the other person's perspective**.
3. *Repeat what the other person said*:
   a. **Try to repeat back what the other person said to you to let him or her know you are listening to him or her**.
   b. *Repeating statements usually starts with:* **"It sounds like…**
      i. **…you're upset."**
      ii. **…you're angry."**
      iii. **…your feelings are hurt."**
   c. **Examples**:
      i. **"I feel bad when you tell jokes about me."**
         1. **Response: "It sounds like I upset you."**
      ii. **"I feel bad when you make fun of me."**
         1. **Response: "It sounds like what I said made you feel bad."**
      iii. "I feel frustrated when you tell jokes about me."
         1. Response: "It sounds like I made you upset."
      iv. "I feel bad when you laugh at me in front of everybody."
         1. Response: "It sounds like I made you feel bad."
      v. "I feel upset when you say those things."
         1. Response: "It sounds like I upset you."
      vi. "I don't like it when you tell other people my secrets."
         1. Response: "It sounds like I hurt your feelings."
4. *Explain your side*.
   a. **Explain your side if there is a misunderstanding**.
   b. **Avoid telling the other person that he or she is wrong**:
      i. **This will only upset the other person and escalate the argument**.
   c. **Calmly explain your side of the story**.

5. ***Say you are sorry***.
   a. **It is helpful to say you are sorry when someone is angry, sad, or upset.**
   b. **Saying that you are sorry does not mean that you admit you did anything wrong.**
   c. **You can simply say you are sorry they feel that way.**
      i. Examples:
         1. "I'm sorry you feel bad."
         2. "I'm sorry you're feeling upset."
         3. "I'm sorry you're mad at me."
         4. "I'm sorry your feelings got hurt."
         5. "I'm sorry this has happened."
6. ***Try to solve the problem***.
   a. ***Tell the other person what you will do differently***.
      i. **Examples**:
         1. **"I'll try not to upset you again."**
         2. **"I'll try not to tell jokes about you."**
         3. **"I'll try not to embarrass you again."**
   b. ***Ask the other person what he or she wants you to do***.
      i. **Examples**:
         1. **"What can I do to make you feel better?"**
         2. **"What would you like me to do?"**
         3. **"What can I do to fix this?"**
   c. ***Suggest what you want the other person to do*** (if you are upset with the other person).
      i. **Examples**:
         1. **"I would like it if you didn't do that again."**
         2. **"I wish you would try not to embarrass me like that again."**
         3. **"I would like it if you wouldn't make fun of me anymore."**
   d. **If you cannot *solve the problem*:**
      i. **Try to *keep your cool*.**
      ii. **Do not expect the other person to admit he or she was wrong.**
         1. **Your goal is not to get the other person to apologize or admit that he or she was wrong.**
         2. **Your goal is to try to end the disagreement.**

Homework Assignments

The parent group leader should go over the homework assignment and trouble-shoot any potential problems with parents.

1. **Teens are to have a friend over for a *get-together*.**
   a. **Make an *out-of-group* call to set up the *get-together*.**
      i. ***Trade information* to find *common interests*.**

    ii. **Decide what you are going to do during your *get-together*.**

  b. **Parents monitor the *get-together* from a *distance*.**

  c. **The *get-together* should be activity-based.**

  d. **If applicable, practice *being a good sport*.**

  e. **Be sure the teen *trades information* with the guest:**

    i. **50% of the *get-together* should be spent *trading information*.**

  f. **First *get-togethers* with a particular teen should be limited to approximately 2 hours (depending on the activity).**

2. **Practice *tease-the-tease* if it comes up this week.**

  a. **Parents and teens may want to practice *tease-the-tease* during the week.**

  b. **Parents and teens should discuss how the teen used *tease-the-tease*:**

    i. ***Tease-the-tease* is generally appropriate to use with peers or siblings of the same age.**

3. **If applicable, practice *handling bullying* or *changing a bad reputation*.**

  a. **Parents and teens should discuss how the teen *handled bullying*.**

  b. **Parents and teens should discuss how their teen is progressing to *change a bad reputation*.**

4. ***Bring outside sports equipment*.**

  a. **Bring outside sports equipment to share with the group (e.g., basketball, soccer ball, volleyball, football, Frisbee).**

    i. **No solitary games or equipment.**

  b. **Do not bring something that you are:**

    i. **Unwilling to share with group members.**

    ii. **Worried about breaking or losing.**

5. **Practice *handling a disagreement* if it comes up this week.**

  a. **Parents and teens should discuss how the teen handled the disagreement.**

    i. **Disagreements with siblings may also be used as practice.**

  b. **Parents and teens may want to practice using role plays.**

Reminder: The PEERS Graduation is in 2 weeks!

Suggestions for How to Present the Graduation

Teen Session

- Explain that the graduation party is for the teens and will be held in the teen room.
- Encourage parents to bring treats for the graduation party to add to the festivities.

- Treats are typically kept in the teen room (but parents are welcome to bring snacks for the parent group too).
- The PEERS team should provide dinner and beverages (usually pizza and soda).
- The treatment team should have a selection of PG-rated DVDs for the teens to watch during the party.
- The treatment team should also have a selection of games from which the teens can choose to play.
- The teens will vote on what they do or which movie they watch.
- Teens should receive graduation prizes at the graduation party.

Parent Session

- Parents will attend their usual parent session.
- The parent group leader will go over suggestions for where to go from here.

Graduation Ceremony

- The ceremony will be held in the parent room (or the largest room).
- Parents and family members are welcome to attend the graduation ceremony.
- Teens should receive a diploma at the graduation ceremony.
- For privacy, no cameras or video cameras are allowed.
- We ask that additional family members who attend the graduation ceremony wait in the lobby until just before the ceremony begins in order to protect confidentiality.

Note: It is recommended that the treatment team provide a graduation flyer to be distributed in the 12th and 13th sessions with the relevant information from above, including the date and time of the graduation, as well as any information about posttesting. A sample graduation flyer is presented in Appendix I.]

Parent Handout 12: Handling Disagreements

Handling Disagreements

1. ***Keep your cool***:
   a. Stay calm.
   b. Do not get upset.
2. ***Listen to the other person first***:
   a. Listen to the other person's side first.
   b. This will help you to understand what the disagreement is about.
   c. Listening is an important part of communication and helps us to understand the other person's perspective.
3. ***Repeat what the other person said***:
   a. Try to repeat back what the other person said to you to let the other person know you are listening to him or her.
   b. *Repeating statements usually start with*: "It sounds like…
      i. …you're upset."
      ii. …you're angry."
      iii. …your feelings are hurt."
   c. Examples:
      i. "I feel bad when you tell jokes about me."
         1. Response: "It sounds like I upset you."
      ii. "I feel bad when you make fun of me."
         1. Response: "It sounds like what I said made you feel bad."
4. ***Explain your side***.
   a. Explain your side if there is a misunderstanding.
   b. Avoid telling the other person that he or she is wrong:
      i. This will only upset the other person and escalate the argument.
   c. Calmly explain your side of the story.
5. ***Say you are sorry***.
   a. It is helpful to say you are sorry when someone is angry, sad, or upset.
   b. Saying that you are sorry does not mean that you admit you did anything wrong.
   c. You can simply say you are sorry the other person feels that way.
6. ***Try to solve the problem***.
   a. ***Tell the other person what you will do differently***.
      i. Examples:
         1. "I'll try not to upset you again."
         2. "I'll try not to tell jokes about you."
         3. "I'll try not to embarrass you again."
   b. ***Ask the other person what he or she wants you to do***.
      i. Examples:
         1. "What can I do to make you feel better?"
         2. "What would you like me to do?"

    3. "What can I do to fix this?"

  c. ***Suggest what you want the other person to do*** (if you are upset with him or her).

    i. Examples:

      1. "I would like it if you didn't do that again."

      2. "I wish you would try not to embarrass me like that again."

      3. "I would like it if you wouldn't make fun of me anymore."

  d. If you cannot *solve the problem*:

    i. Try to keep your cool.

    ii. Do not expect the other person to admit that he or she was wrong.

      1. Your goal is not to get the other person to apologize or admit he or she was wrong.

      2. Your goal is to try to end the disagreement.

Homework Assignments

1. Teens are to have a friend over for a ***get-together***.

  a. Make an ***out-of-group*** call to set up the ***get-together***.

    i. ***Trade information*** to find ***common interests***.

    ii. Decide what you are going to do during your ***get-together***.

  b. Parents monitor the ***get-together*** from a *distance*.

  c. The ***get-together*** should be activity-based.

  d. If applicable, practice ***being a good sport***.

  e. Be sure the teen ***trades information*** with the guest:

    i. 50% of the ***get-together*** should be spent ***trading information***.

  f. First ***get-togethers*** with a particular teen should be limited to approximately 2 hours (depending on the activity).

2. Practice ***tease-the-tease*** if it comes up this week.

  a. Parents and teens may want to practice ***tease-the-tease*** during the week.

  b. Parents and teens should discuss how the teen used ***tease-the-tease***.

    i. ***Tease-the-tease*** is generally appropriate to use with peers or siblings.

3. If applicable, practice ***handling bullying*** or ***changing a bad reputation***.

  a. Parents and teens should discuss how the teen ***handled bullying***.

  b. Parents and teens should discuss how the teen might ***change a bad reputation***.

4. ***Bring outside sports equipment***.

  a. Bring outside sports equipment to share with the group (e.g., basketball, soccer ball, volleyball, football, Frisbee).

    i. No solitary games or equipment.

  b. Do not bring something that you are:

    i. Unwilling to share with group members.

    ii. Worried about breaking or losing.

5. Practice ***handling a disagreement*** if it comes up this week.

    a. Parents and teens should discuss how the teen handled the disagreement.
       i. Disagreements with siblings may also be used as practice.
    b. Parents and teens may want to practice using role plays.

Reminder: The PEERS Graduation is in 2 weeks!

Teen Therapist Guide—Session 12: Handling Disagreements

Guiding Principles of the Teen Session

The purpose of this lesson is to teach some skills to help teens resolve disagreements with peers. Misunderstandings and disagreements are common among teenagers, and when infrequent, do not need to result in the termination of a friendship. Yet some teens who lack skills for resolving arguments may be unable to see any way out of the disagreement and may choose to end the friendship. This may be characteristic of teens with autism spectrum disorders, as they have a tendency to think concretely with little flexibility. An important goal of this session is to help teens understand that occasional arguments with friends do not need to result in the termination of friendship. Rather, through appropriate conflict resolution, friendships should be able to be maintained despite the periodic disagreement. However, some teens who find themselves engaged in frequent conflict with specific friends may need to reexamine the appropriateness of their friendship choices.

This session marks the beginning of termination for the group. At the end of the session, the teen group leader will want to announce to the teens that only two additional sessions remain. Some teens will find this news surprising and many will express disappointment. By this point in the group, many teens have developed close relationships with the other group members and will feel nervous and sad at the prospect of not seeing these peers on a regular basis. Questions may arise about whether or not teens can socialize with each other outside of the group and plan get-togethers. While the program prohibits the occurrence of get-togethers among group members during the course of treatment, when appropriate and sanctioned by parents, some teens may choose to stay in touch with one another. It will be important for the treatment team to remain uninvolved in this process, as the goal of this program is not to facilitate match-making of friends, but to allow teens to learn new skills through instruction and practice with like peers.

Rule Review

Note: Only go over session rules again if the teens are having difficulty following them.

- Have teens identify the rules for the group.
- Give them points for remembering:

1. Listen to the other group members (no talking when others are speaking)
2. Follow directions
3. Raise your hand
4. Be respectful (no teasing or making fun of others)

5. No touching (no hitting, kicking, pushing, hugging, etc.)

Homework Review

Note: Give points for homework *parts*—not just one point per assignment.

1. ***Bring outside sports equipment***.
   a. Have teens identify the outside sports equipment they brought to share with the group (e.g., basketball, soccer ball, volleyball, football, Frisbee).
   b. Only give credit for appropriate items.
   c. To avoid distractions, have a coach put the item away until the teen session activity.
2. ***Handling bullying and bad reputations***.
   a. Say: *One of your assignments this week was to practice handling bullying. Raise your hand if you used one or more of the strategies for handling bullying this week.*
      i. Have teens report what they did to handle bullying.
      ii. Troubleshoot any problems that may have arisen.
      iii. If any teens did not use any of the strategies for handling bullying this week, have them identify a couple of options.
   b. Say: *Another related assignment was to begin to take steps toward changing your reputation. Raise your hand if you did anything new this week to try to change your reputation.*
      i. Have teens report what they did to change their reputation.
         1. [Note: It is likely that very few teens will report making changes in this area. At best, certain teens with bad reputations should be laying low for the moment until they can move onto the other steps.]
      ii. If teens did not use any of the strategies for changing a reputation this week, have them identify the steps for doing this.
         1. ***Lay low***.
         2. ***Follow the crowd***.
            a. ***Try to fit in with the crowd***.
            b. ***Try not to stand out from the crowd***.
         3. ***Change your look to change your reputation***.
         4. ***Own up to your previous reputation***.
         5. ***Find a new group or crowd***.
3. ***Tease-the-tease***.
   a. Say: *Another one of your assignments this week was to practice using tease-the-tease. We know that teasing is very common for teenagers, so I would expect that everyone here had an opportunity to use tease-the-tease with either a peer or a sibling or maybe through practice with your parents. Raise your hand if you were able to practice using tease-the-tease this week.*

      i. [Note: This introduction will help teens save face about being teased.]

   b. Have teens report how ***tease-the-tease*** was used:

      i. Do not allow teens to talk about the specific way someone teased them, instead have them focus only on their response.

   c. Troubleshoot any problems that may have arisen.

   d. If teens did not use ***tease-the-tease*** this week, have them identify and demonstrate using a couple of ***tease-the-tease*** comebacks before moving on.

4. ***Get-together***.

   a. Say: *Your main homework assignment this week was to have a get-together with a friend. Raise your hand if you had a get-together this week.*

      i. Begin by calling on the teens who completed the assignment.

      ii. Briefly ask:

         1. *Who did you have a get-together with?*

         2. *Where was the get-together?*

         3. *Did you make an out-of-group phone call to figure out what you were going to do?*

         4. *What did you end up doing?*

         5. *Who chose the activities?* [Answer should be the guest.]

         6. *Did you trade information at least 50% of the time?*

         7. *Were you able to practice being a good sport?* (If the opportunity came up.)

           a. *What did you do to be a good sport?*

         8. *Did you have a good time?*

         9. *Did your friend have a good time?*

        10. *Is this someone you might want to have a get-together with again?*

      iii. Troubleshoot any problems that may have arisen.

Didactic Lesson: Handling Disagreements

■ Explain: *Today we're going to be talking about how to handle disagreements and arguments. Disagreements with friends are common and **occasional** disagreements should not end your friendship. However, if you're having frequent and explosive arguments with a friend, you may need to consider whether this person is the right friend for you. Because we know that occasional disagreements are common, it's important that we know how to appropriately handle these disagreements with our friends to minimize the negative impact.*

■ Present the following steps for handling disagreements:

1. ***Keep your cool***.

   a. Say: *The first step for handling a disagreement with a friend is to keep your cool. This means you need to stay calm and don't get upset. You may need to take deep breaths or count slowly to yourself, or you may need to take some time to cool down before you talk. Why would it be important to keep your cool in a disagreement?*

 i. Answer: Because if you lose your cool, you may end up saying something you regret or ruining your friendship.

2. ***Listen to the other person first.***

 a. Say: *The next step for handling a disagreement with a friend is to listen. We need to listen to the other person's side first, before we share our side. This will help you to understand what the disagreement is about. Why would it be important to listen to the other person's side first?*

  i. Answer: Listening is an important part of communication and helps us to understand the other person's perspective.

3. ***Repeat what the other person said.***

 a. Say: *The next step is to try to repeat back what the other person said to you to let the other person know you're listening to him or her. Why would it be important to repeat back what the other person said?*

  i. Answer: It shows the other person that you are listening, makes them feel like you care, and makes the other person feel heard.

 b. Explain: *Repeating statements usually start with:* "It sounds like…

  i. …you're upset."

  ii. …you're angry."

  iii. …your feelings are hurt."

 c. Examples:

  i. "I feel bad when you tell jokes about me."

   1. Response: "It sounds like I upset you."

  ii. "I feel bad when you make fun of me."

   1. Response: "It sounds like what I said made you feel bad."

  iii. "I feel frustrated when you tell jokes about me."

   1. Response: "It sounds like I made you upset."

  iv. "I feel bad when you laugh at me in front of everybody."

   1. Response: "It sounds like I made you feel bad."

  v. "I feel upset when you say those things."

   1. Response: "It sounds like I upset you."

  vi. "I don't like it when you tell other people my secrets."

   1. Response: "It sounds like I hurt your feelings."

4. ***Explain your side.***

 a. Say: *The next step is to explain your side if there is a misunderstanding. Many people will jump to do this step first, but you need to **wait** until you've kept your cool, listened, and repeated what the other person said. When you're explaining your side, you should avoid telling the other person that he or she is wrong. Instead, calmly explain your side of the story. Why would we want to avoid telling the other person what we think he or she did wrong?*

  i. Answer: This will only upset the other person and escalate the argument; the other person is not likely to agree; he or she will most likely get more upset with you.

5. ***Say you are sorry****.*
   a. Say: *The next step for resolving a disagreement with a friend is to say you're sorry. It is helpful to say you're sorry when someone is angry, sad, or upset. Why is it important to say you're sorry when someone is upset?*
      i. Answer: Because the person is feeling bad and wants you to acknowledge that you are sorry he or she is feeling that way; often the argument will not be over until you have said you are sorry in some way or other.
   b. Explain: *Saying that you're sorry doesn't mean that you admit you did anything wrong. You can simply say you're sorry they feel that way.*
      i. Examples:
         1. "I'm sorry you feel bad."
         2. "I'm sorry you're feeling upset."
         3. "I'm sorry you're mad at me."
         4. "I'm sorry your feelings got hurt."
         5. "I'm sorry this happened."
6. ***Try to solve the problem****.*
   a. Say: *The last step in handling a disagreement with a friend is to try to solve the problem. This can be done in several ways.*
      i. ***Tell your friend what you will do differently****.*
         1. Examples:
            a. "I'll try not to upset you again."
            b. "I'll try not to tell jokes about you."
            c. "I'll try not to embarrass you again."
      ii. ***Ask the other person what he or she wants you to do****:*
         1. Examples:
            a. "What can I do to make you feel better?"
            b. "What would you like me to do?"
            c. "What can I do to fix this?"
      iii. ***Suggest what you want the other person to do*** (if you are upset with him or her).
         1. Examples:
            a. "I would like it if you didn't do that again."
            b. "I wish you would try not to embarrass me like that again."
            c. "I would like it if you wouldn't make fun of me anymore."
   b. If you cannot solve the problem, try to keep your cool.
      i. Explain: *If you can't solve the problem, try to keep your cool. Don't expect the other person to admit he or she was wrong. Your goal is not to get the other person to apologize or admit he or she was wrong. Your goal is to try to end the disagreement.*

Role Play

■ The teen group leader and coach should demonstrate an *appropriate* role play of a disagreement between friends.
  - Each step of how to handle the disagreement should be presented individually and in succession, adding a new step in each phase of the role play.
  - Explain to the teens that you are going to act out a typical teen dispute several times, each time adding a new step.
    • This will illustrate the importance of following each step.
  - Explain that the first two steps of handling a disagreement are to **keep your cool** and to **listen to the other person first**.
    • Say: *Watch this and tell me which steps I'm following.*
      ■ Demonstrate keeping your cool and listening to the other person first.
■ Example of an *appropriate* role play:

Coach: "I'm so mad at you (insert group leader name)! Carrie told me that you were talking behind my back and you told everyone that I got grounded for getting a bad grade on my math test."

Teen group leader: (keeping cool, not getting upset, listening)

Coach: "I can't believe you told everyone that! That was supposed to be a secret. And now everyone knows. That is so uncool."

Teen group leader: (keeping cool, not getting upset, listening)
  • Say: *Time-out on that. So which of the steps did I follow?*
    ■ Answer: Keep your cool; listen to the other person first.
  • Ask: *Does it feel like the argument is over?*
    ■ Answer: No.
  - Explain that the next step is to **repeat what the person said**.
    • Say: *Watch this and tell me which steps I'm following.*
      ■ Demonstrate keeping your cool, listening to the other person first, and repeating what the person said by saying, "It sounds like…"

Coach: "I'm so mad at you (insert name)! Carrie told me that you were talking behind my back and you told everyone that I got grounded for getting a bad grade on my math test."

Teen group leader: (keeping cool, not getting upset, listening)

Coach: "I can't believe you told everyone that! That was supposed to be a secret. And now everyone knows. That is so uncool."

Teen group leader: "It sounds like you're really upset with me."

Coach: "Yeah, I'm upset! I told you that in secret. You weren't supposed to say anything. Now everyone knows my business and is making fun of me."

Teen group leader: (looks like he or she feels bad)
  • Say: *Time-out on that. So which of the steps did I follow?*
    ■ Answer: Keep your cool; listen to the other person first; repeat what the other person said.
  • Ask: *Does it feel like the argument is over?*
    ■ Answer: No.

  – Explain that the next step is to ***explain your side***.
   • Say: *Watch this and tell me which steps I'm following.*
    ■ Demonstrate keeping your cool, listening to the other person first, repeating what the person said by saying, "It sounds like…," and explaining your side.

Coach: "I'm so mad at you (insert group leader name)! Carrie told me that you were talking behind my back and you told everyone that I got grounded for getting a bad grade on my math test."

Teen group leader: (keeping cool, not getting upset, listening)

Coach: "I can't believe you told everyone that! That was supposed to be a secret. And now everyone knows. That is so uncool."

Teen group leader: "It sounds like you're really upset with me."

Coach: "Yeah, I'm upset! I told you that in secret. You weren't supposed to say anything. Now everyone knows my business and is making fun of me."

Teen group leader: (looks like he or she feels bad) "I didn't realize that was a secret. I didn't think I was talking behind your back because I thought people already knew. I didn't realize people were going to make fun of you."

Coach: "Well they are and it's your fault! If you hadn't said anything then none of this would have happened."

Teen group leader: (looks like he or she feels bad)
   • Say: *Time-out on that. So which of the steps did I follow?*
    ■ Answer: Keep your cool; listen to the other person first; repeat what they said; explain your side.
   • Ask: *Does it feel like the argument is over?*
    ■ Answer: No

  – Explain that the next step is to ***say you are sorry***.
   • Say: *Watch this and tell me which steps I'm following.*
    ■ Demonstrate keeping your cool, listening to the other person first, repeating what the person said by saying, "It sounds like…," explaining your side, and saying that you are sorry.

Coach: "I'm so mad at you (insert name)! Carrie told me that you were talking behind my back and you told everyone that I got grounded for getting a bad grade on my math test."

Teen group leader: (keeping cool, not getting upset, listening)

Coach: "I can't believe you told everyone that! That was supposed to be a secret. And now everyone knows. That is so uncool."

Teen group leader: "It sounds like you're really upset with me."

Coach: "Yeah, I'm upset! I told you that in secret. You weren't supposed to say anything. Now everyone knows my business and is making fun of me."

Teen group leader: (looks like he or she feels bad) "I didn't realize that was a secret. I didn't think I was talking behind your back because I thought people already knew. I didn't realize people were going to make fun of you."

Coach: "Well they are and it's your fault! If you hadn't said anything then none of this would have happened."

Teen group leader: (looks like he or she feels bad) "I'm sorry I upset you. I didn't mean to share your secrets."

Coach: "Well you did, and it's too late to do anything about it now."

- Say: *Time-out on that. So which of the steps did I follow?*
  - ■ Answer: Keep your cool; listen to the other person first; repeat what they said; explain your side; say you are sorry.
- Ask: *Does it feel like the argument is over?*
  - ■ Answer: No.

- Explain that the next step is to ***try to solve the problem***.
  - Say: "Watch this and tell me which steps I'm following."
    - ■ Demonstrate all of the steps by keeping your cool, listening to the other person first, repeating what the person said by saying, "It sounds like…," explaining yourself, saying you are sorry, and trying to solve the problem.

Coach: "I'm so mad at you (insert group leader's name)! Carrie told me that you were talking behind my back and you told everyone that I got grounded for getting a bad grade on my math test."

Teen group leader: (keeping cool, not getting upset, listening)

Coach: "I can't believe you told everyone that! That was supposed to be a secret. And now everyone knows. That is so uncool."

Teen group leader: "It sounds like you're really upset with me."

Coach: "Yeah, I'm upset! I told you that in secret. You weren't supposed to say anything. Now everyone knows my business and is making fun of me."

Teen group leader: (looks like he or she feels bad) "I didn't realize that was a secret. I didn't think I was talking behind your back because I thought people already knew. I didn't realize people were going to make fun of you."

Coach: "Well they are and it's your fault! If you hadn't said anything then none of this would have happened."

Teen group leader: (looks like he or she feels bad) "I'm sorry I upset you. I didn't mean to share your secrets."

Coach: "Well you did, and it's too late to do anything about it now."

Teen group leader: "You're right. But I didn't mean for that to happen. From now on I'll be more careful about not telling people your business and I promise not to talk behind your back."

Coach: (pause) "Okay, fine." (said reluctantly, still a little annoyed)

- Say: *Time-out on that. So which of the steps did I follow?*
  - ■ Answer: Keep your cool; listen to the other person first; repeat what they said; explain your side; say you are sorry; try to solve the problem.
- Ask: *Does it feel like the argument is over?*
  - ■ Answer: Yes; as much as it can be for now.

- Explain that each of the steps does not work alone:

- The steps only work when they are done together.
- If you leave out a step, the argument may not be resolved completely.

Behavioral Rehearsal

■ Go around the room and have each teen practice following each of these steps in a behavioral rehearsal with the teen group leader.
  - The teen group leader should accuse each teen of something different.
  - The teens should feel free to look at the board in order to follow the steps for handling the disagreement.
    • The teen group leader may need to point to a certain step if the teen gets stuck as a reminder of what to do next.
    • If the teen does something inappropriate, call a time-out on the behavioral rehearsal and gently point out the error, then have the teen start again from the beginning until he or she is successful in following the steps.
  - Use different examples of typical teen disputes for each teen behavioral rehearsal.
    • Examples:
      ■ A friend is hurt because the teen made fun of him.
      ■ A friend is upset because the teen told a secret.
      ■ A friend is upset because she felt ignored by the teen in the hallway.
      ■ A friend did not call when she said she would.
      ■ A friend feels betrayed because you did not pick him for your team.
      ■ A friend is mad because you were hanging out with her "enemy."
      ■ A friend is hurt because you did not invite him to your party.
      ■ A friend is angry because you laughed when people were teasing her.
      ■ A friend is upset because you did not save him a seat at lunch.
      ■ A friend feels betrayed because you did not come to his defense when someone accused him of something.

Homework Assignments

■ Briefly explain the homework for the week by saying: *The main homework assignment this week is for each of you to have another get-together with one or more friends. You may need to make a phone call to set up this get-together. During these get-togethers, we want you to practice being a good sport if you play games or sports. We also want you to practice using tease-the-tease if it comes up this week. We know teasing is very common among teenagers, so we expect it to come up for everyone at some point this week. You should also be using the strategies for handling bullying and bad reputations. And if you get into an argument with a friend or a sibling this week, use the steps for handling a disagreement. You may even want to practice these steps with your parents. Next week we will be outside on the play* **deck** *again, so you will need to bring some type of outside sports equipment to share with the group. Again, your homework assignment this week is to:*

- *Have a get-together with one or more friends.*
  - *Make an out-of-group call to schedule the get-together.*
  - *Trade information to figure out what you are going to do.*
  - *Practice being a good sport if applicable.*
- *Practice handling bullying and changing a bad reputation if applicable.*
- *Practice using tease-the-tease with the comebacks we identified in group.*
- *Practice handling an argument following the steps we outlined.*
- *Bring outside sports equipment.*
  - *Bring appropriate equipment for outdoor activities with groups or pairs (e.g., basketball, soccer ball, volleyball, Frisbee, handball, football).*
  - *No solitary equipment is allowed.*

Graduation Announcement

- Notify teens that their graduation is in 2 weeks.
- Explain that the graduation party is for the teens and will be held in the teen room.
- Parents and teens are welcome to bring treats for the graduation party to add to the festivities.
- Treats are typically kept in the teen room (but parents are welcome to bring snacks for the parent group, too).
- The PEERS team should provide dinner and beverages (usually pizza or soda).
- The treatment team should have a selection of PG-rated DVDs for the teens to watch during the party.
- The treatment team should also have a selection of games from which the teens can choose to play.
- The teens will vote on what they do or which movie they watch.
- Teens should receive graduation prizes at the graduation party.

Parent Session

- Parents will attend their usual parent session.
- The parent group leader will go over suggestions for where to go from here.

Graduation Ceremony

- The ceremony will be held in the parent room (or the largest room).
- Parents and family members are welcome to attend the graduation ceremony.
- Teens should receive a diploma at the graduation ceremony.
- For privacy, no cameras or video cameras are allowed.

■ We ask that additional family members who attend the graduation ceremony wait in the lobby until just before the ceremony begins in order to protect confidentiality.

Teen Activity: Good Sportsmanship and Outdoor Activities

Note: See the "Teen Activity Guide" for rules.

■ Teens will be playing outdoor games and sports on the play deck.
■ The outdoor game is chosen from appropriate **outdoor sports equipment** brought by teens and from other available outdoor gear provided by the treatment team.
■ Allow teens to choose what they play so long as it is not aggressive or dangerous (e.g., touch football instead of tackle football).
■ Do not allow any teens to engage in solitary play or isolative behavior.
■ Teens receive points while practicing **being a good sport**:
  – **Praise**
  – **Do not referee**
  – **Do not be a coach**
  – **Share and take turns**
  – **If you get bored, suggest a change**
  – **Do not gloat if you win**
  – **Do not sulk or get angry if you lose**
  – **At the end of the game say: "Good game"**
■ The teen group leader and coaches should monitor points for good sportsmanship using the "PEERS Good Sportsmanship Point Log" (Appendix G).

Reunification With Parents

■ Announce that teens should join their parents.
  – Be sure that the teens are standing or sitting next to their parents.
  – Be sure to have silence and the full attention of the group.
■ Say: *Today we worked on handling arguments and disagreements. Who can tell us the first step for trying to resolve a disagreement?* [Have teens generate all of the steps. Be prepared to give prompts if necessary.]
  – **Keep your cool**.
  – **Listen to the other person first**.
  – **Repeat what the other person said**.
  – **Explain your side**.
  – **Say you are sorry**.
  – **Try to solve the problem**.
  – If you cannot solve the problem—**keep your cool**.
■ Say: *Today we also practiced playing outdoor sports, and this group did a great job of being good sports. Let's give them a round of applause.*

■ Go over the homework for the next week (see below).
■ Individually and separately negotiate with each family:
  – The location of the get-together, the activity planned, who will be present, as well as the parent role in the get-together.
  – What outside sports equipment will be brought next week.

Homework Assignments

1. Teens are to have a friend over for a ***get-together***.
   a. Make an ***out-of-group*** call to set up the ***get-together***:
      i. ***Trade information*** to find ***common interests***.
      ii. Decide what you are going to do during your ***get-together***.
   b. Parents monitor the ***get-together*** from a *distance*.
   c. The ***get-together*** should be activity-based.
   d. If applicable, practice ***being a good sport***.
   e. Be sure the teen ***trades information*** with the guest:
      i. 50% of the ***get-together*** should be spent ***trading information***.
   f. First ***get-togethers*** with a particular teen should be limited to approximately 2 hours (depending on the activity).
2. Practice ***tease-the-tease*** if it comes up this week.
   a. Parents and teens may want to practice ***tease-the-tease*** during the week.
   b. Parents and teens should discuss how the teen used ***tease-the-tease***.
      i. ***Tease-the-tease*** is generally appropriate to use with peers or siblings.
3. If applicable, practice ***handling bullying*** or ***changing a bad reputation***.
   a. Parents and teens should discuss how the teen ***handled bullying***.
   b. Parent and teens should discuss how the teen might ***change a bad reputation***.
4. ***Bring outside sports equipment***.
   a. Bring outside sports equipment to share with the group (e.g., basketball, soccer ball, volleyball, football, Frisbee).
      i. No solitary games or equipment.
   b. Do not bring something that you are:
      i. Unwilling to share with group members.
      ii. Worried about breaking or losing.
4. Practice ***handling a disagreement*** if it comes up this week.
   a. Parents and teens should discuss how the teen handled the disagreement.
      i. Disagreements with siblings may also be used as practice.
   b. Parents and teens may want to practice using role plays.

Calculate Points

Keep track of the following for each week of the intervention.

- Calculate the number of points earned by each teen.
- Add up the total number of points earned by the group.
- Do not calculate the points in the presence of the teens:
  - Do not disclose the individual or group total of points.
  - Discourage attempts to compare number of points earned between teens.
- Remind them that they are working as a team to earn a bigger and better graduation party.

Teen Activity Guide: Session 12

"Good Sportsmanship and Outdoor Activities"

Materials Needed

- Outside sports equipment brought by teens.
- In the event that a teen forgets to bring outdoor sports equipment, have the teens share items or have sports equipment available to use:
  - Soccer ball
  - Basketball
  - Handball
  - Frisbee

Rules

- Have teens negotiate what they will play when they reach the play deck.
  - Give examples of possible games:
    - Basketball
    - Soccer
    - Handball
    - Frisbee
  - If there are enough players, you may have teens play different games.
- Explain the rules for the game:
  - We have a "no contact" rule for all sports—no excessive touching, crowding, or stealing.
  - Must pass the ball in soccer and basketball.
  - Warnings will be given for poor sportsmanship.
- Coaches may need to periodically remind teens of the rules for specific games:
  - Try to avoid acting as a referee if disagreements occur.
  - Encourage teens to work out their differences by being **good sports**.
- You may need to prompt teens to be **good sports** and other **praise** players.
- Give points for **good sportsmanship**:
  - ***Praise***
  - ***Do not referee***

- *Do not be a coach*
- *Share and take turns*
- *If you get bored, suggest a change*
- *Do not gloat if you win*
- *Do not sulk or get angry if you lose*
- *At the end of the game say: "Good game"*

■ Coaches should state why the teen is receiving a point. (e.g., "John gets a point for praising his teammate!")
  - Be sure to keep track of points on the "Good Sportsmanship Point Log" (see Appendix G).
  - Speak loudly when giving out points so other teens can hear.
    • The social comparison will encourage other teens to ***praise*** and be ***good sports***.

Chapter 15

Session 13
Rumors and Gossip

Parent Session Therapist Guide

Guiding Principles of the Parent Session

The major focus of homework review continues to be the get-togethers that the teens have arranged in the past week. Parents should be debriefed about these get-togethers in detail, as there will still be much need for input from the group leader.

The focus of the current lesson is on how to appropriately manage rumors and gossip. Gossip gives us information about the misadventures of others and is a very common form of communication for adolescents and even adults; the latter is evidenced by the popularity of gossip shows and tabloid magazines. It has been proposed that gossip is mostly negative because people learn more from negative instances of others in order to avoid the same mistakes (Baumeister, Zhang, & Vohs, 2004). Rumors (negative information about someone) begin in the context of gossip. Research suggests that denial is the best means to dispel the negative effects of rumors, and the best denial has strong arguments about why the rumor is not true and how the source of the rumor is not credible (Bordia, DiFonzo, Haines, & Chaseling, 2005). The form of denial reviewed in this chapter does not involve confrontation with the originator of gossip. Confronting the source of the gossip may only lead to further retaliation. Teens will be taught to "spread a rumor about themselves" that indirectly denies the original rumor and simultaneously discredits the gossip.

Similar to previous sessions on bullying and disagreements, this lesson is most effective when the teen is aware of rumors and gossip that are currently circulating about him or her. This didactic may be less relevant to teens who are socially withdrawn or isolated, as they may not have been noticed enough by their peers to be the target of gossip or rumors. Parents should still retain this handout on the chance that the issue will surface after PEERS has ended.

Homework Review

1. ***Get-together.***
   a. Identify whether the ***get-together*** was:
      i. Activity-based.
      ii. Monitored by parents from a *distance*.
      iii. No more than 2 hours (depending on the activity).
   b. If relevant, check to see if the teen practiced ***being a good sport***.
   c. Be sure that the teen ***traded information*** with his or her guest and found a ***common interest***:
      i. 50% of the time should have been spent ***trading information***.
2. ***Handling disagreements.***
   a. Have parents report whether the teen practiced ***handling a disagreement*** during the week:
      i. This may have been done in the context of a real disagreement with a friend or sibling, or through practice role plays with parents.
3. ***Handling bullying*** and ***bad reputations.***
   a. If relevant, have parents report:
      i. How the teen ***handled bullying***.
      ii. How the teen might change his or her ***bad reputation***.
         1. ***Lay low.***
         2. ***Follow the crowd***:
            a. ***Try to fit in with the crowd.***
            b. ***Try not to stand out from the crowd.***
         3. ***Change your look to change your reputation.***
         4. ***Own up to your previous reputation.***
         5. ***Find a new group or a crowd.***
   b. Troubleshoot any problems that may have arisen.
4. ***Tease-the-tease.***
   a. Check to see if parents practiced ***tease-the-tease*** with their teen (not an assignment).
   b. Have parents report how ***tease-the-tease*** was used.
      i. ***Tease-the-tease*** may have been used with peers or siblings of the same age.
   c. Troubleshoot any problems that may have arisen.
5. ***Bring outside sports equipment.***
   a. Have parents identify the outside equipment their teen brought to share with the group (e.g., basketball, soccer ball, volleyball, football, Frisbee).
   b. Only give credit for appropriate items.

Didactic Lesson: Rumors and Gossip

- Distribute the Parent Handout.
- Say: *The occurrence of rumors and gossip is very common in middle school and high school. There is very little that you or your teen can do to prevent the occurrence of gossip; however, it can be very helpful to know why people gossip and what to do in situations when the rumor mill is focused on your teen.*
- Explain the following:
  - Rumors and gossip are *social weapons*:
    - They are often mean spirited.
    - They are very common in middle school and high school.
  - Rumors and gossip are sometimes used to hurt others.
    - They are used as a form of retaliation:
      - They may be used to get revenge on someone for something they have done.
    - They are used to damage the reputation of someone unliked or envied.
    - They are used to fulfill a threat (e.g., "If you don't do what I say, I'll tell everyone…").
  - More often, rumors and gossip are just part of teenage conversation.
    - Spreading gossip is a way for some teens to:
      - Get attention.
      - Feel important (i.e., they know something no one else does).
- Rumors are very difficult to disprove:
  - You can never completely disprove a rumor.
  - You can try to undermine the rumor by making fun of it (e.g., acting amazed anyone would believe it).
  - Using this technique, you will be indirectly denying the rumor and discrediting the source of the gossip.
  - This will minimize the impact of the gossip and often *kills the rumor*.

Rules for Handling Rumors and Gossip

- Say: *Now that we are clear on* **why** *teens gossip, it will be helpful to know what our teens can do to make it less likely that people will gossip about them.*
- Go around the room and have parents take turns reading the Parent Handout.
- Sections in **bold print** come directly from the Parent Handout.

How to Avoid Being the Target of Gossip

- *Avoid being friends with gossips* **(this includes casual socializing):**

- *Gossips* are people who like to tell rumors and spread gossip about others.
■ *Do not provoke the gossips*:
  - Do not tell secrets, gossip about, or make fun of *gossip* or their friends.
  - This will only provoke them to retaliate.
■ *Do not spread rumors about other people*:
  - Avoid retaliating against the people who have been gossiping about you.
  - Avoid spreading rumors about people in general:
    • It is hurtful.
    • People will not want to be friends with you.

What to Do When You Are the Target of Gossip

■ Say: *Even though our teens may try their best to avoid being gossiped about, it may still happen, so we need to know what we can do to minimize the impact of gossip when it is focused on our teens. There are some very specific rules about what to do when you are the target of rumors and gossip.*
■ *Do not show that you are upset*.
  - If you show people that you are upset:
    • You will look defensive.
      ■ People will assume you have something to hide.
    • You will add fuel to the *rumor mill*.
    • People will start gossiping about how upset you are.
■ *Do not confront the source of the gossip*.
  - This will only escalate the feud:
    • The person may start spreading even more gossip about you.
    • This may result in an argument or even a fight.
    • The person will feel justified in spreading gossip about you.
  - The source of the gossip is often waiting for you to confront him or her:
    • The source of the gossip may be anticipating an argument.
■ *Avoid the source of the gossip*.
  - Keep your distance from the source of the gossip.
  - The source of the gossip may be expecting a confrontation:
    • Do not give him or her the satisfaction of a confrontation.
      ■ This will only create more gossip and add fuel to the *rumor mill*.
■ *Act amazed*.
  - Give the impression that you are amazed at how ridiculous the rumor is.
  - This is *indirectly* denying the rumor is true.
  - This will also discredit the source of the gossip.

- **Examples**:
  - ■ "I can't believe anyone would believe that...that's just stupid."
  - ■ "I can't believe people are saying that...what a joke."
  - ■ "It's unbelievable anyone would believe that. People need to get a life."
- ■ *Spread a rumor about yourself.*
  - – Acknowledge that the rumor is out there, but tell everyone how stupid it is:
    - This is also *indirectly* denying the rumor is true.
    - By doing this you are discrediting the source of the gossip (without confronting them) and making it less likely that others will spread the rumor.
  - – In particular, tell your friends who will be on your side.
  - – Spread this rumor in the presence of other people who will overhear.
    - **Examples**:
      - ■ "Have you heard about this rumor going around about me? How stupid is that one?"
      - ■ "Did you hear what people are saying about me? It's crazy what some people will believe."
      - ■ "Can you believe this rumor about me? That's too ridiculous for words."
  - – This will often *kill the rumor* because:
    - **The person spreading the gossip looks stupid.**
    - **People are less likely to continue to spread the rumor, because they will look stupid.**
- ■ Go around the room and have parents identify whether their teen has struggled with being the target of rumors and gossip.
- ■ Have parents identify ways in which they might assist their teen in minimizing the negative impact of rumors and gossip in the future by following the suggestions presented.

Homework Assignments

The parent group leader should go over the homework assignment and troubleshoot any potential problems with parents.

1. **Teens should practice *handling rumors and gossip* if it comes up this week.**
   a. **Teens should try avoiding gossip.**
   b. **When relevant, teens should try using the strategies for handling rumors.**
2. **Teens are to have a friend over for a *get-together*.**
   a. **Make an *out-of-group* call to set up the *get-together*.**

    i. ***Trade information*** to find ***common interests***.

    ii. **Decide what you are going to do during your *get-together*.**

  b. **Parents monitor the *get-together* from a *distance*.**

  c. **The *get-together* should be activity-based.**

  d. **If relevant, practice *being a good sport*.**

  e. **Be sure the teen *trades information* with the guest:**

    i. **50% of the *get-together* should be spent *trading information*.**

  f. **First *get-togethers* should be limited to approximately 2 hours (depending on the activity).**

3. **Practice *tease-the-tease* if it comes up this week.**

  a. **Parents and teens may want to practice *tease-the-tease* during the week.**

  b. **Parents and teens should discuss how the teen used *tease-the-tease*.**

    i. ***Tease-the-tease*** **is generally appropriate to use with peers or siblings of the same age.**

4. **If applicable, practice *handling bullying or changing a bad reputation*.**

  a. **Parents and teens should discuss how the teen *handled bullying*.**

  b. **Parents and teens should discuss how their teen is progressing to *change a bad reputation*.**

5. **Practice *handling disagreements* if it comes up this week.**

  a. **Parents and teens should discuss how the teen handled the disagreement.**

    i. **Disagreements with siblings may also be used as practice.**

  b. **Parents and teens may want to practice using role plays.**

Reminder: The PEERS Graduation is next week!

Suggestions for How to Present the Graduation

Telling Parents About the Teen Session

- Explain that the graduation party is for the teens and will be held in the teen room.
- Encourage parents to bring treats for the graduation party to add to the festivities.
- Treats are typically kept in the teen room (but parents are welcome to bring snacks for the parent group too).
- The PEERS team should provide dinner and beverages (usually pizza and soda).
- The treatment team should have a selection of PG-rated DVDs for the teens to watch during the party.

- The treatment team should also have a selection of games from which the teens can choose to play.
- The teens will vote on what they do or which movie they watch.
- Teens should receive graduation prizes at the graduation party.

Telling Parents About the Parent Session

- Parents will attend their usual parent session.
- The parent group leader will go over suggestions for where to go from here.

Telling Parents About the Graduation Ceremony

- The ceremony will be held in the parent room (or the largest room).
- Parents and family members are welcome to attend the graduation ceremony.
- Teens should receive a diploma at the graduation ceremony.
- For privacy, no cameras or video cameras are allowed.
- We ask that additional family members who attend the graduation ceremony wait in the lobby until just before the ceremony begins in order to protect confidentiality.

Note: It is recommended that the treatment team provide a graduation flyer to be distributed in the 12th and 13th sessions with the relevant information from above, including the date and time of the graduation, as well as any information about posttesting. A sample "Graduation Flyer" is presented in Appendix I.

Parent Handout 13: Rumors and Gossip

Rules for Handling Rumors and Gossip

How to Avoid Being the Target of Gossip

- ▪ ***Avoid being friends with gossips*** (this includes casual socializing):
  - ***Gossips*** are people who like to tell rumors and spread gossip about others.
- ▪ ***Do not provoke the gossips***:
  - Do not tell secrets, gossip about, or make fun of ***gossips*** or their friends.
  - This will only provoke them to retaliate.
- ▪ ***Do not spread rumors about other people***:
  - Avoid retaliating against the people who have been gossiping about you.
  - Avoid spreading rumors about people in general:
    - It is hurtful.
    - People will not want to be friends with you.

What to Do When You Are the Target of Gossip

- ▪ ***Do not show that you are upset***.
  - If you show people that you are upset:
    - You will look defensive.
      - ▪ People will assume you have something to hide.
    - You will add fuel to the ***rumor mill***.
    - People will start gossiping about how upset you are.
- ▪ ***Do not confront the source of the gossip***.
  - This will only escalate the feud:
    - The person may start spreading even more gossip about you.
    - This may result in an argument or even a fight.
    - The person will feel justified in spreading gossip about you.
  - The source of the gossip is often waiting for you to confront him or her.
    - The source of the gossip may be anticipating an argument.
- ▪ ***Avoid the source of the gossip***.
  - Keep your distance from the source of the gossip.
  - The source of the gossip may be expecting a confrontation.
    - Do not give him or her the satisfaction of a confrontation.
      - ▪ This will only create more gossip and add fuel to the ***rumor mill***.
- ▪ ***Act amazed***.
  - Give the impression that you are amazed at how ridiculous the rumor is.
  - This is ***indirectly*** denying the rumor is true.
  - This will also discredit the source of the gossip.
    - Examples:
      - ▪ "I can't believe anyone would believe that…that's just stupid."

- ■ "I can't believe people are saying that...what a joke."
- ■ "It's unbelievable anyone would believe that. People need to get a life."

■ ***Spread a rumor about yourself.***
- – Acknowledge that the rumor is out there, but tell everyone how stupid it is:
  - • This is also *indirectly* denying the rumor is true.
  - • By doing this you are discrediting the source of the gossip (without confronting him or her) and making it less likely that others will spread the rumor.
- – In particular, tell your friends, who will be on your side.
- – Spread this rumor in the presence of other people who will overhear.
  - • Examples:
    - ■ "Have you heard about this rumor going around about me? How stupid is that one?"
    - ■ "Did you hear what people are saying about me? It's crazy what some people will believe."
    - ■ "Can you believe this rumor about me? That's too ridiculous for words."
- – This will often **kill the rumor** because:
  - • The person spreading the gossip looks stupid.
  - • People are less likely to continue to spread the rumor, because they will look stupid.

Homework Assignments

1. Teens should practice **handling rumors and gossip** if it comes up this week.
   a. Teens should try avoiding gossips.
   b. When relevant, teens should try using the strategies for handling rumors.
2. Teens are to have a friend over for a **get-together**.
   a. Make an **out-of-group** call to set up the **get-together**.
      i. **Trade information** to find **common interests**.
      ii. Decide what you are going to do during your **get-together**.
   b. Parents monitor the **get-together** from a *distance*.
   c. **Get-together** should be activity-based.
   d. If relevant, practice **being a good sport**.
   e. Be sure the teen **trades information** with the guest.
      i. 50% of the **get-together** should be spent **trading information**.
   f. First **get-togethers** should be limited to approximately 2 hours (depending on the activity).
3. Practice **tease-the-tease** if it comes up this week.
   a. Parents and teens may want to practice **tease-the-tease** during the week.
   b. Parents and teens should discuss how the teen used **tease-the-tease**.

      i. ***Tease-the-tease*** is generally appropriate to use with peers or siblings of the same age.

4. If applicable, practice ***handling bullying*** or ***changing a bad reputation***.

    a. Parents and teens should discuss how the teen ***handled bullying***.

    b. Parent and teens should discuss how their teen is progressing to ***change a bad reputation***.

5. Practice ***handling disagreements*** if it comes up this week.

    a. Parents and teens should discuss how the teen handled the disagreement.

       i. Disagreements with siblings may also be used as practice.

    b. Parents and teens may want to practice using role plays.

Teen Therapist Guide—Session 13: Rumors and Gossip

Guiding Principles of the Teen Session

The purpose of this session is to give teens the necessary tools for handling situations in which they are the target of rumors or gossip. Teens are taught that it is ineffective to confront people who spread rumors about them. Instead it is best to "act amazed" that anyone would believe such things, thereby indirectly denying the rumor is true and making the rumor seem silly. This will make it less "cool" for others to continue to spread the rumor. Teens are also taught to "spread a rumor about yourself" when they are the target of gossip. This involves discrediting the rumor (indirectly) and discrediting the source of the gossip without the need for a confrontation.

For teens who are socially isolated or withdrawn, this skill may be less relevant. However, for teens who have had a history of greater social rejection associated with a bad reputation, this skill may be critical in helping to diffuse what is often a very challenging social situation.

Rule Review

Note: Only go over session rules again if the teens are having difficulty following them.

- Have teens identify the rules for the group.
- Give them points for remembering:

1. Listen to the other group members (no talking when others are speaking)
2. Follow directions
3. Raise your hand
4. Be respectful (no teasing or making fun of others)
5. No touching (no hitting, kicking, pushing, hugging, etc.)

Homework Review

Note: Give points for homework *parts*—not just one point per assignment.

1. ***Bring outside sports equipment***.
   a. Have teens identify the outside sports equipment they brought to share with the group (e.g., basketball, soccer ball, volleyball, football, Frisbee).
   b. Only give credit for appropriate items.
   c. To avoid distractions, have a coach put the item away until the teen session activity.

2. ***Handling disagreements***.
  a. Say: *One of your assignments was to practice handling a disagreement with a friend or a sibling if it came up this week. You may also have practiced handling a disagreement with your parent during a role play. Raise your hand if you had a chance to practice handling a disagreement this week.*
    i. Begin by calling on the teens who completed the assignment.
    ii. Briefly ask:
      1. *Who did you practice handling a disagreement with?*
      2. *Which steps did you follow to resolve the disagreement?*
      3. Troubleshoot any problems that may have arisen.
    iii. If teens did not practice, have them go over the steps for handling disagreements.
      1. ***Keep your cool***.
      2. ***Listen to the other person first***.
      3. ***Repeat what the other person said***.
      4. ***Explain your side***.
      5. ***Say you are sorry***.
      6. ***Try to solve the problem***.
3. ***Handling bullying and bad reputations***.
  a. Say: *Another one of your assignments this week was to practice handling bullying. Raise your hand if you used one or more of the strategies for handling bullying this week.*
    i. Have teens report what they did to handle bullying.
    ii. Troubleshoot any problems that may have arisen.
    iii. If teens did not use any of the strategies for handling bullying this week, have them identify a couple of options.
  b. Say: *Another related assignment was to begin to take steps toward changing your reputation. Raise your hand if you did anything new this week to try to change your reputation.*
    i. Have teens report what they did to change their reputation.
      1. [Note: It is likely that very few teens will report making changes in this area. At best, certain teens with bad reputations should be laying low for the moment until they can move onto the other steps.]
    ii. If teens did not use any of the strategies for changing a reputation this week, have them identify the steps for doing this.
      1. ***Lay low***.
      2. ***Follow the crowd***:
        a. ***Try to fit in with the crowd***.
        b. ***Try not to stand out from the crowd***.
      3. ***Change your look to change your reputation***.
      4. ***Own up to your previous reputation***.
      5. ***Find a new group or crowd***.

4. ***Tease-the-tease***.

    a. Say: *Another one of your assignments this week was to practice using tease-the-tease. We know that teasing is very common for teenagers, so I would expect that everyone here had an opportunity to use tease-the-tease with either a peer or a sibling or maybe through practice with your parents. Raise your hand if you were able to practice using tease-the-tease this week.*

        i. [Note: This introduction will help teens save face about being teased.]

    b. Have teens report how ***tease-the-tease*** was used.

        i. Do not allow teens to talk about the specific way someone teased them, instead have them focus on their response only.

    c. Troubleshoot any problems that may have arisen.

    d. If any teens did not use ***tease-the-tease*** this week, have them identify and practice using a couple of ***tease-the-tease*** comebacks.

5. ***Get-together***.

    a. Say: *Your main homework assignment this week was to have a get-together with a friend. Raise your hand if you had a get-together this week.*

        i. Begin by calling on the teens who completed the assignment.

        ii. Briefly ask:

            1. *Who did you have a get-together with?*

            2. *Where was the get-together?*

            3. *Did you make an out-of-group phone call to figure out what you were going to do?*

            4. *What did you end up doing?*

            5. *Who chose the activities?* [Answer should be the guest.]

            6. *Did you trade information at least 50% of the time?*

            7. *Were you able to practice being a good sport?* (If relevant.)

               a. *What did you do to be a good sport?*

            8. *Did you have a good time?*

            9. *Did your friend have a good time?*

          10. *Is this someone you might want to have a get-together with again?*

        iii. Troubleshoot any problems that may have arisen.

Didactic Lesson: Rumors and Gossip

■ Say: *Rumors and gossip are very common in middle school and high school. There is very little that you can do to prevent people from gossiping or spreading rumors. However, it can be very helpful to know why people gossip and what to do in situations when the rumor mill is focused on you.*

■ Explain the following:

    – Rumors and gossip are ***social weapons***:

        • They are often mean spirited.

        • They are very common in middle school and high school.

    – Rumors and gossip are sometimes used to hurt others.

        • Used as a form of retaliation:

■ Used to get revenge on someone for something they have done.
- Used to damage the reputation of someone unliked or envied.
- Used to fulfill some threat (e.g., "If you don't do what I say, I'll tell everyone…").

- More often, rumors and gossip are just part of teenage conversation.
  - Spreading gossip is a way for some teens to:
    ■ Get attention.
    ■ Feel important (i.e., they know something no one else does).

- Rumors are very difficult to disprove:
  - You can never completely disprove a rumor.
  - You can try to undermine the rumor by making fun of it (e.g., acting amazed anyone would believe it).
    ■ In this process you will be indirectly denying the rumor and discrediting the source of the gossip.
    ■ This will minimize the impact of the gossip and often ***kills the rumor***.

Rules for Handling Rumors and Gossip

How to Avoid Being the Target of Gossip

Say: *Now that we are clear on **why** people gossip, it will be helpful to know what we can do to make it less likely that people will gossip about us.*

■ ***Avoid being friends with gossips*** (this includes casual socializing).
- Say: *The first rule for avoiding being the target of rumors and gossip is to avoid being friends with gossips. "Gossips" are people who like to tell rumors and spread gossip about others. What would be the problem with being friends with a gossip?*
  - Answer: They are likely to spread rumors about you if they get mad at you; it is difficult to trust someone who is a gossip; other people may not want to be friends with you because they know you associate with the gossip.

■ ***Do not provoke the gossips***.
- Say: *The next rule for avoiding being the target of rumors and gossip is not to provoke the "gossips." This means don't tell secrets, gossip about, or make fun of "gossips" or their friends. What is the problem with making a "gossip" or their friends angry?*
  - Answer: This will only provoke them to retaliate against you; you are likely to become the object of gossip.

■ ***Do not spread rumors about other people***.
- Say: *Our last rule for avoiding being the target of rumors and gossip is not to spread rumors about other people. This means you should avoid retaliating against the people who have been gossiping about you and* avoid

spreading rumors about people in general. Why should you never spread rumors about other people?

- Answer: Because it is hurtful and people will not want to be friends with you.

What to Do When You Are the Target of Gossip

Say: *Even though we may try our best to avoid being gossiped about, it may still happen, so we need to know what we can do to minimize the impact of gossip when it is focused on us. There are some very specific rules about what to do when you are the target of rumors and gossip.*

- ■ ***Do not show that you are upset**.*
  - Say: *One of the rules for handling rumors and gossip in which we are the target is not to show you are upset. What is the problem with letting people know you are upset about a rumor?*
    - Answer: If you show people that you are upset, you will look defensive; people will assume you have something to hide; you will add fuel to the ***rumor mill***; people will start gossiping about how upset you are.
- ■ ***Do not confront the source of the gossip**.*
  - Say: *Another rule for handling rumors and gossip in which we are the target is not to confront the source of the gossip. This means that if there is a rumor spread about you, don't confront the person who started it. This will only escalate the feud. What is the problem with confronting the source of the gossip?*
    - Answer: The person may start spreading even more gossip about you; this may result in an argument or even a fight; the person will feel justified in spreading gossip about you.
- ■ ***Avoid the source of the gossip**.*
  - Say: *Another rule for handling rumors and gossip in which we are the target is to avoid the source of the gossip. This means that if you know someone has spread a rumor about you, keep your distance from that person. Why would it be a good idea to avoid the person spreading the rumor about you?*
    - Answer: They may be expecting a confrontation; any type of confrontation will only serve to add fuel to the ***rumor mill***; if you avoid the source of the gossip, there will be no confrontation and no additional rumors.
- ■ ***Act amazed**.*
  - Say: *Another rule for handling rumors and gossip in which we are the target is to act amazed. This means that when you hear that a rumor is being spread about you, act like you're amazed that anyone would believe*

it. This is a way of indirectly denying the rumor is true, without sounding defensive. It also discredits the source of the gossip.

- Examples of what to say:
  - "I can't believe anyone would believe that...that's just stupid."
  - "I can't believe people are saying that...what a joke."
  - "It's unbelievable anyone would believe that. People need to get a life."

- Ask: *Why would acting amazed that anyone would believe such a rumor be a good idea?*
  - Answer: Because it makes the rumor seems silly; people will be less likely to believe the rumor; people will be less likely to continue to spread the rumor.

■ **Spread a rumor about yourself.**
  - Say: *Another important rule for handling rumors and gossip in which we are the target is to spread a rumor about yourself. This involves acknowledging that the rumor is out there, but telling everyone how stupid it is. This is another way of indirectly denying the rumor and discrediting the person who spread it without confronting them and causing more gossip through a confrontation. In particular, you will want to tell your friends, who will be on your side, and try to spread the rumor when there are other people around who will overhear the conversation.*
    - Examples of what to say:
      - "Have you heard about this rumor going around about me? How stupid is that one?"
      - "Did you hear what people are saying about me? It's crazy what some people will believe."
      - "Can you believe this rumor about me? That's too ridiculous for words."
  - Ask: *Why would it be a good idea to spread a rumor about yourself?*
    - Answer: Because the new rumor will be how stupid the old rumor was; no one will want to spread the old rumor because that would make them look silly.
  - Explain: *Spreading a rumor about yourself will often kill the rumor because the person spreading the gossip looks stupid and people will be less likely to continue to spread the rumor, because they will look like they don't know what they're talking about. Even if the rumor is true, you can act amazed that anyone would care enough to gossip about it. This also takes all of the shock value and power out of the rumor.*

Role Play

■ The teen group leader demonstrates an *appropriate* role play of spreading a rumor about yourself.

- Examples of *appropriate* role plays:
  - Say: *The rumor is I got caught cheating on a test.*
    - Response: "Can you believe this stupid rumor about me? People are saying how I got caught cheating on a test. How lame!"
  - Say: *The rumor is I got grounded for ditching school.*
    - Response: "Have you heard this rumor going around?! People are saying I got grounded for ditching school. How stupid!"
  - Say: *The rumor is my best friend and I got into a big fight.*
    - Response: "Hey, did you hear that people are saying I got into this big fight with my friend?! How dumb! People need to get a life."

Behavioral Rehearsal

- Go around the room and have each teen practice handling rumors and gossip.
- The group leader should inform teens that a rumor has been spread about them and that they need to **spread a rumor about themselves**.
  - Use different examples of typical teen gossip.
  - Examples:
    - "The rumor is you are failing a class."
    - "The rumor is you got detention for talking back to a teacher."
    - "The rumor is you have a crush on (insert name)."
    - "The rumor is you got grounded for staying out late."
    - "The rumor is you were talking behind your friend's back."
    - "The rumor is you don't like (insert name)."
    - "The rumor is you may not graduate."
    - "The rumor is you got caught driving your parent's car without permission."
    - "The rumor is you might get kicked off the track team."
    - "The rumor is that you're going to ask (insert name) out."

Homework Assignments

- Briefly explain the homework for the week by saying: *The main homework assignment this week is for each of you to have another get-together with one or more friends. You may need to make a phone call to set up this get-together. During these get-togethers, we want you to practice being a good sport if you play games or sports. We also want you to practice using tease-the-tease if it comes up this week. We know teasing is very common among teenagers, so we expect it to come up for everyone at some point this week. You should also be using the strategies for handling bullying and bad reputations. If you get into an argument with a friend or a sibling this week, use the steps for handling a disagreement. You may even want to practice these steps with your parents. And if it is relevant, use the strategies for handling rumors and gossip. Again, your homework assignment this week is to:*

- *Have a get-together with one or more friends.*
  - *Make an out-of-group call to schedule the get-together.*
  - *Trade information to figure out what you're going to do.*
  - *Practice being a good sport if relevant.*
- *Practice handling bullying and changing a bad reputation if relevant.*
- *Practice using tease-the-tease with the comebacks we identified in group.*
- *Practice handling an argument following the steps we outlined.*
- *Practice handling rumor and gossip if it comes up this week.*

Graduation Announcement

Explain the following to the teens.

- Remind teens that their graduation is next week.
- Explain that the graduation party is for the teens and will be held in the teen room.
- Parents and teens are welcome to bring treats for the graduation party to add to the festivities.
- Treats are typically kept in the teen room (but parents are welcome to bring snacks for the parent group, too).
- The PEERS team should provide dinner and beverages (usually pizza and soda).
- The treatment team should have a selection of PG-rated DVDs for the teens to watch during the party.
- The treatment team should also have a selection of games from which the teens can choose to play.
- The teens will vote on what they do or which movie they watch.
- Teens should receive graduation prizes at the graduation party.

Parent Session

- Parents will attend their usual parent session.
- The parent group leader will go over suggestions for where to go from here.

Graduation Ceremony

- The ceremony will be held in the parent room (or the largest room).
- Parents and family members are welcome to attend the graduation ceremony.
- Teens should receive a diploma at the graduation ceremony.
- For privacy, no cameras or video cameras are allowed.
- We ask that additional family members who attend the graduation ceremony wait in the lobby until just before the ceremony begins in order to protect confidentiality.

Teen Activity: Good Sportsmanship and Outdoor Activities

Note: See the "Teen Activity Guide" for rules.

- Teens will be playing outdoor games and sports on the play deck.
- The outdoor game is chosen from appropriate **outdoor sports equipment** brought by teens and from other available outdoor gear provided by the treatment team.
- Allow teens to choose what they play so long as it is not aggressive or dangerous (e.g., touch football instead of tackle football).
- Do not allow any teens to engage in solitary play or isolative behavior.
- Teens receive points while practicing **being a good sport**:
  - **Praise**
  - **Do not referee**
  - **Do not be a coach**
  - **Share and take turns**
  - **If you get bored, suggest a change**
  - **Do not gloat if you win**
  - **Do not sulk or get angry if you lose**
  - **At the end of the game say, "Good game"**
- The teen group leader and coaches should monitor points for good sportsmanship using the "PEERS Good Sportsmanship Point Log" (Appendix G).

Reunification With Parents

- Announce that teens should join their parents.
  - Be sure that the teens are standing or sitting next to their parents.
  - Be sure to have silence and the full attention of the group.
- Say: *Today we worked on handling rumors and gossip. Remember there are a number of rules related to managing the negative impact of rumors and gossip. What are some of the rules for avoiding being the target of gossip?* [Have teens generate all of the rules. Be prepared to give prompts if necessary.]
  - **Avoid being friends with gossips**.
  - **Do not provoke the gossips**.
  - **Do not spread rumors about other people**.
- Ask: *What are the rules for handling rumors and gossip in which we are the target?* [Have teens generate all of the rules. Be prepared to give prompts if necessary.]
  - **Do not show that you are upset**.
  - **Do not confront the source of the gossip**.
  - **Avoid the source of the gossip**.
  - **Act amazed**.
  - **Spread a rumor about yourself**.

■ Say: *Today we also practiced spreading rumors about ourselves, and this group did a great job. Let's give them a round of applause.*
■ Go over the homework for the next week (see below).
■ Individually and separately negotiate with each family:
  – The location of the get-together, the activity planned, who will be present, as well as the parent role in the get-together.
  – What graduation party treat will be brought next week.

Homework Assignments

1. Teens should practice **handling rumors and gossip** if it comes up this week.
   a. Teens should try avoiding gossips.
   b. When relevant, teens should try using the strategies for handling rumors.
2. Teens are to have a friend over for a **get-together**:
   a. Make an **out-of-group** call to set up the **get-together**.
      i. **Trade information** to find **common interests**.
      ii. Decide what you are going to do during your **get-together**.
   b. Parents monitor the **get-together** from a **distance**.
   c. **Get-together** should be activity-based.
   d. If relevant, practice **being a good sport**.
   e. Be sure the teen **trades information** with the guest:
      i. 50% of the **get-together** should be spent **trading information**.
      ii. First *get-togethers* should be limited to approximately 2 hours (depending on the activity).
3. Practice **tease-the-tease** if it comes up this week.
   a. Parents and teens may want to practice **tease-the-tease** during the week.
   b. Parents and teens should discuss how the teen used **tease-the-tease**.
      i. **Tease-the-tease** is generally appropriate to use with peers or siblings of the same age.
4. If applicable, practice **handling bullying** or **changing a bad reputation**.
   a. Parents and teens should discuss how the teen **handled bullying.**
   b. Parents and teens should discuss how their teen is progressing to **change a bad reputation.**
5. Practice **handling disagreements**.
   a. Parents and teens should discuss the handling of a disagreement that comes up this week.
      i. Disagreements with siblings may also be used as practice.
   b. Parents and teens may want to practice using role plays.

Calculate Points

Keep track of the following for each week of the intervention.

- Calculate the number of points earned by each teen.
- Add up the total number of points earned by the group.
- Do not calculate the points in the presence of the teens:
  - Do not disclose the individual or group total of points.
    Discourage attempts to compare number of points earned between teens.
- Remind them that they are working as a team to earn a bigger and better graduation party.

Teen Activity Guide: Session 13

"Good Sportsmanship and Outdoor Activities"

Materials Needed

- ***Outside sports*** equipment brought by teens.
- In the event that a teen forgets to bring outdoor sports equipment, have the teens share items or have sports equipment available to use:
  - Soccer ball
  - Basketball
  - Handball
  - Frisbee

Rules

- Have teens negotiate what they will play when they reach the play deck.
  - Give examples of possible games:
    - Basketball
    - Soccer
    - Handball
    - Frisbee
  - If there are enough players, you may have teens play different games.
- Explain the rules for the game:
  - We have a "no contact" rule for all sports—no excessive touching, crowding, or stealing.
  - Must pass the ball in soccer and basketball.
  - Warnings will be given for poor sportsmanship.
- Coaches may need to periodically remind teens of the rules for specific games:
  - Try to avoid acting as a referee if disagreements occur.
  - Encourage teens to work out their differences by being ***good sports***.
- You may need to prompt teens to be ***good sports*** and ***praise*** other players.
- Give points for ***good sportsmanship***:
  - ***Praise***
  - ***Do not referee***

- *Do not be a coach*
- *Share and take turns*
- *If you get bored, suggest a change*
- *Do not gloat if you win*
- *Do not sulk or get angry if you lose*
- *At the end of the game say, "Good game"*

■ Coaches should state why the teen is receiving a point. (e.g., "John gets a point for praising his teammate!")
  - Be sure to keep track of points on the "PEERS Good Sportsmanship Point Log" (see Appendix G).
  - Speak loudly when giving out points so other teens can hear.
  - The social comparison will encourage other teens to **praise** and be **good sports**.

Chapter 16

Session 14
Graduation and Termination

Parent Session Therapist Guide

Guiding Principles of the Parent Session

The major focus of the homework review continues to be the get-togethers that the teens have arranged in the past week. Parents should debrief about these get-togethers in detail as there will still be much need for input from the group leader.

The major focus of this session is termination from this brief intervention. The knee-jerk reaction of many parents is to inquire if there is another series of classes they can enroll their teen in, before the ink is dry on the graduation certificate. If the intervention was successful, then there should not be a need for continuing treatment. The basic skills have been taught and the behaviors interfering with forming friendships have been addressed. The parent and teen should have worked together to find a suitable crowd, and friendships should be emerging. Development of these friendships will further embed the teen into the identified crowd, which will hopefully be the setting for continued instruction on social competence and a source of new friendships. The parents have also been taught how to help their teen promote friendships and how to help their teen deal with conflict, change a bad reputation, deal with rumors and gossip, and deal with teasing and bullying from peers. The only remaining issues are to communicate these points to the parents and teens, and end the treatment formally with a ceremony. There is no new material presented in the didactic lesson, just a brief review of the principle material that composes PEERS.

Administer Posttreatment Outcome Measures

Allow sufficient time to administer posttreatment measures. These measures should duplicate the measures completed before treatment began. See Chapter 2 for suggestions for outcome measures.

Homework Review

1. ***Get-together***.
   a. Identify whether the ***get-together*** was:
      i. Activity-based.
      ii. Monitored by parents from a ***distance***.
      iii. No more than 2 hours (depending on the activity).
   b. If relevant, check to see if the teen practiced ***being a good sport***.
   c. Be sure that the teen ***traded information*** with his or her guest and found a ***common interest***:
      i. 50% of the time should have been spent ***trading information***.
2. ***Handling disagreements***.
   a. Have parents report whether the teen practiced ***handling a disagreement*** during the week:
      i. This may have been done in the context of a real disagreement with a friend or sibling, or through practice role plays with parents.
3. ***Handling bullying and bad reputations***.
   a. If relevant, have parents report:
      i. How the teen ***handled bullying***.
      ii. How the teen might change his or her ***bad reputation***.
         1. ***Lay low***.
         2. ***Follow the crowd***:
            a. ***Try to fit in with the crowd***.
            b. ***Try not to stand out from the crowd***.
         3. ***Change your look to change your reputation***.
         4. ***Own up to your previous reputation***.
         5. ***Find a new group or crowd***.
   b. Troubleshoot any problems that may have arisen.
4. ***Tease-the-tease***.
   a. Check to see if parents practiced ***tease-the-tease*** with their teen (not an assignment).
   b. Have parents report how ***tease-the-tease*** was used:
      i. ***Tease-the-tease*** may have been used with peers or siblings.
   c. Troubleshoot any problems that may have arisen.
5. ***Handling rumors and gossip***.
   a. If relevant, have parents identify whether their teen used the strategies for handling rumors and gossip.
   b. Troubleshoot any problems that may have arisen.

Didactic Lesson: Final Thoughts / Where to Go From Here

- Distribute the Parent Handout.
- Explain: *Tonight is the last session of PEERS, but just because the group is coming to an end does not mean that your work has also come to an end. Tonight we are going to focus on exactly what you will need to do to help your teen continue to make and keep friends.*
- Go around the room and have parents take turns reading the Parent Handout.
- Sections in **bold print** come directly from the Parent Handout.

Where to Go From Here

1. *Extracurricular activities*.
   a. **It is essential that your teen participate in extracurricular activities in order to make friends**.
   b. **We recommend *at least one extracurricular activity* at a time**:
      i. **More than one activity can be overly demanding**.
   c. **If your teen has a bad reputation at school, he or she may need to find an extracurricular activity in the community, rather than at school**.
   d. **Parents should *discuss* and *decide* on extracurricular activities with their teen based on their teen's interests**.
   e. **Parents may need to come up with *options* for their teen to choose from**.
   f. **Be sure that the extracurricular activity regularly exposes them to other teens**.
   g. **Parents are responsible for ensuring that their teen enroll in these activities**:
      i. **Do not wait for your teen to enroll himself or herself**.
      ii. **Some parents will need to make extracurricular activities mandatory for their teens; other parents will just need to strongly suggest them**.
   h. **When presenting new activities, ask your teen: "Which one do you want to join?" rather than "Do you want to join?"**
      i. **Participating in activities should not be negotiable**.
      ii. **Choosing which activities to join should be negotiable**.
2. *Get-togethers*.
   a. **It is also essential that your teen have regular *get-togethers* with friends**.
   b. ***Get-togethers* are the method by which teens form and keep close friendships**.
   c. **When your teen is first becoming friends with a new teen, you should encourage him or her to have *get-togethers* in your home where you can *unobtrusively* observe them**:

        i. **Be sure that each new friend is appropriate (e.g., does not tease, ignore, argue, or get your teen in trouble).**

   d. **On average, most teenagers have one to two *get-togethers* per week:**

        i. **We recommend that you set a goal with your teen of at least one *get-together* per week.**

   e. **Initial *get-togethers* with a particular teen should be limited to 2 hours (depending on the activity):**

        i. ***Get-togethers* can be much longer as teens maintain friendships.**

3. ***Teasing and bullying.***

   a. **Parents should be able to assist their teens with handling teasing and bullying from peers.**

   b. ***How to use tease-the-tease*:**

        i. **Response should be brief, simple, and give the impression that you do not care.**

        ii. **Examples:**

           1. **"Whatever!"**
           2. **"Anyway…"**
           3. **"Big deal!"**
           4. **"So what!"**
           5. **"Who cares?"**
           6. **"Yeah, and?"**
           7. **"And your point is?"**
           8. **"Tell me when you get to the funny part."**
           9. **"Am I supposed to care?"**
          10. **"Is that supposed to be funny?"**
          11. **"And why do I care?"**
          12. **Shrug shoulders, shake your head, and walk away.**
          13. **Roll your eyes and walk away.**

   c. ***How to handle bullying*:**

        i. ***Lay low.***

        ii. ***Avoid the bully.***

       iii. ***Do not provoke the bully.***

           1. **Only use *tease-the-tease* with teens who are *verbally* aggressive; not *physically* aggressive.**

        iv. ***Hang out with other people.***

        v. ***If you are in danger—get help from an adult.***

   d. **When your teen is bullied or teased at school:**

        i. **Allow him or her to *briefly* discuss how it felt to be teased or bullied, if he or she appears to want to talk about these feelings.**

      1. **If your teen does not automatically bring up his or her feelings around the bullying, do not encourage the discussion (this may only further upset your teen).**

   ii. **Assess how your teen handled the teasing or bullying.**

  iii. **If he or she did not follow the correct steps, discuss how your teen might have handled the situation differently.**

      1. **Do this by collaborating with your teen about the appropriate steps.**

      2. **Do not outright tell him or her that he or she handled the situation incorrectly.**

   iv. **Discuss how your teen might handle the situation differently in the future (i.e., follow the rules/steps).**

   v. **If your teen appears to be in danger from bullying, contact the school *immediately*.**

4. *Changing a bad reputation.*

  a. **It will be your primary responsibility to help your teen change his or her bad reputation following treatment (if necessary).**

   i. **This is a lengthy process and would not have been possible in the short time of treatment.**

  b. **You will want to engage in a routine discussion about your teen's reputation and the strategies he or she is currently working on to change any negative impressions.**

  c. **Stay familiar with the steps for changing a bad reputation and be able to present them to your teen during these conversations:**

   i. ***Lay low*:**

      1. **Keep a low profile.**

      2. **Do not draw attention to yourself.**

   ii. ***Follow the crowd*:**

      1. ***Try to fit in with the crowd.***

      2. ***Try not to stand out from the crowd.***

  iii. ***Change your look to change your reputation.***

  iv. ***Own up to your previous reputation.***

  v. ***Find a new group or crowd.***

  d. **While you are waiting for your teen's reputation to die down, be sure to be assisting in finding alternative sources of friends outside of school (i.e., nonschool-related extracurricular activities).**

5. *PEERS skills.*

  a. **Encourage your teen to use the skills learned in PEERS to make new friends.**

  b. **Remember that the *ideal* time to make new friends is at the beginning of the school year.**

  c. **You may need to go over the Parent Handouts with your teen periodically to remind him or her of the skills or how to handle**

disagreement, rumors or gossip, teasing and bullying from peers, or how to change a bad reputation.

■ Allow parents to ask any final questions.
■ Remind parents that they are welcome to call the treatment team should they have questions in the future.

Reunification and Graduation Ceremony

■ Reunite parents and teens for the graduation ceremony (allot approximately 15 minutes for the ceremony and good-byes).
■ Remind parents there is no picture taking allowed in order to preserve confidentiality:
 – Families are free to take pictures once they have left the group.
■ Parent and teen group leaders conduct the graduation ceremony:
 – Parents and teens should be standing or sitting near each other.
 – The treatment team members will be standing at the front of the room in a line.
 – The parent group leader begins by complimenting both parents and teens on the hard work they have done:
  • Comment on the progress the group has made as a whole.
   ■ Avoid mentioning specifics about group members.
 – The teen group leader compliments both parents and teens on the hard work they have done:
  • Provide additional comments on the progress the group has made as a whole.
   ■ Avoid mentioning specifics about group members.
 – The teen group leader announces the start of the graduation ceremony.
  • Explain how the ceremony will work:
   ■ When they hear their names called, teens will come to the front of the room to receive their Certificate of Completion.
   ■ Everyone will clap and cheer for them.
   ■ The teen group leader will hand the teen his or her certificate and shake his or her hand.
   ■ The teen will shake the hand of each of the treatment team members.
   ■ Everyone will continue to clap and cheer.
 – The teen group leader presents the Certificates of Completion:
  • Call each teen up to the front of the room and present him or her with a Certificate of Completion.
  • Be sure the teen shakes everyone's hand.
  • Encourage the group to clap for each teen individually.
■ Once the final Certificate of Completion is awarded:
 – Thank the group for coming.
 – Make a few final comments about the wonderful progress that has been made.

– Remind the families that just because the group is over, that does not
  mean that they should stop using the skills.
– Encourage them to keep practicing what they have learned so that they
  can continue to make and keep friends.
– Wish them well.
– Parents will often want to personally thank the group leaders before they
  leave.

Parent Handout 14: Where to Go From Here

Final Thoughts

1. ***Extracurricular activities***.
   a. It is essential that your teen participate in extracurricular activities in order to make friends.
   b. We recommend ***at least one extracurricular activity*** at a time:
      i. More than one activity can be overly demanding.
   c. If your teen has a bad reputation at school, he or she may need to find an extracurricular activity in the community, rather than at school.
   d. Parents should ***discuss*** and ***decide*** on extracurricular activities with their teen based on their teen's interests.
   e. Parents may need to come up with ***options*** for their teen to choose from.
   f. Be sure that the extracurricular activity regularly exposes the teen to other teens.
   g. Parents are responsible for ensuring that their teen enrolls in these activities:
      i. Do not wait for your teen to enroll himself or herself.
      ii. Some parents will need to make extracurricular activities mandatory for their teens; other parents will just need to strongly suggest them.
   h. When presenting new activities, ask your teen, "Which one do you want to join?" rather than "Do you want to join?"
      i. Participating in activities should not be negotiable.
      ii. Choosing which activities to join should be negotiable.
2. ***Get-togethers***.
   a. It is also essential that your teen have regular ***get-togethers*** with friends.
   b. ***Get-togethers*** are the method by which teens form and keep close friendships.
   c. When your teen is first becoming friends with a new teen, you should encourage him or her to have ***get-togethers*** in your home where you can ***unobtrusively*** observe them:
      i. Be sure that each new friend is appropriate (e.g., does not tease, ignore, argue, or get your teen in trouble).
   d. On average, most teenagers have one to two ***get-togethers*** per week:
      i. We recommend that you set a goal with your teen of at least one ***get-together*** per week.
   e. Initial ***get-togethers*** with a particular teen should be limited to 2 hours (depending on the activity):
      i. ***Get-togethers*** can be much longer as teens maintain friendships.
3. ***Teasing and bullying***.
   a. **Parents should be able to assist their teens with handling teasing and bullying from peers**.
   b. ***How to use tease-the-tease***:

   i. Response should be brief and simple and give the impression that you do not care.

   ii. Examples:

    1. "Whatever!"

    2. "Anyway…"

    3. "Big deal!"

    4. "So what!"

    5. "Who cares?"

    6. "Yeah, and?"

    7. "And your point is?"

    8. "Tell me when you get to the funny part."

    9. "Am I supposed to care?"

    10. "Is that supposed to be funny?"

    11. "And why do I care?"

    12. Shrug your shoulders, shake your head, and walk away.

    13. Roll your eyes and walk away.

 c. ***How to handle bullying***:

   i. ***Lay low***.

   ii. ***Avoid the bully***.

   iii. ***Do not provoke the bully***.

    1. Only use ***tease-the-tease*** with teens who are *verbally* aggressive, not *physically* aggressive.

   iv. ***Hang out with other people***.

   v. ***If you are in danger—get help from an adult***.

 d. When your teen is bullied or teased at school:

   i. Allow him or her to *briefly* discuss how it felt to be teased or bullied, if he or she appears to want to talk about these feelings.

    1. If your teen does not automatically bring up his or her feelings around the bullying, do not encourage the discussion (this may only further upset your teen).

   ii. Assess how your teen handled the teasing or bullying.

   iii. If he or she did not follow the correct steps, discuss how your teen might have handled the situation differently:

    1. Do this by collaborating with your teen about the appropriate steps.

    2. Do not outright tell him or her that he or she handled the situation incorrectly.

   iv. Discuss how your teen might handle the situation differently in the future (i.e., follow the rules/steps).

   v. If your teen appears to be in danger from bullying, contact the school *immediately*.

4. ***Changing a bad reputation***.

 a. It will be your primary responsibility to help your teen change his or her bad reputation following treatment (if necessary).

      i. This is a lengthy process and would not have been possible in the short time of treatment.

  b. You will want to engage in a routine discussion about your teen's reputation and the strategies he or she is currently working on to change any negative impressions.

  c. Stay familiar with the steps for changing a bad reputation and be able to present them to your teen during these conversations:

      i. ***Lay low***:

        1. Keep a low profile.

        2. Do not draw attention to yourself.

      ii. ***Follow the crowd***:

        1. ***Try to fit in with the crowd***.

        2. ***Try not to stand out from the crowd***.

      iii. ***Change your look to change your reputation***.

      iv. ***Own up to your previous reputation***.

      v. ***Find a new group or crowd***.

  d. While you are waiting for your teen's reputation to die down, be sure to be assisting in finding alternative sources of friends outside of school (i.e., nonschool-related extracurricular activities).

5. ***PEERS skills***.

  a. Encourage your teen to use the skills learned in PEERS to make new friends.

  b. Remember that the ***ideal*** time to make new friends is at the beginning of the school year.

  c. You may need to go over the Parent Handouts with your teen periodically to remind him or her of the skills or how to handle disagreement, rumors or gossip, teasing and bullying from peers, or how to change a bad reputation.

Thank you for being a part of PEERS! Congratulations on all of your hard work. We wish you the best of luck in the future!

Teen Therapist Guide—Session 14: Graduation and Termination

Guiding Principles of the Teen Session

The purpose of this final session is to reward teens for their hard work throughout the intervention and to provide closure with fun and celebration. The teens have been earning points throughout the intervention toward the graduation party and graduation prizes by completing weekly socialization assignments, participating in the group, and following the rules.

The majority of teens will be cheerful throughout the graduation party and generally in a festive mood. However, there are typically one or two teens who exhibit visible anxiety or sadness in response to treatment termination. Although it will be important for the group leader to empathize with this reaction, it is also helpful to focus on all the progress each teen has made.

Some teens will also ask what comes next. They will often express an interest in coming back to future groups or having reunions with the other group members. Although the group members are free to socialize with one another after the termination of the group, we do not promote the organization of reunions by the group leaders. Although it is unlikely that reunions would do any harm, the added effectiveness to the treatment delivery is unknown.

Administer Posttreatment Outcome Measures

Allow sufficient time to administer posttreatment measures. These measures should duplicate the measures completed before treatment began. See Chapter 2 for suggestions for outcome measures.

Homework Review

- Very briefly identify who completed their homework assignments and give credit as appropriate:
  - This should take no more than 5 minutes.
- Do not go into details unless there were significant problems, simply make a note of the points.
  - Ask if there were any problems.
  - Troubleshoot problems as necessary.
    - You may need to troubleshoot problems later and privately with the teen so that the graduation party can begin.
- Points for homework completion should be added to the total number of points for each teen.
- Teens will be awarded graduation prizes at the end of the session in order of the number of points received.

1. **Handling rumors and gossip**.
   a. Say: *Raise your hand if you used one or more of the strategies for handling rumors and gossip this week.*
2. ***Handling arguments and disagreements***.
   a. Say: *Raise your hand if you used one or more of the strategies for handling arguments or disagreements this week.*
3. ***Handling bullying and bad reputations***.
   a. Say: *Raise your hand if you used one or more of the strategies for handling bullying this week.*
4. ***Tease-the-tease***.
   a. Say: *Raise your hand if you were able to use tease-the-tease this week.*
5. ***Get-together***.
   a. Say: *Raise your hand if you had a get-together this week.*

Teen Activity

Suggestions for the graduation party.

- Teens often enjoy watching a movie of their choosing or playing games and talking.
  - It is recommended that a selection of PG-rated movies be provided by the treatment team:
    - Teens should be able to vote on which movie to watch.
      - Teens will often enjoy narrating or joking about the movie.
  - Have a selection of games available in the event that teens prefer to play games and talk.
- It is recommended that pizza and beverages be provided by the treatment team.
- Other snacks and desserts should be provided by parents.
- Teens should be encouraged to talk and socialize during the movie or games, much like they would during a group get-together.
- These activities were chosen because they are favorite teen activities done during parties and get-togethers.

Calculate the Points

- While the teens are having their party, calculate the total earned points for each teen:
  - Include points for this week's completed homework assignments.
- Determine the order of distribution for the graduation prizes.
- Do not calculate the points in the presence of the teens.
- Do not disclose the individual or group total of points publicly.
- Remind the teens that they worked as a team to earn a bigger and better graduation party and prizes.

Graduation Prizes

■ Approximately 5 to 10 minutes before the graduation ceremony, announce the graduation prize winners in order of highest number of points:
- Everyone will win a graduation prize.
- Do not mention the total number of points earned publicly.
  • You may tell each teen privately what he or she earned if asked, but do not share other participant totals.
- Allow teens to quickly choose their graduation prizes.
  • Teens will have had an opportunity to see graduation prizes in advance, so they will most likely have an idea of what they want.
- Encourage teens to clap for one another.
- Congratulate all of the prize winners.

Reunification and Graduation Ceremony

■ Reunite parents and teens for the graduation ceremony (allot approximately 15 minutes for the ceremony and good-byes).
■ Parent and teen group leaders conduct the graduation ceremony.
- Parents and teens should be standing or sitting near each other.
- The treatment team members will be standing at the front of the room in a line.
- The parent group leader begins by complimenting both parents and teens on the hard work they have done.
  • Comment on the progress the group has made as a whole:
    ■ Avoid mentioning specifics about group members.
- The teen group leader compliments both parents and teens on the hard work they have done.
  • Provide additional comments on the progress the group has made as a whole:
    ■ Avoid mentioning specifics about group members.
- The teen group leader announces the start of the graduation ceremony.
  • Explain how the ceremony will work:
    ■ When they hear their name called, teens will come to the front of the room to receive their Certificate of Completion.
    ■ Everyone will clap and cheer for them.
    ■ The teen group leader will hand the teen his or her certificate and shake his or her hand.
    ■ The teen will shake the hand of each of the treatment team members.
    ■ Everyone will continue to clap and cheer.
- The teen group leader presents the Certificates of Completion:
  • Call each teen up to the front of the room and present him or her with a Certificate of Completion.

- Be sure the teen shakes everyone's hand.
- Encourage the group to clap for each teen individually.

■ Once the final Certificate of Completion is awarded:
  - Thank the group for coming.
  - Make a few final comments about the wonderful progress that has been made.
  - Remind the families that just because the group is over, that does not mean that they should stop using the skills.
  - Encourage them to keep practicing what they have learned so that they can continue to make and keep friends.
  - Wish them well.
  - Parents will often want to personally thank the group leaders before they leave.

Chapter 17

Case Examples

Case Example: "Martin"

"Martin" (pseudonym) was a 14-year-old Caucasian male. Martin was diagnosed with autism at the age of 3 by the California Regional Center when his parents became concerned about his lack of expressive language and lack of social awareness. Shortly after being diagnosed, Martin began to receive intensive early intervention, which resulted in improved language development. At the time of admission into PEERS, Martin's expressive and receptive language skills were well above average and his cognitive functioning was assessed to be in the high average range. He was mainstreamed and reported by his parents to be an excellent student, but was experiencing a great deal of social rejection from his classmates. He was reported to have virtually no friends and was often teased by peers.

Upon intake, Martin indicated that although he would really like to have friends, he just did not think that was possible. He said he had tried numerous times, but "no one wanted to hang out" with him, so he had given up trying. Martin also described frequent instances of teasing from his classmates. In describing this social rejection, Martin became visibly agitated and angry. He explained that the other students in his small middle school would sometimes make fun of him when he would talk about politics (his restricted interest and a major social hurdle for him). This led Martin to retaliate by teasing back, which only appeared to distance him further from his classmates. Martin was not only steadfast in his political beliefs, but was adamantly and openly opposed to anyone who did not share his political ideals. He would often approach acquaintances, inappropriately requesting information about their political ideology. If they had the occasion to disagree with him, he became visibly upset and argumentative.

Martin's tendency to get into heated political debates became quickly evident in the early sessions of the PEERS intervention. Martin would quickly turn the conversation to politics during behavioral rehearsal exercises, while his peers preferred to talk about video games or movies. He would attempt to engage in long monologues in which he would extol the virtues of Nixon and Reagan, much to the boredom of his listener. That the purpose of the exercise was to trade information and find common interests was a revelation to Martin.

Martin was eventually able to find other topics of interest upon which to converse. He soon discovered that he enjoyed talking about movies and favorite television shows (like the other teens), and he eventually spent most behavioral rehearsals discussing these topics, with very little reference to politics. That is, with one exception. Martin had a particular fondness for the *Colbert Report*—a political satire about a conservative talk show host. He believed the political satire of the *Colbert Report* to be real and did not understand the humor intended. The treatment team worked with Martin on developing a better understanding about the satirical nature of this particular television show, so that he was ultimately able to converse about the show more appropriately with peers.

In the process of Martin improving his conversational skills (i.e., being less of a conversation hog, trading information about topics other than politics, and finding common interests with peers), Martin joined the debate team at his school. This was an ideal venue in which Martin could explore and discuss his political beliefs with other teenagers who held a passion for debate and an interest in politics. Martin began to comprehend the importance of different viewpoints, and discovered methods for challenging opposing views in a mutually respectful and appropriate manner. Martin began to find new sources of friends with similar interests. Each week in PEERS, he reported using his peer entry skills to slip into conversations with other members before and after debate. He found it easy to converse with the other members because they already shared common interests. He also successfully organized multiple get-togethers with various members of his debate team, which eventually led to Martin planning his first adolescent birthday party, in which nearly all 10 members of his debate team attended with much fun, amusement—and debate!

Martin's pretest and posttest outcome measures documented that he made substantial progress in the program. Self-reports of friendship quality, social skills knowledge, and self-esteem improved, as did parent reports of social skills and frequency of hosted get-togethers.

Martin and his parents returned to the program 3 months after the intervention had ended to take part in a follow-up assessment. Martin's social skills knowledge, friendship quality, and parent-reported social skills had maintained at posttreatment levels, and he also significantly improved his self-esteem, increased the frequency of hosted get-togethers, and was now a guest on significantly more invited get-togethers. However, according to anecdotal parent report, Martin continued to require reminding from parents not to be a "conversation hog," particularly when discussing politics, and needed periodic parental assistance in resolving conflicts and arguments with peers. Arguments generally centered around differences of opinion related to political philosophy, and Martin needed occasional reminding that these differences did not have to result in the loss of a friendship.

Case Example: "Tina"

"Tina" (pseudonym) was a 13-year-old Asian American female. She was diagnosed with Asperger's disorder at the age of 10 when her parents and teachers became concerned that she was having significant social problems. Tina was reported to be a good student and a well-behaved child, but she was extremely socially isolated. At the time of her diagnosis, Tina had never had a play date with a peer, had no friends, and had never even attended a birthday party for a classmate. For approximately 1 year, Tina attended a weekly social skills group with other children her age with autism spectrum disorders. This program had no parental involvement, and consequently, her parents had little idea of what Tina did in the group. However, Tina's parents reported that she demonstrated moderate success in this program in that she was able to make a couple of friends from among the other group members.

At the time of intake for PEERS, Tina was mainstreamed at a large public middle school. Her parents indicated that Tina had struggled with the transition from elementary to middle school and was finding it very difficult to make friends. Of the few friends she had from elementary school, most had moved on to new schools or new friends. Tina was described as "socially immature" and "awkward" by her teachers, and her parents indicated that she had begun to socially withdraw again. Tina explained that when she was in elementary school it was easier to interact with her peers because social exchanges were primarily focused on play, whereas in middle school social interactions revolved around conversations with others—an area Tina admittedly struggled with.

During the first couple sessions of PEERS, Tina was extremely quiet and did not participate voluntarily, but she would provide thoughtful responses when called upon and willingly participated in behavioral rehearsals with other group members. While practicing conversational skills with her peers in the group, Tina had a particular interest in anime and comic books (both reading and drawing them). Fortunately, two of the other group members had similar interests, which made it easier for this trio to converse. In an effort to encourage continued use of newly learned conversational skills, Tina was paired with these group members for the first couple of in-group phone assignments. Tina's father soon commented on how surprised he was by Tina's willingness to make the phone calls and her ability to carry on a two-way conversation. This was something Tina's father had seen little of from Tina before. He reflected that Tina had always been a "follower" in the few friendships she previously developed. She rarely had much to say in conversations with peers. Tina had never approached conversations with the goal of finding common interests. The result was that those who knew her (who might share her interest) rarely knew of her love of anime and comic books.

With the goal of finding common interests in mind, Tina quickly improved her conversational skills and found other peers who shared the same love of anime. With the help of her parents, Tina discovered a comic book club in her school and joined its ranks. She slowly made friends with the other kids in the club, and by the time she reached the end of PEERS, she was having regular get-togethers organized around attending comic book conventions and going to comic book stores.

At a 3-month follow-up assessment, Tina reported that she was continuing to have regular get-togethers with her new friends and had even been invited to a party by one of the comic book club members. She no longer felt uncomfortable conversing with people she knew, and her parents indicated that Tina was no longer socially isolated. Bridging upon Tina's love for anime and comic books, her parents also reported that they had enrolled her in art classes. Through these classes, Tina was able to meet new friends with a similar passion for drawing comics. Tina's main issues around socialization following the intervention included repetitive themes in conversations and minimal peer entry attempts. According to her parents, although Tina made great progress in the program, she still needed frequent reminding to shift conversational topics from time to time. Her love of anime resulted in her desire to talk about it obsessively, a habit that sometimes appeared to annoy her friends. Additionally, Tina's parents reported that she continued to be "shy" around those she did not know well, and was reluctant at times to use her peer entry skills in novel situations. However, with appropriate parent coaching, Tina continued to improve in these areas over time.

Case Example: "Daniel"

"Daniel" (pseudonym) was a 16-year-old Latino male diagnosed with autism at the age of 4, when his parents became concerned that his language was not developing at an adequate pace. As a young child, Daniel was described by his parents as "withdrawn and disconnected." They indicated that he rarely spoke, unless attempting to get his needs met. After years of receiving intensive behavioral therapy and speech and language services, Daniel improved his language skills but continued to struggle with social deficits. At the time of enrolling in PEERS, he attended general education classes and received additional classroom support in the form of a resource class 1 hour per day to help him organize his homework assignments.

Daniel had a very pedantic style of speaking with a monotone delivery and very little inflection. He had an unusual gait, poor gross motor skills, and was considered rather clumsy. His teacher stated that his fellow classmates considered him "odd."

At intake, Daniel indicated that he was very eager to join PEERS. He explained that he wanted to make friends but just did not know how. He often felt lonely, sometimes felt depressed, and wished he were different. In discussing his social challenges, Daniel stated, "Other kids treat me differently. Some of them tease me, but most people ignore me."

Although Daniel had an effortful style of speaking, he appeared to enjoy conversing with the other group members in PEERS. He frequently talked about computer games and video games with the other teens, but his favorite conversational topic related to his restricted interest: World of Warcraft. Daniel was "obsessed" with this multiplayer online role-playing game where players control an "avatar" character while acting out a storyline. Daniel was thrilled when he discovered other PEERS group members liked World of Warcraft and this became a common topic of conversation during behavioral rehearsals and in-group phone call assignments. When choosing extracurricular activities, Daniel joined a video game club at his high school, where he was able to meet other teens with similar interests. During a homework review, his father recounted a very successful out-of-group phone call with a member from this club in which the two spent nearly an hour talking about World of Warcraft with much delight. Although Daniel's father was ecstatic to have Daniel trading information on the phone, he was concerned that the entire conversation was focused on this fantasy world. The teen group leader gave Daniel the added assignment to trade information about something other than World of Warcraft (or any other online game) for at least 25% of his next phone call. Daniel agreed to this suggestion and eventually included other topics of conversation, including favorite movies and TV shows. By the time Daniel had his first get-together for PEERS, he was conversing about a variety of topics with friends and enjoying the development of a few close friendships.

At a 3-month follow-up, Daniel's parents reported that he was having regular get-togethers with three new friends he met in the video game club at school. He had been invited on several group get-togethers to these friends' houses, where he had met other teens with similar interests and was beginning to develop new friendships among these peers. Although Daniel continued to need reminding from his parents to occasionally switch topics in conversations and avoid only talking about his online fantasy world, he was reckoned to have made great progress in his overall friendship skills.

References

Altman, I., & Taylor, D. (1973). *Social penetration: The development of interpersonal relationships*. New York: Holt, Rinehart & Winston.

Baumeister, R. F., Zhang, L., & Vohs, K. D. (2004). Gossip as cultural learning. *Review of General Psychology, 8*, 111–121.

Baxter, A. (1997). The power of friendship. *Journal of Developmental Disabilities, 5*(2), 112–117.

Bordia, P., DiFonzo, N., Haines, R., & Chaseling, E. (2005). Rumor denials as persuasive messages: Effects of personal relevance, source, and message characteristics. *Journal of Applied Social Psychology, 35*, 1301–1331.

Buhrmester, D. (1990). Intimacy of friendship, interpersonal competence, and adjustment during preadolescence and adolescence. *Child Development, 61*, 1101–1111.

Coie, J. D., Dodge, K. A., & Kupersmidt, J. B. (1990). Peer group behavior and social status. In S. R. Asher & J. D. Coie (Eds.), *Peer rejection in childhood* (pp. 17–59). New York: Cambridge University Press.

Coie, J. D., & Kupersmidt, J. B. (1983). A behavioral analysis of emerging social status. *Child Development, 54*, 1400–1416.

Crick, N. R., & Ladd, G. W. (1990). Children's perceptions of the outcomes of social strategies: Do the ends justify being mean? *Developmental Psychology, 26*, 612–620.

Dodge, K. A., Schlundt, D. C., Schocken, I., & Delugach, J. D. (1983). Social competence and children's sociometric status: The role of peer group entry strategies. *Merrill-Palmer Quarterly, 29*, 309–336.

Emerich, D. M., Creaghead, N. A., Grether, S. M., Murray, D., & Grasha, C. (2003). The comprehension of humorous materials by adolescents with high-functioning autism and Asperger's syndrome. *Journal of Autism and Developmental Disorders, 33*, 253–257.

Frankel, F. (1996). *Good friends are hard to find: Help your child find, make, and keep friends*. Los Angeles: Perspective.

Frankel, F., Erhardt, D., Renenger, K., & Pataki, C. (in press). Child knowledge of key peer relationship behaviors: Relationship with teacher-reported social skills. Manuscript submitted for publication.

Frankel, F., Gorospe, C. M., Chang, Y., & Sugar, C. A. (in press). Mothers' reports of play dates and observation of school playground behavior of children having high-functioning autism spectrum disorders. Manuscript submitted for publication.

Frankel, F., & Mintz, J. (in press). Measuring the quality of play dates. Manuscript submitted for publication.

Frankel, F., & Myatt, R. (2003). *Children's friendship training*. New York: Brunner-Routledge.

Frankel, F., Myatt, R., Whitham, C., Gorospe, C. M., & Laugeson, E. (in press). A controlled study of parent-assisted children's friendship training with children having autism spectrum disorders. *Journal of Autism and Developmental Disorders*.

Frankel, F., & Simmons, J. Q. (1992). Parent behavioral training: Why and when some parents drop out. *Journal of Clinical Child Psychology, 21,* 322–330.

Frankel, F., Sinton, M., & Wilfley, D. (2007). Social skills training and the treatment of pediatric overweight. In W. T. O'Donohue, B. A. Moore, & B. J. Scott (Eds.), *Handbook of pediatric and adolescent obesity treatment* (pp. 105–116). New York: Routledge.

Garvey, C. (1984). *Children's talk.* Cambridge, MA: Harvard University Press.

Gralinski, J. H., & Kopp, C. (1993). Everyday rules for behavior: Mother's requests to young children. *Developmental Psychology, 29,* 573–584.

Gresham, F. M., & Elliott, S. N. (2008). *Social Skills Improvement System (SSIS) Rating Scales Manual.* Minneapolis, MN: Pearson Education.

Hartup, W. W. (1993). Adolescents and their friends. In B. Laursen (Ed.), *Close friendships in adolescence* (Series: New directions for child development) (W. Damon, series Ed.), Number 60, 3–22, San Francisco: Jossey Bass.

Hibbs, E. D., Clarke, G., Hechtman, L., Abikoff, H., Greenhill, L., & Jensen, P. (1997). Manual development for the treatment of child and adolescent disorders. *Psychopharmacology Bulletin, 33,* 619–629.

Hodges, E. V. E., & Perry, D. G. (1999). Personal and interpersonal antecedents and consequences of victimization by peers. *Journal of Personality & Social Psychology, 76,* 677–685.

Laugeson, E. A., Frankel, F., Mogil, C., & Dillon, A. R. (2009). Parent-assisted social skills training to improve friendships in teens with Autism Spectrum Disorders. *Journal of Autism & Developmental Disorders, 39,* 596–606.

Laursen, B., & Koplas, A. L. (1995). What's important about important conflicts? Adolescents' perceptions of daily disagreements. *Merrill-Palmer Quarterly, 41,* 536–553.

Little, L. (2001). Peer victimization of children with Asperger Spectrum Disorders. *Journal of the American Academy of Child & Adolescent Psychiatry, 40,* 995–996.

Marlowe, D. B., Kirby, K. C., Festinger, D. S., Husband, S. D., & Platt, J. J. (1997). Impact of comorbid personality disorders and personality disorder symptoms on outcomes of behavioral treatment for cocaine dependence. *Journal of Nervous & Mental Disease, 185,* 483–490.

Marriage, K. J., Gordon, V., & Brand, L. (1995). A social skills group for boys with Asperger's syndrome. *Australian & New Zealand Journal of Psychiatry, 29,* 58–62.

McGuire, K. D., & Weisz, J. R. (1982). Social cognition and behavior correlates of preadolescent chumship. *Child Development, 53,* 1478–1484.

Miller, P. M., & Ingham, J. G. (1976). Friends, confidants, and symptoms. *Social Psychiatry, 11,* 51–58.

O'Connor, M. J., Frankel, F., Paley, B., Schonfeld, A. M., Carpenter, E., Laugeson, E., & Marquardt, R. (2006). A controlled social skills training for children with fetal alcohol spectrum disorders. *Journal of Consulting and Clinical Psychology, 74,* 639–648.

Olweus, D. (1993). Bullies on the playground: The role of victimization. In C. H. Hart (Ed.), *Children on playgrounds* (pp. 45–128). Albany: State University of New York Press.

Perry, D. G., Kusel, S. J., & Perry, L. C. (1988). Victims of aggression. *Developmental Psychology, 24,* 807–814.

Perry, D. G., Williard, J. C., & Perry, L. C. (1990). Peer perceptions of the consequences that victimized children provide aggressors. *Child Development, 61,* 1310–1325.

Phillips, C. A., Rolls, S., Rouse, A., & Griffiths, M. D. (1995). Home video game playing in schoolchildren: A study of incidence and patterns of play. *Journal of Adolescence, 18,* 687–691.

Putallaz, M., & Gottman, J. M. (1981). An interactional model of children's entry into peer groups. *Child Development, 52,* 986–994.

Rubin, Z., & Sloman, J. (1984). In M. Lewis (Ed.), *Beyond the dyad* (pp. 223–250). New York: Plenum Press.

Shantz, D. W. (1986). Conflict, aggression and peer status: An observational study. *Child Development, 57,* 1322–1332.

Thurlow, C., & McKay, S. (2003). Profiling "new" communication technologies in adolescence. *Journal of Language and Social Psychology, 22,* 94–103.

Van Bourgondien, M. E., & Mesibov, G. B. (1987). Humor in high functioning autistic adults. *Journal of Autism and Developmental Disorders, 17,* 417–424.

Warm, T. R. (1997). The role of teasing in development and vice versa. *Journal of Developmental & Behavioral Pediatrics, 18,* 97–101.

Wolfberg, P. J., & Schuler, A. L. (1993). Integrated play groups: A model for promoting the social and cognitive dimensions of play in children with autism. *Journal of Autism & Developmental Disorders, 23,* 467–489.

List of Key Terms

Bullying
Buzzwords
Challenging parent behaviors
Characteristics of good friendships
Children's Friendship Training
Cold calling
Cover stories (phone call examples)
Cover stories (slipping out of a conversation)
Cover story (ending a get-together)
Crowds (varieties of)
Cyberbullying
Embarrassing feedback
Friendship Qualities Scale
Gaze aversion
Gold standard for choosing a friend for a get-together
Good and bad places to make friends
Good Sportsmanship Point Log
Graduation flyer
Group leader's homework review skills
Handling disagreements
Handling misbehavior
Helicopter parents
Homework compliance sheet
How to handle bullying
Humor feedback
Importance of having a crowd/clique
In-group Phone Call Assignment Sheet
Jeopardy game
Outcome assessments
Parent saving face for no get-together
PEERS Phone Screen Data Sheet
Personality disorder
Phone Screen Data Sheet
Phone roster

Phone Screening Script
Planned absence sheet
Quality of Play Questionnaire
Reasons for being turned down (entering a conversation)
Rules about using humor
Rules for changing a bad reputation
Rules for good sportsmanship
Rules for handling bullying
Rules for handling disagreements
Rules for handling rumors and gossip
Rules for having a good get-together
Rules for leaving a voice-mail message
Rules for phone calls
Rules for slipping into a conversation
Rules for slipping out of a conversation
Rules for text messages
Rules for using the Internet
Social Responsiveness Scale
Social Skills Improvement System
Sources of friends
Starting and ending a phone call
Steps for slipping into a conversation
Suggestions for activity-based get-togethers
Tease-the-tease
Teasing
Teen Intake Interview Checklist
Test of Adolescent Social Skills Knowledge
Tips for changing a bad reputation
Too cool for school syndrome
Trading information
Two message rule
Weekly total point log
Welcome letter

Appendices

Assessment Measures

Appendix A: Test of Adolescent Social Skills Knowledge (TASSK)

Appendix B: Quality of Play Questionnaire—Parent (QPQ-P)

Quality of Play Questionnaire—Adolescent (QPQ-A)

Session Materials

Appendix C: Phone Roster

Appendix D: Planned Absence Sheet

Appendix E: In-Group Phone Call Assignment Log

Appendix F: PEERS Weekly Point Log

Appendix G: PEERS Good Sportsmanship Point Log

Appendix H: PEERS Homework Compliance Sheet

Appendix I: Graduation Party Flyer

Appendix A

Test of Adolescent Social Skills Knowledge* (TASSK)

Instructions:

The following items are about making and keeping friends. After you read each item, there will be a couple of choices to choose from. Decide which choice is the best by bubbling in the best answer. Only choose one answer per item.

1. The most important part of having a conversation is to:
   - ☐ Trade information.
   - ☐ Make sure the other person is laughing and smiling.
2. The goal of a conversation is to:
   - ☐ Make the other person like you.
   - ☐ Find common interests.
3. One of the rules for having a two-way conversation is to:
   - ☐ Be an interviewer.
   - ☐ Do not be an interviewer.
4. When you are *first* getting to know someone, it is important to be:
   - ☐ Funny and silly.
   - ☐ Serious.
5. When you are calling a friend on the telephone, it is important to:
   - ☐ Tell him or her your first and last name and where you go to school.
   - ☐ Have a cover story for calling.
6. When you are calling a peer on the telephone, you should:
   - ☐ Avoid cold calling.
   - ☐ Let him or her do most of the talking.
7. After you make a joke, it is a good idea to pay attention to:
   - ☐ Whether the other person is laughing.
   - ☐ Your humor feedback.

---

* Modification of the Test of Social Skills Knowledge (Frankel, F., Erhardt, D., Renenger, K., & Pataki, C., 2009) by permission of authors.

8. It is *always* a good sign if someone laughs at your jokes:
   □ True.
   □ False.

9. It is *always* a good idea to try to make friends with:
   □ Someone who is more popular than you.
   □ Someone who likes the same things as you.

10. It is a good idea to have a group or a crowd because:
    □ You are more likely to be popular.
    □ It protects you from bullying.

11. When you are trying to join a conversation, the *first* thing you should do is:
    □ Watch and listen to observe the conversation.
    □ Make a comment about what they are saying.

12. When joining a conversation, you should wait for:
    □ Someone to invite you to talk.
    □ A pause in the conversation.

13. If you try to join a conversation and the people ignore you:
    □ Slip out of the conversation.
    □ Make sure they can hear you.

14. If you try to join 10 different conversations, on average, how many times out of 10 are you likely to be rejected:
    □ 7 out of 10.
    □ 5 out of 10.

15. When having a friend over for a get-together at your home:
    □ Tell your friend what you are going to do.
    □ Have your friend choose the activity.

16. If you are having a friend over for a get-together and someone else unexpectedly calls that you really like, you should:
    □ Invite your other friend over.
    □ Tell them that you are busy and will call them later.

17. Teens like to play sports with other teens who:
    □ Score points and play well.
    □ Praise them.

18. When people are not playing by the rules, you should:
    □ Nicely remind them what the rules are.
    □ Do not referee them.

19. If another kid teases you or calls you a name, you should:
    □ Tease the tease.
    □ Tell an adult.

20. When someone teases you, the best thing to do is:
    □ Ignore that person and walk away.
    □ Act like what he or she said did not bother you.

21. If someone is bullying you, the *first* thing you should do is:
    □ Get help from an adult.
    □ Avoid the bully.

22. If you are trying to change your bad reputation, you should:
    ☐ Lay low for a while.
    ☐ Make sure that people get to know you better.
23. The *first* thing you should do when you get into an argument with a friend is:
    ☐ Listen and keep your cool.
    ☐ Explain your side.
24. When a friend accuses you of doing something you did not do:
    ☐ Say you are sorry that this happened.
    ☐ Explain your side until he or she believes you.
25. If someone spreads a rumor about you that is not true, you should:
    ☐ Confront the person who started the rumor.
    ☐ Spread a rumor about yourself.
26. If someone is gossiping behind your back, you should:
    ☐ Let that person know that the gossip hurts your feelings.
    ☐ Act amazed that anyone would believe the gossip.

Test of Adolescent Social Skills Knowledge (TASSK)

Administration

- ■ The TASSK is intended to provide an assessment of the social skills knowledge of the teen.
- ■ The TASSK is completed by each teen individually.
    - For teens with significant language delay or reading impairment, it is recommended that the TASSK be administered orally.
    - Administration may be completed in group or individual format.
- ■ The TASSK may be used as a pre-, post-, or follow-up assessment of treatment outcome.
- ■ The 26 items that make up the TASSK are derived from teen session content.
    - Two items are taken from each didactic lesson.
- ■ These items are considered to be central to the social skills lessons.

Scoring Key

SCORING: Items in bold type reflect the correct answer. One point should be given for each correct answer. Scores range from 0 to 26. Higher scores reflect better knowledge of teen social etiquette.

1. The most important part of having a conversation is to:
   ☐ **Trade information**.
   ☐ Make sure the other person is laughing and smiling.
2. The goal of a conversation is to:

☐ Make the other person like you.

☐ **Find common interests**.

3. One of the rules for having a two-way conversation is to:

☐ Be an interviewer.

☐ **Do not be an interviewer**.

4. When you are *first* getting to know someone, it is important to be:

☐ Funny and silly.

☐ **Serious**.

5. When you are calling a friend on the telephone, it is important to:

☐ Tell him or her your first and last name and where you go to school.

☐ **Have a cover story for calling**.

6. When you are calling a peer on the telephone, you should:

☐ **Avoid cold calling**.

☐ Let him or her do most of the talking.

7. After you make a joke, it is a good idea to pay attention to:

☐ Whether the other person is laughing.

☐ **Your humor feedback**.

8. It is *always* a good sign if someone laughs at your jokes:

☐ True.

☐ **False**.

9. It is *always* a good idea to try to make friends with:

☐ Someone who is more popular than you.

☐ **Someone who likes the same things as you**.

10. It is a good idea to have a group or a crowd because:

☐ You are more likely to be popular.

☐ **It protects you from bullying**.

11. When you are trying to join a conversation, the *first* thing you should do is:

☐ **Watch and listen to observe the conversation**.

☐ Make a comment about what they are saying.

12. When joining a conversation, you should wait for:

☐ Someone to invite you to talk.

☐ **A pause in the conversation**.

13. If you try to join a conversation and the people ignore you:

☐ **Slip out of the conversation**.

☐ Make sure they can hear you.

14. If you try to join 10 different conversations, on average, how many times out of 10 are you likely to be rejected:

☐ 7 out of 10.

☐ **5 out of 10**.

15. When having a friend over for a get-together at your home:

☐ Tell your friend what you are going to do.

☐ **Have your friend choose the activity**.

16. If you are having a friend over for a get-together and someone else unexpectedly calls that you really like, you should:

☐ Invite your other friend over.

☐ **Tell them that you are busy and will call them later**.

17. Teens like to play sports with other teens who:

☐ Score points and play well.

☐ **Praise them**.

18. When people are not playing by the rules, you should:

☐ Nicely remind them what the rules are.

☐ **Do not referee them**.

19. If another kid teases you or calls you a name, you should:

☐ **Tease-the-tease**.

☐ Tell an adult.

20. When someone teases you, the best thing to do is:

☐ Ignore that person and walk away.

☐ **Act like what he or she said did not bother you**.

21. If someone is bullying you, the *first* thing you should do is:

☐ Get help from an adult.

☐ **Avoid the bully**.

22. If you are trying to change your bad reputation, you should:

☐ **Lay low for a while**.

☐ Make sure that people get to know you better.

23. The *first* thing you should do when you get into an argument with a friend is:

☐ **Listen and keep your cool**.

☐ Explain your side.

24. When a friend accuses you of doing something you did not do:

☐ **Say you are sorry that this happened**.

☐ Explain your side until he or she believes you.

25. If someone spreads a rumor about you that is not true, you should:

☐ Confront the person who started the rumor.

☐ **Spread a rumor about yourself**.

26. If someone is gossiping behind your back, you should:

☐ Let that person know that the gossip hurts your feelings.

☐ **Act amazed that anyone would believe the gossip**.

Appendix B

Quality of Play Questionnaire—Parent (QPQ-P)*

We would like information on your teen's friendships. We **only** want to know about the friends that your teen has invited for a **get-together.** Do not consider friends who only did homework together.

Please indicate how many get-togethers your teen has **hosted in the past month**: _____

Please fill in the **first names** of the friends who have attended a get-together **hosted by your teen in the past month**. If your teen has not had any friends over for a get-together in the past month, leave the section below blank.

Friend's first name _____   Friend's first name _____

Friend's first name _____   Friend's first name _____

Friend's first name _____   Friend's first name _____

Friend's first name _____   Friend's first name _____

What the teens did during the last visit you observed:
Consider the last get-together your teen hosted in which you were around to see or hear what was happening. Circle the number below that describes how true the preceding statement is.

	Not at All	Just a Little	Pretty Much	Very Much
1. They did things without each other.	0	1	2	3
2. They did not share games, personal items, etc.	0	1	2	3
3. They got upset at each other.	0	1	2	3
4. They argued with each other.	0	1	2	3

---

* Adapted from Frankel & Mintz (2008) by permission of the authors.

5. They criticized or teased each other.	0	1	2	3
6. They were bossy with each other.	0	1	2	3
7. They allowed a sibling to join the get-together unexpectedly.	0	1	2	3
8. They allowed other teens to join the get-together unexpectedly.	0	1	2	3
9. They needed a parent to solve problems.	0	1	2	3
10. They annoyed each other.	0	1	2	3

Get-togethers at another teen's house:

Please indicate how many get-togethers your teen has attended at another teen's house in the past month: _____

Please try to recall the times your teen went to a get-together at another teen's house in the past month. Fill in the first names of your teen's friends who hosted the get-togethers. Do not consider friends who only did homework together. If your teen did not attend a get-together at another teen's house in the past month, leave the section below blank.

Friend's first name _____   Friend's first name _____
Friend's first name _____   Friend's first name _____
Friend's first name _____   Friend's first name _____
Friend's first name _____   Friend's first name _____

Quality of Play Questionnaire—Adolescent (QPQ-A)[2]

Please indicate how many get-togethers you **hosted in the last month**. _____
Please list the **first names** of all of the friends who have come to a get-together hosted by you the past month for a get-together. Do not include friends who only came over to do homework. If you did not have a get-together in the past month, leave the section below blank.

Friend's first name _____   Friend's first name _____
Friend's first name _____   Friend's first name _____
Friend's first name _____   Friend's first name _____
Friend's first name _____   Friend's first name _____

What you did during the last get-together:

Consider the **last get-together you hosted**. Circle the number on the next page that describes how true the sentence is.

	Not at All	Just a Little	Pretty Much	Very Much
1. We did things without each other.	0	1	2	3
2. We did not share games, personal items, etc.	0	1	2	3
3. We got upset at each other.	0	1	2	3
4. We argued with each other.	0	1	2	3
5. We criticized or teased each other.	0	1	2	3
6. We were bossy with each other.	0	1	2	3
7. We allowed a sibling to join the get-together unexpectedly.	0	1	2	3
8. We allowed other teens to join the get-together unexpectedly.	0	1	2	3
9. We needed a parent to solve problems.	0	1	2	3
10. We annoyed each other.	0	1	2	3

Get-togethers at another teen's house:

Please indicate how many get-togethers you attended **at another teen's house in the past month**: _____

Think of all of the times when you went to a get-together **at another teen's house** in the **past month.** Fill in the **first names** of your friends who hosted the get-togethers. Do not include friends you only did homework with. If you did not go to a get-together at another teen's house in the past month, leave the section below blank.

Friend's first name _____   Friend's first name _____
Friend's first name _____   Friend's first name _____
Friend's first name _____   Friend's first name _____

Quality of Play Questionnaire

Administration

- The QPQ-P takes approximately 5 minutes to complete and should be completed independently by the parent.
- The QPQ-A takes approximately 5 minutes to complete. Most teens can complete this independently. However, it should be orally administered to teens with reading or comprehension difficulties.

Scoring Key (Both Parent and Teen Versions)

■ Important scores to use as outcome measures:
  – The number of get-togethers the teen **hosted** in the last month.
  – The number of different friends who were **invited** over for **hosted** get-togethers in the last month.
  – The number of get-togethers the teen was **invited to attend** in the last month.
  – The number of different friends who **invited the teen** over for get-togethers in the last month.
■ Calculate the total Conflict scale score by summing the scores from items 2 through 7, 9, and 10. Scores greater than 3.5 indicate significant conflict.

Appendix C

Phone Roster

This phone roster is to be used to complete the *in-group phone calls*. Please use this table to keep track of the person your teen is assigned to call each week, and note the day and time of the scheduled call. If you would prefer that a different number be used than the one listed below, please let us know.

Teen Name	Parent/ Guardian Name	Phone Number	Week 1 Day/ Time	Week 2 Day/ Time	Week 3 Day/ Time	Week 4 Day/ Time	Week 5 Day/ Time	Week 6 Day/ Time

Appendix D

Planned Absence Sheet

It is very important for you and your teen to attend *every session* of PEERS. However, if you know that you have to be absent for a session, *please mark those dates that you know you will not be able to attend below.*

Teen's Name: _____

Parent's Name: _____

Session	Date	Planned Absence
1		
2		
3		
4		
5		
6		
7		
8		
9		
10		
11		
12		
13		
14		Graduation

Advanced information about planned absences will be used to determine if a particular session needs to be rescheduled based on the anticipated number of absences.

Please return this memo at the *second* group meeting if you have any planned absences.

Appendix E

In-Group Phone Call Assignment Log

Week 1

Caller		Receiver	
Caller	_____	Receiver	_____
Caller	_____	Receiver	_____
Caller	_____	Receiver	_____
Caller	_____	Receiver	_____
Caller	_____	Receiver	_____

Week 2

Caller		Receiver	
Caller	_____	Receiver	_____
Caller	_____	Receiver	_____
Caller	_____	Receiver	_____
Caller	_____	Receiver	_____
Caller	_____	Receiver	_____

Week 3

Caller		Receiver	
Caller	_____	Receiver	_____
Caller	_____	Receiver	_____
Caller	_____	Receiver	_____
Caller	_____	Receiver	_____
Caller	_____	Receiver	_____

Week 4

Caller		Receiver	
Caller	_____	Receiver	_____
Caller	_____	Receiver	_____
Caller	_____	Receiver	_____
Caller	_____	Receiver	_____
Caller	_____	Receiver	_____

Week 5

Caller		Receiver	
Caller	_____	Receiver	_____
Caller	_____	Receiver	_____
Caller	_____	Receiver	_____
Caller	_____	Receiver	_____
Caller	_____	Receiver	_____

Week 6

Caller		Receiver	
Caller	_____	Receiver	_____
Caller	_____	Receiver	_____
Caller	_____	Receiver	_____
Caller	_____	Receiver	_____
Caller	_____	Receiver	_____

Appendix F

PEERS Weekly Point Log

Name	1	2	3	4	5	6	7	8	9	10	11	12	13	14	Total
Total															

Appendix G

PEERS Good Sportsmanship Point Log

Name	Week 9	Week 10	Week 11	Week 12	Week 13	Total
Total						

Appendix H

PEERS Homework Compliance Sheet

Session #	1	2	3	4	5	6	7	8	9	10	11	12	13	14
Date														

C = Complete   P = Partially Complete   I = Incomplete

Teen / Parent	Present and/or Minutes Late	Personal Item / Game / Equipment	Trading Info with Parent	In-Group Call	Out-of-Group Call	Humor Feedback	Source of Friends	Slipping In and/or Slipping Out	Get-together and/or Good Sport	Tease-the-Tease	Bullying / Bad Reputations	Handling Arguments and/or Rumors and Gossip	Comments:
T = First, Last Initial Age; Grade; School setting P = Parent first name													
T =													
P =													
T =													
P =													
T =													
P =													
T =													
P =													
T =													
P =													
T =													
P =													
T =													
P =													

Appendix I

[Insert day of week and date]

Testing: [insert time of post-testing]
Graduation party: [insert time]

Please Note the Time Change

[Insert date] is the last meeting of PEERS. We will begin the evening by doing post-testing with parents and teens. **Please plan to arrive 30 minutes earlier.**

We will wrap-up our 14th meeting with the parents, while the teens attend their graduation party. At the end of the meeting, we will all assemble for a brief graduation ceremony.

We would kindly appreciate it if all of our families could bring a treat to the party.

Patient confidentiality prohibits photography.

Author Index

A

Abikoff, H., 380
Altman, I., 68, 379
Asher, S. R., 379

B

Baumeister, R. F., 337, 379
Baxter, A., 11, 379
Bordia, P., 337, 379
Brand, L., 12, 380
Buhrmester, D., 12, 379

C

Carpenter, E., 380
Chang, Y., xxiii, 223, 379
Chaseling, E., 337, 379
Clarke, G., 380
Coie, J. D., 171, 294, 379
Creaghead, N. A., 147, 379
Crick, N. R., 252, 379

D

Delugach, J. D., 171, 379
DiFonzo, N., 337, 379
Dillon, A. R., xxiii, 12, 380
Dodge, K. A., 171, 294, 379

E

Elliott, S. N., 33, 380
Emerich, D. M., 147, 379
Erhardt, D., 379, 387

F

Festinger, D. S., 38, 380

Frankel, F., 379, 380, 387, 393
    bad reputation intervention, 294
    best friendships, 12, 68, 135
    Children's Friendship Training, xxi, 3, 67
        research, 5,
    PEERS research, 12, 13
    PEERS development, 3, 38, 40, 171, 223, 252
    Quality of Play Questionnaire, 34
    tease-the-tease technique 268
    teasing described, 267
    teen intake interview checklist, 27

G

Garvey, C., 171, 380
Gordon, V., 380
Gorospe, C. M., xxiii, 223, 379, 380
Gottman, J. M., 294, 381
Gralinski, J. H., 11, 380
Grasha, C., 147, 379
Greenhill, L., 380
Gresham, F. M., 33, 380
Grether, S. M., 147, 379
Griffiths, M. D., 235, 381

H

Haines, R., 337, 379
Hart, C. H., 380
Hartup, W. W., 135, 380
Hechtman, L., 380
Hibbs, E. D., 4, 380
Hodges, E. V. E., 267, 380
Husband, S. D., 38, 380

I

Ingham, J. G., 12, 380

J

Jensen, P., 380

K

Kirby, K. C., 38, 380
Koplas, A. L., 313, 380
Kopp, C., 380
Kupersmidt, J. B., 171, 294, 379
Kusel, S. J., 267, 380

L

Ladd, G. W., 252, 379
Laugeson, E. A., xxi, 12, 34, 380
Laursen, B., 313, 380
Lewis, M., 381
Little, L., 293, 380

M

Marlowe, D. B., 38, 380
Marquardt, R., 380
Marriage, K. J., 12, 380
McGuire, K. D., 12, 380
McKay, S., 381
Mesibov, G. B., 147, 381
Miller, P. M., 12, 380
Mintz, J., 34, 379, 393
Mogil, C., xiii, 12, 380
Moore, B. A., 380
Murray, D., 147, 379
Myatt, R., 25, 28, 379, 380
   bad reputation intervention, 294
   best friendships, 12, 68, 135
   Children's Friendship Training, xxi, 3, 67
      research, 5
   PEERS development, 38, 40, 171, 223, 252
   tease-the-tease technique, 268
      teasing described, 267

O

O'Connor, M. J., 5, 380
O'Donohue, W. T., 380
Olweus, D., 293

P

Paley, B., xxiii, 380

Pataki, C., 379, 387
Perry, D. G., 267, 380, 381
Perry, L. C., 267, 380, 381
Phillips, C. A., 235, 381
Platt, J. J., 38, 380
Putallaz, M., 294, 381

R

Renenger, K., 379, 387
Rolls, S., 235, 381
Rouse, A., 235, 381
Rubin, Z., 11, 381

S

Schlundt, D. C., 171, 379
Schocken, I., 379
Schonfeld, A. M., 380
Schuler, A. L., 12, 381
Scott, B. J., 380
Shantz, D. W., 267, 381
Simmons, J. Q., 13, 380
Sinton, M., 5, 267, 380
Sloman, J., 11, 381
Sugar, C. A., 223, 379

T

Taylor, D., 68, 379
Thurlow, C., 95, 381

V

Van Bourgondien, M. E., 147, 381
Vohs, K. D., 337, 379

W

Warm, T. R., 267, 381
Weisz, J. R., 12, 380
Whitham, C., 5, 380
Wilfley, D., 5, 267, 380
Williard, J. C., 267, 381
Wolfberg, P. J., 12, 381

Z

Zhang, L., 337, 379

Subject Index

A

Appropriate Use of Humor (Parent Handout), 154–157
Attention-deficit-hyperactivity disorder (ADHD), 5, 11
Autism spectrum disorders (ASD), 11, 12
  benefits from PEERS, 5, 12, 13
  bullying, 293
  grouping with other teens with ASD, 30
  importance of get-togethers, 223
  understanding jokes, 147

B

Bad reputation; *see also* Negative reputation
  and cyberbullying, 116
  and handling teasing, 294
  and humor feedback, 158
  and insult jokes, 162
  and offensive jokes, 149
  and poor sport, 259
  and stalking, 115
  slipping in, unsuccessful, 208
  tips for changing, 295–298, 299, 307–309
Behavioral control techniques, 30–31; *see also* Handling misbehavior
Body boundaries, good, 84–85
Bullying, 304–306
  ASD research, 293
  defined, 268, 293
  handling, 295–296
  teasing *vs.*, 277, 283
Bullying and Bad Reputations (Parent Handout), 299 301
Buzzwords, defined, 10, 33

C

Call Assignment Log, 402

D

Didactic presentations; *see* Teen Therapist Guides

E

Electronic Communication (Parent Handout), 103–106
Embarrassing feedback, 267, 271–272, 285
  vs. teasing, 271
    examples, 271, 286
Entering a Conversation (Parent Handout), 177–180

Challenging parent behaviors, 60–70; *see also* Personality disorder and session interference
Children's Friendship Training
  ADHD, 5
  extension of PEERS, xxi, 3
  format for PEERS, 4
Choosing Appropriate Friends (Parent Handout), 132–134
Cliques; *see* Crowds
Cold calling, 114
Confidentiality, 40
Conversation hog, 81–82
Cover stories
  first contact, 100
    examples, 104
  phone call ending, 99
    examples, 99
  slipping out of a conversation, 202
    ending a get–together, 244
Crowds (varieties of), 97, 138
  and fitting in, 138
  importance of, 127, 139
Cyberbullying, 116
  and Internet use, 101

Exiting a Conversation (Parent Handout),
    205–207
Extracurricular activities, 95, 208
    importance of, 128
    intake assessment, 24
Eye contact, 85–86, 173
    assessing receptiveness of others, 45, 174
    gaze aversion, 188–189
    gender differences, 73, 86
    slipping in, 273
    slipping out, 202
    two-way conversations, 72

F

Friendship Qualities Scale, 34

G

Gaze aversion, 188–189; *see also* Eye contact
Get-Togethers (Parent Handout), 232–234
Get-togethers
    activity-based, suggestions, 239–240,
        226–227
    cover story for ending, 244
    gold standard, 224
    parent jobs, 228
    research about, 223
    suitable activities for, 226, 239
Good Sportsmanship (Parent Handout),
    256–257
Good sportsmanship, 253–254, 259–262
Good Sportsmanship Point Log, 31, 405
    in get-togethers, 289
    and social goals, 252
Gossip, 337; *see also* Rumors
Graduation
    ceremony, 318, 354, 364–365
    how to present, 317–318, 342–343
    flyer, 410
    parent session, 318
    prizes, 371
    teen session, 318
Group leaders, requirements of, 4

H

Handling Disagreements (Parent Handout),
    319–321
Handling disagreements, 314–316, 324–326

Handling misbehavior, 42, 51, 53; *see also*
    Behavioral control techniques;
    Misbehavior
Helicopter parents, 224, 235, 252
    defined, 46, 224
Homework
    getting better compliance on, 96
    how to help teens with, 46
Humor
    feedback,
        from parent, 149
        from peers, 150–151, 155, 162–163, 164–166
    rules about use, 149–150, 154, 160–164

I

Intake interview
    parent, 23–24
    teen, 22–23
        checklist, 27–28
Interviewer (conversational error), 82
Introduction and Trading Information (Parent
    Handout), 48–50

J

"Jeopardy" teen activity, 62, 90, 120
    answer sheets, 65, 93, 123
Joke; *see also* Humor
    receiver, 158
    research, ASD, 147
    rule for telling, 160–162
    teen misbehavior, 53, 76
    teller, 158

L

Lateness, parent
    responses to chronic, 69–70

M

Misbehavior; *see also* Handling misbehavior;
    Behavioral control techniques
    explaining to teens, 42
    how to handle, 52, 53
    minimizing, 51
Missed sessions, providing handouts for, 9

N

Negative reputation, 98; *see also* Bad
    reputation
    and crowd, 135
    and phone call, 171
    and slipping in, 225
    research, 294

O

Outcome assessments, 33–34
    posttreatment, 360, 369
    Quality of Play Questionnaire, 393–395
        administration and scoring, 395–396
        described, 34
    Social Responsiveness Scale (SRS), 33
    Social Skills Improvement System (SSIS), 33
    Test of Adolescent Social Skills Knowledge
        (TASSK), 387–389
        administration, 395
        described, 34
        parent, 393
        scoring, 396
        teen, 394

P

Parent Handouts
    Appropriate Use of Humor (Session 5),
        154–157
    Bullying and Bad Reputations (Session 11),
        299–301
    Choosing Appropriate Friends (Session 4),
        132–134
    Electronic Communication (Session 3),
        103–106
    Entering a Conversation (Session 6),
        177–180
    Exiting a Conversation (Session 7), 205–207
    Get-Togethers (Session 8), 232–234
    Good Sportsmanship (Session 9), 256–257
    Handling Disagreements (Session 12),
        319–321
    Introduction and Trading Information
        (Session 1), 48–50
    Rumors and Gossip (Session 13), 344–346
    Teasing and Embarrassing Feedback
        (Session 10), 274–276
    Two-Way Conversations (Session 2), 74–75
    Where to Go From Here (Session 14),
        366–368

Parent Session Therapist Guide
    overview of, 9
    Session 1, 37–47
    Session 2, 67–73
    Session 3, 95–102
    Session 4, 125–129
    Session 5, 147–151
    Session 6, 171–175
    Session 7, 199–203
    Session 8, 223–231
    Session 9, 251–254
    Session 10, 267–272
    Session 11, 293–298
    Session 12, 313–318
    Session 13, 337–343
    Session 14, 359–364
Peer entry skills, 173; *see also* Slipping in
Personality disorder and session interference,
        38–40; *see also* Challenging parents
Phone call
    assignment log (in-group), 60, 402
    basis of assignment, 40
    cover story, 100
        examples, 111
    ending calls, 109
    starting calls, 103, 109
    two-message rule, 114
Phone Roster, 397
Phone Screen Data Sheet, 21
Phone Screening Script, 18–20
Planned Absence Sheet, 399
Preparing for treatment, 17–33
    facilities, 30
    food and beverages, 32
    forming groups, 30
    group composition, 30
    intake interview, 22
        parent/guardian, 23
        teen, 22
        teen interview checklist, 27
    phone screening, 18
        data sheet, 21
    required materials, 31
    screening, 17
Program for the Evaluation and Education for
        Relational Skills (PEERS)
    ASD, 12
    coaches, 4–5
    earning points, 55–6
    manual
        organization, 5
        use, 3

use in school setting, 13
    use with young adults, 13–14
required materials, 31–32
required personnel, 4
research evidence, 11, 12–13
session structure, 55
who may benefit, 5

Q

Quality of Play Questionnaire (QPQ), 34

R

Reasons for being turned down (entering a
        conversation), 201, 205
Rules for
    changing a bad reputation, 307–309
    e-mails, 100–101, 104
    good sportsmanship, 253, 259–262
    handling bullying, 295–296, 305–306
    handling disagreements, 315–316, 324–326
    handling rumors and gossip, 344, 349
    having a good get-together, 237–241
    instant message (IM), 104
    Internet use, 101, 105
    "Jeopardy" (teen activity), 120
    leaving a voice-mail message, 99–100
    phone calls, 98–99, 103, 109–113
    slipping into a conversation, 184–189, 196
    slipping out of a conversation, 211–213
    text messages, 100–101, 104, 113
    trading information, 45, 49
    two-way conversation, 71–73, 79–86
    using humor, 149–150, 160–164
    voice-mail message, 99–100
Rumors
    handling, 339–341, 349–352
    research, 337
Rumors and Gossip (Parent Handout), 344–346

S

Slipping into a conversation; *see also* Rules for
        slipping in
    good and bad times and places, 184
    reasons for being turned down, 201, 211
    steps for conversations, 173, 177
Slipping out of a conversation, 211–213
Social contact between group members,
        reasons to prohibit, 25
Social Responsiveness Scale, 33

Social Skills Improvement System, 33
Socratic method, 52
Sources of friends, 128–129

T

Teasing
    vs. bullying, 268, 277
    vs. embarrassing feedback, 271–272,
        285–286
    research, 267
    tease-the-tease, 269–270, 274, 279–283
Teasing and Embarrassing Feedback (Parent
        Handout), 274–276
Teen Activity Guides
    get-togethers, 248–249
    get-togethers and good sportsmanship,
        265–266, 287
    good sportsmanship and outdoor activities,
        310, 332, 357–358
    "Jeopardy," 62–65, 90–93, 120–123
        answer sheets, 65, 93, 123
    slipping in and out of conversations,
        221–222
    slipping into conversations, 196–197
    trading information: personal items,
        144–145, 170
Teen intake interview checklist, 23, 27
Teen Session Plans
    Session 1, 51
    Session 2, 76
    Session 3, 107
    Session 4, 135
    Session 5, 158
    Session 6, 181
    Session 7, 208
    Session 8, 235
    Session 9, 258
    Session 10, 277
    Session 11, 302
    Session 12, 322
    Session 13, 347
    Session 14, 369
Teen Therapist Guides
    Appropriate Use of Humor (Session 5),
        158–169
    Bullying and Bad Reputations (Session 11),
        302–311
    Choosing Appropriate Friends (Session 4),
        135–144
    Electronic Communication (Session 3),
        107–120

Entering a Conversation (Session 6), 181–191
Get-Togethers (Session 8), 235–245
Good Sportsmanship (Session 9), 258–264
Graduation and Termination (Session 14), 369–371
Handling Disagreements (Session 12), 322–334
Rumors and Gossip (Session 13), 347–356
Slipping Out of a Conversation (Session 7), 208–217
Teasing and Embarrassing Feedback (Session 10), 277–289
Trading Information (Session 1), 51–62
Two-Way Conversations (Session 2), 76–89
Test of Adolescent Social Skills Knowledge (TASSK); *see* Outcome assessments
"Too cool for school" syndrome, 51, 158
Two-message rule, 114

Two-Way Conversations (Parent Handout), 74–75
script writers, 69

V

Video games
get-togethers, 227, 232, 240
conversational topics, 79
crowds, 97, 103, 138
research, 235
sources of friends, 71, 74, 128

W

Weekly Point Log, 403
Welcome Letter, 29
Where to Go From Here (Parent Handout), 366–368